Term *Rewriting* and *All That*

This is the first English language textbook offering a unified and self-contained introduction to the field of term rewriting. It covers all the basic material (abstract reduction systems, termination, confluence, completion, and combination problems), but also some important and closely connected subjects: universal algebra, unification theory, and Gröbner bases. The main algorithms are presented both informally and as programs in the functional language Standard ML (an appendix contains a quick and easy introduction to ML). Certain crucial algorithms like unification and congruence closure are covered in more depth and efficient Pascal programs are developed. The book contains many examples and over 170 exercises.

This text is also an ideal reference book for professional researchers: results that have been spread over many conference and journal articles are collected together in a unified notation, detailed proofs of almost all theorems are provided, and each chapter closes with a guide to the literature.

Term *Rewriting* and *All That*

Franz Baader

RWTH, Aachen

and

Tobias Nipkow

Technische Universität, München

CAMBRIDGE
UNIVERSITY PRESS

CAMBRIDGE UNIVERSITY PRESS
Cambridge, New York, Melbourne, Madrid, Cape Town, Singapore, São Paulo

Cambridge University Press
The Edinburgh Building, Cambridge CB2 2RU, UK

Published in the United States of America by Cambridge University Press, New York

www.cambridge.org
Information on this title: www.cambridge.org/9780521455206

First published 1998
First paperback edition 1999

Typeset by the authors

A catalogue record for this publication is available from the British Library

Library of Congress Cataloguing in Publication data

Baader, Franz.
Term rewriting and all that / Franz Baader and Tobias Nipkow.
p. cm.
Includes bibliographical references and index.
ISBN 0 521 45520 0 (hc : alk. paper)
1. Rewriting systems (Computer science). I. Nipkow, Tobias, 1958–
II. Title.
QA267.B314 1998
005.13′1–dc21 97-28286 CIP

ISBN-13 978-0-521-45520-6 hardback
ISBN-10 0-521-45520-0 hardback

ISBN-13 978-0-521-77920-3 paperback
ISBN-10 0-521-77920-0 paperback

Transferred to digital printing 2006

Contents

Preface

Term rewriting is a branch of theoretical computer science which combines elements of logic, universal algebra, automated theorem proving and functional programming. Its foundation is equational logic. What distinguishes term rewriting from equational logic is that equations are used as *directed* replacement rules, i.e. the left-hand side can be replaced by the right-hand side, but not vice versa. This constitutes a Turing-complete computational model which is very close to functional programming. It has applications in algebra (e.g. Boolean algebra, group theory and ring theory), recursion theory (what is and is not computable with certain sets of rewrite rules), software engineering (reasoning about equationally defined data types such as numbers, lists, sets etc.), and programming languages (especially functional and logic programming). In general, term rewriting applies in any context where efficient methods for reasoning with equations are required.

To date, most of the term rewriting literature has been published in specialist conference proceedings (especially *Rewriting Techniques and Applications* and *Automated Deduction* in Springer's LNCS series) and journals (e.g. *Journal of Symbolic Computation* and *Journal of Automated Reasoning*). In addition, several overview articles provide introductions into the field, and references to the relevant literature [141, 74, 204]. This is the first English book devoted to the theory and applications of term rewriting. It is ambitious in that it tries to serve two masters:

- The researcher, who needs a unified theory that covers, in detail and in a single volume, material that has previously only been collected in overview articles, and whose technical details are spread over the literature.
- The teacher or student, who needs a readable textbook in an area where there is hardly any literature for the non-specialist.

Our choice of material is fairly canonical: abstract reduction systems and universal algebra (the foundation), word problems (the motivation), unification (a central algorithm), termination, confluence and completion (the *sine qua non* of term rewriting). The inclusion of combination problems is also uncontroversial, except maybe for the rather technical topic of combining word problems. Two further topics show our own preferences and are not strictly core material: equational unification is included because of its significance for rewriting based theorem provers, Gröbner bases because they form an essential link between term rewriting and computer algebra.

Prerequisites are minimal: readers who have taken introductory courses such as discrete mathematics, (linear) algebra, or theoretical computer science are well equipped for this book. The basic notions of ordered sets are summarized in an appendix.

How to teach this book

The diagram below shows the dependencies between the different sections of the book.

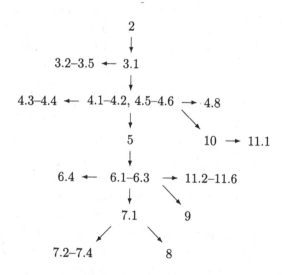

An introductory undergraduate course should cover the trunk of the above tree. To give the students a more algorithmic understanding of completion, it is helpful also to introduce Huet's completion procedure (7.4) without formally justifying its correctness. The course should conclude with 11.2–11.6. A more advanced introduction at graduate level would also include 4.3–4.4, 4.8, 6.4, 7.2–7.4, 9.1–9.3, and (initial segments of) 10. For a mathematically oriented audience, 3.2–3.5 is mandatory and 8 contains an excellent application of rewriting methods in mathematics.

Chapter 2 on abstract reduction systems is the foundation that term rewriting rests on. Nevertheless we recommend not to teach this chapter *en bloc* but to interleave it with the rest of the book. Only Section 2.1 needs to be covered right at the start. The dependency of the remaining sections is as follows:

$$2.2\text{–}2.5 \longrightarrow 5 \longrightarrow 2.7 \longrightarrow 6.$$

This groups together the abstract and concrete treatments of termination (2.2–2.5 and 5) and confluence (2.7 and 6).

Chapter 5 on termination has a special status in the dependency diagram. It is not the case that all of Chapter 5 is a prerequisite for the remainder of the book. In fact, almost the opposite is the case: one could read most of the remainder quite happily, except that one would not be able to follow particular termination arguments. However, due to the overall importance of termination, we recommend that students should be exposed at least to 5.1–5.3 and possibly one of the simplification orders in 5.4. The general theory of simplification orders should be reserved for a graduate-level course.

A final word of warning. A book also aimed at researchers is written with a higher level of formality than a pure textbook. In places, the formal rigour of the book needs to be adjusted to the requirements of the classroom.

The rôle of ML

Most of the theory in this book is constructive. Either we explicitly deal with particular algorithms, e.g. unification, or the proof of some theorem is essentially an algorithm, e.g. a decision procedure. We find that many computer science students take more easily to logical formalisms once they understand how to represent formulae as data structures and how to transform them. Therefore we have tried to accompany every major algorithm in this book by an implementation. As an implementation language we have chosen ML: functional languages are closest to our algorithms and ML is one of its best-known representatives. For those readers not familiar with ML, a concise summary of the core of the language is provided as an appendix.

It should be emphasized that our ML programs are strictly added value: they reside in separate sections and are not required for an understanding of the main text (although we believe that their study enhances this understanding).

We should also point out that the programs are intentionally unoptimized.

They are written for clarity rather than efficiency. Nevertheless they cope well with small to medium sized examples. Their simplicity makes them an ideal vehicle for further developments, and we encourage our readers to experiment with them. They are available on the internet at

`http://www4.informatik.tu-muenchen.de/~nipkow/`

Acknowledgments

David Basin, Eric Domenjoud, Harald Ganzinger, Bernhard Gramlich, Henrik Linnestad, Aart Middeldorp, Monica Nesi, Vincent van Oostrom, Larry Paulson, Manfred Schmidt-Schauß, Klaus Schulz, Wayne Snyder, Cesare Tinelli, and Markus Wenzel read individual chapters and commented extensively on them. In particular Aart Middeldorp's amazing scrutiny uncovered a number of embarrassing mistakes.

Michael Hanus, Maribel Fernández and Femke van Raamsdonk provided additional comments.

Can A. Albayrak and Volker Braun produced first versions of some of the figures.

The DFG funded a sabbatical of the second author at Cambridge University Computer Laboratory where Larry Paulson greatly contributed to a very productive four months.

Alison Woollatt of CUP provided essential TeXpertise. David Tranah, our very patient editor, suggested the title.

We wish to thank them all.

1

Motivating Examples

Equational reasoning is concerned with a rather restricted class of first-order languages: the only predicate symbol is equality. It is, however, at the heart of many problems in mathematics and computer science, which explains why developing specialized methods and tools for this type of reasoning is very popular and important. For example, in mathematics one often defines classes of algebras (such as groups, rings, etc.) by giving defining identities (which state associativity of the group operation, etc.). In this context, it is important to know which other identities can be derived from the defining ones. In algebraic specification, new operations are defined from given ones by stating characteristic identities that must hold for the defined operations. As a special case we have functional programs where functions are defined by recursion equations.

For example, assume that we want to define addition of natural numbers using the constant 0 and the successor function s. This can be done with the identities†

$$x + 0 \approx x,$$
$$x + s(y) \approx s(x + y).$$

By applying these identities, we can calculate the sum of 1 (encoded as $s(0)$) and 2 (encoded as $s(s(0))$):

$$s(0) + s(s(0)) \approx s(s(0) + s(0)) \approx s(s(s(0)) + 0) \approx s(s(s(0))).$$

In this calculation, we have interpreted the identities as rewrite rules that tell us how a subterm of a given term can be replaced by another term.

This brings us to one of the key notions of this book, namely **term rewriting systems**. What do we mean by **terms**? They are built from **variables**,

---

† Throughout this book, we use $\approx$ for identities to make a clear distinction between the object level sign for identity and our use of $=$ for equality on the meta-level.

constant symbols, and **function symbols**. In the above example, $+$ is a binary function symbol, s is a unary function symbol, 0 is a constant symbol, and x, y are variables. Examples of terms over these symbols are 0, x, $s(s(0))$, $x + s(0)$, $s(s(s(0)) + 0)$. In our example calculation, we have used the identities only from left to right, but in general, identities can be applied in both directions.

In the following, we give two examples that illustrate some of the key issues arising in connection with identities and rewrite systems, and which will be treated in detail in this book. In the first example, the rewrite rules are intended to be used only in one direction (which is expressed by writing $\rightarrow$ instead of $\approx$). This is an instance of rewriting as a computation mechanism. In the second, we consider the identities defining groups, which are intended to be used in both directions. This is an instance of rewriting as a deduction mechanism.

Symbolic Differentiation

We consider symbolic differentiation of arithmetic expressions that are built with the operations $+$, $*$, the indeterminates X, Y, and the numbers $0, 1$. For example, $((X+X)*Y)+1$ is an admissible expression. These expressions can be viewed as terms that are built from the constant symbols 0, 1, X, and Y, and the binary function symbols $+$ and $*$. For the partial derivative with respect to X, we introduce the additional (unary) function symbol D_X. The following rules are (some of the) well-known rules for computing the derivative:

$$
\begin{array}{lrcl}
\text{(R1)} & D_X(X) & \rightarrow & 1, \\
\text{(R2)} & D_X(Y) & \rightarrow & 0, \\
\text{(R3)} & D_X(u + v) & \rightarrow & D_X(u) + D_X(v), \\
\text{(R4)} & D_X(u * v) & \rightarrow & (u * D_X(v)) + (D_X(u) * v).
\end{array}
$$

In terms like $D_X(u+v)$, the symbols u and v are variables, with the intended meaning that they can be replaced by arbitrary expressions.† Thus, rule (R3) can be applied to terms having the same pattern as the left-hand side, i.e. a D_X followed by a $+$-expression.

Starting with the term $D_X(X*X)$, the rules (R1)–(R4) lead to the possible reductions depicted in Fig. 1.1. We can use this example to illustrate two of the most important properties of term rewriting systems:

---

† These variables should not be confused with the indeterminates X, Y of the arithmetic expressions, which are constant symbols.

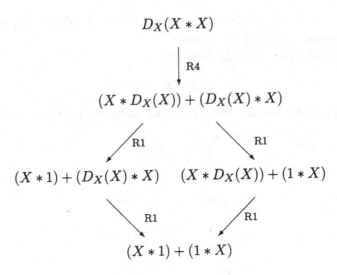

Fig. 1.1. Symbolic differentiation of the expression $D_X(X * X)$.

Termination: Is it always the case that after finitely many rule applications we reach an expression to which no more rules apply? Such an expression is then called a **normal form**.

For the rules (R1)–(R4) this is the case. It is, however, not completely trivial to show this because rule (R4) leads to a considerable increase in the size of the expression.

An example of a non-terminating rule is

$$u + v \rightarrow v + u,$$

which expresses commutativity of addition. The sequence $(X * 1) + (1 * X) \rightarrow (1 * X) + (X * 1) \rightarrow (X * 1) + (1 * X) \rightarrow \dots$ is an example for an infinite chain of applications of this rule. Of course, non-termination need not always be caused by a single rule; it could also result from the interaction of several rules.

Confluence: If there are different ways of applying rules to a given term t, leading to different derived terms t_1 and t_2, can t_1 and t_2 be joined, i.e. can we always find a common term s that can be reached both from t_1 and from t_2 by rule application?

In Fig. 1.1 this is the case, and more generally, one can prove (but how?) that (R1)–(R4) are confluent. This shows that the symbolic differentiation of a given expression always leads to the same derivative (i.e. the term to which no more rules apply), independent of the strategy for applying rules.

If we add the simplification rule

$$(\text{R5}) \quad u + 0 \rightarrow u$$

to (R1)–(R4), we lose the confluence property (see Fig. 1.2).

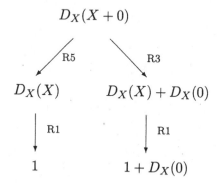

Fig. 1.2. $D_X(X)$ and $D_X(X) + D_X(0)$ cannot be joined.

In our example, non-confluence of (R1)–(R5) can be overcome by adding the rule $D_X(0) \rightarrow 0$. More generally, one can ask whether this is always possible, i.e. can we always make a non-confluent system confluent by adding implied rules (**completion** of term rewriting systems).

Because of their special form, the rules (R1)–(R4) constitute a functional program (on the left-hand side, the defined function D_X occurs only at the very outside). Termination of the rules means that D_X is a total function. Confluence of the rules means that the result of a computation is independent of the evaluation strategy. Confluence of (R1)–(R4) is not a lucky coincidence. We will prove that all term rewriting systems that constitute functional programs are confluent.

Group Theory

Let $\circ$ be a binary function symbol, i be a unary function symbol, e be a constant symbol, and x, y, z be variable symbols. The class of all groups is defined by the identities

$$
\begin{array}{lrcl}
(\text{G1}) & (x \circ y) \circ z & \approx & x \circ (y \circ z), \\
(\text{G2}) & e \circ x & \approx & x, \\
(\text{G3}) & i(x) \circ x & \approx & e,
\end{array}
$$

i.e. a set G equipped with a binary operation $\circ$, a unary operation i, and containing an element e is a group iff the operations satisfy the identities (G1)–(G3). Identity (G3) states only that for every group element g, the element $i(g)$ is a left-inverse of g with respect to the left-unit e. The identities (G1)–(G3) can be used to show that this left-inverse is also a right-inverse. In fact, using these identities, the term e can be transformed into the term $x \circ i(x)$:

$$
\begin{aligned}
e &\overset{\text{G3}}{\approx} i(x \circ i(x)) \circ (x \circ i(x)) \\
&\overset{\text{G2}}{\approx} i(x \circ i(x)) \circ (x \circ (e \circ i(x))) \\
&\overset{\text{G3}}{\approx} i(x \circ i(x)) \circ (x \circ ((i(x) \circ x) \circ i(x))) \\
&\overset{\text{G1}}{\approx} i(x \circ i(x)) \circ ((x \circ (i(x) \circ x)) \circ i(x)) \\
&\overset{\text{G1}}{\approx} i(x \circ i(x)) \circ (((x \circ i(x)) \circ x) \circ i(x)) \\
&\overset{\text{G1}}{\approx} i(x \circ i(x)) \circ ((x \circ i(x)) \circ (x \circ i(x))) \\
&\overset{\text{G1}}{\approx} (i(x \circ i(x)) \circ (x \circ i(x))) \circ (x \circ i(x)) \\
&\overset{\text{G3}}{\approx} e \circ (x \circ i(x)) \\
&\overset{\text{G2}}{\approx} x \circ i(x).
\end{aligned}
$$

This example illustrates that it is nontrivial to find such derivations, i.e. to solve the so-called **word problem** for sets of identities: given a set of identities E and two terms s and t, is it possible to transform the term s into the term t, using the identities in E as rewrite rules that can be applied in both directions?

One possible way of approaching this problem is to consider the identities as uni-directional rewrite rules:

$$
\begin{aligned}
\text{(RG1)} \qquad (x \circ y) \circ z &\;\to\; x \circ (y \circ z), \\
\text{(RG2)} \qquad e \circ x &\;\to\; x, \\
\text{(RG3)} \qquad i(x) \circ x &\;\to\; e.
\end{aligned}
$$

The basic idea is that the identities are only applied in the direction that "simplifies" a given term. One is now looking for normal forms, i.e. terms to which no more rules apply. In order to decide whether the terms s and t are equivalent (i.e. can be transformed into each other by applying identities in both directions), we use the uni-directional rewrite rules to reduce s to a normal form $\hat{s}$ and t to a normal form $\hat{t}$. Then we check whether $\hat{s}$ and $\hat{t}$ are syntactically equal. There are, however, two problems that must be overcome before this method for deciding the word problem can be applied:

- Equivalent terms can have distinct normal forms. In our example, both $x \circ i(x)$ and e are normal forms with respect to (RG1)–(RG3), and we have shown that they are equivalent. However, the above method for deciding the word problem would fail because it would find that the normal forms of $x \circ i(x)$ and e are distinct.

- Normal forms need not exist: the process of reducing a term may lead to an infinite chain of rule applications.

We will see that termination and confluence are the important properties that ensure existence and uniqueness of normal forms. If a given set of identities leads to a non-confluent rewrite system, we do not have to give up. We can again apply the idea of completion to extend the rewrite system to a confluent one. In the case of groups, a confluent and terminating extension of (RG1)–(RG3) exists (see Exercise 7.12 on page 184).

2

Abstract Reduction Systems

This chapter is concerned with the abstract treatment of reduction, where reduction is synonymous with the traversal of some directed graph, the stepwise execution of some computation, the gradual transformation of some object (e.g. a term), or any similar step by step activity. Mathematically this means we are simply talking about binary relations. An **abstract reduction system** is a pair $(A, \rightarrow)$, where the **reduction** $\rightarrow$ is a binary relation on the set A, i.e. $\rightarrow \subseteq A \times A$. Instead of $(a, b) \in \rightarrow$ we write $a \rightarrow b$.

The term "reduction" has been chosen because in many applications something decreases with each reduction step, but cannot decrease forever. Yet this need not be the case, as witnessed by the reduction $0 \rightarrow 1 \rightarrow 2 \rightarrow \cdots$.

Unless noted otherwise, all our discussions take place in the context of some arbitrary but fixed abstract reduction system $(A, \rightarrow)$.

2.1 Equivalence and reduction

We can view reduction in two ways: the first is as a directed computation, which, starting from some point a_0, tries to reach a normal form by following the reduction $a_0 \rightarrow a_1 \rightarrow \cdots$. This corresponds to the idea of program evaluation. Or we may consider $\rightarrow$ merely as a description of $\overset{*}{\leftrightarrow}$, where $a \overset{*}{\leftrightarrow} b$ means that there is a path between a and b where the arrows can be traversed in both directions, for example, as in $a_0 \leftarrow a_1 \rightarrow a_2 \leftarrow a_3$. This corresponds to the idea of identities which can be used in both directions. The key question here is to decide if two elements a and b are **equivalent**, i.e. if $a \overset{*}{\leftrightarrow} b$ holds. Settling this question by an undirected search along both $\rightarrow$ and $\leftarrow$ is bound to be expensive. Wouldn't it be nice if we could decide equivalence by reducing both a and b to their normal forms and testing if the normal forms are identical? As explained in the first chapter, this idea is only going to work if reduction terminates and normal forms are unique.

Formally, we talk about *termination* and *confluence* of reduction, and the study of these two notions is one of the central themes of this book.

2.1.1 Basic definitions

In the sequel, we define a great many symbols, not all of which will be put to immediate use. Therefore you may treat these definitions as a table of relevant notions which can be consulted when necessary.

Given two relations $R \subseteq A \times B$ and $S \subseteq B \times C$, their **composition** is defined by

$$R \circ S := \{(x, z) \in A \times C \mid \exists y \in B. \ (x, y) \in R \wedge (y, z) \in S\}$$

Definition 2.1.1 We are particularly interested in composing a reduction with itself and define the following notions:

$$
\begin{array}{lll}
\xrightarrow{0} & := & \{(x,x) \mid x \in A\} \quad \text{identity} \\
\xrightarrow{i+1} & := & \xrightarrow{i} \circ \rightarrow \qquad\qquad (i+1)\text{-fold composition}, i \geq 0 \\
\xrightarrow{+} & := & \bigcup_{i>0} \xrightarrow{i} \qquad\quad \text{transitive closure} \\
\xrightarrow{*} & := & \xrightarrow{+} \cup \xrightarrow{0} \qquad \text{reflexive transitive closure} \\
\xrightarrow{=} & := & \rightarrow \cup \xrightarrow{0} \qquad \text{reflexive closure} \\
\xrightarrow{-1} & := & \{(y,x) \mid x \rightarrow y\} \quad \text{inverse} \\
\leftarrow & := & \xrightarrow{-1} \qquad\qquad\quad \text{inverse} \\
\leftrightarrow & := & \rightarrow \cup \leftarrow \qquad\quad \text{symmetric closure} \\
\xleftrightarrow{+} & := & (\leftrightarrow)^+ \qquad\qquad \text{transitive symmetric closure} \\
\xleftrightarrow{*} & := & (\leftrightarrow)^* \qquad\qquad \text{reflexive transitive symmetric closure}
\end{array}
$$

Some remarks are in order:

1. Notations like $\xrightarrow{*}$ and $\leftarrow$ only work for arrow-like symbols. In the case of arbitrary relations $R \subseteq A \times A$ we write R^*, R^{-1} etc.
2. Some of the constructions can also be expressed nicely in terms of *paths*:

   $x \xrightarrow{n} y$ if there is a path of length n from x to y,

   $x \xrightarrow{*} y$ if there is some finite path from x to y,

   $x \xrightarrow{+} y$ if there is some finite nonempty path from x to y.
3. The word **closure** has a precise meaning: the P closure of R is the least set with property P which contains R. For example, $\xrightarrow{*}$, the reflexive transitive closure of $\rightarrow$, is the least reflexive and transitive relation which contains $\rightarrow$. Note that for arbitrary P and R, the P closure of R need not exist, but in the above cases they always do because reflexivity, transitivity and symmetry are closed under arbitrary intersections. In

such cases the P closure of R can be defined directly as the intersection of all sets with property P which contain R.

4. It is easy to show that $\overset{*}{\leftrightarrow}$ is the least equivalence relation containing $\rightarrow$.

Let us add some terminology to this notation:

1. x is **reducible** iff there is a y such that $x \rightarrow y$.
2. x is **in normal form (irreducible)** iff it is not reducible.
3. y is **a normal form of** x iff $x \overset{*}{\rightarrow} y$ and y is in normal form. If x has a uniquely determined normal form, the latter is denoted by $x\downarrow$.
4. y is a **direct successor** of x iff $x \rightarrow y$.
5. y is a **successor** of x iff $x \overset{+}{\rightarrow} y$
6. x and y are **joinable** iff there is a z such that $x \overset{*}{\rightarrow} z \overset{*}{\leftarrow} y$, in which case we write $x \downarrow y$.

Example 2.1.2

1. Let $A := \mathbb{N} - \{0,1\}$ and $\rightarrow := \{(m,n) \mid m > n \text{ and } n \text{ divides } m\}$. Then

   (a) m is in normal form iff m is prime.
   (b) p is a normal form of m iff p is a prime factor of m.
   (c) $m \downarrow n$ iff m and n are not relatively prime.
   (d) $\overset{+}{\rightarrow} = \rightarrow$ because $>$ and "divides" are already transitive.
   (e) $\overset{*}{\leftrightarrow} = A \times A$.

2. Let $A := \{a,b\}^*$ (the set of words over the alphabet $\{a,b\}$) and $\rightarrow := \{(ubav, uabv) \mid u,v \in A\}$. Then

   (a) w is in normal form iff w is sorted, i.e. of the form a^*b^*.
   (b) Every w has a unique normal form $w\downarrow$, the result of sorting w.
   (c) $w_1 \downarrow w_2$ iff $w_1 \overset{*}{\leftrightarrow} w_2$ iff w_1 and w_2 contain the same number of as and bs.

Finally we come to some of the central notions of this book.

Definition 2.1.3 A reduction $\rightarrow$ is called

Church-Rosser†	iff $x \overset{*}{\leftrightarrow} y \Rightarrow x \downarrow y$	(see Fig. 2.1).
confluent	iff $y_1 \overset{*}{\leftarrow} x \overset{*}{\rightarrow} y_2 \Rightarrow y_1 \downarrow y_2$	(see Fig. 2.1).
terminating	iff there is no infinite descending chain $a_0 \rightarrow a_1 \rightarrow \cdots$	
normalizing	iff every element has a normal form.	
convergent	iff it is both confluent and terminating.	

Both reductions in Example 2.1.2 terminate, but only the second one is Church-Rosser and confluent.

† Alonzo Church and J. Barkley Rosser proved that the λ-calculus has this property [51].

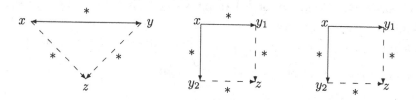

Fig. 2.1. Church-Rosser property, confluence and semi-confluence.

Remarks:

1. The diagrams in Fig. 2.1 have a precise meaning and are used throughout the book in this manner: solid arrows represent universal and dashed arrows existential quantification; the whole diagram is an implication of the form $\forall \overline{x}.\ P(\overline{x}) \Rightarrow \exists \overline{y}.\ Q(\overline{x}, \overline{y})$. For example, the confluence diagram becomes $\forall x, y_1, y_2.\ y_1 \xleftarrow{*} x \xrightarrow{*} y_2 \Rightarrow \exists z.\ y_1 \xrightarrow{*} z \xleftarrow{*} y_2$.
2. Because $x \downarrow y$ implies $x \overset{*}{\leftrightarrow} y$, the Church-Rosser property can also be phrased as an equivalence: $x \overset{*}{\leftrightarrow} y \Leftrightarrow x \downarrow y$.
3. Any terminating relation is normalizing, but the converse is not true, as the example in Fig 2.2 shows.

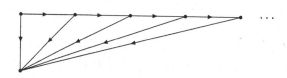

Fig. 2.2. Confluent, normalizing and acyclic but not terminating.

Thus we have come back to our initial motivation: the Church-Rosser property is exactly what we were looking for, namely the ability to test equivalence by the search for a common successor. We will now see how it relates to termination and confluence.

2.1.2 Basic results

It turns out that the Church-Rosser property and confluence coincide. The fact that any Church-Rosser relation is confluent is almost immediate, and the reverse implication has a beautiful diagrammatic proof which is shown in Fig. 2.3. It is based on the observation that any equivalence $x \overset{*}{\leftrightarrow} y$ can be

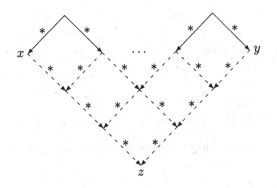

Fig. 2.3. Confluence implies the Church-Rosser property.

written as a series of peaks as in the top of the diagram. Now you can use confluence to complete the diagram from the top to the bottom. The formal proof below yields some additional information by involving an intermediate property:

Definition 2.1.4 A relation $\rightarrow$ is **semi-confluent** (Fig. 2.1) iff

$$y_1 \leftarrow x \xrightarrow{*} y_2 \Rightarrow y_1 \downarrow y_2.$$

Although semi-confluence looks weaker than confluence, it turns out to be equivalent:

Theorem 2.1.5 *The following conditions are equivalent:*

1. $\rightarrow$ *has the Church-Rosser property.*
2. $\rightarrow$ *is confluent.*
3. $\rightarrow$ *is semi-confluent.*

Proof We show that the implications $1 \Rightarrow 2 \Rightarrow 3 \Rightarrow 1$ hold.

   ($1 \Rightarrow 2$) If $\rightarrow$ has the Church-Rosser property and $y_1 \xleftarrow{*} x \xrightarrow{*} y_2$ then $y_1 \xleftrightarrow{*} y_2$ and hence, by the Church-Rosser property, $y_1 \downarrow y_2$, i.e. $\rightarrow$ is confluent.

   ($2 \Rightarrow 3$) Obviously any confluent relation is semi-confluent.

   ($3 \Rightarrow 1$) If $\rightarrow$ is semi-confluent and $x \xleftrightarrow{*} y$ then we show $x \downarrow y$, i.e. the Church-Rosser property, by induction on the length of the chain $x \xleftrightarrow{*} y$. If $x = y$, this is trivial. If $x \xleftrightarrow{*} y \leftrightarrow y'$ we know $x \downarrow y$ by induction hypothesis, i.e. $x \xrightarrow{*} z \xleftarrow{*} y$ for some suitable z. We show $x \downarrow y'$ by case distinction:

$y \leftarrow y'$: $x \downarrow y'$ follows directly from $x \downarrow y$.

$y \rightarrow y'$: semi-confluence implies $z \downarrow y'$ and hence $x \downarrow y'$.

The reasoning is displayed graphically in Fig. 2.4.   □

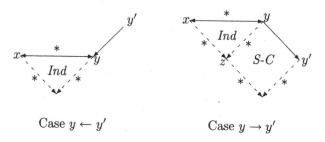

Case $y \leftarrow y'$ Case $y \rightarrow y'$

Fig. 2.4. Semi-confluence implies the Church-Rosser property.

This theorem has some easy consequences:

Corollary 2.1.6 *If $\rightarrow$ is confluent and $x \stackrel{*}{\leftrightarrow} y$ then*

1. $x \stackrel{*}{\rightarrow} y$ *if y is in normal form, and*
2. $x = y$ *if both x and y are in normal form.*

Now we know that for confluent relations, two elements are equivalent iff they are joinable. Of course the test for joinability can be difficult (and even undecidable) if the relation does not terminate: given two elements which are not joinable, when should you stop the search for a common successor in case of an infinite reduction starting from one of the two elements, as in the following example?

$$a_0 \rightarrow a_1 \rightarrow a_2 \rightarrow \cdots,$$
$$b_0 \rightarrow b_1 \rightarrow b_2 \rightarrow \cdots.$$

It turns out that normalization suffices for determining joinability. To see this, let us explore the relationship between termination, normalization, confluence and the uniqueness of normal forms.

Fact 2.1.7 *If $\rightarrow$ is confluent, every element has at most one normal form.*

Since every element has at least one normal form if $\rightarrow$ is normalizing, it follows that for confluent and normalizing relations every element x has exactly one normal form which we write $x{\downarrow}$:

Lemma 2.1.8 *If $\rightarrow$ is normalizing and confluent, every element has a unique normal form.*

Having established under what conditions the notation $x{\downarrow}$ is well-defined, we immediately obtain our main theorem:

Theorem 2.1.9 *If $\rightarrow$ is confluent and normalizing then $x \stackrel{*}{\leftrightarrow} y \Leftrightarrow x{\downarrow} = y{\downarrow}$.*

Proof The $\Leftarrow$-direction is trivial. Conversely, if $x \overset{*}{\leftrightarrow} y$ then $x{\downarrow} \overset{*}{\leftrightarrow} y{\downarrow}$ and hence $x{\downarrow} = y{\downarrow}$ by Corollary 2.1.6. □

Thus we have finally arrived at a very goal-directed equivalence test: simply check if the normal forms of both elements are identical. Provided normal forms are computable and identity is decidable, equivalence also becomes decidable.

Many authors prefer to work with termination instead of normalization and state Theorem 2.1.9 with "convergent" instead of "confluent and normalizing". Although normalization suffices for finding normal forms, it means that breadth-first rather than depth-first search may be required, for example in Fig. 2.2. For this reason we will also concentrate on termination rather than normalization in the sequel.

Exercises

2.1 Which closure operations commute? Find a proof or counterexample:

    (a) Is the reflexive closure of the transitive closure the same as the transitive closure of the reflexive closure, i.e. are $(\overset{+}{\rightarrow})^=$ and $(\overset{=}{\rightarrow})^+$ the same and do they coincide with $\overset{*}{\rightarrow}$?

    (b) What about the transitive and the symmetric closure? Do $(\leftrightarrow)^+$ and $(\overset{+}{\rightarrow}) \cup (\overset{+}{\rightarrow})^{-1}$ coincide?

2.2 Show that $\rightarrow$ is confluent and normalizing iff every element has a unique normal form.

2.3 Find a reduction $\rightarrow$ on $\mathbb{N}$ such that $\rightarrow$ is decidable but it is undecidable if some n is in normal form.

2.2 Well-founded induction

This section introduces the important proof principle of well-founded induction and shows that it is enjoyed by all terminating relations. As a motivation, recall the principle of induction for natural numbers: a property $P(n)$ holds for all natural numbers n if we can show that $P(n)$ holds under the (induction) hypothesis that $P(m)$ holds for all $m < n$. Why is this proof principle sound? Because there is no infinitely descending chain $m_0 > m_1 > \cdots$ of natural numbers. The principle of **well-founded induction** is a generalization of induction from $(\mathbb{N}, >)$ to any terminating reduction system $(A, \rightarrow)$. Formally, it is expressed by the following inference rule:

$$\frac{\forall x \in A. \ (\forall y \in A. \ x \xrightarrow{+} y \ \Rightarrow \ P(y)) \ \Rightarrow \ P(x)}{\forall x \in A. \ P(x)} \quad \text{(WFI)}$$

where P is some property of elements of A. The horizontal line is simply another symbol for implication.

In words: to prove $P(x)$ for all x, it suffices to prove $P(x)$ under the assumption that $P(y)$ holds for all successors y of x.

It may come as a bit of a surprise to see an induction schema without explicit base case. The solution to this puzzle is that the premise of WFI subsumes the base case. If $\rightarrow$ is terminating, the "base case" of the induction consists of showing that $P(x)$ holds for all elements without successor, i.e. all normal forms. Hence the assumption $(\forall y \in A. \ x \xrightarrow{+} y \ \Rightarrow \ P(y))$ is trivially true and the premise of WFI degenerates to $P(x)$, just as expected.

WFI is not correct for arbitrary $\rightarrow$, but for terminating ones it is:

Theorem 2.2.1 *If $\rightarrow$ terminates then WFI holds.*

Proof by contraposition. Assume that WFI does not hold for $\rightarrow$, i.e. there is some P such that the premise of WFI holds but the conclusion does not, i.e. $\neg P(a_0)$ for some $a_0 \in A$. But then the premise of WFI implies that there must exist some a_1 such that $a_0 \xrightarrow{+} a_1$ and $\neg P(a_1)$. By the same argument, there must exist some a_2 such that $a_1 \xrightarrow{+} a_2$ and $\neg P(a_2)$. Hence there is an infinite chain $a_0 \xrightarrow{+} a_1 \xrightarrow{+} a_2 \xrightarrow{+} \cdots$, i.e. $\rightarrow$ does not terminate. $\square$

As a first application of WFI, we can prove the converse of this theorem:

Theorem 2.2.2 *If WFI holds, then $\rightarrow$ terminates.*

Proof by WFI where $P(x) :=$ "there is no infinite chain starting from x". The induction step is simple: if there is no infinite chain starting from any successor of x, then there is no infinite chain starting from x either. Hence the premise of WFI holds and we can conclude that $P(x)$ holds for all x, i.e. $\rightarrow$ terminates. $\square$

A few words on terminology. Terminating relations are usually called **well-founded** in the mathematical literature. Hence the term "well-founded induction". In the computer science literature the terms **Noetherian**† and **Noetherian induction** are sometimes used instead. Strictly speaking, a reduction system $(A, \rightarrow)$ is well-founded if every nonempty $B \subseteq A$ has a minimal element, i.e. some $b \in B$ such that $b \rightarrow b'$ for no $b' \in B$. With

---

† In honour of the mathematician Emmy Noether.

the help of the Axiom of Choice it can be shown that well-foundedness and termination are equivalent.

We will now use well-founded induction to study some further properties of reductions which are related to termination.

Definition 2.2.3 A relation $\to$ is called

finitely branching if each element has only finitely many direct successors,
globally finite if each element has only finitely many successors,
acyclic if there is no element a such that $a \xrightarrow{+} a$.

Note that $\to$ is globally finite iff $\xrightarrow{+}$ is finitely branching.

Lemma 2.2.4 *A finitely branching relation is globally finite if it is terminating.*

Proof Let $\to$ be finitely branching and terminating. We use well-founded induction to prove that for every element the set of all its successors is finite. Since this is true for all its direct successors (by induction hypothesis), of which there are only finitely many, it is also true for the element itself. $\square$

It is not true that a finitely branching relation is terminating if it is globally finite. The reason is cycles. However, we have the following weaker implication:

Lemma 2.2.5 *Any acyclic relation is terminating if it is globally finite.*

The combination of the last two lemmas says that a finitely branching and acyclic relation is globally finite iff it is terminating. The special case of an acyclic relation induced by a tree is known as **König's Lemma**:

A finitely branching tree is infinite iff it contains an infinite path.

Exercises

2.4 Show that $\xrightarrow{+}$ is terminating iff $\to$ is.

2.5 Show that $\xrightarrow{+}$ is a strict partial order iff $\to$ is acyclic.

2.6 A relation $\to$ is called **bounded** iff for each element the length of all paths starting from it is bounded: $\forall x. \exists n. \not\exists y. x \xrightarrow{n} y$.

 (a) Is every terminating relation bounded?
 (b) Show that a finitely branching relation terminates iff it is bounded.

2.7 Prove Lemma 2.2.5.

2.3 Proving termination

The importance of termination hardly needs emphasizing: it is essential not just for programmers but also for theoreticians, as the previous sections, in particular the connection with well-founded induction, have shown. We will now examine a number of constructions for proving termination, a hard (because undecidable) task, as computer scientists well know. These constructions are on the level of relations and are applicable to termination proofs of programs as well as to purely mathematical questions, for example from the realm of group theory.

In connection with termination, it frequently pays to work with transitive relations or even partial orders. One reason is that there is a vast body of mathematical literature on partial orders. Another is that some of our constructions (e.g. the multiset order) are simpler for partial orders than for arbitrary relations. Fortunately, the transition to partial orders is without loss of generality: $\xrightarrow{+}$ terminates iff $\rightarrow$ does, in which case $\xrightarrow{+}$ is a strict order (Exercises 2.4 and 2.5).

The most basic method for proving termination of some $(A, \rightarrow)$ is to embed it into another abstract reduction system $(B, >)$ which is known to terminate. This requires a monotone mapping $\varphi : A \rightarrow B$, where **monotone** means that $x \rightarrow x'$ implies $\varphi(x) > \varphi(x')$. Now $\rightarrow$ terminates because an infinite chain $x_0 \rightarrow x_1 \rightarrow \cdots$ would induce an infinite chain $\varphi(x_0) > \varphi(x_1) > \cdots$. The mapping φ is often called a **measure function** and the whole construction is known as the **inverse image** construction (because $\rightarrow \subseteq \varphi^{-1}(>) := \{(x, x') \mid \varphi(x) > \varphi(x')\}$). Note that if φ is the identity, this yields that any subset of a terminating relation is terminating.

Example 2.3.1 The most popular choice for termination proofs is an embedding into $(\mathbb{N}, >)$, which is known to terminate. For strings, i.e. $A := X^*$ for some set X, there are two natural choices:

1. Length. φ is defined by $\varphi(w) := |w|$. This proves termination of all length-decreasing reductions like $uabbv \rightarrow_1 uaav$, where $u, v \in A$ are arbitrary and $a, b \in X$ are fixed.

2. Letters. For each $a \in X$ define $\varphi_a(w) :=$ "the number of occurrences of a in w". This can cope with reductions like $uav \rightarrow_2 vbu$ where $u, v \in A$ are arbitrary and $a, b \in X$, $a \neq b$, are fixed.

How about $\rightarrow_1 \cup \rightarrow_2$? We claim it also terminates, in which case Lemma 2.3.3 below tells us that there exists a measure function into $\mathbb{N}$. Can you find one?

Many program termination proofs follow the same schema by showing that every computation step (e.g. loop iteration or recursive call) decreases the value of some expression $\varphi(\bar{x})$ in terms of the program variables $\bar{x}$.

Example 2.3.2 Assume all variables in the following program range over natural numbers:

```
while ub > lb + 1 do
begin r := (ub + lb) div 2;
      if Φ then ub := r else lb := r
end
```

Termination is independent of the test Φ (provided Φ terminates and has no side effect) and can be proved with the measure function $\varphi(ub, lb) := ub - lb$ which decreases with every loop iteration.

The popularity of measure functions into $\mathbb{N}$ is in part explained by the following completeness result:

Lemma 2.3.3 *A finitely branching reduction terminates iff there is a monotone embedding into* $(\mathbb{N}, >)$.

Proof The $\Leftarrow$-direction follows from the soundness of the measure function approach. For the other direction, let $\rightarrow$ be a terminating and finitely branching reduction. Define $\varphi(x)$ as the number of successors of x which, by Lemma 2.2.4, must be finite. Since $\rightarrow$ is terminating and hence acyclic, $x \rightarrow x'$ implies that x' has strictly fewer successors than x. Alternatively, $\varphi(x)$ can be defined as the length of the longest reduction starting from x. Since $\rightarrow$ terminates, Exercise 2.6 implies that $\varphi(x)$ is well-defined. □

The restriction to finitely branching relations is necessary, as the following example shows.

Example 2.3.4 Let $A := \mathbb{N} \times \mathbb{N}$ and let $\rightarrow$ be defined by the two rules $(i+1, j) \rightarrow (i, k)$ and $(i, j+1) \rightarrow (i, j)$ for all $i, j, k \geq 0$. This reduction is not finitely branching because the value of k in the first rule is not constrained by the left-hand side. Termination of $\rightarrow$ can be shown by a simple lexicographic construction (see Section 2.4). Yet there is no monotone function φ from $(\mathbb{N} \times \mathbb{N}, \rightarrow)$ into $(\mathbb{N}, >)$. For if there were such a function φ, observe that monotonicity implies $k := \varphi(1, 1) > \varphi(0, k) > \varphi(0, k - 1) > \cdots > \varphi(0, 0)$. This is a contradiction because there are only k natural numbers below k and yet the chain $\varphi(0, k) > \cdots > \varphi(0, 0)$ has length $k + 1$.

Even in the context of finitely branching reductions, an embedding into $\mathbb{N}$ can be tricky to find.

Example 2.3.5 Let $A = \mathbb{N} \times \mathbb{N}$ and define the reduction by $(i, j+1) \to (i, j)$ and $(i+1, j) \to (i, i)$. This reduction terminates at $(0, 0)$ for every start point. It is also finitely branching. Hence there is a measure function into $\mathbb{N}$. In this particular case $\varphi(i, j) = i^2 + j$ does the job, but it takes a moment to find this function and prove that it is monotone.

We will now discuss how to get around the above problems with measure functions into $\mathbb{N}$ by building complex orders from simpler ones using fixed constructions which preserve termination.

Exercises

2.8   Find a measure function into $\mathbb{N}$ which proves termination of $\to$ in Example 2.1.2, part 2.

2.9   Find a measure function into $\mathbb{N}$ which proves termination of $\to_1 \cup \to_2$ in Example 2.3.1.

2.4 Lexicographic orders

Given two strict orders $(A, >_A)$ and $(B, >_B)$, the **lexicographic product** $>_{A \times B}$ on $A \times B$ is defined by

$$(x, y) >_{A \times B} (x', y') \; :\Leftrightarrow \; (x >_A x') \lor (x = x' \land y >_B y').$$

If A and B are obvious from the context we write $>$ instead of $>_{A \times B}$. Sometimes we also write $>_A \times_{lex} >_B$.

The following property is routine to prove:

Lemma 2.4.1 *The lexicographic product of two strict orders is again a strict order.*

More interestingly we have

Theorem 2.4.2 *The lexicographic product of two terminating relations is again terminating.*

Proof by contradiction. Assume there is an infinitely descending chain $(a_0, b_0) > (a_1, b_1) > \cdots$. This implies $a_0 \geq_A a_1 \geq_A \cdots$. Since $>_A$ terminates, this chain cannot contain an infinite number of strict steps $a_i >_A a_{i+1}$. Hence there is a k such that $a_i = a_{i+1}$ for all $i \geq k$. But this implies $b_i >_B b_{i+1}$ for all $i \geq k$, which contradicts the termination of $>_B$. $\qquad\square$

This theorem proves termination of $\to$ on $\mathbb{N} \times \mathbb{N}$ in Examples 2.3.4 and 2.3.5: $(i, j) \to (i', j')$ is defined such that (i, j) is lexicographically greater than (i', j'), i.e. $\to$ is a subset of the terminating relation $>_{N \times N}$. It also proves termination of $\to_1 \cup \to_2$ in Example 2.3.1: $\to_1$ decreases the length whereas $\to_2$ leaves the length invariant but decreases the number of as.

Lexicographic products are essential in building up more complex orders from simpler ones. By iteration, we can form lexicographic products over any number of strict orders $(A_i, >_i)$, $i = 1, \ldots, n$: $>_{1 \ldots n}$, where $n > 1$, is the lexicographic product of $>_1$ and $>_{2 \ldots n}$. Unwinding the recursion and writing $>$ instead of $>_{1 \ldots n}$ we get

$$(x_1, \ldots, x_n) > (y_1, \ldots, y_n) :\Leftrightarrow \exists k \le n. \ (\forall i < k. \ x_i = y_i) \wedge x_k >_k y_k. \quad (2.1)$$

If all $(A_i, >_i)$ are the same we write $>_{lex}^n$ for the n-fold lexicographic product.

The above results for the binary lexicographic product carry over to n-fold products: $>$ is again a strict order and it terminates if all the $>_i$ terminate. The proofs are by induction on n.

Instead of tuples of fixed length, we can also consider strings of arbitrary but finite length: given a strict order $(A, >)$, the **lexicographic order** $>_{lex}^*$ on A^* is defined as

$$u >_{lex}^* v :\Leftrightarrow (|u| > |v|) \vee (|u| = |v| \wedge u >_{lex}^{|u|} v)$$

where $|w|$ is the length of w and $>_{lex}^{|w|}$ is the order on $A^{|w|}$ defined in (2.1) above. More concisely, we can define $>_{lex}^*$ as the lexicographic product of $>_{len}$ and $\bigcup_{i \in N} >_{lex}^i$, where $u >_{len} v :\Leftrightarrow |u| > |v|$. Since A^i and A^j are disjoint if $i \ne j$, the second component of this product is a union of orders over disjoint sets. Since such unions (this is easy to see) and lexicographic products (as shown above) preserve strict orders and termination, we have

Lemma 2.4.3 *If $>$ is a strict order, so is $>_{lex}^*$. If $>$ terminates, so does $>_{lex}^*$.*

Despite its name, $>_{lex}^*$ is not the order used in dictionaries. The latter does not terminate: $a >_{dict} aa >_{dict} aaa >_{dict} \cdots$.

Yet another interesting variation on lexicographic orders compares strings from left to right as follows: $w_1 >_{Lex} w_2$ if w_2 is a proper prefix of w_1 or if $w_1 = uav$, $w_2 = ubw$ and $a > b$, where $>$ is the underlying strict order. For example, if $a > b$, then $aaaa >_{Lex} aaa >_{Lex} abba$. Unfortunately, $>_{Lex}$ need not terminate either, even if $>$ does (exercise!). Nevertheless, $>_{Lex}$ can be a useful component in more complicated orders.

Lemma 2.4.4 *If $>$ is a strict order, so is $>_{Lex}$.*

The proof, a simple case analysis, is left as an exercise.

A final word of warning about our definition of the lexicographic product. Although we assume the component relations to be strict orders, the definition works just as well for arbitrary relations. In fact, Theorem 2.4.2 depends on termination only. Nevertheless, the lexicographic product of two arbitrary relations may not be what you expect. For example $\geq_N \times_{lex} \geq_N$ relates all (i, j) and (i, k), simply because $i \geq_N i$. Hence you should not use $\times_{lex}$ directly with reflexive relations. Given two partial orders $\geq_A$ and $\geq_B$, their lexicographic product should be defined as the reflexive closure of $>_A \times_{lex} >_B$. (Remember that the strict part of a partial order $\geq$ is written $>$.) Of course this can be written more succinctly, if slightly ambiguously, as $\geq_{A \times B}$. Alternatively, we can define the lexicographic product directly for partial orders:

$$(x, y) \geq_{A \times B} (x', y') \quad :\Leftrightarrow \quad (x >_A x') \vee (x = x' \wedge y \geq_B y').$$

It is easy to show that these two definitions of $\geq_{A \times B}$ are equivalent and that $\geq_{A \times B}$ is a partial order if $\geq_A$ and $\geq_B$ are partial orders (exercise!).

Exercises

2.10   Prove Theorem 2.4.2 by well-founded induction.

2.11   Show that the following process always terminates. There is a box full of black and white balls. Each step consists of removing an arbitrary ball from the box. If it happens to be a black ball, one also adds an arbitrary (but finite) number of white balls to the box.

2.12   Show that $v_1 >_{lex}^* v_2$ implies $uv_1w >_{lex}^* uv_2w$.

2.13   Show that $>_{A \times B}$ is linear if both $>_A$ and $>_B$ are.

2.14   Show that $>_{lex}^*$ is linear if $>$ is.

2.15   Why do the following two programs terminate, provided all variables range over positive natural numbers?

```
while m ≠ n do
   if m > n then m := m − n else n := n − m

while m ≠ n do
   if m > n then m := m − n
   else begin h := m; m := n; n := h end
```

What if the variables range over positive rational numbers?

2.16 Show that the evaluation of the following recursively defined function, also known as **Ackermann's function**, terminates for all $m, n \in \mathbb{N}$:

$$
\begin{aligned}
ack(0, n) &= n + 1, \\
ack(m + 1, 0) &= ack(m, 1), \\
ack(m + 1, n + 1) &= ack(m, ack(m + 1, n)).
\end{aligned}
$$

2.17 Does termination of $>$ imply termination of $>_{Lex}$?

2.18 Prove Lemma 2.4.4.

2.19 Show that $>_{Lex}$ is linear if $>$ is.

2.20 Formalize the order used in dictionaries.

2.21 The lexicographic product of two quasi-orders $\gtrsim_A$ and $\gtrsim_B$ is defined as follows:

$$(x, y) \gtrsim (x', y') \quad :\Leftrightarrow \quad x >_A x' \vee (x \sim_A x' \wedge y \gtrsim_B y').$$

(a) Show that $\gtrsim$ is a quasi-order if both $\gtrsim_A$ and $\gtrsim_B$ are.

(b) Show that $>$, the strict part of $\gtrsim$, terminates if $>_A$ and $>_B$ do.

2.5 Multiset orders

Consider the following reduction on $\mathbb{N}^*$: $u(i+1)v \to uiiv$ for all $u, v \in \mathbb{N}^*$ and $i \in \mathbb{N}$. It turns out that $\to$ terminates, and because it is finitely branching, there should also exist a measure function into $\mathbb{N}$. If you want to spare yourself the torture of finding that function, you should read on.

One of the most powerful ways of building terminating orders is *multisets*. They are usually defined as "sets with repeated elements", which the purist will find a contradiction in terms, but which conveys their nature quite well. Examples are $\{a, a, b\}$ and $\{a, b, a\}$, which are identical, and $\{a, b, b\}$, which is distinct from them. Of course, we can also be more formal:

Definition 2.5.1 A **multiset** M over a set A is a function $M : A \to \mathbb{N}$. Intuitively, $M(x)$ is the number of copies of $x \in A$ in M.

A multiset M is **finite** if there are only finitely many x such that $M(x) > 0$. Let $\mathcal{M}(A)$ denote the set of all finite multisets over A.

Although multisets can be infinite, and much of the theory works for infinite multisets, the bit that is crucial for us fails: termination. Therefore all our multisets are assumed to be finite unless stated otherwise.

We use standard set notation like $\{a, a, b\}$ as an abbreviation of the function $\{a \mapsto 2, b \mapsto 1, c \mapsto 0\}$ over the base set $A = \{a, b, c\}$. It will be obvious from the context if we refer to a set or a multiset.

Most set operations are easily generalized to multisets by replacing the underlying Boolean operations by similar ones on $\mathbb{N}$.

Definition 2.5.2 Some basic operations and relations on $\mathcal{M}(A)$ are:

Element : $x \in M :\Leftrightarrow M(x) > 0$.
Inclusion : $M \subseteq N :\Leftrightarrow \forall x \in A.\ M(x) \le N(x)$.
Union : $(M \cup N)(x) := M(x) + N(x)$.
Difference : $(M - N)(x) := M(x) \dot{-} N(x)$
      where $m \dot{-} n$ is $m - n$ if $m \ge n$ and is 0 otherwise.

Some typical examples: $\emptyset \subseteq \{a, a\} \subseteq \{a, a, a\}$, $\{a, b\} \cup \{b, a\} = \{a, a, b, b\}$ and $\{a, b, b, b\} - \{a, a, b, c\} = \{b, b\}$.

Now we come to the central concept of this section, an order on multisets: the smaller multiset is obtained from the larger one by removing a nonempty subset X and adding only elements which are smaller than some element in X.

Definition 2.5.3 Given a strict order $>$ on a set A, we define the corresponding **multiset order** $>_{mul}$ on $\mathcal{M}(A)$ as follows:

$$M >_{mul} N \quad \text{iff} \quad \text{there exist } X, Y \in \mathcal{M}(A) \text{ such that}$$
$$\emptyset \ne X \subseteq M \text{ and}$$
$$N = (M - X) \cup Y \text{ and}$$
$$\forall y \in Y.\ \exists x \in X.\ x > y.$$

For example, $\{5, 3, 1, 1\} >_{mul} \{4, 3, 3, 1\}$ is verified by replacing $X = \{5, 1\}$ by $Y = \{4, 3\}$. Note that X and Y are not uniquely determined: $X = \{5, 3, 1, 1\}$ and $Y = \{4, 3, 3, 1\}$ work just as well.

Sometimes it can be useful to realize that $M >_{mul} N$ holds iff you can get from M to N by carrying out the following procedure one or more times: remove an element x and add a finite number of elements, all of which are smaller than x (see Exercise 2.22).

On finite multisets, the multiset order is again a strict order:

Lemma 2.5.4 *If $>$ is a strict order, so is $>_{mul}$.*

Proof Irreflexivity: if $M >_{mul} M$, there are X and Y such that $X \subseteq M$, $M = (M - X) \cup Y$, i.e. $X = Y$, and $\forall y \in Y.\exists x \in X.\ x > y$, which implies $\forall y \in X.\exists x \in X.\ x > y$. Since $>$ is a strict order this implies that X is infinite, a contradiction.

Transitivity is more involved. If $M_1 >_{mul} M_2 >_{mul} M_3$ then $M_2 = (M_1 - X_1) \cup Y_1$ and $M_3 = (M_2 - X_2) \cup Y_2$, for multisets X_i and Y_i satisfying the appropriate conditions in the definition of $>_{mul}$. We now claim that

$X := X_1 \cup (X_2 - Y_1)$ and $Y := (Y_1 - X_2) \cup Y_2$ prove $M_1 >_{mul} M_3$. Let us look at the required conditions in turn.

- $X \neq \emptyset$ is implied by $X_1 \neq \emptyset$.
- $X_2 \subseteq M_2 = (M_1 - X_1) \cup Y_1$ implies $X_2 - Y_1 \subseteq M_1 - X_1$ and hence, because $X_1 \subseteq M_1$, $X = X_1 \cup (X_2 - Y_1) \subseteq M_1$.
- We need to show that $M_3 = (M_1 - X) \cup Y =: M_3'$, which follows if we can show $M_3(a) = M_3'(a)$ for an arbitrary $a \in A$. We have $M_3'(a) = (M_1(a) \dot{-} (X_1(a) + (X_2(a) \dot{-} Y_1(a)))) + ((Y_1(a) \dot{-} X_2(a)) + Y_2(a))$. Because $X \subseteq M_1$, the first "$\dot{-}$" in this expression can be replaced by an ordinary minus "$-$", which (after some arithmetic rearrangement) yields $M_3'(a) = (M_1(a) - X_1(a)) + ((Y_1(a) \dot{-} X_2(a)) - (X_2(a) \dot{-} Y_1(a))) + Y_2(a)$. Obviously, $(m \dot{-} n) - (n \dot{-} m) = m - n$, and thus we obtain $M_3'(a) = (((M_1(a) - X_1(a)) + Y_1(a)) - X_2(a)) + Y_2(a) = (M_2(a) - X_2(a)) + Y_2(a) = M_3(a)$.
- To prove $\forall y \in Y. \exists x \in X. x > y$ let $y \in Y$. If $y \in Y_1$, $M_1 >_{mul} M_2$ implies $x > y$ for some $x \in X_1 \subseteq X$. If $y \in Y_2$, $M_2 >_{mul} M_3$ implies $x > y$ for some $x \in X_2$. If $x \in X_2 - Y_1 \subseteq X$, we are done. Otherwise $x \in Y_1$, in which case $M_1 >_{mul} M_2$ implies $x_1 > x$ for some $x_1 \in X_1 \subseteq X$ and hence $x_1 > y$ by transitivity of $>$ on A. $\square$

The really important nontrivial property of $>_{mul}$ is

Theorem 2.5.5 *The multiset order $>_{mul}$ is terminating iff $>$ is.*

Proof If $>$ does not terminate, there is an infinite chain $a_0 > a_1 > \cdots$ which induces an infinite chain $\{a_0\} >_{mul} \{a_1\} >_{mul} \cdots$ of multisets. Hence $>_{mul}$ does not terminate either.

If $>$ terminates, we show by contradiction that $>_{mul}$ terminates. Assume there is an infinite chain $M_0 >_{mul} M_1 >_{mul} \cdots$. We can then build a finitely branching but infinite tree where the nodes are labelled with elements of A such that along each path the labels decrease w.r.t. $>$. Using König's Lemma, it follows that this tree must have an infinite branch, which yields an infinitely descending sequence in A, the desired contradiction. It remains to be seen how to construct this tree.

Let $\perp$ be an arbitrary element not in A, let $A_\perp := A \cup \{\perp\}$, and extend $>$ by defining $a > \perp$ for all $a \in A$. Obviously $(A_\perp, >)$ is still terminating. Now we grow the following tree whose nodes are labelled with elements of $A_\perp$. At stage i of the construction the non-$\perp$ leaf nodes form the multiset M_i. The initial tree has a root with an arbitrary label and a successor node for each element of M_0, e.g. $M_0 = \{5, 3, 1, 1\}$:

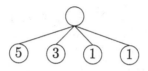

Since $M_0 >_{mul} M_1$, there are finite multisets X and Y with the properties stated in the definition of $>_{mul}$. For every $y \in Y$ add a new node labelled y and make it the child of some leaf node labelled x where $x > y$. By definition of $>_{mul}$ such an x must exist in $X \subseteq M_0$ and hence x is among the current leaf nodes. In addition we add a son labelled $\bot$ to each $x \in X$. This ensures that even if Y is empty, the tree has grown. Example: $M_1 = \{4, 3, 3, 1\}$, $X = \{5, 1\}$ and $Y = \{4, 3\}$:

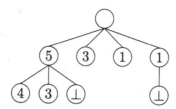

This process can be continued for M_2, M_3, ... Thus we are constructing a finitely branching (the M_i are finite) but infinite (for each M_i at least one node is added) tree. Ignoring the root node, the labels on each path are strictly decreasing by construction. $\qquad\square$

Note that the proof does not require $>$ to be a strict order but works for any relation.

It is now easy to see that the reduction $u(i+1)v \to uiiv$ considered at the beginning of this section terminates: the mapping $\varphi : \mathbb{N}^* \to \mathcal{M}(\mathbb{N})$ defined by $\varphi(i_1 \ldots i_n) := \{i_1, \ldots, i_n\}$ is obviously monotone ($\varphi(u(i+1)v) = \varphi(u) \cup \{i+1\} \cup \varphi(v) >_{mul} \varphi(u) \cup \{i, i\} \cup \varphi(v) = \varphi(uiiv)$) and $>_{mul}$ on $\mathcal{M}(\mathbb{N})$ terminates because $>$ on $\mathbb{N}$ does.

The above definition of $>_{mul}$ is quite intuitive but also a little cumbersome because of its many quantifiers and conditions. Therefore the following alternative characterization is useful:

Lemma 2.5.6 *If $>$ is a strict order and $M, N \in \mathcal{M}(A)$, then*

$$M >_{mul} N \iff M \neq N \wedge \forall n \in N - M. \exists m \in M - N. m > n.$$

Proof For the $\Rightarrow$-direction, assume $M >_{mul} N$, in which case there are X and Y as in the definition of $>_{mul}$. $M \neq N$ follows from irreflexivity of $>_{mul}$. For the second conjunct, let $y_1 \in N - M = ((M - X) \cup Y) - M = ((M \cup Y) - X) - M = ((M \cup Y) - M) - X = Y - X$. Hence there is a $y_2 \in X$ such that $y_2 > y_1$. Either $y_2 \in X - Y = (M - (M - X)) - Y =$

$M - ((M - X) \cup Y) = M - N$, in which case we are done, or $y_2 \in X \cap Y$ (where $(X \cap Y)(x) := min(X(x), Y(x))$), in which case there is a $y_3 \in X$ such that $y_3 > y_2$. Because our multisets are finite and $>$ is a strict order, there is no infinite ascending chain $y_1 < y_2 < y_3 < \cdots$ in $X \cap Y$, i.e. this process must always terminate with some $y_n \in X - Y = M - N$. Transitivity yields $y_n > y_1$.

The $\Leftarrow$-direction is left as an exercise. $\qquad\qquad\qquad\qquad\qquad\square$

It is worth noting that if $>$ is linear, then $M >_{mul} N$ can be computed quite efficiently: sort M and N into descending order (w.r.t. $>$) and compare the resulting lists lexicographically w.r.t. $>_{Lex}$. Let $\vec{M}$ be the sorted version of M. It is easy to see that $\vec{M} >_{Lex} \vec{N}$ implies $M >_{mul} N$: either $\vec{N}$ is a proper prefix of $\vec{M}$, in which case $M \supset N$ and hence $M >_{mul} N$; or $\vec{M} = umv$, $\vec{N} = unw$ such that $m > n$, in which case m is larger than all elements in w, which again implies $M >_{mul} N$. Conversely, if $\vec{M} \not>_{Lex} \vec{N}$ then either $M = N$ or $\vec{N} >_{Lex} \vec{M}$ (Exercise 2.19) and thus $N >_{mul} M$; since $>_{mul}$ is strict, this implies $M \not>_{mul} N$ in both cases. Thus we conclude that

$$M >_{mul} N \Leftrightarrow \vec{M} >_{Lex} \vec{N}. \qquad (2.2)$$

Let us briefly look at the multiset extension of partial orders. As in the lexicographic case, we have to be a bit careful. If we simply replace $>$ by $\geq$ we end up with $\{1\} \geq_{mul} \{1, 1\}$, which is not desirable. Instead, $\geq_{mul}$, the multiset extension of a partial order $\geq$, is defined as follows:

$$M \geq_{mul} N :\Leftrightarrow M >_{mul} N \lor M = N.$$

Given a quasi-order $(A, \gtrsim)$, we define its multiset extension via the induced partial order $\geq$ on $A/_\sim$:

$$M \gtrsim N :\Leftrightarrow M/_\sim \geq_{mul} N/_\sim$$

where $\{a_1, \ldots, a_k\}/_\sim := \{[a_1]_\sim, \ldots, [a_k]_\sim\}$.

Exercises

2.22 Given a strict order $(A, >)$, define the following single-step relation on $\mathcal{M}(A)$:

$$M >^1_{mul} N :\Leftrightarrow \exists x \in M, Y \in \mathcal{M}(A). \; N = (M - \{x\}) \cup Y \land \\ \forall y \in Y. \; x > y.$$

Show that $>_{mul}$ is the same as the transitive closure of $>^1_{mul}$. (*Hint:* show that each relation is contained in the other using appropriate inductions.) Conclude that $>_{mul}$ is transitive.

2.23 Show that X and Y in the definition of $>_{mul}$ can always be chosen such that they are disjoint.

2.24 Give a counterexample to Lemma 2.5.4 for infinite multisets. Show that Lemma 2.5.4 also holds for infinite multisets provided there is no infinitely *ascending* chain $x_0 < x_1 < \cdots$.

2.25 Prove the $\Leftarrow$-direction of Lemma 2.5.6.

2.26 Show that if $\geq$ is a partial order, so is $\geq_{mul}$, and that $\gtrsim_{mul}$ is a quasi-order if $\gtrsim$ is one.

2.6 Orders in ML

How should we implement strict/partial orders in general? The obvious implementation as a function $ord\colon \tau * \tau \to bool$ has its problems:

- If $ord(x,y)$ implements $x > y$, we cannot recover $x \geq y$ by writing $ord(x,y)$ orelse x = y because in general we cannot assume that the mathematical equality $=$ on the base set A coincides with the programming language equality = on the type τ used to implement A. For example, if sets are implemented by lists, we do not have [1,2] = [2,1] although they are equal as sets.

- If $ord(x,y)$ implements $x \geq y$, we can compute $x > y$ as $ord(x,y)$ andalso $not(ord(y,x))$. This is mathematically correct but inefficient because of the two calls to ord. The performance penalty is exponential in the depth of the nesting of orders.

- Implementing both $>$ and $\geq$ is likely to duplicate much of the code.

To overcome these problems we introduce

        datatype *order* = *GR* | *EQ* | *NGE*;

which represents the three outcomes $>$, $=$ and $\not\gtrsim$. We say that a function ord computes a strict/partial order $>/\geq$ if

$$ord(x,y) = \begin{cases} GR & \text{if } x > y, \\ EQ & \text{if } x = y, \\ NGE & \text{if } x \not\geq y. \end{cases}$$

Note that by $x = y$ we mean equality on the abstract, not the implementation level. The latter is x = y, which is too weak, as the set/list example demonstrates: on the implementation level, a partial order may turn into a quasi-order. The purpose of EQ instead of = is to hide that fact. On the other hand, we may even start with a quasi-order $\gtrsim$, in which case GR, EQ and NGE represent $>$, $\sim$ and $\not\gtrsim$.

2.6.1 Lexicographic orders

Unsurprisingly, $\times$ is implemented by $*$ and $*$ by *list*. The corresponding constructions $>_{A \times B}$ and $>^*_{lex}$ are equally straightforward. Note that A^n should be implemented not as an n-fold product but as a list, in which case $>^n_{lex}$ has the following simple recursive implementation:

```
(* lex: (α * β -> order) -> α list * β list -> order *)
fun lex ord ([],[]) = EQ
  | lex ord (x::xs,y::ys) = case ord(x,y) of
        GR => GR
      | EQ => lex ord (xs,ys)
      | NGE => NGE;
```

If *ord* implements $>$ then *lex ord* implements $>^n_{lex}$ for any n. Note that *lex ord* is undefined if the two argument lists have different lengths.

The type of *lex* is slightly more general than one might have expected because *ord* could potentially compare elements of two different types. This kind of unexpected generalization is a frequent ML phenomenon which we will not comment on in the future.

2.6.2 Multiset orders

We represent finite multisets over a type τ by τ *list*, which leads to very simple algorithms. For example, $\cup$ becomes @. Multiset difference, however, needs to be parameterized by the order on τ because we need to compare elements for *EQuality* on the abstract level:

```
(* rem1: (α * β -> bool) -> α list -> β -> α list *)
fun rem1 ord ([], _)    = []
  | rem1 ord (x::xs, y) = if ord(x,y) = EQ then xs
                          else x :: (rem1 ord (xs, y));

(* mdiff: (α * β -> bool) -> α list -> β list -> α list *)
fun mdiff ord (xs, [])    = xs
  | mdiff ord (xs, y::ys) = mdiff ord (rem1 ord (xs,y), ys);
```

The starting point for an implementation of $>_{mul}$ is not its actual definition, which is marred by existential quantifiers, but Lemma 2.5.6 which can be expressed in ML almost verbatim:

```
(* mul: (α * α -> order) -> α list * α list -> order *)
fun mul ord (ms,ns) =
  let val nms = mdiff ord (ns,ms)
      val mns = mdiff ord (ms,ns)
  in if null(nms) andalso null(mns) then EQ
     else if forall (fn n => exists (fn m => ord(m,n)=GR) mns) nms
          then GR else NGE
  end;
```

The "almost" is a consequence of the fact that we cannot use $=$ to compare ms and ns. The test $null(nms)$ $\mathtt{andalso}$ $null(mns)$ is justified by the equivalence $M = N \Leftrightarrow (M - N) = \emptyset = (N - M)$ on the multiset level.

Assuming that the running time of ord is constant, $mdiff\ ord\ (ms, ns)$ has time complexity $O(mn)$, where m and n are the lengths of ms and ns. This is inherited by $mul\ ord\ (ms, ns)$ because $O(mn + nm + |m - n||n - m|) = O(mn)$. If ord is a linear order, condition (2.2) above allows an implementation of mul which runs in time $O(m+n)$, provided multisets are represented by sorted lists.

Exercises

2.27 Implement $>_{Lex}$.

2.28 Implement multisets as association lists which pair every element with the number of times it occurs in the multiset. Update the code for $mdiff$ and mul accordingly.

2.7 Proving confluence

Proving confluence can be hard work because one has to consider forks $y_1 \overset{*}{\leftarrow} x \overset{*}{\rightarrow} y_2$ of arbitrary length. We will now look at ways of *localizing* the confluence test to single-step forks $y_1 \leftarrow x \rightarrow y_2$.

Definition 2.7.1 A relation $\rightarrow$ is **locally confluent** (Fig. 2.5) iff

$$y_1 \leftarrow x \rightarrow y_2 \Rightarrow y_1 \downarrow y_2.$$

Fig. 2.5. Local confluence, strong confluence, and the diamond property.

Local confluence is strictly weaker than confluence. A simple example is shown in Fig. 2.6 on the left: both local forks $a \leftarrow 0 \rightarrow 1$ and $0 \leftarrow 1 \rightarrow b$ can be closed, yet the reduction is not confluent. One might suspect that the cycle between 0 and 1 is responsible, but the second example in Fig. 2.6 (only an initial segment of the infinite graph generated by $2n \rightarrow a$, $2n + 1 \rightarrow b$ and $n \rightarrow n + 1$, is shown) proves that this is not the case: even for acyclic

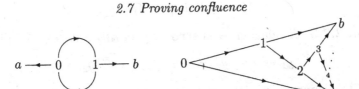

Fig. 2.6. Local confluence does not imply confluence.

relations, local confluence does not imply confluence. Both example are nonterminating. This is a consequence of **Newman's Lemma** [185]:

Lemma 2.7.2 *A terminating relation is confluent if it is locally confluent.*

Proof Let $\rightarrow$ be terminating and locally confluent. We show confluence by well-founded induction using the predicate

$$P(x) \ = \ \forall y, z. \ y \stackrel{*}{\leftarrow} x \stackrel{*}{\rightarrow} z \Rightarrow y \downarrow z.$$

Obviously $\rightarrow$ is confluent if $P(x)$ holds for all x. Well-founded induction requires us to show $P(x)$ under the assumption $P(t)$ for all t such that $x \stackrel{+}{\rightarrow} t$. To prove $P(x)$, we analyse the fork $y \stackrel{*}{\leftarrow} x \stackrel{*}{\rightarrow} z$. If $x = y$ or $x = z$, $y \downarrow z$ is immediate. Otherwise we have $x \rightarrow y_1 \stackrel{*}{\rightarrow} y$ and $x \rightarrow z_1 \stackrel{*}{\rightarrow} z$ as shown in Fig. 2.7. The existence of u follows by local confluence, the

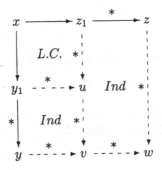

Fig. 2.7. Proof of Newman's Lemma.

existence of v and w by induction hypothesis because $x \stackrel{+}{\rightarrow} y_1$ and $x \stackrel{+}{\rightarrow} z_1$, respectively. Thus we get $y \downarrow z$, i.e. $P(x)$. $\square$

Of course the other direction of the implication holds trivially.

Termination opens a particularly easy path to confluence via local confluence. For nonterminating relations we can still localize the confluence test if we restrict the way in which forks are closed.

Definition 2.7.3 A relation $\to$ is **strongly confluent** (Fig. 2.5) iff

$$y_1 \leftarrow x \to y_2 \Rightarrow \exists z.\ y_1 \overset{*}{\to} z \overset{=}{\leftarrow} y_2.$$

Beware of the symmetry in this definition: $y_1 \leftarrow x \to y_2$ must imply both $y_1 \overset{*}{\to} z_1 \overset{=}{\leftarrow} y_2$ and $y_1 \overset{=}{\to} z_2 \overset{*}{\leftarrow} y_2$ for suitable z_1 and z_2. Therefore neither of the relations in Fig. 2.6 is strongly confluent.

Lemma 2.7.4 *Any strongly confluent relation is confluent.*

Proof By Theorem 2.1.5 it suffices to show that strong confluence implies semi-confluence:

$$
\begin{array}{ccccccc}
x_1 & \longrightarrow & x_2 & \cdots\cdots & x_{n-1} & \longrightarrow & x_n \\
\downarrow & & \vdots & & \vdots & & \vdots \\
& S.C. =\! & & =\! & S.C. =\! & & \\
\downarrow & & \vdots & & \vdots & & \vdots \\
y_1 & \dashrightarrow & y_2 & \cdots\cdots & y_{n-1} & \dashrightarrow & y_n
\end{array}
$$

Formally, this is a proof of $y_1 \leftarrow x_1 \overset{n}{\to} x_n \Rightarrow \exists y_n.\ y_1 \overset{*}{\to} y_n \overset{=}{\leftarrow} x_n$ by induction on n. $\qquad\square$

The reader may wonder if such a strong property can be of practical use. The trick is not to apply Lemma 2.7.4 directly to the real object of interest $\to$ but to define a strongly confluent relation $\to_s$ such that $\overset{*}{\to} = \overset{*}{\to}_s$. Now Lemma 2.7.4 yields confluence of $\to_s$ which carries over to $\to$ using the following observation:

Fact 2.7.5 *If $\overset{*}{\to}_1 = \overset{*}{\to}_2$ then $\to_1$ is confluent iff $\to_2$ is confluent.*

The following lemma facilitates the application of this fact:

Lemma 2.7.6 *If $\to_1 \subseteq \to_2 \subseteq \overset{*}{\to}_1$ then $\overset{*}{\to}_1 = \overset{*}{\to}_2$.*

Proof Because the reflexive transitive closure is a monotone and idempotent operation, $\to_1 \subseteq \to_2 \subseteq \overset{*}{\to}_1$ implies $\overset{*}{\to}_1 \subseteq \overset{*}{\to}_2 \subseteq (\overset{*}{\to}_1)^* = \overset{*}{\to}_1$ and thus $\overset{*}{\to}_1 = \overset{*}{\to}_2$. $\qquad\square$

Putting Lemma 2.7.4, Fact 2.7.5 and Lemma 2.7.6 together we obtain

Corollary 2.7.7 *If $\to_1 \subseteq \to_2 \subseteq \overset{*}{\to}_1$ and $\to_2$ is strongly confluent, then $\to_1$ is confluent.*

In practice we are able to work with a yet stronger property:

Definition 2.7.8 A relation $\to$ has the **diamond property** (Fig. 2.5)† iff

$$y_1 \leftarrow x \to y_2 \Rightarrow \exists z.\ y_1 \to z \leftarrow y_2.$$

† For layout reasons, our diamonds frequently turn into squares.

The name is inspired not just by the corresponding diagram but also because the property is hard to obtain and precious.

Obviously, the diamond property implies strong confluence. Hence Corollary 2.7.7 also holds if $\to_2$ has the diamond property. Note further that $\to$ is confluent iff $\overset{*}{\to}$ has the diamond property.

2.7.1 Commutation

Confluence proofs can also be localized by splitting a reduction up into several smaller reductions and proving them confluent separately. In the sequel let $\to_1$ and $\to_2$ be two reductions on A. Clearly, confluence of $\to_1$ and $\to_2$ does not in general imply confluence of $\to_1 \cup \to_2$ (counterexample?). However, it does if $\to_1$ and $\to_2$ commute:

Definition 2.7.9 (See Fig. 2.8.) We say that $\to_1$ and $\to_2$

> **commute iff** $\qquad y_1 \overset{*}{\leftarrow}_1 x \overset{*}{\to}_2 y_2 \Rightarrow \exists z. \, y_1 \overset{*}{\to}_2 z \overset{*}{\leftarrow}_1 y_2,$
>
> **strongly commute iff** $\quad y_1 \leftarrow_1 x \to_2 y_2 \Rightarrow \exists z. \, y_1 \overset{=}{\to}_2 z \overset{*}{\leftarrow}_1 y_2,$
>
> have the **commuting diamond property iff**
>
> $$y_1 \leftarrow_1 x \to_2 y_2 \Rightarrow \exists z. \, y_1 \to_2 z \leftarrow_1 y_2.$$

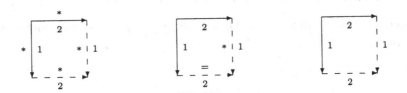

Fig. 2.8. Commutation, strong commutation, the commuting diamond property.

Note that "$\to_1$ and $\to_2$ commute" does not mean $\to_1 \circ \to_2 = \to_2 \circ \to_1$ but $\overset{*}{\leftarrow}_1 \circ \overset{*}{\to}_2 \subseteq \overset{*}{\to}_2 \circ \overset{*}{\leftarrow}_1$. Note also that "$\to_1$ and $\to_2$ strongly commute" is an asymmetric property, but will be used only in situations where this does not matter.

Commutation can be seen as a generalization of confluence to two relations. In fact, we could have introduced commutation first and confluence later on as a derived notion: $\to$ is confluent iff $\to$ and $\to$ commute. We prefer to generalize matters in stages.

The **Commutative Union Lemma** tells us that in certain cases union preserves confluence:

Lemma 2.7.10 *If $\to_1$ and $\to_2$ are confluent and commute, then $\to_1 \cup \to_2$ is also confluent.*

Proof Every $(\to_1 \cup \to_2)^*$ reduction consists of alternating segments of $\overset{*}{\to}_1$ and $\overset{*}{\to}_2$ reductions. Hence the following tiling argument proves the claim:

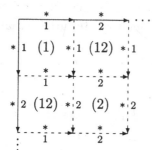

(1)   Confluence of $\to_1$
(2)   Confluence of $\to_2$
(12) Commutation of $\to_1$ and $\to_2$

The above proof is a bit informal because of the "...". It can easily be made completely formal by observing that the diagram without the "..." clearly proves that $\overset{*}{\to}_1 \circ \overset{*}{\to}_2$ has the diamond property and is therefore strongly confluent. It is also easy to see that (for arbitrary $\to_1$ and $\to_2$) we have

$$(\to_1 \cup \to_2) \subseteq (\overset{*}{\to}_1 \circ \overset{*}{\to}_2) \subseteq (\to_1 \cup \to_2)^*.$$

By Corollary 2.7.7 it follows that $\to_1 \cup \to_2$ is confluent. □

Commutation proofs are often simplified by the **Commutation Lemma**:

Lemma 2.7.11 *Two strongly commuting reductions commute.*

This generalizes Lemma 2.7.4. Generalizing the proof is recommended as an exercise.

Exercises

2.29 Give an indirect proof of Newman's Lemma by showing that if $\to$ is locally confluent but not confluent, then $\to$ contains an infinite reduction sequence. (*Hint:* show that an element with two distinct normal forms has a direct successor with two distinct normal forms.)

2.30 A reduction $\to_r$ is a **refinement** of $\to$ if $\to \subseteq \overset{*}{\to}_r$ and a **compatible refinement** if additionally $x \overset{*}{\to}_r y \Rightarrow x \downarrow y$. Show the following:

(a) Let $\to_r$ be a refinement of $\to$. Then $\to_r$ is a compatible refinement of $\to$ iff $x \to_r y \overset{*}{\to} z \Rightarrow x \downarrow z$.

(b) Let $\to_r$ be a compatible refinement of $\to$. Then $\to_r$ is confluent iff $\to$ is confluent.

2.31 Does strong confluence imply the following property?

$$y_1 \leftarrow x \to y_2 \;\Rightarrow\; \exists z. \; y_1 \overset{=}{\to} z \overset{=}{\leftarrow} y_2.$$

Give a proof or counterexample.

2.32   Show that if → has the diamond property, every element either is in normal form or has no normal form.

2.33   Let → satisfy the following weak form of the diamond property: if $y \leftarrow x \rightarrow z$ and $y \neq z$ then there is a u such that $y \rightarrow u \leftarrow z$. Show that if an element a has a normal form, then

(a) there is no infinite reduction sequence starting from a, and

(b) all reductions from a to its normal form have the same length.

2.34   Let $\rightarrow_i$, $i \in I$, be a set of reductions. Show that $\bigcup_{i \in I} \rightarrow_i$ is confluent if $\rightarrow_i$ and $\rightarrow_j$ commute for every $i, j \in I$.

2.35   Show that $(\rightarrow_1 \cup \rightarrow_2)^* = (\overset{*}{\rightarrow}_1 \cup \overset{*}{\rightarrow}_2)^*$.

2.36   Prove the Commutation Lemma.

2.37   Let $\rightarrow_1$ and $\rightarrow_2$ be two reductions on A such that $\rightarrow_1 \cup \rightarrow_2$ is transitive. Show that $\rightarrow_1 \cup \rightarrow_2$ is terminating iff $\rightarrow_1$ and $\rightarrow_2$ are terminating. (*Hint:* indirect proof.)

2.8 Bibliographic notes

Much of the material in this chapter is mathematical folklore found in introductory books on ordered sets, relations, or graphs.

The multiset order is due to Dershowitz and Manna [76].

The slick inductive proof of Newman's Lemma is due to Huet [119]. Confluence proofs based on the diamond property (Corollary 2.7.7) were pioneered by Tait and Martin-Löf [21, Chapter 3] in the context of λ-calculus. The Commutative Union Lemma and the Commutation Lemma were discovered by both Hindley [112] and Rosen [217].

3

Universal Algebra

The purpose of this chapter is twofold. On the one hand, it introduces basic notions from universal algebra (such as terms, substitutions, and identities) on a syntactic level that does not require (or give) much mathematical background. On the other hand, it presents the semantic counterparts of these syntactic notions (such as algebras, homomorphisms, and equational classes), and proves some elementary results on their connections. Most of the definitions and results presented in subsequent chapters can be understood knowing only the syntactic level introduced in Section 3.1. In order to obtain a deeper understanding of the meaning of these results, and of the context in which they are of interest, a study of the other sections in this chapter is recommended, however. For more information on universal algebra see, for example, [100, 55, 173].

3.1 Terms, substitutions, and identities

Terms will be built from function symbols and variables in the usual way. For example, if f is a binary function symbol, and x, y are variables, then $f(x, y)$ is a term. To make clear which function symbols are available in a certain context, and which arity they have, one introduces *signatures*.

Definition 3.1.1 A **signature** Σ is a set of **function symbols**, where each $f \in \Sigma$ is associated with a non-negative integer n, the **arity** of f. For $n \geq 0$, we denote the set of all n-ary elements of Σ by $\Sigma^{(n)}$. The elements of $\Sigma^{(0)}$ are also called **constant symbols**.

For example, if we want to talk about *groups*, which are equipped with an identity element, a unary inversion operation, and a binary multiplication operation, we use the signature $\Sigma_G := \{e, i, f\}$, where e has arity 0, i is unary, and f is binary. If we consider the *set of non-negative integers*, we may use the same signature, but now e denotes the smallest non-negative integer, i denotes the successor function, and f denotes addition.

In many applications (such as algebraic specification), one is faced with the problem that some operations are not defined on the whole domain. For example, the multiplicative inverse in a field is not defined on 0, and if we want to consider lists of non-negative integers, *addition* is not defined on lists, and *append* is not defined on non-negative integers. To cope with such situations, one usually introduces *sorts*, which (in the simplest version) just partition the domain (for example, into the set of non-negative integers, NAT, and the set of lists of non-negative integers, LIST). The signature now determines on which sorts a function is defined, and to which sort the result of the function application belongs. For example, the operation *cons*, which adds a new element to the beginning of a list, would be of signature NAT × LIST → LIST. In order to simplify notation, we shall not consider different sorts here. All the results and definitions can, however, easily be extended to the **many-sorted** case, where sorts are simply assumed to partition the domain. It should be noted that such an easy transfer of results is no longer possible when considering an **order-sorted** framework [224], where one sort can be a subsort of another (e.g. NAT $\leq$ INT).

Definition 3.1.2 Let Σ be a signature and X be a set of **variables** such that $\Sigma \cap X = \emptyset$. The set $T(\Sigma, X)$ of all Σ-**terms** over X is inductively defined as

- $X \subseteq T(\Sigma, X)$ (i.e. every variable is a term),
- for all $n \geq 0$, all $f \in \Sigma^{(n)}$, and all $t_1, \ldots, t_n \in T(\Sigma, X)$, we have $f(t_1, \ldots, t_n) \in T(\Sigma, X)$ (i.e. application of function symbols to terms yields terms).

For example, for the signature $\Sigma_G = \{e, i, f\}$ from above, $f(e, f(x, i(x)))$ is a Σ_G-term that contains the variable x. For the 0-ary function symbol e, we have written the corresponding term simply as e instead of $e()$ (i.e. e applied to the sequence of terms of length 0). Binary function symbols (such as $+$ and $*$) are often written in infix form, with parentheses if necessary; e.g. $(x + y) + z$ instead of $+(+(x, y), z)$. If g is a unary function symbol, then $g^n(t)$ abbreviates the term $g(g(\ldots g(t) \ldots))$, the n-fold application of g to t. In the context of terms, symbols f, g, h usually stand for function symbols (of arity > 0), a, b, c for constant symbols, and x, y, z for variables.

The structure of a term can be nicely illustrated by representing it as a tree, where function symbols are nodes and arrows point to the arguments of the function. The tree in Fig. 3.1 depicts the term t of our example.

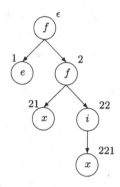

Fig. 3.1. Tree representation of $t = f(e, f(x, i(x)))$.

Using a standard numbering of the nodes of the tree by strings of positive integers (as illustrated in the example), we can refer to positions in a term. In our example, position ϵ (the empty string) refers to the symbol f on the top level, and position 2 refers to the symbol f that occurs as second argument of the top-level f. The subterm of t at position 2 is $f(x, i(x))$, and the subterm of t at position 22 is $i(x)$. More formally, notions like position and subterm can be defined by induction on the structure of terms.

Definition 3.1.3 Let Σ be a signature, X be a set of variables disjoint from Σ, and $s, t \in T(\Sigma, X)$.

1. The set of **positions** of the term s is a set $\mathcal{P}os(s)$ of strings over the alphabet of positive integers, which is inductively defined as follows:
   - If $s = x \in X$, then $\mathcal{P}os(s) := \{\epsilon\}$, where ϵ denotes the empty string.
   - If $s = f(s_1, \ldots, s_n)$, then

$$\mathcal{P}os(s) := \{\epsilon\} \cup \bigcup_{i=1}^{n} \{ip \mid p \in \mathcal{P}os(s_i)\}.$$

   The position ϵ is called the **root position** of the term s, and the function or variable symbol at this position is called the **root symbol** of s. The **prefix order** defined as

$$p \leq q \text{ iff there exists } p' \text{ such that } pp' = q$$

   is a partial order on positions. We say that the positions p, q are **parallel** ($p \parallel q$) iff p and q are incomparable with respect to $\leq$. The position p is **above** q if $p \leq q$ and p is **strictly above** q if $p < q$ (**below** is defined analogously).

2. The **size** $|s|$ of a term s is the cardinality of $\mathcal{P}os(s)$.

3. For $p \in Pos(s)$, the **subterm of** s **at position** p, denoted by $s|_p$, is defined by induction on the length of p:

$$s|_\epsilon \; := \; s,$$
$$f(s_1, \ldots, s_n)|_{iq} \; := \; s_i|_q.$$

Note that, for $p = iq$, $p \in Pos(s)$ implies that s is of the form $s = f(s_1, \ldots, s_n)$ with $i \leq n$.

4. For $p \in Pos(s)$, we denote by $s[t]_p$ the term that is obtained from s by **replacing the subterm at position** p **by** t, i.e.

$$s[t]_\epsilon \; := \; t,$$
$$f(s_1, \ldots, s_n)[t]_{iq} \; := \; f(s_1, \ldots, s_i[t]_q, \ldots, s_n).$$

5. By $Var(s)$ we denote the set of **variables occurring in** s, i.e.

$$Var(s) := \{x \in X \mid \text{there exists } p \in Pos(s) \text{ such that } s|_p = x\}.$$

We call $p \in Pos(t)$ a **variable position** if $t|_p$ is a variable.

For the term t of the above example, $Pos(t) = \{\epsilon, 1, 2, 21, 22, 221\}$, $t|_{22} = i(x)$, $t[e]_2 = f(e, e)$, $Var(t) = \{x\}$, and $|t| = 6$. Note that the size of t is just the number of nodes in the tree representation of t. The set of positions of a term is obviously closed under taking prefixes, i.e. if $q \in Pos(t)$ then $p \in Pos(t)$ for all $p \leq q$. The following lemma states some useful rules for computing with positions and subterms.

Lemma 3.1.4 *Let s, t, r be terms and p, q be strings over the positive integers.*

1. *If $pq \in Pos(s)$, then $s|_{pq} = (s|_p)|_q$.*
2. *If $p \in Pos(s)$ and $q \in Pos(t)$, then*

$$(s[t]_p)|_{pq} \; = \; t|_q,$$
$$(s[t]_p)[r]_{pq} \; = \; s[t[r]_q]_p.$$

3. *If $pq \in Pos(s)$, then*

$$(s[t]_{pq})|_p \; = \; (s|_p)[t]_q,$$
$$(s[t]_{pq})[r]_p \; = \; s[r]_p.$$

4. *If p and q are parallel positions in s (i.e. $p \parallel q$), then*

$$(s[t]_p)|_q \; = \; s|_q,$$
$$(s[t]_p)[r]_q \; = \; (s[r]_q)[t]_p.$$

Proof These rules are quite obvious when we consider the intuitive meaning of positions in the tree representation of a term, but they can, of course, also be proved by induction according to the formal definitions given above. As an example, we show, by induction on the length of p, that $s|_{pq} = (s|_p)|_q$ holds for all $pq \in \mathcal{P}os(s)$.

For $p = \epsilon$, we have $pq = q$, and thus $s|_{pq} = s|_q$. In addition, $p = \epsilon$ implies $s|_p = s$, which shows $s|_q = (s|_p)|_q$.

Now, assume that $p = ip'$. Because $ip'q \in \mathcal{P}os(s)$, we know that s is of the form $s = f(s_1, \ldots, s_n)$ with $i \le n$. By definition, $s|_{pq} = s|_{ip'q} = s_i|_{p'q}$, and by induction $s_i|_{p'q} = (s_i|_{p'})|_q$. Again by definition, we obtain $s_i|_{p'} = s|_{ip'} = s|_p$, which finishes the proof of the induction step.   □

Terms that do not contain variables will sometimes play a particular rôle.

Definition 3.1.5 Let Σ be a signature, and X be a set of variables disjoint from Σ. A term $t \in T(\Sigma, X)$ is called **ground** iff $\mathcal{V}ar(t) = \emptyset$. The set of all ground terms over Σ is denoted by $T(\Sigma, \emptyset)$ or simply $T(\Sigma)$.

The main difference between constant symbols and variables is that the latter may be replaced by substitutions.

Definition 3.1.6 Let Σ be a signature and V be a countably infinite set of variables. A $T(\Sigma, V)$-**substitution**—or simply substitution, if the set of terms is irrelevant or clear from the context—is a function $\sigma : V \to T(\Sigma, V)$ such that $\sigma(x) \ne x$ for only finitely many xs. The (finite) set of variables that σ does not map to themselves is called the **domain** of σ: $\mathcal{D}om(\sigma) := \{x \in V \mid \sigma(x) \ne x\}$. If $\mathcal{D}om(\sigma) = \{x_1, \ldots, x_n\}$, then we may write σ as

$$\sigma = \{x_1 \mapsto \sigma(x_1), \ldots, x_n \mapsto \sigma(x_n)\}.$$

The **range** of σ is $\mathcal{R}an(\sigma) := \{\sigma(x) \mid x \in \mathcal{D}om(\sigma)\}$, and the **variable range** of σ consists of the variables occurring in $\mathcal{R}an(\sigma)$:

$$\mathcal{V}\mathcal{R}an(\sigma) := \bigcup_{x \in \mathcal{D}om(\sigma)} \mathcal{V}ar(\sigma(x)).$$

We say that σ **instantiates** x if $x \in \mathcal{D}om(\sigma)$. The set of all $T(\Sigma, V)$-substitutions will be denoted by $\mathcal{S}ub(T(\Sigma, V))$ or simply $\mathcal{S}ub$.

Any $T(\Sigma, V)$-substitution σ can be **extended** to a mapping $\hat{\sigma} : T(\Sigma, V) \to T(\Sigma, V)$ as follows: for $x \in V$, $\hat{\sigma}(x) := \sigma(x)$, and for a non-variable term $s = f(s_1, \ldots, s_n)$ we define $\hat{\sigma}(s) := f(\hat{\sigma}(s_1), \ldots, \hat{\sigma}(s_n))$.

The application of a substitution σ to a term simultaneously replaces all occurrences of variables by their respective σ-images. For example, let $s = f(e, x)$ and $t = f(y, f(x, y))$, and let $\sigma = \{x \mapsto i(y), y \mapsto e\}$. Then $\hat{\sigma}(s) =$

$f(e, i(y))$ and $\hat{\sigma}(t) = f(e, f(i(y), e))$. The restriction to finite domains allows for an easy finite representation of substitutions. It is justified by the fact that we are usually only interested in the effect of applying a substitution to a finite set of terms $\{s_1, \ldots, s_n\}$, and thus only the images of the finitely many variables in $Var(s_1) \cup \ldots \cup Var(s_n)$ are of interest.

The **composition** $\sigma\tau$ of two substitutions σ and τ is defined as $\sigma\tau(x) := \hat{\sigma}(\tau(x))$. Obviously, $\sigma\tau$ is a mapping of V into $T(\Sigma, V)$, and since $\sigma\tau(x) = x$ holds for all variables $x \in V - (\mathcal{D}om(\sigma) \cup \mathcal{D}om(\tau))$, we know that it is again a substitution. In addition, it is easy to see that composition of substitutions is an associative operation. The definition of composition makes sure that the extension of the composition $\sigma\tau$ is just the composition of the extensions of σ and τ, i.e. $\widehat{\sigma\tau} = \hat{\sigma}\hat{\tau}$ (where $\hat{\sigma}\hat{\tau}$ denotes just the usual composition of mappings). To simplify notation, we usually do not distinguish between a substitution $\sigma : V \to T(\Sigma, V)$ and its extension $\hat{\sigma} : T(\Sigma, V) \to T(\Sigma, V)$. In the following, σ will be used to denote both. In addition, we sometimes simply write σt instead of $\sigma(t)$ for the application of the substitution σ to the term t.

A term t is called an **instance** of a term s iff there exists a substitution σ such that $\sigma(s) = t$. In this case, we write $t \gtrsim s$. If t is an instance of s but not vice versa then we write $t > s$ (i.e. $>$ is the strict partial order associated with the quasi-order $\gtrsim$).

Definition 3.1.7 Let Σ be a signature and V a countably infinite set of variables disjoint from Σ. A Σ-**identity** (or simply identity) is a pair $(s, t) \in T(\Sigma, V) \times T(\Sigma, V)$. Identities will be written as $s \approx t$. We call s the **left-hand side (lhs)** and t the **right-hand side (rhs)** of the identity $s \approx t$.

A given identity consists of two terms, and thus contains only finitely many variables. We have chosen a countably infinite set of variables to allow for identities containing an arbitrary finite number of different variables. Identities can be used to transform terms into other "equivalent" terms by replacing instances of the left-hand side with the corresponding instances of the right-hand side and vice versa. For example, the identity $f(x, f(y, z)) \approx f(f(x, y), z)$, which we interpret as saying that f is associative, can be used to transform $f(e, f(i(e), e))$ into $f(f(e, i(e)), e)$.

Definition 3.1.8 Let E be a set of Σ-identities. The **reduction relation** $\to_E \subseteq T(\Sigma, V) \times T(\Sigma, V)$ is defined as

$$s \to_E t \quad \text{iff}$$
$$\exists (l, r) \in E, \; p \in Pos(s), \; \sigma \in \mathcal{S}ub. \; s|_p = \sigma(l) \text{ and } t = s[\sigma(r)]_p.$$

We sometimes write $s \rightarrow^p_E t$ to indicate at which position the reduction takes place.

This situation is illustrated in Fig. 3.2.

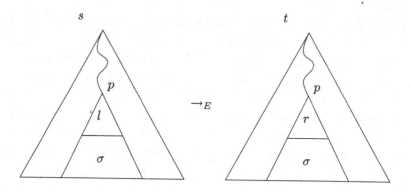

Fig. 3.2. In the term s, the instance $\sigma(l)$ of l, which occurs at position p, is replaced by the corresponding instance $\sigma(r)$ of r.

For example, let

$$G := \{f(x, f(y, z)) \approx f(f(x, y), z),\ f(e, x) \approx x,\ f(i(x), x) \approx e\}.$$

Then $f(i(e), f(e, e)) \rightarrow_G f(f(i(e), e), e) \rightarrow_G f(e, e) \rightarrow_G e$, where the first reduction takes place at position $p_1 = \epsilon$ with the first identity and with the substitution $\sigma_1 = \{x \mapsto i(e), y \mapsto e, z \mapsto e\}$, the second reduction takes place at position $p_2 = 1$ with the third identity and the substitution $\sigma_2 = \{x \mapsto e\}$, and the third reduction takes place at position $p_3 = \epsilon$ with the second identity and the substitution $\sigma_3 = \{x \mapsto e\}$.

As defined in Chapter 2, $\xrightarrow{*}_E$ denotes the reflexive transitive closure of $\rightarrow_E$, and $\xleftrightarrow{*}_E$ denotes the reflexive transitive symmetric closure of $\rightarrow_E$. One important goal of equational reasoning is to design decision procedures for $\xleftrightarrow{*}_E$ (see Chapter 4 for more details). In the subsequent sections of this chapter, we present a semantic characterization of $\xleftrightarrow{*}_E$, which makes clear why this relation is of great interest in universal algebra. But first, we give another syntactic characterization of $\xleftrightarrow{*}_E$ in terms of closure under certain operations.

Definition 3.1.9 Let $\equiv$ be a binary relation on $T(\Sigma, V)$.

1. The relation $\equiv$ is **closed under substitutions** if $s \equiv t$ implies $\sigma(s) \equiv \sigma(t)$ for all $s, t \in T(\Sigma, V)$ and substitutions σ.

2. The relation $\equiv$ is **closed under Σ-operations** iff $s_1 \equiv t_1, \ldots, s_n \equiv t_n$ imply $f(s_1, \ldots, s_n) \equiv f(t_1, \ldots, t_n)$ for all $n \geq 0$, $f \in \Sigma^{(n)}$ and $s_1, \ldots, s_n, t_1, \ldots, t_n \in T(\Sigma, V)$.

3. The relation $\equiv$ is **compatible with Σ-operations** iff $s \equiv t$ implies $f(s_1, \ldots, s_{i-1}, s, s_{i+1}, \ldots, s_n) \equiv f(s_1, \ldots, s_{i-1}, t, s_{i+1}, \ldots, s_n)$ for all $n \geq 0$, $f \in \Sigma^{(n)}$, $i = 1, \ldots, n$, and $s_1, \ldots, s_{i-1}, s, t, s_{i+1}, \ldots, s_n \in T(\Sigma, V)$.

4. The relation $\equiv$ is **compatible with Σ-contexts** iff $s \equiv s'$ implies $t[s]_p \equiv t[s']_p$ for all Σ-terms t and positions $p \in \mathcal{P}os(t)$.

The following lemma is an easy consequence of the definition of $\rightarrow_E$.

Lemma 3.1.10 *Let E be a set of Σ-identities. The reduction relation $\rightarrow_E$ is closed under substitutions and compatible with Σ-operations.*

In general, $\rightarrow_E$ is not closed under Σ-operations because the reduction takes place only at a single position.

Lemma 3.1.11 *Let $\equiv$ be a binary relation on $T(\Sigma, V)$.*

1. *The relation $\equiv$ is compatible with Σ-operations iff it is compatible with Σ-contexts.*

2. *If $\equiv$ is reflexive and transitive, then it is compatible with Σ-operations iff it is closed under Σ-operations.*

Proof The $\Leftarrow$-direction of the first statement is obvious, and the $\Rightarrow$-direction can be shown by an easy induction argument on the length of the position p. Reflexivity yields the $\Leftarrow$-direction of the second statement, and transitivity the $\Rightarrow$-direction. $\qquad\square$

Theorem 3.1.12 *Let E be a set of Σ-identities. The relation $\overset{*}{\leftrightarrow}_E$ is the smallest equivalence relation on $T(\Sigma, V)$ that contains E and is closed under substitutions and Σ-operations.*

Proof By definition, $\overset{*}{\leftrightarrow}_E$ is an equivalence relation. Using Lemma 3.1.10, one can easily show by induction that $\overset{*}{\leftrightarrow}_E$ is also closed under substitutions and compatible with Σ-operations. Since $\overset{*}{\leftrightarrow}_E$ is reflexive and transitive, this implies that $\overset{*}{\leftrightarrow}_E$ is closed under Σ-operations.

Now, assume that $\equiv$ is an equivalence relation on $T(\Sigma, V)$ that contains E and is closed under substitutions and Σ-operations. We prove that $s \rightarrow_E t$ implies $s \equiv t$. Since, by definition, $\overset{*}{\leftrightarrow}_E$ is the smallest equivalence relation containing $\rightarrow_E$, we can then deduce that $\overset{*}{\leftrightarrow}_E \subseteq \equiv$.

From $s \rightarrow_E t$ it follows that there exist an identity $(l, r) \in E$, a position $p \in \mathcal{P}os(s)$, and a substitution σ such that $s|_p = \sigma(l)$ and $t = s[\sigma(r)]_p$. Since $\equiv$ contains E, we know that $l \equiv r$, which implies that $\sigma(l) \equiv \sigma(r)$ because

$\equiv$ is closed under substitutions. Since $\equiv$ is reflexive and closed under Σ-operations, it is also compatible with Σ-operations, and thus compatible with Σ-contexts. This yields $s = s[\sigma(l)]_p \equiv s[\sigma(r)]_p = t$. $\qquad\square$

The theorem says that $\overset{*}{\leftrightarrow}_E$ can also be obtained by starting with the binary relation E, and then closing the relation under reflexivity, symmetry, transitivity, substitutions, and Σ-operations. Describing the closing process by inference rules leads to **equational logic**:

$$\frac{(s \approx t) \in E}{E \vdash s \approx t}$$

$$\frac{}{E \vdash t \approx t} \qquad \frac{E \vdash s \approx t}{E \vdash t \approx s} \qquad \frac{E \vdash s \approx t \quad E \vdash t \approx u}{E \vdash s \approx u}$$

$$\frac{E \vdash s \approx t}{E \vdash \sigma(s) \approx \sigma(t)} \qquad \frac{E \vdash s_1 \approx t_1 \quad \dots \quad E \vdash s_n \approx t_n}{E \vdash f(s_1, \dots, s_n) \approx f(t_1, \dots, t_n)}$$

The notation $E \vdash s \approx t$ stands for "$s \approx t$ is a syntactic consequence of E". The horizontal lines in the above rules separate the premises of the inference rule from their conclusion, i.e. if the premises are already derived, then one can also derive the conclusion. The first rule is the **assumption rule** and asserts that any element of E is a syntactic consequence of E. The next three rules express reflexivity, symmetry, and transitivity. Finally we have instantiation with an arbitrary substitution σ and closure under all n-ary function symbols f.

Inference rules can be composed to form **proof trees**:

1. Every instance of the assumption and the reflexivity rule is a proof tree.
2. Given an instance $\frac{E \vdash s_1 \approx t_1 \; \dots \; E \vdash s_n \approx t_n}{E \vdash s \approx t}$ of one of the above inference rules and proof trees T_i with conclusions $E \vdash s_i \approx t_i$, $i = 1, \dots, n$,

$$\frac{T_1 \; \dots \; T_n}{E \vdash s \approx t}$$

is also a proof tree.

Example 3.1.13 Let $E = \{a \approx b, f(x) \approx g(x)\}$. The following tree depicts a proof of $E \vdash g(b) \approx f(a)$:

$$\frac{\dfrac{E \vdash a \approx b}{E \vdash f(a) \approx f(b)} \quad \dfrac{E \vdash f(x) \approx g(x)}{E \vdash f(b) \approx g(b)}}{\dfrac{E \vdash f(a) \approx g(b)}{E \vdash g(b) \approx f(a)}}$$

Contrast this with the derivation of $g(b) \overset{*}{\leftrightarrow}_E f(a)$: $g(b) \leftrightarrow_E g(a) \leftrightarrow_E f(a)$.

Although Theorem 3.1.12 tells us that $s \overset{*}{\leftrightarrow}_E t$ holds iff $E \vdash s \approx t$ can be derived using the above inference rules, there are two important differences:

1. The rewriting approach (which generates $\overset{*}{\leftrightarrow}_E$) allows the replacement of a subterm at an arbitrary position in a single step; the inference rule approach (which allows us to derive statements of the form $E \vdash$) needs to simulate this by many small steps of closure under single operations.

2. Closure under operations in the inference rule approach allows the simultaneous replacement in each argument of an operation; the rewriting approach needs to simulate this by a number of replacements steps in sequence.

Exercises

3.1   Let Σ be a signature consisting of one binary function symbol, and let X be a nonempty set of variables. Characterize those subsets of $\mathbb{N}^*$ (i.e. sets of strings of positive integers) that are of the form $\mathcal{P}os(t)$ for some term $t \in T(\Sigma, X)$.

3.2   Give inductive proofs for (2)–(4) of Lemma 3.1.4.

3.3   Show that the composition of substitutions is an associative operation.

3.4   Let σ and τ be substitutions.

  (a) Describe the variable range $\mathcal{VRan}(\sigma\tau)$ of the composition of σ and τ.

  (b) Under what conditions do we have $\sigma\tau = \tau$? What are the conditions for $\tau\tau = \tau$ to hold?

3.5   Let $T(\Sigma, \{x\})$ be the set of Σ-terms over one variable x. The reduction relation $\rightarrow_I$ on $T(\Sigma, \{x\})$ is defined by $s \rightarrow_I t$ iff s is an instance of t and $s \neq t$. Show that $\rightarrow_I$ is terminating and confluent. Can this result be generalized to the case of more than one variable?

3.6   Let f be a binary function symbol, and

$$G = \{f(x, f(y, z)) \approx f(f(x, y), z), \; f(e, x) \approx x, \; f(i(x), x) \approx e\}.$$

  Show that $f(x, e) \overset{*}{\leftrightarrow}_G x$.

3.7   Let f be a binary function symbol, and

$$E = \{f(x, f(y, z)) \approx f(f(x, y), z), \; f(f(x, y), x) \approx x\}.$$

  Show that $f(x, x) \overset{*}{\leftrightarrow}_E x$ and $f(f(x, y), z) \overset{*}{\leftrightarrow}_E f(x, z)$.

3.8   Let $\Sigma = \{f\}$ for a binary function symbol f, and $E = \{f(x, f(y, z)) \approx f(f(x, y), z), \; f(x, x) \approx x, \; f(f(x, y), z) \approx f(x, y)\}$. Show that it is decidable whether two given Σ-terms s, t satisfy $s \overset{*}{\leftrightarrow}_E t$ or not. (*Hint:*

for a given Σ-term s, try to determine what the smallest terms in the $\overset{*}{\leftrightarrow}_E$-equivalence class of s look like.)

3.9   Prove Lemma 3.1.10 and Lemma 3.1.11.

3.2 Algebras, homomorphisms, and congruences

For a given signature Σ, a Σ-algebra provides an interpretation of all the function symbols in Σ.

Definition 3.2.1 Let Σ be a signature. A Σ**-algebra** $\mathcal{A}$ consists of

- a **carrier** set (domain) A, and
- a mapping that associates with each function symbol $f \in \Sigma^{(n)}$ a function $f^{\mathcal{A}} : A^n \to A$ (for all $n \geq 0$).

If the signature is irrelevant or clear from the context, we shall sometimes simply use the term "algebra" in place of "Σ-algebra".

As an example, let us again consider the signature $\Sigma_G = \{e, i, f\}$, where e has arity 0, i is unary, and f is binary. The additive group of integers, $\mathcal{Z}$, has as carrier the set of all integers $\mathbb{Z}$, and interprets f as addition of integers, i as (unary) negation, and e as 0.

One can construct new Σ-algebras from given ones by forming subalgebras, homomorphic images, quotient algebras, and direct products.

Definition 3.2.2 Let Σ be a signature.

1. The Σ-algebra $\mathcal{B}$ is a Σ**-subalgebra** of the Σ-algebra $\mathcal{A}$ iff its carrier B is a subset of the carrier A of $\mathcal{A}$, and for all $n \geq 0$, all $f \in \Sigma^{(n)}$, and all $b_1, \ldots, b_n \in B$ we have $f^{\mathcal{A}}(b_1, \ldots, b_n) = f^{\mathcal{B}}(b_1, \ldots, b_n) \in B$.

2. If X is a subset of the carrier of the Σ-algebra $\mathcal{A}$, then the Σ**-subalgebra of** $\mathcal{A}$ **generated by** X is the smallest subalgebra of $\mathcal{A}$ (w.r.t. inclusion of carrier sets) that contains X. If this subalgebra is already the whole algebra $\mathcal{A}$, then we say that $\mathcal{A}$ is **generated by** X. Note that the smallest subalgebra of $\mathcal{A}$ containing X always exists since the intersection of all subalgebras of $\mathcal{A}$ containing X is again a subalgebra of $\mathcal{A}$ containing X.

For example, the set $E := \{2z \mid z \in \mathbb{Z}\}$ of all even integers is the carrier of a subalgebra $\mathcal{E}$ of $\mathcal{Z}$, and this subalgebra is generated by $\{2\}$. The algebra $\mathcal{Z}$ itself is generated either by $\{1\}$ or by $\{-1\}$, but it is not generated by any other singleton set.

Definition 3.2.3 Let Σ be a signature, and let $\mathcal{A}$, $\mathcal{B}$ be Σ-algebras. A Σ**-homomorphism** $\phi : \mathcal{A} \to \mathcal{B}$ is a mapping of A into B such that for all $n \geq 0$, $f \in \Sigma^{(n)}$, and $a_1, \ldots, a_n \in A$ we have $\phi(f^{\mathcal{A}}(a_1, \ldots, a_n)) = f^{\mathcal{B}}(\phi(a_1), \ldots, \phi(a_n))$. If the mapping ϕ is onto, then $\mathcal{B}$ is called a **homomorphic image** of $\mathcal{A}$. A homomorphism $\phi : \mathcal{A} \to \mathcal{A}$ is called an **endomorphism**, and a homomorphism that is a bijection is called an **isomorphism**. $\mathcal{A}$ and $\mathcal{B}$ are **isomorphic** ($\mathcal{A} \cong \mathcal{B}$) iff there is an isomorphism $\phi : \mathcal{A} \to \mathcal{B}$.

As with substitutions, we denote the **composition** of homomorphisms by juxtaposition, i.e. $\phi\psi$ denotes the composition of the homomorphisms $\psi :$ $\mathcal{A} \to \mathcal{B}$ and $\phi : \mathcal{B} \to \mathcal{C}$, which is a homomorphism of $\mathcal{A}$ into $\mathcal{C}$. In our example, the mapping $\phi : \mathbb{Z} \to \mathbb{Z} : z \mapsto 2z$ is an endomorphism of $\mathcal{Z}$, and it is an isomorphism between $\mathcal{Z}$ and $\mathcal{E}$.

Definition 3.2.4 Let $\mathcal{A}$ be a Σ-algebra. An equivalence relation $\equiv$ on its carrier A is called a **congruence** on $\mathcal{A}$ iff it is compatible with the interpretation of all function symbols of Σ, i.e. for all $n \geq 0$, all $f \in \Sigma^{(n)}$, and all $a_1 \equiv b_1, \ldots, a_n \equiv b_n$ in A we have

$$f^{\mathcal{A}}(a_1, \ldots, a_n) \equiv f^{\mathcal{A}}(b_1, \ldots, b_n).$$

The **quotient algebra** $\mathcal{A}/_{\equiv}$ has as carrier the set of equivalence classes $[a]_{\equiv} := \{b \in A \mid a \equiv b\}$, and interprets the symbols $f \in \Sigma^{(n)}$ (for all $n \geq 0$) as $f^{\mathcal{A}/_{\equiv}}([a_1]_{\equiv}, \ldots, [a_n]_{\equiv}) := [f^{\mathcal{A}}(a_1, \ldots, a_n)]_{\equiv}$.

Note that the definition of a congruence makes sure that the definition of $f^{\mathcal{A}/_{\equiv}}$ is independent of the choice of representatives from each congruence class. In our example, the relation $\equiv_2 := \{(z_1, z_2) \mid 2 \text{ is a divisor of } z_1 - z_2\}$ is a congruence on $\mathcal{Z}$. The quotient algebra is the (unique) Abelian group of order 2, with carrier set $\{[0]_{\equiv_2}, [1]_{\equiv_2}\}$.

There is a close connection between homomorphic images and quotient algebras.

Lemma 3.2.5 *Let Σ be a signature, and $\mathcal{A}, \mathcal{B}$ be Σ-algebras.*

1. *Let $\equiv$ be a congruence on $\mathcal{A}$. The quotient algebra $\mathcal{A}/_{\equiv}$ is the homomorphic image of $\mathcal{A}$ under the **canonical homomorphism** $\pi_{\equiv} : A \to A/_{\equiv} : a \mapsto [a]_{\equiv}$.*

2. *Let $\phi : \mathcal{A} \to \mathcal{B}$ be a surjective homomorphism of $\mathcal{A}$ onto $\mathcal{B}$. Then $\mathcal{B}$ is isomorphic to $\mathcal{A}/_{\equiv_\phi}$, where $\equiv_\phi$ denotes the **kernel** of ϕ, i.e. the congruence $\equiv_\phi := \{(a, a') \mid \phi(a) = \phi(a')\}$.*

3. *Let $\phi : \mathcal{A} \to \mathcal{B}$ be a homomorphism and $\equiv$ be a congruence on $\mathcal{A}$. If $\equiv \subseteq \equiv_\phi$, then there exist a homomorphism $\phi_{\equiv} : \mathcal{A}/_{\equiv} \to \mathcal{B}$ such that $\phi = \phi_{\equiv}\pi_{\equiv}$.*

Proof (1) Obviously, the mapping $\pi_\equiv$ is onto. Thus, it is sufficient to prove that $\pi_\equiv$ is a homomorphism. This is an immediate consequence of the definition of $\pi_\equiv$ and the interpretation of the function symbols in $\mathcal{A}/_\equiv$.

(2) By definition, $\equiv_\phi$ is an equivalence relation, and since ϕ was assumed to be a homomorphism, it is even a congruence. In addition, it is easy to see that the mapping $\psi : A/_{\equiv_\phi} \to B : [a]_{\equiv_\phi} \mapsto \phi(a)$ is an isomorphism.

(3) Let us define the mapping $\phi_\equiv : A/_\equiv \to B$ by $\phi_\equiv([a]_\equiv) := \phi(a)$. By assumption, $a \equiv a'$ implies $\phi(a) = \phi(a')$, which shows that this definition is independent of the choice of the representative for the congruence class $[a]_\equiv$. In addition, $\phi = \phi_\equiv \pi_\equiv$ by the definition of $\phi_\equiv$. The fact that ϕ is a homomorphism can easily be used to show that $\phi_\equiv$ is a homomorphism as well. $\qquad\square$

Definition 3.2.6 Let I be an arbitrary index set, and assume that $(\mathcal{A}_i)_{i \in I}$ is an I-indexed family of Σ-algebras. The **direct product** of this family is the Σ-algebra $\mathcal{P} = \prod_{i \in I} \mathcal{A}_i$ that has the Cartesian product $P := \prod_{i \in I} A_i$ of the carrier sets A_i as its carrier, and which interprets the function symbols component-wise, i.e. if π_i denotes the projection to the ith component, then for all $n \geq 0$, all $f \in \Sigma^{(n)}$, all $p_1, \ldots, p_n \in P$, and all $i \in I$

$$\pi_i(f^\mathcal{P}(p_1, \ldots, p_n)) = f^{\mathcal{A}_i}(\pi_i(p_1), \ldots, \pi_i(p_n)).$$

Exercises

3.10 Let $\mathcal{Z}$ be the additive group of the integers.

(a) Determine all subalgebras of $\mathcal{Z}$ and all congruences on $\mathcal{Z}$.

(b) Characterize those subsets of $\mathbb{Z}$ of cardinality 2 that generate $\mathcal{Z}$.

(c) Given the integers $a, b, c \in \mathbb{Z}$, we define the mapping $h_{(a,b,c)} : \mathbb{Z} \to \mathbb{Z}$ by

$$h_{(a,b,c)}(z) := az^2 + bz + c.$$

For what triples (a, b, c) is $h_{(a,b,c)}$ an endomorphism of $\mathcal{Z}$?

(d) Given the integers a, b, we define the mapping $g_{(a,b)} : \mathbb{Z} \times \mathbb{Z} \to \mathbb{Z}$ by

$$g_{(a,b)}(z_1, z_2) := az_1 + bz_2.$$

Show that $g_{(a,b)}$ is a homomorphism of the direct product $\mathcal{Z} \times \mathcal{Z}$ into $\mathcal{Z}$. For what tuples (a, b) is $g_{(a,b)}$ onto?

3.3 Free algebras

If an algebra A is generated by a subset X of its carrier, then any homomorphism of A into an algebra B is uniquely determined by the images of the elements of X.

Lemma 3.3.1 *Let A, B be two Σ-algebras, and assume that A is generated by X. If ϕ and ψ are homomorphisms of A into B, and if ϕ and ψ coincide on X, then they coincide on A, i.e. $\phi = \psi$.*

Proof First, it is easy to see that the carrier set of the Σ-subalgebra of A generated by X is obtained as $\bigcup_{i \geq 0} A_i$, where $A_0 := X$, and $A_{i+1} := A_i \cup \{f(a_1, \ldots, a_n) \mid n \geq 0, f \in \Sigma^{(n)}, a_1, \ldots, a_n \in A_i\}$.

Second, since A is generated by X, we know that $A = \bigcup_{i \geq 0} A_i$, and it is easy to show by induction on i that ϕ and ψ coincide on A_i for all $i \geq 0$. $\square$

In general, however, not every mapping of X into B can be extended to a homomorphism of A into B. Algebras for which this is always possible (under certain restrictions) are called *free*.

Definition 3.3.2 Let Σ be a signature, X be a set, and $\mathcal{K}$ be a class of Σ-algebras. The Σ-algebra A is called **free in $\mathcal{K}$ with generating set X** iff the following three properties are satisfied:

1. A is generated by $X \subseteq A$,
2. $A \in \mathcal{K}$, and
3. for every Σ-algebra B in $\mathcal{K}$, every mapping $\varphi : X \to B$ can be extended to a homomorphism $\widehat{\varphi} : A \to B$.†

An algebra free in $\mathcal{K}$ with an *empty* generating set is called an **initial algebra in $\mathcal{K}$**.

For example, the algebra $\mathcal{Z}$ is the free Abelian group with one generator, i.e. $\mathcal{Z}$ is free in the class of all Abelian groups, and it is generated by $X = \{1\}$. Not every class of algebras contains free algebras (see Example 3.3.4 below), but if a free algebra (for a given cardinality of the set of generators) exists, then it is unique up to isomorphism.

Theorem 3.3.3 *Let Σ be a signature, X, Y be sets, and $\mathcal{K}$ be a class of Σ-algebras. If A is free in $\mathcal{K}$ with generating set X, B is free in $\mathcal{K}$ with generating set Y, and $|X| = |Y|$, then $A \cong B$.*

---

† Since A is generated by X, this extension is unique by Lemma 3.3.1.

Proof Because X and Y are of the same cardinality, we know that there exist bijections $\varphi : X \to Y$ and $\vartheta : Y \to X$ such that $\vartheta = \varphi^{-1}$. Since $\mathcal{A}$ is free in $\mathcal{K}$ with generating set X, the mapping φ can be extended to a homomorphism $\widehat{\varphi} : \mathcal{A} \to \mathcal{B}$. Similarly, ϑ has an extension to a homomorphism $\widehat{\vartheta} : \mathcal{B} \to \mathcal{A}$.

The composition $\widehat{\vartheta}\widehat{\varphi}$ is a homomorphism from $\mathcal{A}$ into $\mathcal{A}$, and its restriction to X is $\vartheta\varphi = Id_X$, i.e. the identity mapping on X. Now, both $\widehat{\vartheta}\widehat{\varphi}$ and $Id_{\mathcal{A}}$ are homomorphisms from $\mathcal{A}$ into $\mathcal{A}$ that extend Id_X. This implies $\widehat{\vartheta}\widehat{\varphi} = Id_{\mathcal{A}}$, since $\mathcal{A}$ is generated by X.

A symmetry argument shows that $\widehat{\varphi}\widehat{\vartheta} = Id_{\mathcal{B}}$. Thus $\widehat{\varphi}$ and $\widehat{\vartheta}$ are isomorphisms that are inverse to each other. In particular, it follows that $\mathcal{A} \cong \mathcal{B}$.

$\square$

As an obvious corollary we obtain that the initial algebra in a given class is unique up to isomorphism, if it exists. The following example shows that a class of algebras need not contain initial algebras.

Example 3.3.4 Let $\Sigma = \{a, b, c\}$ be a signature that consists of three constant symbols. We consider the class

$$\mathcal{K} := \{\mathcal{A} \mid \mathcal{A} \text{ is a } \Sigma\text{-algebra that satisfies } a^{\mathcal{A}} = b^{\mathcal{A}} \text{ or } a^{\mathcal{A}} = c^{\mathcal{A}}\}.$$

Now, assume that $\mathcal{A}_0$ is an initial algebra in $\mathcal{K}$. Since $\mathcal{A}_0$ is an element of $\mathcal{K}$, we know that $a^{\mathcal{A}_0} = b^{\mathcal{A}_0}$ or $a^{\mathcal{A}_0} = c^{\mathcal{A}_0}$ holds. Without loss of generality we assume that $a^{\mathcal{A}_0} = b^{\mathcal{A}_0}$ is satisfied. (The other case can be treated analogously.)

Let us define the Σ-algebra $\mathcal{B}$ as follows: it has carrier set $B = \{0, 1\}$, and interprets the constants as $a^{\mathcal{B}} = 0$, $b^{\mathcal{B}} = 1$, and $c^{\mathcal{B}} = 0$. Because of $a^{\mathcal{B}} = c^{\mathcal{B}}$, we know that $\mathcal{B}$ belongs to $\mathcal{K}$. Since $\mathcal{A}_0$ was assumed to be initial in $\mathcal{K}$, there exists a homomorphism $\phi : \mathcal{A}_0 \to \mathcal{B}$. But then $a^{\mathcal{A}_0} = b^{\mathcal{A}_0}$ implies $a^{\mathcal{B}} = \phi(a^{\mathcal{A}_0}) = \phi(b^{\mathcal{A}_0}) = b^{\mathcal{B}}$, which contradicts the definition of the interpretation of a and b in $\mathcal{B}$.

Exercises

3.11 Show that $\mathcal{Z} \times \mathcal{Z}$ is the free Abelian group with two generators, i.e. there exists a subset X of $\mathbb{Z} \times \mathbb{Z}$ of cardinality 2 such that $\mathcal{Z} \times \mathcal{Z}$ is free with generating set X in the class of all Abelian groups.

3.12 Let $\mathcal{A}, \mathcal{B} \in \mathcal{K}$, where $\mathcal{K}$ is a class of Σ-algebras that contains a finite algebra of cardinality larger than 1, and assume that $\mathcal{A}$ is free in $\mathcal{K}$ with finite generating set X and that $\mathcal{B}$ is free in $\mathcal{K}$ with finite generating set Y. Show that the following holds: if $\mathcal{A}$ is isomorphic to $\mathcal{B}$ then $|X| = |Y|$.

3.4 Term algebras

For a signature Σ and a (disjoint) set of variables X, one can use $T(\Sigma, X)$ as carrier of a Σ-algebra in which the function symbols "interpret themselves".

Definition 3.4.1 Let Σ be a signature and X be a set of variables disjoint from Σ. The Σ-**term algebra** $T(\Sigma, X)$ has $T(\Sigma, X)$ as carrier set, and interprets the function symbols $f \in \Sigma^{(n)}$ (for $n \geq 0$) as follows:

$$f^{T(\Sigma, X)} : T(\Sigma, X)^n \to T(\Sigma, X) : (t_1, \ldots, t_n) \mapsto f(t_1, \ldots, t_n).$$

Σ-term algebras play an important rôle in universal algebra since they are free in the class of all Σ-algebras.

Theorem 3.4.2 $T(\Sigma, X)$ *is free with generating set* X *in the class of all* Σ-*algebras.*

Proof Obviously, $T(\Sigma, X)$ is a Σ-algebra (i.e. it belongs to the given class), and it satisfies $X \subseteq T(\Sigma, X)$. As an easy consequence of the inductive definition of Σ-terms we obtain that $T(\Sigma, X)$ is generated by X.

Assume that $\mathcal{B}$ is a Σ-algebra and that $\varphi : X \to B$ is an arbitrary mapping. Define an extension $\widehat{\varphi} : T(\Sigma, X) \to B$ of φ by induction on the structure of terms:

- if $x \in X$ then $\widehat{\varphi}(x) := \varphi(x)$,
- if $f \in \Sigma^{(n)}$ for $n \geq 0$, and if $s_1, \ldots, s_n$ are terms for which the images $\widehat{\varphi}(s_1), \ldots, \widehat{\varphi}(s_n)$ are already defined, then

$$\widehat{\varphi}(f(s_1, \ldots, s_n)) := f^{\mathcal{B}}(\widehat{\varphi}(s_1), \ldots, \widehat{\varphi}(s_n)).$$

By definition, $\widehat{\varphi}$ is a Σ-homomorphism that extends φ. $\square$

In Section 3.1, we have introduced $T(\Sigma, V)$-substitutions, which were defined as mappings $\sigma : V \to T(\Sigma, V)$ that change only finitely many variables. In addition, we have shown how to extend a given substitution to a mapping $\widehat{\sigma} : T(\Sigma, V) \to T(\Sigma, V)$. Obviously, the definition of this extension is just a special case of what we have done in the above proof. Thus, $\widehat{\sigma}$ is the unique extension of σ to an endomorphism of $T(\Sigma, V)$. Since we usually do not distinguish between a substitution and its extension, we can thus say that a substitution is an endomorphism of the term algebra that coincides with the identity mapping on almost all variables.

3.5 Equational classes

Recall that a Σ-*identity* is a pair $s \approx t$ of terms in $T(\Sigma, V)$, for a countably infinite set of variables V. Intuitively, an identity holds in a Σ-algebra $\mathcal{A}$ if it is true for all possible ways of replacing the variables in s, t by elements of A. The formal definition given below makes use of the fact that a given mapping of variables to elements of A can be uniquely extended to a homomorphism.

Definition 3.5.1 The Σ-identity $s \approx t$ **holds** in the Σ-algebra $\mathcal{A}$ ($\mathcal{A} \models s \approx t$) iff for all homomorphisms $\phi : \mathcal{T}(\Sigma, V) \to \mathcal{A}$ we have $\phi(s) = \phi(t)$.

We use the name "identity" for a pair of terms $s \approx t$ to express that this equality is assumed to *hold* in an algebra, and distinguish this from the notion of an "equation", which must be *solved* in an algebra. Logically, the difference is that identities are (implicitly) universally quantified whereas equations are (implicitly) existentially quantified. It should be noted, however, that some authors do not make this distinction, and use the term "equation" for what we call identity. For this reason, varieties (as defined below) are sometimes also called equational classes.

Definition 3.5.2 Let Σ be a signature and E be a set of Σ-identities.

1. The Σ-algebra $\mathcal{A}$ is a **model** of E ($\mathcal{A} \models E$) iff every identity of E holds in $\mathcal{A}$.
2. The class of all models of E is called the Σ-**variety** defined by E. It is denoted by $\mathcal{V}(E)$.

As an example, consider the set of identities

$$G = \{f(x, f(y, z)) \approx f(f(x, y), z),\ f(e, x) \approx x,\ f(i(x), x) \approx e\}.$$

The Σ_G-algebra $\mathcal{Z}$ is a model of G, and $\mathcal{V}(G)$ is the class of all groups. We might now ask ourselves what kind of identities can be deduced from G, i.e. what Σ_G-identities hold in all groups.

Definition 3.5.3 Let E be a set of Σ-identities.

1. The identity $s \approx t$ is a **semantic consequence** of E ($E \models s \approx t$) iff it holds in all models of E, i.e. for all $\mathcal{A} \in \mathcal{V}(E)$ we have that $s \approx t$ holds in $\mathcal{A}$.
2. The relation

$$\approx_E := \{(s, t) \in T(\Sigma, V) \times T(\Sigma, V) \mid E \models s \approx t\}$$

is called the **equational theory** induced by E.
3. The set of identities E is called **trivial** iff $\approx_E = T(\Sigma, V) \times T(\Sigma, V)$.

Obviously $s \approx t \in E$ implies that $s \approx_E t$. In addition, it is easy to see that the relation $\approx_E$ is a congruence relation on $\mathcal{T}(\Sigma, V)$. Thus, we can build the quotient algebra $\mathcal{T}(\Sigma, V)/_{\approx_E}$.

Lemma. 3.5.4 *Let E be a set of Σ-identities, and $\approx_E$ be the equational theory induced by E.*

1. *The congruence $\approx_E$ is **fully invariant**, where fully invariant means that it is closed under endomorphisms, i.e. $s \approx_E t$ implies $\phi(s) \approx_E \phi(t)$ for all endomorphisms ϕ of $T(\Sigma, V)$.*

2. *For any homomorphism $\phi : T(\Sigma, V) \to T(\Sigma, V)/_{\approx_E}$ there exists an endomorphism ψ of $T(\Sigma, V)$ such that $\phi = \pi_{\approx_E}\psi$, where $\pi_{\approx_E}$ denotes the canonical homomorphism of $T(\Sigma, V)$ onto $T(\Sigma, V)/_{\approx_E}$.*

Proof (1) Let ϕ be an endomorphism of $T(\Sigma, V)$ and assume that $s \approx_E t$ holds. We must show that $\phi(s) \approx_E \phi(t)$ holds as well, i.e. that the identity $\phi(s) \approx \phi(t)$ holds in all models of E. Thus, let $\mathcal{A} \in \mathcal{V}(E)$, and let $\psi : T(\Sigma, V) \to \mathcal{A}$ be a homomorphism. We must show that $\psi(\phi(s)) = \psi(\phi(t))$. Since $\mathcal{A} \in \mathcal{V}(E)$, we know that $s \approx_E t$ implies that $s \approx t$ holds in $\mathcal{A}$. Consequently, $\psi(\phi(s)) = \psi\phi(s) = \psi\phi(t) = \psi(\phi(t))$, since $\psi\phi$ is a homomorphism of $T(\Sigma, V)$ into $\mathcal{A}$. This concludes the proof that $\phi(s) \approx \phi(t)$ holds in $\mathcal{A}$.

(2) Let $\phi : T(\Sigma, V) \to T(\Sigma, V)/_{\approx_E}$ be a homomorphism. Let us define the endomorphism ψ of $T(\Sigma, V)$ as follows: for all $x \in V$, let t_x be an arbitrary element of the $\approx_E$-class $\phi(x)$. Now ψ is the unique endomorphism of $T(\Sigma, V)$ that extends the mapping $V \to T(\Sigma, V) : x \mapsto t_x$. (Recall that $T(\Sigma, V)$ is free for the class of all Σ-algebras, and thus this extension exists.) By definition of ψ, the homomorphism $\pi_{\approx_E}\psi$ coincides with ϕ on V, and since $T(\Sigma, V)$ is generated by V, we can deduce $\phi = \pi_{\approx_E}\psi$. $\square$

Lemma 3.5.5 *Let E be a set of Σ-identities.*

1. *E is trivial iff $x \approx_E y$ holds for some pair of distinct variables $x, y \in V$.*
2. *E is trivial iff $\mathcal{V}(E)$ consists of algebras of cardinality less than or equal to 1.*

Proof (1) Obviously, if $\approx_E = T(\Sigma, V) \times T(\Sigma, V)$, then $x \approx_E y$ holds for all $x, y \in V$. Conversely, assume that $x \approx_E y$ holds for distinct variables $x, y \in V$. For every $s, t \in T(\Sigma, V)$ there exists an endomorphism ϕ of $T(\Sigma, V)$ such that $\phi(x) = s$ and $\phi(y) = t$. Because $\approx_E$ is fully invariant, we can thus deduce $s \approx_E t$ by applying ϕ to $x \approx_E y$.

(2) Assume that E is trivial, and let $\mathcal{A}$ be a model of E. By the first part of the lemma, there are distinct variables $x, y \in V$ such that $x \approx_E y$, and thus the identity $x \approx y$ holds in $\mathcal{A}$. For every $a_1, a_2 \in A$ there exists a homomorphism $\phi : T(\Sigma, V) \to \mathcal{A}$ such that $\phi(x) = a_1$ and $\phi(y) = a_2$. Thus, we can deduce that $a_1 = a_2$, which shows that $\mathcal{A}$ is of cardinality at most 1. Conversely, assume that E is non-trivial, and let V be a countably infinite set of variables. By the first part of the lemma, we have $x \not\approx_E y$ for every

pair x, y of distinct elements of V. Thus, the cardinality of the quotient algebra $\mathcal{T}(\Sigma, V)/_{\approx_E}$ is greater than 1. In addition, $\mathcal{T}(\Sigma, V)/_{\approx_E}$ belongs to $\mathcal{V}(E)$ (as will be shown in the proof of Theorem 3.5.6 below). □

Theorem 3.5.6 *Let V be a countably infinite set of variables. The quotient algebra $\mathcal{T}(\Sigma, V)/_{\approx_E}$ is the free algebra in $\mathcal{V}(E)$ with generating set $V/_{\approx_E} :=$ $\{[x]_{\approx_E} \mid x \in V\}$. If E is not trivial, then $V/_{\approx_E}$ is countably infinite.*

Proof Since $\mathcal{T}(\Sigma, V)$ is generated by V, we know that $\mathcal{T}(\Sigma, V)/_{\approx_E}$ is generated by the congruence classes of the elements of V.

In order to prove that $\mathcal{T}(\Sigma, V)/_{\approx_E}$ belongs to $\mathcal{V}(E)$, we must show that every identity $s \approx t \in E$ holds in $\mathcal{T}(\Sigma, V)/_{\approx_E}$. Since V is countably infinite, we may assume without loss of generality that $s, t \in \mathcal{T}(\Sigma, V)$. Thus, let $\phi : \mathcal{T}(\Sigma, V) \to \mathcal{T}(\Sigma, V)/_{\approx_E}$ be a homomorphism. By (2) of Lemma 3.5.4, there exists an endomorphism ψ of $\mathcal{T}(\Sigma, V)$ such that $\phi = \pi_{\approx_E}\psi$. Now, $s \approx t \in E$ implies $s \approx_E t$, and thus (1) of Lemma 3.5.4 yields $\psi(s) \approx_E \psi(t)$, which shows that $\phi(s) = \pi_{\approx_E}(\psi(s)) = \pi_{\approx_E}(\psi(t)) = \phi(t)$.

Let $\mathcal{A}$ be a model of E, and let $\varphi : V/_{\approx_E} \to \mathcal{A}$ be a mapping. Since $\mathcal{T}(\Sigma, V)$ is free with generators V for the class of all Σ-algebras, the mapping $\vartheta : V \to \mathcal{A} : x \mapsto \varphi([x]_{\approx_E})$ can be extended to a homomorphism $\widehat{\vartheta} :$ $\mathcal{T}(\Sigma, V) \to \mathcal{A}$. Because $\mathcal{A}$ is a model of E, we know that $\approx_E$ is contained in the kernel $\equiv_{\widehat{\vartheta}}$ of this homomorphism. Thus, there exists a homomorphism $\widehat{\vartheta}_{\approx_E} : \mathcal{T}(\Sigma, V)/_{\approx_E} \to \mathcal{A}$ with $\widehat{\vartheta} = \widehat{\vartheta}_{\approx_E}\pi_{\approx_E}$, by Lemma 3.2.5. In particular, for all $x \in X$,

$$\varphi([x]_{\approx_E}) = \vartheta(x) = \widehat{\vartheta}(x) = \widehat{\vartheta}_{\approx_E}(\pi_{\approx_E}(x)) = \widehat{\vartheta}_{\approx_E}([x]_{\approx_E}),$$

which shows that $\widehat{\vartheta}_{\approx_E}$ extends φ. This completes the proof that $\mathcal{T}(\Sigma, V)/_{\approx_E}$ is the free algebra in $\mathcal{V}(E)$ with generating set $V/_{\approx_E}$.

If E is not trivial, then Lemma 3.5.5 implies that the mapping $V \to V/_{\approx_E} :$ $x \mapsto [x]_{\approx_E}$ is a bijection, which shows that $V/_{\approx_E}$ is countably infinite. □

An easy consequence of this theorem is that an identity belongs to $\approx_E$ iff it holds in $\mathcal{T}(\Sigma, V)/_{\approx_E}$.

Corollary 3.5.7 *Let V be a countably infinite set of variables, and $s, t \in$ $\mathcal{T}(\Sigma, V)$. Then $\mathcal{T}(\Sigma, V)/_{\approx_E} \models s \approx t$ iff $s \approx_E t$.*

Proof We have already shown that $\mathcal{T}(\Sigma, V)/_{\approx_E} \in \mathcal{V}(E)$, and thus $s \approx_E t$ implies that $s \approx t$ holds in $\mathcal{T}(\Sigma, V)/_{\approx_E}$.

For the other implication, assume that $s \approx t$ holds in $\mathcal{T}(\Sigma, V)/_{\approx_E}$. In particular, if we consider the canonical homomorphism $\pi_{\approx_E} : \mathcal{T}(\Sigma, V) \to$ $\mathcal{T}(\Sigma, V)/_{\approx_E}$, we obtain $\pi_{\approx_E}(s) = \pi_{\approx_E}(t)$, which shows that $s \approx_E t$. □

For any subset X of V, the restriction of $\approx_E$ to $T(\Sigma, X)$ will also be denoted by $\approx_E$.

Corollary 3.5.8 *The quotient algebra $T(\Sigma, X)/\!\approx_E$ is the free algebra in $\mathcal{V}(E)$ with generating set $X/\!\approx_E := \{[x]_{\approx_E} \mid x \in X\}$. In particular, the algebra $T(\Sigma, \emptyset)/\!\approx_E$ is the initial algebra in $\mathcal{V}(E)$. If E is nontrivial, then $|X| = |X/\!\approx_E|$.*

For $X \subseteq V$, Corollary 3.5.7 holds in an appropriately modified version: for any $s, t \in T(\Sigma, X)$ we have $T(\Sigma, X)/\!\approx_E \models s \approx t$ iff $s \approx_E t$. It should be noted, however, that for finite sets X, the algebra $T(\Sigma, X)/\!\approx_E$ may satisfy identities $s \approx t$ that contain more than $|X|$ variables and are not satisfied in $T(\Sigma, V)/\!\approx_E$. In particular, the initial algebra in $\mathcal{V}(E)$ usually satisfies identities $s \approx t$ that contain variables and are not satisfied in the free algebra in countably many generators.

Example 3.5.9 Let $\Sigma := \{a, b, f\}$ be a signature consisting of two constant symbols a, b and a binary function symbol f. We consider the set of identities $E := \{f(f(x, y), z) \approx f(x, f(y, z)), f(a, b) \approx f(b, a)\}$.

It is easy to see that the commutativity identity $f(x, y) \approx f(y, x)$ holds in the initial algebra, even though $f(x, y) \approx_E f(y, x)$ does not hold.

In some applications, such as algebraic specification, one is actually more interested in the identities holding in the initial algebra than in those contained in the equational theory induced by E. Since such identities are often proved by induction on the structure of ground terms, one calls the set of these identities an inductive theory.

Definition 3.5.10 Let Σ be a signature containing at least one constant symbol, and let E be a set of Σ-identities. The **inductive theory** induced by E is defined as

$$\approx_E^I := \{(s, t) \in T(\Sigma, V) \times T(\Sigma, V) \mid T(\Sigma, \emptyset)/\!\approx_E \models s \approx t\}.$$

We have seen that a variety $\mathcal{V}(E)$ defined by a nontrivial set of identities E contains free algebras with generating sets of arbitrary finite or countably infinite cardinality. In addition, the free algebra with a countably infinite generating set satisfies exactly the identities belonging to $\approx_E$, whereas a finitely generated free algebra may satisfy more identities. Now, we shall show that $\mathcal{V}(E)$ contains free algebras with generating sets of arbitrarily large infinite cardinality. It is, however, not really necessary to consider these free algebras since they satisfy the same identities satisfied by the free algebra with a countably infinite set of generators.

Proposition 3.5.11 *Let E be a nontrivial set of identities, and let α be an uncountable cardinal. The variety $\mathcal{V}(E)$ contains a free algebra with generating set of cardinality α, and this algebra satisfies exactly the identities in $\approx_E$.*

Proof Let X be a set of variables of cardinality α. Obviously, any pair $(s,t) \in T(\Sigma, X) \times T(\Sigma, X)$ can also be considered as the identity $s \approx t$. Such an identity $s \approx t$ holds in an algebra $\mathcal{A}$ iff $\phi(s) = \phi(t)$ for all homomorphisms $\phi : T(\Sigma, X) \to \mathcal{A}$. Let us define the relation $\equiv_E$ on $T(\Sigma, X)$ by

$$\equiv_E := \{(s,t) \in T(\Sigma, X) \times T(\Sigma, X) \mid s \approx t \text{ holds for all } \mathcal{A} \in \mathcal{V}(E)\}.$$

(1) First, note that $\equiv_E \subseteq T(\Sigma, X) \times T(\Sigma, X)$ is just a syntactic variant of $\approx_E \subseteq T(\Sigma, V) \times T(\Sigma, V)$, i.e. every identity in $\equiv_E$ can be obtained from an identity in $\approx_E$ by renaming of variables, and vice versa. In fact, let $s, t \in T(\Sigma, X)$ be terms, and let $\{x_1, \ldots, x_n\}$ be the (finite) set of variables occurring in s and t. Since V is countably infinite, it contains at least n different variables, say $v_1, \ldots, v_n$. Let $\hat{s}, \hat{t} \in T(\Sigma, V)$ be the terms that are obtained from s, t by replacing x_i with v_i (for $i = 1, \ldots, n$). Obviously, the identity $s \approx t$ holds in an algebra $\mathcal{A}$ iff $\hat{s} \approx \hat{t}$ holds in $\mathcal{A}$. This implies that $s \equiv_E t$ holds iff $\hat{s} \approx_E \hat{t}$ holds. Similarly, it can be shown that for given terms $s, t \in T(\Sigma, V)$ there exist syntactic variants $s', t' \in T(\Sigma, X)$ (obtained by renaming variables) such that an algebra satisfies $s \approx t$ iff it satisfies $s' \approx t'$, and thus $s' \equiv_E t'$ holds iff $s \approx_E t$ holds.

(2) As in the case of a countably infinite set of variables, one can show the following:

- $\equiv_E$ is a fully invariant congruence on $T(\Sigma, X)$.
- The quotient algebra $T(\Sigma, X)/_{\equiv_E}$ is the free algebra in $\mathcal{V}(E)$ with generating set $X/_{\equiv_E} := \{[x]_{\equiv_E} \mid x \in X\}$.
- $\alpha = |X| = |X/_{\equiv_E}|$ since E is nontrivial.
- $T(\Sigma, X)/_{\equiv_E}$ satisfies exactly the identities in $\equiv_E$.

(3) It remains to be shown that $T(\Sigma, X)/_{\equiv_E}$ satisfies exactly the identities in $\approx_E$. First, assume that $T(\Sigma, X)/_{\equiv_E}$ satisfies the identity $s \approx t$ for $s, t \in T(\Sigma, V)$. Let $s', t' \in T(\Sigma, X)$ be syntactic variants of s, t (see part (1) of the proof). Because $T(\Sigma, X)/_{\equiv_E}$ satisfies $s \approx t$, we can deduce that $T(\Sigma, X)/_{\equiv_E}$ also satisfies $s' \approx t'$. By part (2) of the proof, this implies $s' \equiv_E t'$, which in turn implies $s \approx_E t$, because $s \approx t$ is a syntactic variant of $s' \approx t'$.

Now, assume that $s \approx_E t$ holds for $s, t \in T(\Sigma, V)$. Again, we consider syntactic variants $s', t' \in T(\Sigma, X)$ of s, t. Now, $s \approx_E t$ yields $s' \equiv_E t'$, and, by part (2) of the proof, this implies that $s' \approx t'$ holds in $T(\Sigma, X)/_{\equiv_E}$. Since

$s \approx t$ is a syntactic variant of $s' \approx t'$, we can deduce that $T(\Sigma, X)/_{\equiv_E}$ also satisfies $s \approx t$. $\qquad\square$

An important theorem due to Birkhoff says that the relation $\approx_E$, which we have defined in this section in a model-theoretic way, coincides with the syntactically defined relation $\overset{*}{\leftrightarrow}_E$ (see Section 3.1). First, we show that $\overset{*}{\leftrightarrow}_E$ is contained in $\approx_E$. Obviously, this is an immediate consequence of the next lemma, since $\approx_E$ is a fully invariant congruence containing E.

Lemma 3.5.12 *The relation $\overset{*}{\leftrightarrow}_E$ is the smallest fully invariant congruence on $T(\Sigma, V)$ that contains E.*

Proof This lemma is just a reformulation of Theorem 3.1.12, since the fully invariant congruences on $T(\Sigma, V)$ are just the equivalence relations on $T(\Sigma, V)$ that are closed under substitutions and Σ-operations. $\qquad\square$

The other direction of Birkhoff's Theorem is an immediate consequence of the next lemma.

Lemma 3.5.13 *Any fully invariant congruence $\equiv$ on $T(\Sigma, V)$ containing E contains $\approx_E$ as well.*

Proof It is sufficient to show that the quotient algebra $T(\Sigma, V)/_{\equiv}$ is a model of E. In fact, if this is the case then $s \approx_E t$ implies that $s \approx t$ holds in $T(\Sigma, V)/_{\equiv}$, and thus the canonical homomorphism $\pi_{\equiv}$ satisfies $\pi_{\equiv}(s) = \pi_{\equiv}(t)$, i.e. $s \equiv t$.

To see that $T(\Sigma, V)/_{\equiv} \models s \approx t$ for every identity $s \approx t \in E$, recall the second paragraph of the proof of Theorem 3.5.6, which shows this fact for $\approx_E$ in place of $\equiv$. The only property of $\approx_E$ that is used there is that it is fully invariant and contains E. In addition, the second statement of Lemma 3.5.4 is applied. It is, however, easy to see that this statement also holds with $\equiv$ in place of $\approx_E$. $\qquad\square$

Thus, we have proved Birkhoff's Theorem:

Theorem 3.5.14 *Let E be a set of identities. The syntactic consequence relation $\overset{*}{\leftrightarrow}_E$ coincides with the semantic consequence relation $\approx_E$.*

Alternatively, we can say that $\vdash$ and $\models$ coincide.

We close this chapter by giving an alternative characterization of varieties in terms of closure operations. For the interested reader, we include a proof of the characterization theorem stated below. It should be noted, however, that this characterization and its proof will not be referred to in any of the subsequent chapters. Thus, skipping the proof will not cause problems later on.

Theorem 3.5.15 *For a class $\mathcal{K}$ of Σ-algebras, the following statements are equivalent:*

1. *$\mathcal{K}$ is a variety, i.e. $\mathcal{K} = \mathcal{V}(E)$ for a set E of Σ-identities.*
2. *$\mathcal{K}$ is closed under building subalgebras, homomorphic images, and direct products.*

Proof $(1 \Rightarrow 2)$ It is quite obvious that an identity $s \approx t$ that holds in an algebra $\mathcal{A}$ also holds in any subalgebra and any homomorphic image of $\mathcal{A}$. In addition, if $s \approx t$ holds in the algebras $\mathcal{A}_i$, for $i \in I$, then it also holds in the direct product $\prod_{i \in I} \mathcal{A}_i$.

$(2 \Rightarrow 1)$ Let $\mathcal{K}$ be a class of Σ-algebras that is closed under building subalgebras, homomorphic images, and direct products. Define

$$E := \{(s, t) \in T(\Sigma, V) \times T(\Sigma, V) \mid \mathcal{A} \models s \approx t \text{ for all } \mathcal{A} \in \mathcal{K}\},$$

where V is a countably infinite set of variables. It is easy to see that E is a fully invariant congruence on $T(\Sigma, V)$, and thus we know that $E = \overset{*}{\leftrightarrow}_E = \approx_E$, by Lemma 3.5.12 and Birkhoff's Theorem. We claim that $\mathcal{K} = \mathcal{V}(E)$. By definition, the algebras in $\mathcal{K}$ satisfy all identities in E, which shows that $\mathcal{K} \subseteq \mathcal{V}(E)$.

To prove the other inclusion, let $\mathcal{A}$ be an algebra in $\mathcal{V}(E)$. We consider an infinite set W of variables, whose cardinality is not smaller than the cardinality of A. Since identities contain only finitely many variables, the relation

$$\equiv := \{(s, t) \in T(\Sigma, W) \times T(\Sigma, W) \mid \mathcal{B} \models s \approx t \text{ for all } \mathcal{B} \in \mathcal{K}\}$$

on $T(\Sigma, W)$ is just a syntactic variant of the relation $E = \approx_E$ (see the proof of Proposition 3.5.11). In particular, $\equiv$ is a fully invariant congruence on $T(\Sigma, W)$, and $\mathcal{V}(E)$ is the class of algebras that satisfy all identities $s \approx t$ with $s \equiv t$.

Before we can prove that $\mathcal{A} \in \mathcal{K}$, we need to show that $T(\Sigma, W)/_{\equiv}$ belongs to $\mathcal{K}$. By definition of $\equiv$, a tuple (s, t) belongs to $\equiv$ iff all $\mathcal{B} \in \mathcal{K}$ and all homomorphisms $\phi : T(\Sigma, W) \to \mathcal{B}$ satisfy $\phi(s) = \phi(t)$. Thus, if $\equiv_{\mathcal{B}, \phi}$ denotes the kernel of $\phi : T(\Sigma, W) \to \mathcal{B}$, then $\equiv = \bigcap_{\mathcal{B} \in \mathcal{K}, \phi} \equiv_{\mathcal{B}, \phi}$ (where, for every $\mathcal{B}$, ϕ ranges over all homomorphisms $T(\Sigma, W) \to \mathcal{B}$). By Lemma 3.2.5, the image $\phi(T(\Sigma, W))$ of $T(\Sigma, W)$ under ϕ is isomorphic to $T(\Sigma, W)/_{\equiv_{\mathcal{B}, \phi}}$. Since this image is a subalgebra of $\mathcal{B} \in \mathcal{K}$, we can deduce that $T(\Sigma, W)/_{\equiv_{\mathcal{B}, \phi}}$ belongs to $\mathcal{K}$. Now, let ψ be the homomorphism of $T(\Sigma, W)$ into the product

$\prod_{B\in\mathcal{K},\phi} T(\Sigma, W)/_{\equiv_{B,\phi}}$ that maps every term t into the tuple consisting of its $\equiv_{B,\phi}$-classes. It is easy to see that the kernel of this homomorphism is $\equiv = \bigcap_{B\in\mathcal{K},\phi} \equiv_{B,\phi}$, which shows that $T(\Sigma, W)/_{\equiv}$ is a subalgebra of the product (Lemma 3.2.5). Since every component of the product is in $\mathcal{K}$, the product itself and all its subalgebras are in $\mathcal{K}$.

Since $T(\Sigma, W)/_{\equiv} \in \mathcal{K}$ and $\mathcal{K}$ is closed under building homomorphic images, we can conclude the proof of the theorem by showing that the algebra $\mathcal{A}$ is a homomorphic image of $T(\Sigma, W)/_{\equiv}$. Since the cardinality of W is at least as large as the cardinality of A, there is a mapping ϑ of W *onto* A. As in the third paragraph of the proof of Theorem 3.5.6 we can show that there exists a homomorphism $\phi : T(\Sigma, W)/_{\equiv} \to \mathcal{A}$ that satisfies $\phi([x]_{\equiv}) = \vartheta(x)$. Since ϑ is onto, this homomorphism is also onto. $\qquad\qquad\square$

Exercises

3.13   Let $G' := \{f(x, f(y, z)) \approx f(f(x, y), z),\ f(e, x) \approx x,\ f(x, i(x)) \approx e\}$. Show that $f(x, e) \approx_{G'} x$ does not hold. (*Hint:* construct a model of G' in which the identity $f(x, e) \approx x$ is not satisfied.)

3.14   Let $\Sigma := \{f\}$ for a binary function symbol f, and

$$AC := \{f(x, f(y, z)) \approx f(f(x, y), z),\ f(x, y) \approx f(y, x)\}.$$

Consider the Σ-algebra $\mathcal{N}$ that has $\mathbb{N} \times \mathbb{N} \times \mathbb{N} - \{(0, 0, 0)\}$ as carrier set, and which interprets f as component-wise addition. Show that $\mathcal{N}$ is the free algebra in $\mathcal{V}(AC)$ with a generating set of cardinality 3.

3.15   Let Σ consist of the binary function symbol h and the unary function symbols g_1, g_2, and consider the set of identities

$$E := \{h(g_1(x), g_2(x)) \approx x,\ g_1(h(x, y)) \approx x,\ g_2(h(x, y)) \approx y\}.$$

Show that E has an infinite model, and that $g_1(x) \approx_E g_2(x)$ does not hold. (*Hint:* take a countably infinite carrier set A, and interpret h as a bijection of $A \times A$ into A.)

3.16   The purpose of this exercise is to show that the converse of Theorem 3.3.3 need not hold, even if $\mathcal{K}$ is a variety defined by a nontrivial set of identities. Let Σ and E be as in Exercise 3.15, and let $\mathcal{A} := T(\Sigma, \{x\})/_{\approx_E}$ be the free algebra in $\mathcal{V}(E)$ with generating set $\{[x]_{\approx_E}\}$. Show that $[g_1(x)]_{\approx_E} \neq [g_2(x)]_{\approx_E}$, and that $\mathcal{A}$ is free in $\mathcal{V}(E)$ with generating set $\{[g_1(x)]_{\approx_E}, [g_2(x)]_{\approx_E}\}$.

4

Equational Problems

This chapter deals with the central problems of equational reasoning: validity and satisfiability of equations. Given a set of identities E and an equation $s \approx t$, we say that $s \approx t$ is

valid in E iff $s \approx_E t$, and
satisfiable in E iff there is a substitution σ such that $\sigma(s) \approx_E \sigma(t)$.

Instead of "$s \approx t$ is valid in E" we also say "$s \approx_E t$ is valid", and similarly for satisfiable. Both questions turn out to be undecidable for arbitrary E.

The main topics of this chapter are the following methods for solving special cases of equational problems:

1. *term rewriting* decides $\approx_E$ if $\to_E$ is convergent.
2. *congruence closure* decides $\approx_E$ if E is variable-free.
3. *syntactic unification* computes σ such that $\sigma(s) = \sigma(t)$.

All three methods are of great practical importance. We pay particular attention to efficient implementations of congruence closure and syntactic unification, which also benefits term rewriting, because the latter is based on a special case of syntactic unification.

To see that validity and satisfiability are closely related, we briefly consider their interpretation in first-order logic. The equation $s \approx t$ is valid in E iff the formula $\forall \bar{x}.\ s \approx t$, where $\bar{x}$ are the variables in s and t, holds in all models of E. This is just the definition of $\approx_E$. Dually we have that $s \approx t$ is satisfiable in E iff $\exists \bar{x}.\ s \approx t$ holds in all nonempty models of E. The $\Leftarrow$-direction follows from Corollary 3.5.7 because $\mathcal{T}(\Sigma, V)/_{\approx_E}$ is a nonempty model of E. For the $\Rightarrow$-direction assume $\sigma(s) \approx_E \sigma(t)$ and let $\mathcal{A}$ be a nonempty model of E. Since $\mathcal{A} \models E$, we know that $\mathcal{A} \models \sigma(s) \approx \sigma(t)$, and since $\mathcal{A}$ is nonempty, there exists a homomorphism $\phi : \mathcal{T}(\Sigma, V) \to \mathcal{A}$. Thus we have $\phi(\sigma(s)) = \phi(\sigma(t))$, which yields the required witnesses for $\exists \overline{x}.\ s \approx t$: for each variable x in s or t, take $\phi(\sigma(x))$.

In the sequel, we work with fixed Σ and V. The term $f(s_1, \ldots, s_n)$ is sometimes written $f(\overline{s_n})$.

Recall that the syntactic and the semantic view of equational logic ($\overset{*}{\leftrightarrow}_E$ and $\approx_E$) coincide (Birkhoff's Theorem). We shall use them interchangeably.

4.1 Deciding $\approx_E$

From Theorem 2.1.9 it follows that $\overset{*}{\leftrightarrow}_E$ is decidable if $\to_E$ is convergent, provided we can effectively compute $\downarrow_E$. For this purpose it is essential that we can decide if one term (the term to be reduced) is an instance of another term (the lhs of an identity in E). This is also called the **matching problem**: given two terms s and l, determine if there exists a substitution σ such that $\sigma(l) = s$, and compute σ if it exists. At the end of Section 4.6 we show that matching and satisfiability problems are closely related. A linear time algorithm for matching is the subject of Exercise 4.24.

Theorem 4.1.1 *If E is finite and $\to_E$ is convergent, then $\approx_E$ is decidable.*

Proof Theorem 2.1.9 tells us that $s \overset{*}{\leftrightarrow}_E t$ iff $s\!\downarrow_E = t\!\downarrow_E$. The normal form operator $\downarrow_E$ is computable because we can

1. decide if a term u is already in normal form (w.r.t. $\to_E$) and
2. compute some u' such that $u \to_E u'$ if u is not in normal form.

To decide if u is already in normal form, it suffices to check for all identities $(l \approx r) \in E$ and all positions $p \in \mathcal{P}os(u)$ if there is a substitution σ such that $u|_p = \sigma l$. Since the matching problem is decidable and there are only finitely many identities and positions, either we find that u is already in normal form or we can reduce u to $u[\sigma r]_p$ and iterate the process. This iteration must eventually terminate because $\to_E$ is terminating. $\qquad\square$

This is the key result that explains the importance of convergent reductions.

In general, things are not so rosy: there are finite sets E such that $s \approx_E t$ is undecidable, even if s and t are ground terms.

Definition 4.1.2 The **word problem** for E is the problem of deciding $s \approx_E t$ for arbitrary $s, t \in T(\Sigma, V)$. The **ground word problem** for E is the word problem restricted to ground terms s and t.

We stress that the ground word problem covers only ground terms over the given signature Σ. If we were allowed to use additional free constants, they could take the place of variables and we would be back to the general word problem. Formally: $s \approx_E t \Leftrightarrow \sigma(s) \approx_E \sigma(t)$, where σ is injective and $\mathcal{VR}an(\sigma)$ is a set of constants disjoint from Σ. Two classic examples of undecidable ground word problems follow.

Example 4.1.3 Combinatory logic is one of the earliest formalisms for encoding all computable functions. It is based on the signature $\Sigma = \{\cdot, S, K\}$, where $\cdot$ is a binary infix function and S and K are constants. Computations in this system are described by the identities

$$E := \{((S \cdot x) \cdot y) \cdot z \approx (x \cdot z) \cdot (y \cdot z), \; (K \cdot x) \cdot y \approx x\}.$$

Any program can be encoded as a ground term over Σ, which causes the undecidability of the word problem for E [62].

Example 4.1.4 Fig. 4.1 shows a finitely presented semigroup with undecidable ground word problem due to Matijasevič [170]. In the terminology of this book we have one binary infix function $\cdot$ and two constants a and b, together with the identities in Fig. 4.1. For readability $x \cdot y$ and $x \cdots x$ are written xy and x^n. Associativity allows us to drop brackets.

$$\begin{aligned}
(xy)z &\approx x(yz) \\
aba^2b^2 &\approx b^2a^2ba \\
a^2bab^2a &\approx b^2a^3ba \\
aba^3b^2 &\approx ab^2aba^2 \\
b^3a^2b^2a^2ba &\approx b^3a^2b^2a^4 \\
a^4b^2a^2ba &\approx b^2a^4
\end{aligned}$$

Fig. 4.1. A finitely presented semigroup with undecidable ground word problem.

We can recast this example in terms of unary function symbols only: drop "$\cdot$" and the associativity rule, turn a and b into unary functions, and interpret an identity like $ab \approx ba$ as $a(b(x)) \approx b(a(x))$. Because there are no ground terms, this only yields the undecidability of the word problem.

Obviously the word problem for E is undecidable if the ground word problem is. The converse does not hold in general.

Exercises

4.1   Give a trivial example of a finite set of identities E such that the ground word problem for E is decidable but the word problem is not.

4.2   Show that the word problem for E is decidable if all $\approx_E$-equivalence classes are finite.

4.3 Show that $\approx_D$, equality modulo distributivity, is decidable.

$$D := \{x * (y + z) \approx (x * y) + (x * z),\ (x + y) * z \approx (x * z) + (y * z)\}.$$

4.2 Term rewriting systems

The previous section has shown the importance of $\to_E$, i.e. of using equations from left to right only. Thus we have finally arrived at the main topic of this book, *term rewriting*. It comes with its own terminology, which emphasizes the left-to-right replacement process:

Definition 4.2.1 A **rewrite rule** is an identity $l \approx r$ such that l is not a variable and $Var(l) \supseteq Var(r)$. In this case we may write $l \to r$ instead of $l \approx r$. A **term rewriting system (TRS)** is a set of rewrite rules. Unless noted otherwise, R is always a TRS.

A **redex** (**reducible expression**) is an instance of the lhs of a rewrite rule. **Contracting** the redex means replacing it with the corresponding instance of the rhs of the rule.

The two restrictions that distinguish a rewrite rule from an identity avoid certain pathological cases and obvious sources of nontermination. Much of term rewriting theory carries over to arbitrary identities with only minor modifications. In the interest of compatibility this book sticks to the standard definition that requires the above restrictions.

Since any TRS R is in particular a set of identities, the notation $\to_R$, the rewrite relation induced by R, is well-defined. We also take the liberty of saying that R is terminating, confluent, convergent, etc., if $\to_R$ has the corresponding properties. We simply write $\to$ instead of $\to_R$ if R is obvious from the context.

Because termination of $\to_E$ requires E to be a TRS (why?), we can reformulate Theorem 4.1.1 as follows:

If R is a finite convergent TRS, $\approx_R$ is decidable: $s \approx_R t \Leftrightarrow s{\downarrow}_R = t{\downarrow}_R$.

Let us now examine some basic properties of $\to_R$.

Definition 4.2.2 A relation on $T(\Sigma, V)$ is a **rewrite relation** iff it is compatible with Σ-operations and closed under substitutions.

Lemma 3.1.10 states that $\to_R$ is a rewrite relation. It is a simple exercise to show that $\to_R$ is in fact the least rewrite relation containing R. By induction on the length of derivations one can furthermore show that relatives of $\to_R$ like $\xrightarrow{*}_R$, $\xrightarrow{+}_R$ and $\leftrightarrow_R$ are also rewrite relations. The case of $\xleftrightarrow{*}_R$ is already covered by Theorem 3.1.12.

Recall that, by Lemma 3.1.11, $\to_R$ and its relatives are compatible not just with Σ-operations but also with Σ-contexts. Compatibility with contexts and closure under substitution are very basic properties, which is why we shall rarely refer to them explicitly.

This concludes our initial exposition of term rewriting systems. With the exception of Section 4.7, which presents, almost as a by-product, an implementation of term rewriting, the remainder of the chapter returns to validity and satisfiability of equations. The in-depth study of term rewriting is the subject of the following chapters.

Exercises

4.4   Show that if $(l \approx r) \in E$ and $Var(l) \supseteq Var(r)$ does not hold, then E is nonterminating.

4.5   Show that $\to_R$ is the least rewrite relation containing R. (*Hint:* see the proof of Theorem 3.1.12.)

4.3 Congruence closure

Although $\approx_E$ is undecidable for arbitrary E, there is an important subclass for which it is decidable: if E is finite and contains no variables.

Definition 4.3.1 An identity $l \approx r$ is a **ground identity** if it contains no variables, i.e. $Var(l) = Var(r) = \emptyset$.

While studying congruence closure, G always denotes a set of ground identities. In this case, instantiation is redundant (see Exercise 4.6). Hence it follows from Theorem 3.1.12 that $\approx_G$ is just the **congruence closure** of G, i.e. the least congruence on $T(\Sigma, V)$ containing G.

A more operational description of congruence closure is based on a functional version of the rules of equational logic:

$$
\begin{aligned}
R(E) &:= \{(t,t) \mid t \in T(\Sigma, V)\}, \\
S(E) &:= \{(t,s) \mid (s,t) \in E\}, \\
T(E) &:= \{(s,u) \mid \exists t.\ (s,t), (t,u) \in E\}, \\
C(E) &:= \{(f(\overline{s_n}), f(\overline{t_n})) \mid f \in \Sigma^{(n)} \wedge (s_1,t_1), \ldots, (s_n,t_n) \in E\}.
\end{aligned}
$$

We say that a set A is **closed** under a function F from sets to sets if $F(A) \subseteq A$. As observed above, $\approx_G$ is the least congruence, i.e. set closed under R, S, T and C, that contains G. Defining

$$Cong(E) := E \cup R(E) \cup S(E) \cup T(E) \cup C(E)$$

we find that G is a congruence iff it is closed under $Cong$. Monotonicity of R, S, T and C implies monotonicity of $Cong$:

Lemma 4.3.2 $E_1 \subseteq E_2 \Rightarrow Cong(E_1) \subseteq Cong(E_2)$.

The process of closing G under $Cong$ is an iteration from below:

$$G_0 := G,$$
$$G_{i+1} := Cong(G_i).$$

It follows easily that $CC(G) := \bigcup_{i \geq 0} G_i$ is indeed the congruence closure:

Lemma 4.3.3 $CC(G) = \approx_G$.

Proof ($\subseteq$) We show by induction on i that $G_i \subseteq \approx_G$. For $i = 0$ this is trivial. If $G_i \subseteq \approx_G$ then monotonicity of $Cong$ and the fact that $\approx_G$ is a congruence imply $G_{i+1} = Cong(G_i) \subseteq Cong(\approx_G) = \approx_G$.

($\supseteq$) First note that $CC(G)$ is a congruence because it is closed under $Cong$, which can be seen by checking R, S, T and C in turn: for example, if $(s,t), (t,u) \in CC(G)$, i.e. $(s,t) \in G_i$ and $(t,u) \in G_j$ for suitable i and j, take $k := max(i,j)$ to obtain $(s,t), (t,u) \in G_k$ and hence $(s,u) \in G_{k+1} \subseteq CC(G)$. Since $CC(G)$ also contains G it must contain $\approx_G$, the least congruence containing G. $\qquad \square$

Unfortunately, $CC(G)$ is in general infinite. For example, given two constants a and b and a unary function f, $CC(\{a \approx b\})$ contains all identities $f^i(a) \approx f^i(b)$ (recall that $f^i(t)$ abbreviates $f(f(\ldots f(t)\ldots)))$. We can easily determine that $f^2(a) \approx_G f^2(b)$ when we find this identity in G_2, but how can we conclude that $f^2(a) \not\approx_G f^3(b)$? Do we need to examine all G_i? It turns out that because G is ground, the search space is finite: we need to consider only those terms that occur in G or in the input terms to be tested for equivalence.

Given a term t, let $Subterms(t)$ denote the (not necessarily proper) subterms of t:

$$Subterms(t) := \{t|_p \mid p \in Pos(t)\}.$$

This extends to a set of identities E as follows:

$$Subterms(E) := \bigcup_{(l \approx r) \in E} (Subterms(l) \cup Subterms(r)).$$

In the sequel, we fix a finite set of ground identities G and two terms s and t and define $S := Subterms(G) \cup Subterms(s) \cup Subterms(t)$, again a finite set. We will decide $s \approx_G t$ by restricting our attention to S.

Starting with G, we define the sequence

$$H_0 := G,$$
$$H_{i+1} := Cong(H_i) \cap (S \times S).$$

By definition we have $H_i \subseteq S \times S$. Monotonicity of $Cong$ implies $H_i \subseteq H_{i+1}$. Since $S \times S$ is finite, the sequence must eventually converge:

Lemma 4.3.4 *There is some m such that $H_{m+1} = H_m$.*

The limit H_m is denoted by $CC_S(G)$. Although $CC_S(G)$ is transitive and symmetric, it is reflexive only for terms in S and hence it is not a congruence. For example, if $G = \{a \approx b\}$, $s = f(a)$, $t = b$ then $S = \{a, b, f(a)\}$, $H_1 = G \cup \{a \approx a, b \approx b, f(a) \approx f(a), b \approx a\}$ and $H_2 = H_1$. Nevertheless, $CC_S(G)$ is just what we need:

Theorem 4.3.5 $CC_S(G) = \approx_G \cap (S \times S)$.

Proof Because by definition $H_i \subseteq G_i \cap (S \times S)$, we also have $CC_S(G) \subseteq CC(G) \cap (S \times S)$. Conversely, assume $u, v \in S$ and $u \leftrightarrow^n_G v$. We prove $(u, v) \in H_m$, the limit of the H_i, by well-founded induction on the lexicographically ordered pair $(n, |u|)$.

If $n = 0$, then $u = v$ and hence $(u, v) \in H_1 \subseteq H_m$.

If $u \leftrightarrow^{n+1}_G v$, we distinguish two cases:

(1) There is a rewrite step at the root, i.e. $u \leftrightarrow^{n_1}_G l \leftrightarrow_G r \leftrightarrow^{n_2}_G v$ for some $l \approx r \in G \cup G^{-1}$. Note that because G is ground, no substitutions are involved. Since $n_1, n_2 \leq n$ and $l, r \in S$, the induction hypothesis implies $(u, l) \in H_m$ and $(r, v) \in H_m$. The pair (l, r) is either in H_0 or, because of symmetry, in H_1 and hence in H_m. Transitivity of H_m implies $(u, v) \in H_m$.

(2) There is no rewrite step at the root, i.e. $u = f(\overline{u_k})$, $v = f(\overline{v_k})$ and $u_i \leftrightarrow^{n_i}_G v_i$ for all $1 \leq i \leq k$. Since $n_i \leq n + 1$, $|u_i| < |u|$, and $u_i, v_i \in S$, the induction hypothesis yields $(u_i, v_i) \in H_m$ for all i. It follows by congruence that $(u, v) \in H_{m+1} = H_m$. □

Since $CC_S(G)$ is computable (simply enumerate the H_i until you reach the stable point H_m), we can decide $u \approx_G v$ for all $u, v \in S$, in particular for s and t.

Corollary 4.3.6 *The word problem for finite sets of ground identities is decidable.*

Since $CC_S(G)$ decides $u \approx_G v$ for all $u, v \in S$, we could have started not just with a single pair s and t, but with any finite set of terms U, in which case $CC_S(G)$ decides $\approx_G$ for all terms in U.

Lemma 4.3.7 *The time complexity of the above decision algorithm is polynomial in the size of the input, namely G, s and t.*

Proof Let n be the size of the input. The cardinality of S is $O(n)$. Hence the cardinalities of $S \times S$ and each H_i are $O(n^2)$, and so is m. Each step from H_i to H_{i+1} takes polynomial time. For example, computation of $T(H_i)$ is of order n^5: one iteration over H_i for each premise $(n^2 \cdot n^2)$, and a linear equality test for the term in the middle. □

Example 4.3.8 Let $\Sigma := \{f, a\}$ and $G := \{f^3(a) \approx a, f^2(a) \approx a\}$, $S := \{f^i(a) \mid 0 \le i \le 3\}$ and assume $s, t \in S$. $CC_S(G)$ can be computed in three steps. To keep matters readable, reflexive identities are shown as "...":

$$
\begin{aligned}
H_0 &= \{f^3(a) \approx a, f^2(a) \approx a\}, \\
H_1 &= H_0 \cup \{a \approx f^3(a), a \approx f^2(a), f^3(a) \approx f(a), \ldots\}, \\
H_2 &= H_1 \cup \{f(a) \approx f^3(a), f^3(a) \approx f^2(a), f^2(a) \approx f^3(a), a \approx f(a)\}, \\
H_3 &= H_2 \cup \{f(a) \approx a, f(a) \approx f^2(a), f^2(a) \approx f(a)\}.
\end{aligned}
$$

Note that $H_3 = S \times S$, at which point the iteration stops. In general, the iteration may stop before $S \times S$ is reached, i.e. not all terms are identified.

So why does congruence closure fail for non-ground identities?

Example 4.3.9 Let $E := \{f(f(x)) \approx g(x)\}$. Then every derivation of $f(g(a)) \approx_E g(f(a))$, for example $f(g(a)) \approx_E f(f(f(a))) \approx_E g(f(a))$, involves a "detour", i.e. a term not in S.

Exercise

4.6   Show that if G is a set of ground identities, then instantiation is redundant: if $G \vdash s \approx t$ then there is a proof of $G \vdash s \approx t$ that does not involve instantiation.

4.4 Congruence closure on graphs

In order to obtain an efficient version of the above congruence closure algorithm we represent terms as directed acyclic graphs. This allows for shared subterms, but not for cycles. For example, $f(g(a), g(a))$ can have the three different representations shown in Fig. 4.2. Unless we explicitly say so, we do not assume that the graph representation is maximally shared (as in (3)) or even shared at all. In fact, the congruence closure algorithm below can transform (1) via (2) into (3).

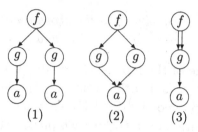

(1)   (2)   (3)

Fig. 4.2. Three term graphs for $f(g(a), g(a))$.

For each node u of the graph the following functions are defined:

$label(u)$ the function symbol attached to u,
$\delta(u)$ the number of successors of u,
$u[i]$ ith successor of u for $i = 1, \ldots, \delta(u)$.

We assume that $label(u) = label(v)$ implies $\delta(u) = \delta(v)$ and call such graphs **term graphs**. The term represented by a node u in a term graph is defined by

$$term(u) := label(u)(term(u[1]), \ldots, term(u[\delta(u)])).$$

The details of representing term graphs as pointer structures in an imperative programming language can be found in Section 4.8.

A relation $\sim$ on the nodes of a term graph is a **congruence** if it is an equivalence and if for all nodes u and v with $label(u) = label(v)$

$$(\forall 1 \leq i \leq \delta(u).\ u[i] \sim v[i]) \Rightarrow u \sim v.$$

The **congruence closure** of $\sim$, denoted by $\sim^{CC}$, is the smallest congruence containing $\sim$.

The congruence closure of a relation on a term graph is a compact representation of $CC_S(G)$ defined earlier: the terms in S correspond to the nodes of the graph, G corresponds to $\sim$ and $CC_S(G)$ corresponds to $\sim^{CC}$. The correspondence between $CC_S(G)$ and $\sim^{CC}$ hinges on the fact that the definition of $CC_S(G)$ includes an intersection with $S \times S$ while the same effect is achieved in the definition of $\sim^{CC}$ by talking about a fixed graph whose nodes correspond to S. Thus we have the following relationship:

Fact 4.4.1 $(s_1, s_2) \in CC_S(G)$ *iff there is* $(u_1, u_2) \in \sim^{CC}$ *such that* $s_i = term(u_i)$, $i = 1, 2$.

In the sequel, we work directly on the graph representation.

As a first application that utilizes the graph view, consider what happens when we compute the congruence closure of the empty relation, for example on the graph (1) in Fig. 4.2. Because the two nodes labelled a have no successors, all their successors are related and thus those two nodes must be in the congruence closure. But now the two nodes labelled g must also be in the congruence closure, because their successors are. At this point we have identified all isomorphic subgraphs and the process stops. Collapsing those isomorphic subgraphs in Fig. 4.2 transforms (1) into (3). Hence a congruence closure algorithm can be used to eliminate common subexpressions, for example in optimizing compilers.

In general we have

Lemma 4.4.2 *Let $\sim$ be a congruence. Then $u \sim v$ if u and v are the roots of isomorphic subgraphs.*

Proof by induction on the structure of $term(u) = term(v)$. □

In particular $\emptyset^{CC}$ identifies two nodes iff they represent the same terms.

The congruence closure algorithm is essentially a computation on equivalence classes of nodes. We need the test whether two nodes are equivalent, i.e. if $u \sim v$, and a procedure $Union(u, v)$ for merging the equivalence class of u with the one of v. Note that we are now in an imperative world: we operate on a single graph and $Union$ updates the equivalence relation $\sim$ on the nodes of that graph.

Because it is good software engineering practice to decouple system layers, our description of the congruence closure algorithm only assumes the existence of $\sim$ and $Union$ with certain properties, without relying on a particular implementation. The latter is provided later on.

For each node u let $preds(u)$ be the set of all predecessors of all nodes equivalent to u:

$$preds(u) := \{v \mid \exists 1 \le i \le \delta(v).\ v[i] \sim u\}.$$

We also define an auxiliary predicate *congruent*:

$$congruent(p, q) := (label(p) = label(q)) \wedge \forall 1 \le i \le \delta(p).\ p[i] \sim q[i].$$

Note that $congruent(p, q)$ implies $p \sim^{CC} q$.

The key component in the congruence closure algorithm is procedure *merge* shown in Fig. 4.3.

Starting from a congruence, $merge(u, v)$ adds (u, v) and again closes the relation under congruence:

Theorem 4.4.3 *If R is closed under congruence and $\sim = R$ before the execution of $merge(u, v)$, then $\sim = (R \cup \{(u, v)\})^{CC}$ afterwards.*

```
procedure merge(u, v);
begin if u ≁ v then
      begin P := preds(u);  Q := preds(v);
            Union(u, v);
            for all (p, q) ∈ P × Q do
                  if p ≁ q and congruent(p, q) then merge(p, q)
      end
end;
```

Fig. 4.3. Procedure *merge*.

Proof Soundness of *merge* is easy: $\sim \subseteq (R \cup \{(u,v)\})^{CC}$ is invariant during the execution of $merge(u,v)$ because $Union(p,q)$ is called only if $(p,q) = (u,v)$ or if $congruent(p,q)$. In both cases it means $(p,q) \in (R \cup \{(u,v)\})^{CC}$.

Completeness of *merge* is proved by recourse to the inductive nature of $(.)^{CC}$. Although we did not spell this out at the time, $(.)^{CC}$ can be defined completely analogously to $CC_S(.)$. Thus we obtain $(R \cup \{(u,v)\})^{CC}$ as the stable point of the sequence $R_0 := R \cup \{(u,v)\}$, $R_{i+1} := Cong(R_i)$. *Cong* on the nodes of a graph is defined analogously to its counterpart on terms, except that we never create new terms but work with a fixed set of nodes. Now let $\sim_0 := R$ and let $\sim_i$, $i > 0$, be the state of the equivalence after the *i*th call to *Union* during the execution of $merge(u,v)$. We prove by induction on i that

$$\forall u', v'. \ (u', v') \in R_i \ \Rightarrow \ \exists j. \ u' \sim_j v'.$$

For $i = 0$ take $j := 1$, i.e. the state after the initial call $Union(u,v)$.

For the induction step assume $(u', v') \in R_{i+1} = Cong(R_i)$. If (u', v') is the result of reflexivity, symmetry or transitivity, the proof is routine because each $\sim_j$ is an equivalence. We concentrate on closure under congruence, i.e. we assume $label(u') = label(v')$ and $(u'[l], v'[l]) \in R_i$ for $l = 1, \ldots, \delta(u')$. Let $K := \{k \mid (u'[k], v'[k]) \notin R\}$. If $K = \emptyset$ then $(u', v') \in R$ because R is a congruence. Therefore $u' \sim_0 v'$. If $K \neq \emptyset$ then there must be some point in the computation and some k such that $u'[k] \not\sim_{j-1} v'[k]$ before a call $Union(u'', v'')$ and $u'[l] \sim_j v'[l]$ for all l afterwards. But this means that $u'[k] \sim_{j-1} u''$ and $v'[k] \sim_{j-1} v''$, i.e. $(u', v') \in preds(u'') \times preds(v'')$. Thus either $merge(u', v')$ is called later on or $u' \sim v'$ is achieved beforehand, in which case the guard if $p \not\sim q$ suppresses the superfluous call. □

Thus we have proved partial correctness of *merge*. Termination is obvious: every call $merge(u,v)$ either terminates immediately (if $u \sim v$) or decreases the number of equivalence classes by one (if $u \not\sim v$).

To compute the congruence closure of $R = \{(u_0, v_0), \ldots, (u_n, v_n)\}$ we start

with the relation $\emptyset^{CC}$ and execute $merge(u_0, v_0); \ldots; merge(u_n, v_n)$. Iterating Theorem 4.4.3 proves that at the end $\sim = R^{CC}$. This leaves us with
the small problem of generating the initial relation $\emptyset^{CC}$, i.e. identifying all
common subgraphs. This can be accomplished very elegantly by identifying
all constants with the same label and letting $merge$ propagate these identi-
fications up the tree (see Exercise 4.8).

Before we look at an example, we have to discuss the implementation of
equivalence classes. The following is a short summary of the $Union/Find$
implementation found in most books on algorithms [3]. Equivalence classes
are represented by sets of (converse) trees, where each child is linked to its
parent. Each tree represents an equivalence class. For example, the partition
$\{\{u_1, u_2, u_3\}, \{u_4, u_5\}, \{u_6\}\}$ can be represented as follows:

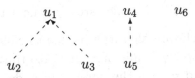

Note that we always use dashed arrows in $Union/Find$-trees in order to
distinguish them from the arrows of the term graphs.

There are two operations on nodes:

$Find(u)$ returns the root of the tree u belongs to. For example, $Find(u_3) =$
u_1 and $Find(u_6) = u_6$. As a side effect, $Find$ also compresses the
path between u and the root by making all the nodes on that path
point directly to the root. This speeds up subsequent calls of $Find$.

$Union(u, v)$ finds the roots of the trees u and v belong to and creates a link
from the smaller tree to the larger one, thus increasing the length
of the path to the root for fewer nodes. For example, $Union(u_2, u_6)$
creates a link from u_6 to u_1.

The implementation of $Union$ and $Find$ is routine. Based on it we define

$$u \sim v := (Find(u) = Find(v)).$$

Example 4.4.4 We come back to $G = \{f^3(a) \approx a, f^2(a) \approx a\}$ from
Example 4.3.8. The initial graph containing $f^3(a)$, $f^2(a)$, $f(a)$ and a is
shown in Fig. 4.4, as are all further steps of the algorithm. We start with a
fully shared graph.

The result of merging the nodes corresponding to $f^3(a)$ and a is shown in
the next graph. Since $f^3(a)$ has no predecessor, nothing much happens.

The final graph shows the result of merging $f^2(a)$ and a as well. Before
$Union(f^2(a), a)$ is executed we have $preds(f^2(a)) = \{f^3(a)\}$ and $preds(a) =$

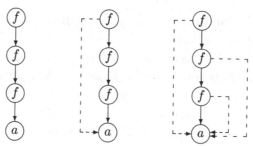

Fig. 4.4. Initial graph, after $merge(f^3(a), a)$, and after $merge(f^2(a), a)$.

$\{f(a)\}$. This causes a recursive call $merge(f^3(a), f(a))$ which in turn leads to $Union(f^3(a), f(a))$ which creates an arrow from $Find(f(a)) = f(a)$ to $Find(f^3(a)) = a$. In the end, all nodes are equivalent to a.

The above congruence closure algorithm is due to Nelson and Oppen [184] who prove that $O(n)$ top-level calls of $merge$ take time $O(m^2)$, where m is the number of edges and $n \le m$ the number of nodes of the initial graph. This requires a fast implementation of $preds$. First note that $u \sim v$ implies $preds(u) = preds(v)$. Hence it suffices to compute $preds$ once for each equivalence class and attach it to the root of the class. (At this point we start to rely on the representation of equivalence classes.) Now $Union$ needs to combine the attached $preds$ sets as well. If they are represented as linked lists without duplicates, they can be merged in time proportional to the sum of their lengths, provided they are sorted w.r.t. some arbitrary but fixed order on the nodes.

Note that the initial identification of common subgraphs sketched above is included in $O(m^2)$. Identifying all constants and variables with the same label takes time $O(m \log n)$ (see Subsection 4.8.3), which does not add anything to $O(m^2)$. Since there are at most n variables and constants, this can only lead to $O(n)$ calls to $merge$.

Exercises

4.7   Let $\Sigma = \{f, a\}$ and $G := \{f^5(a) \approx a, f^3(a) \approx a\}$. Prove $f(a) \approx_G a$ using congruence closure both on sets of identities and on graphs.

4.8   Assume initially $\sim$ is empty. Show that calling $merge(u, v)$ for all nodes u and v such that $label(u) = label(v)$ and $\delta(u) = \delta(v) = 0$ identifies all isomorphic subgraphs: at the end, $term(u) = term(v)$ implies $u \sim v$ for all nodes u and v.

4.9   Implement congruence closure in your favourite programming language.

4.5 Syntactic unification

Unification is the process of solving the satisfiability problem: given E, s and t, find a substitution σ such that $\sigma s \approx_E \sigma t$. If s and t are ground, unification degenerates to solving the ground word problem. Because the latter is undecidable, so is unification. Therefore this chapter concentrates on the special case $E = \emptyset$ which is both theoretically interesting and practically important, as it is the heart of many symbolic computation algorithms, in particular interpreters for the programming language Prolog and the confluence tests based on critical pairs in Chapter 6. This case is also known as "syntactic unification" because we try to find σ such that $\sigma s = \sigma t$, i.e. σs and σt are syntactically identical (recall that $s \approx_E t \Leftrightarrow s = t$ if $E = \emptyset$). In this case σ is called a unifier of s and t or a solution of the equation $s =^? t$.

Let us look at some simple examples to get an idea of the different facets of the problem:

$f(x) =^? f(a)$ has exactly one unifier $\{x \mapsto a\}$.
$x =^? f(y)$ has many unifiers: $\{x \mapsto f(y)\}$, $\{x \mapsto f(a), y \mapsto a\}$, ...
$f(x) =^? g(y)$ has no unifier.
$x =^? f(x)$ has no unifier.

None of these is terribly surprising (except maybe the last one) but it shows that equations may have zero, one or more solutions. However, some solutions are better than others: $\{x \mapsto f(y)\}$ is a more general unifier of $x =^? f(y)$ than $\{x \mapsto f(a), y \mapsto a\}$. In fact, $\{x \mapsto f(y)\}$ is a most general unifier of $x =^? f(y)$: all other unifiers are instances of it.

Definition 4.5.1 A substitution σ is **more general** than a substitution σ' if there is a substitution δ such that $\sigma' = \delta\sigma$. In this case we write $\sigma \lesssim \sigma'$. We also say that σ' is an **instance** of σ.

If $\sigma = \{x \mapsto f(y)\}$ and $\sigma' = \{x \mapsto f(a), y \mapsto a\}$ then $\sigma \lesssim \sigma'$ because $\sigma' = \delta\sigma$ where $\delta = \{y \mapsto a\}$. You can easily check $\sigma' = \delta\sigma$: $\sigma'(x) = f(a) = \delta(\sigma(x))$, $\sigma'(y) = a = \delta(\sigma(y))$ and $\sigma'(z) = z = \delta(\sigma(z))$ for all other variables z.

Lemma 4.5.2 *The relation $\lesssim$ on substitutions is a quasi-order.*

Proof Reflexivity is trivial: simply let δ be the identity. For transitivity suppose $\sigma_2 = \delta_1\sigma_1$ and $\sigma_3 = \delta_2\sigma_2$. Thus $\sigma_3 = \delta_2\sigma_2 = \delta_2(\delta_1\sigma_1) = (\delta_2\delta_1)\sigma_1$ because composition of substitutions is associative. $\square$

We write $\sigma \sim \sigma'$ if $\sigma \lesssim \sigma'$ and $\sigma \gtrsim \sigma'$, as is customary for quasi-orders.

As the symbol indicates, $\lesssim$ is not antisymmetric. For example, let $\sigma = \{x \mapsto y\}$ and $\sigma' = \{y \mapsto x\}$. Then $\sigma \lesssim \sigma'$ because $\sigma' = \sigma'\sigma$, and $\sigma \gtrsim \sigma'$ because $\sigma = \sigma\sigma'$. This situation can be made more precise using the notion of a **renaming**, an injective substitution ρ such that $\mathcal{R}an(\rho) \subseteq V$, i.e. ρ is a bijection on V (because $\mathcal{D}om(\rho)$ is finite) and hence also on $T(\Sigma, V)$.

Lemma 4.5.3 $\sigma \sim \sigma' \Leftrightarrow \exists renaming\ \rho.\ \sigma = \rho\sigma'$.

The proof is left as an exercise.

Now we generalize our setting slightly by solving sets of equations.

Definition 4.5.4 A **unification problem** is a finite set of equations $S = \{s_1 =^? t_1, \ldots, s_n =^? t_n\}$. A **unifier** or **solution** of S is a substitution σ such that $\sigma s_i = \sigma t_i$ for $i = 1, \ldots, n$. $\mathcal{U}(S)$ denotes the set of all unifiers of S. S is **unifiable** if $\mathcal{U}(S) \neq \emptyset$.

A substitution σ is a **most general unifier (mgu)** of S if σ is a least element of $\mathcal{U}(S)$:

- $\sigma \in \mathcal{U}(S)$ and
- $\forall \sigma' \in \mathcal{U}(S).\ \sigma \lesssim \sigma'$.

Example 4.5.5 It is easy to check that $\sigma := \{x \mapsto y\}$ is an mgu of $x =^? y$. Given any unifier θ, $\sigma \lesssim \theta$ because $\theta = \theta\sigma$: $\theta x = \theta y = \theta\sigma x$, $\theta y = \theta\sigma y$, and $\theta z = \theta\sigma z$ for all other variables z.

Certain other consequences of the above definition of mgu are less obvious.

1. $\sigma' := \{x \mapsto z, y \mapsto z\}$ is a unifier of $x =^? y$, but not an mgu: $\sigma = \{x \mapsto y\}$ is not an instance of σ' because $\{z \mapsto y\}\sigma'$ is $\{x \mapsto y, z \mapsto y\}$ but not σ. There are more complex definitions of mgu (see Chapter 10) that take into account that σ and $\{z \mapsto y\}\sigma'$ only differ on variables (z) not present in the unification problem. For the time being we prefer the simpler definition.

2. $\sigma'' := \{x \mapsto y, z_1 \mapsto z_2, z_2 \mapsto z_1\}$ is an mgu of $x =^? y$ because σ, and hence any other unifier, is an instance of σ'': $\sigma = \{z_1 \mapsto z_2, z_2 \mapsto z_1\}\sigma''$.

The second point can be ruled out by restricting to certain well-behaved substitutions:

Definition 4.5.6 A substitution σ is **idempotent** if $\sigma = \sigma\sigma$.

Clearly σ'' above is not idempotent because, for example, $\sigma''(z_1) = z_2$ whereas $\sigma''(\sigma''(z_1)) = z_1$. Non-idempotent substitutions can be very cumbersome to work with. They can be spotted very easily:

Lemma 4.5.7 A substitution σ is idempotent iff $\mathcal{D}om(\sigma) \cap \mathcal{V}\mathcal{R}an(\sigma) = \emptyset$.

The proof is left as an exercise.

Section 4.6 yields an algorithmic proof of the following key theorem:

Theorem 4.5.8 *If a unification problem S has a solution then it has an idempotent mgu.*

Lemma 4.5.3 tells us that mgus are unique only up to renaming. Even idempotent mgus are not unique. For example both $\{x \mapsto y\}$ and $\{y \mapsto x\}$ are idempotent mgus of $x =^? y$.

Exercises

4.10 Prove Lemmas 4.5.3 and 4.5.7.

4.11 Show that if $\sigma \lesssim \sigma'$ then $\sigma\theta \lesssim \sigma'\theta$. Does $\sigma \lesssim \sigma'$ imply $\theta\sigma \lesssim \theta\sigma'$?

4.12 Show that if $Dom(\sigma) \cap Dom(\sigma') = \emptyset$ and $Dom(\sigma) \cap VRan(\sigma') = \emptyset$, then $\sigma\sigma' = \sigma \cup \sigma'$.

4.13 Does $\sigma \subseteq \sigma'$ always imply $\sigma \lesssim \sigma'$? Prove that the implication holds if σ' is idempotent.

4.14 Prove that if $\sigma s = \sigma' s$ then σ and σ' coincide on $Var(s)$.

4.15 Show that if σ is an idempotent mgu of S then $\forall\theta.\ \theta \in \mathcal{U}(S) \Leftrightarrow \theta = \theta\sigma$.

4.6 Unification by transformation

Unification can be expressed as a repeated transformation of a set of equations until the solution stares you in the face. In fact, it is very reminiscent of solving systems of linear equations by Gaussian elimination, as in the following example:

$$\boxed{\begin{array}{l} x + 3y = 0 \\ 2x + 8y = 2z \end{array}} \rightsquigarrow \boxed{\begin{array}{l} x + 3y = 0 \\ 2y = 2z \end{array}} \rightsquigarrow \boxed{\begin{array}{l} x + 3y = 0 \\ y = z \end{array}}$$

$$\rightsquigarrow \boxed{\begin{array}{l} x + 3z = 0 \\ y = z \end{array}} \rightsquigarrow \boxed{\begin{array}{l} x = -3z \\ y = z \end{array}}$$

We leave it to the reader to compare the individual steps of Gaussian elimination and the transformations below.

Definition 4.6.1 A unification problem $S = \{x_1 =^? t_1, \ldots, x_n =^? t_n\}$ is in **solved form** if the x_i are pairwise distinct variables, none of which occurs in any of the t_i. In this case we define

$$\vec{S} := \{x_1 \mapsto t_1, \ldots, x_n \mapsto t_n\}.$$

Lemma 4.6.2 *If S is in solved form then $\sigma = \sigma\vec{S}$ for all $\sigma \in \mathcal{U}(S)$.*

Proof Let $S = \{x_1 =^? t_1, \ldots, x_n =^? t_n\}$. We show by case distinction that σ and $\sigma\vec{S}$ behave the same on all variables, i.e. $\forall x \in V. \ \sigma x = \sigma\vec{S}x$:

1. $x \in \{x_1, \ldots, x_n\}$, e.g. $x = x_k$: $\sigma x = \sigma t_k = \sigma\vec{S}x$ (because $\sigma \in \mathcal{U}(S)$).
2. $x \notin \{x_1, \ldots, x_n\}$: $\sigma x = \sigma\vec{S}x$ (because $\vec{S}x = x$). $\qquad\qquad\square$

Lemma 4.6.3 *If S is in solved form then $\vec{S}$ is an idempotent mgu of S.*

Proof Idempotence follows directly from Lemma 4.5.7 because none of the x_i occurs in the t_i. For the same reason we have $\vec{S}x_i = t_i = \vec{S}t_i$, i.e. $\vec{S} \in \mathcal{U}(S)$. Finally, $\vec{S}$ is an mgu because $\vec{S} \lesssim \sigma$ for all $\sigma \in \mathcal{U}(S)$ by Lemma 4.6.2. $\qquad\square$

Thus we know how to extract an idempotent mgu once we have reached a solved form. In order to get there we employ the following transformation rules:

Delete	$\{t =^? t\} \uplus S$	$\Longrightarrow$	S
Decompose	$\{f(\overline{t_n}) =^? f(\overline{u_n})\} \uplus S$	$\Longrightarrow$	$\{t_1 =^? u_1, \ldots, t_n =^? u_n\} \cup S$
Orient	$\{t =^? x\} \uplus S$	$\Longrightarrow$	$\{x =^? t\} \cup S \quad$ if $t \notin V$
Eliminate	$\{x =^? t\} \uplus S$	$\Longrightarrow$	$\{x =^? t\} \cup \{x \mapsto t\}(S)$
			if $x \in Var(S) - Var(t)$

The application of a substitution to S means its application to both sides of all equations in S. The symbol $\uplus$ denotes disjoint union. This enforces that the particular equation selected by the left-hand side is removed from set of equations (although Eliminate reinserts it). The individual rules are easy to grasp:

Delete deletes trivial equations.

Decompose replaces equations between terms by equations between their subterms.

Orient moves variables to the left-hand side.

Eliminate broadcasts solutions, thereby eliminating the solved variable in the remaining part of the problem.

Dropping the side conditions can cause looping. For example $x \in Var(t)$ in Eliminate has the following consequence:

$$\{x =^? f(x), \ \ldots x \ldots\} \ \Longrightarrow \ \{x =^? f(x), \ \ldots f(x) \ldots\}$$
$$\Longrightarrow \ \{x =^? f(x), \ \ldots f(f(x)) \ldots\} \ \Longrightarrow \ \cdots.$$

Example 4.6.4 The following sequence of transformations illustrates the workings of the above rules:

$$\{x =^? f(a), \; g(x,x) =^? g(x,y)\} \qquad \Longrightarrow \text{Eliminate}$$
$$\{x =^? f(a), \; g(f(a),f(a)) =^? g(f(a),y)\} \quad \Longrightarrow \text{Decompose}$$
$$\{x =^? f(a), \; f(a) =^? f(a), \; f(a) =^? y\} \quad \Longrightarrow \text{Delete}$$
$$\{x =^? f(a), \; f(a) =^? y\} \qquad \Longrightarrow \text{Orient}$$
$$\{x =^? f(a), \; y =^? f(a)\}.$$

Note that the choice of rules is nondeterministic. We could start with De-compose instead of Eliminate. Would this lead to a different solved form?

The solved form we end up with yields an mgu $\{x \mapsto f(a), y \mapsto f(a)\}$ for our initial unification problem. This is not a coincidence. We claim that the following function *Unify* computes a most general unifier if one exists and fails otherwise.

$$Unify(S) \;\; = \;\; \textbf{while} \text{ there is some } T \text{ such that } S \Longrightarrow T \textbf{ do } S := T;$$
$$\text{if } S \text{ is in solved form } \textbf{then return } \vec{S} \textbf{ else fail}.$$

Note that the above algorithm is nondeterministic: if there is more than one applicable transformation rule, e.g. $S \Longrightarrow T_1$ and $S \Longrightarrow T_2$, the algorithm may choose an *arbitrary* one. Termination of *Unify* thus depends on termination of $\Longrightarrow$. The latter is not completely trivial because Eliminate may increase the size of a unification problem, as Example 4.6.4 shows.

Lemma 4.6.5 *Unify terminates for all inputs.*

Proof We call a variable x **solved** if it occurs exactly once in S, namely on the left-hand side of some equation $x =^? t$ where $x \notin Var(t)$.

Termination of $\Longrightarrow$ is proved by a measure function that maps a unification problem S to a triple (n_1, n_2, n_3) of natural numbers such that

n_1 is the number of variables in S that are not solved,

n_2 is the size of S, i.e. $\sum_{(s=^?t)\in S}(|s| + |t|)$, and

n_3 is the number of equations $t =^? x$ in S.

The following table shows that each step decreases the triples w.r.t. the lexicographic order:

	n_1	n_2	n_3
Delete	$\geq$	$>$	
Decompose	$\geq$	$>$	
Orient	$\geq$	$=$	$>$
Eliminate	$>$		

The interpretation is obvious: Eliminate decreases n_1, which none of the other rules can increase. Delete and Decompose decrease n_2. Orient leaves n_2 unchanged but decreases n_3.

For example, the transformations sequence in Example 4.6.4 is mapped to $(2,9,0) >_{lex} (1,12,0) >_{lex} (1,10,1) >_{lex} (1,6,1) >_{lex} (0,6,0)$.   □

The key property of $\Longrightarrow$ is preservation of unifiers:

Lemma 4.6.6 *If* $S \Longrightarrow T$ *then* $\mathcal{U}(S) = \mathcal{U}(T)$.

Proof For Delete, Decompose and Orient this is obvious.

For Eliminate let $\theta := \{x \mapsto t\}$. Applying Lemma 4.6.2 to $x =^? t$, which is in solved form, we get that $\sigma = \sigma\theta$ if $\sigma x = \sigma t$. Thus we conclude that

$$
\begin{aligned}
\sigma \in \mathcal{U}(\{x =^? t\} \uplus S) \quad &\Leftrightarrow \quad \sigma x = \sigma t \wedge \sigma \in \mathcal{U}(S) \\
&\Leftrightarrow \quad \sigma x = \sigma t \wedge \sigma\theta \in \mathcal{U}(S) \\
&\Leftrightarrow \quad \sigma x = \sigma t \wedge \sigma \in \mathcal{U}(\theta S) \\
&\Leftrightarrow \quad \sigma \in \mathcal{U}(\{x =^? t\} \cup \theta S).
\end{aligned}
$$
    □

The following lemma expresses soundness of *Unify* and follows directly from Lemmas 4.6.3 and 4.6.6 above.

Lemma 4.6.7 *If Unify(S) returns a substitution* σ *then* σ *is an idempotent mgu of S.*

The completeness proof requires two fundamental properties of terms:

Lemma 4.6.8 *An equation* $f(\overline{s_m}) =^? g(\overline{t_n})$, *where* $f \neq g$, *has no solution.*

Proof $\sigma(f(\overline{s_m})) = f(\overline{\sigma(s_m)}) \neq g(\overline{\sigma(t_n)}) = \sigma(g(\overline{t_n}))$.   □

Lemma 4.6.9 *An equation* $x =^? t$, *where* $x \in Var(t)$ *and* $x \neq t$, *has no solution.*

Proof If $x \neq t$ then t is of the form $f(\overline{t_n})$ with $x \in Var(t_i)$ for some i. Hence $\sigma(x)$ and $\sigma(t)$ cannot be identical because $|\sigma(x)| \leq |\sigma(t_i)| < |\sigma(t)|$.   □

Now we obtain completeness of *Unify*, i.e. every solvable system is solved:

Lemma 4.6.10 *If S is solvable, Unify(S) does not fail.*

Proof By Lemma 4.6.6 it suffices to show that if S is solvable and in normal form w.r.t. $\Longrightarrow$, then S is in solved form.

S cannot contain equations of the form $f(\ldots) =^? f(\ldots)$ (because of Decompose), $f(\ldots) =^? g(\ldots)$ (because of Lemma 4.6.8), $x =^? x$ (because of Delete), and $t =^? x$ where $t \notin V$ (because of Orient). Hence all equations in S are of the form $x =^? t$ where $x \notin Var(t)$ (because of Lemma 4.6.9).

Because of Eliminate, x cannot occur twice in S. Hence S is in solved form. □

Theorem 4.5.8 is now a direct consequence of soundness, completeness and termination of *Unify*.

Detecting unsolvability with the above rules for $\Longrightarrow$ can be a lengthy affair because one has to compute a normal form first. Therefore we introduce a special unification problem $\bot$ that has no solution, and add the two rules

Clash	$\{f(\overline{t_m}) =^? g(\overline{u_n})\} \uplus S \implies \bot$	if $f \neq g$
Occurs-Check	$\{x =^? t\} \uplus S \implies \bot$	if $x \in \mathcal{V}(t)$ and $x \neq t$

which are immediately justified by Lemmas 4.6.8 and 4.6.9. Here is a very simple example of the behaviour of the extended set of rules:

$$\{f(x,x) =^? f(y, g(y))\} \Longrightarrow \{x =^? y, \ x =^? g(y)\} \Longrightarrow \{x =^? y, \ y =^? g(y)\}$$
$$\Longrightarrow \bot.$$

Since $\bot$ is not in solved form, *Unify* fails on problems with normal form $\bot$.

The complexity of *Unify* is (at least) exponential in both time and space.

Example 4.6.11 It is easy to see that the unification problem

$$\{x_1 =^? f(x_0, x_0), \ x_2 =^? f(x_1, x_1), \ \ldots, \ x_n =^? f(x_{n-1}, x_{n-1})\}$$

has the idempotent mgu

$$\{x_1 \mapsto f(x_0, x_0), x_2 \mapsto f(f(x_0, x_0), f(x_0, x_0)), \ldots\}$$

which maps x_i to a complete binary tree of height i. Thus the size of every mgu of this example is exponential in the size of the input (because mgus are equal modulo renaming).

The above unification problem can also be obtained by unifying only two terms containing just variables and the binary f:

$$
\begin{aligned}
s_n(x) &= f(x_1, & f(x_2, & f(\ldots, x_n &)\ldots)), \\
t_n(x) &= f(f(x_0, x_0), & f(f(x_1, x_1), & f(\ldots, f(x_{n-1}, x_{n-1}))\ldots)).
\end{aligned}
$$

Note that the names of the x_i on the rhs depend directly on the x on the lhs. This becomes relevant in a later example where we need different instances of s_n and t_n with different variable names x and y.

Computing the mgu in this example requires exponential space because of copying. If the underlying implementation is based on graphs and sharing, as opposed to trees, linear space complexity is obtained. We come back to this implementation technique in Section 4.8.

Before we concentrate on algorithmic issues, let us briefly explore the connection between unification and matching. Recall that (syntactic) matching is the problem of finding a substitution σ such that $\sigma(s) = t$. We denote the matching problem by $s \lesssim^? t$ and call σ a solution of $s \lesssim^? t$ or a **matcher** of s and t, in which case we say that s **matches** t. The extension to finite sets of matching problems is analogous to unification.

Note that all solutions of $s \lesssim^? t$ coincide on $Var(s)$ (see Exercise 4.14). Thus a matcher is unique, as far as s and t are concerned.

We can easily reduce matching to unification: simply regard all variables in t as constants, for example by introducing a new constant c_x for each variable x.

Example 4.6.12 The matching problem $f(x, y) \lesssim^? f(g(z), x)$ becomes the unification problem $f(x, y) =^? f(g(c_z), c_x)$. The unifier $\{x \mapsto g(c_z), y \mapsto c_x\}$ becomes the matcher $\{x \mapsto g(z), y \mapsto x\}$.

In many applications of matching we may assume that t is ground. In that case unification and matching trivially coincide. From a complexity point of view, unification and matching do not differ very much either: both can be implemented in linear time. However, linear implementations of matching are quite straightforward (see Exercise 4.24), whereas linear unification requires sophisticated data structures and will occupy us for much of the rest of this chapter. Therefore matching should be implemented separately from unification if efficiency is an issue.

Exercises

4.16 Let S and T be unification problems. Show that if σ is an mgu of S and θ an mgu of $\sigma(T)$ then $\theta\sigma$ is an mgu of $S \cup T$.

4.17 Show that after the addition of the rules Clash and Occurs-Check, the second line in function *Unify* can be rephrased as follows:

$$\text{if } S = \bot \text{ then fail else return } \vec{S}.$$

4.18 Check if the following unification/matching problems are solvable:

    (a) $f(x, y) =^? / \lesssim^? f(h(a), x)$;
    (b) $f(x, y) =^? / \lesssim^? f(h(x), x)$;
    (c) $f(x, b) =^? / \lesssim^? f(h(y), z)$;
    (d) $f(x, x) =^? / \lesssim^? f(h(y), y)$.

4.19 Modify the transformation rules for unification (including Occurs-Check and Clash) such that they directly solve the matching problem (rather than first replacing all variables on the right-hand sides by

constants). Allow for variables on both sides and detect unsolvability
as early as possible.

4.20 Does every matching problem have an idempotent solution? Can you
find a sufficient condition for the existence of an idempotent solution?

4.7 Unification and term rewriting in ML

This section lays the foundations for our little ML-based term rewriting laboratory: it implements terms, substitutions, unification, matching and, while
we are at it, term rewriting. The emphasis is on succinctness. Efficiency is
catered for in the next section.

Terms have a very straightforward representation:

```
type vname = string * int;
```

```
datatype term = V of vname | T of string * term list;
```

Variable names consist of a name and an index. The index component
simplifies renaming but is not made use of in the current context. The
constructors V and T distinguish variables and proper terms. For example,
x_1 is $V("x",1)$ and $f(a,y_2)$ is $T("f",[T("a",[]),V("y",2)])$.

Substitutions are implemented by so-called association lists:

```
type subst = (vname * term) list;
```

Clearly, the mapping $\{x_1 \mapsto t_1,\ldots\}$ is represented as $[(x_1,t_1),\ldots]$. Although *subst* also contains elements like $[(x,s),(x,t)]$, our algorithms never construct such lists that associate a variable with more than one term.
The test $x \in Dom(\sigma)$ is implemented as *indom x σ*:

```
(* indom: vname -> subst -> bool *)
fun indom x s = exists (fn (y,_) => x = y) s;
```

The application of a substitution to a variable is performed by *app*:

```
(* app: subst -> vname -> term *)
fun app ((y,t)::s) x  =  if x=y then t else app s x;
```

Note that *app s x* is defined iff *indom x s* is *true*. The homomorphic extension
of a substitution to terms, introduced as $\hat{\sigma}$ in Section 3.1 but subsequently
identified with σ, is performed by *lift*:

```
(* lift: subst -> term -> term *)
fun lift s (V x)    = if indom x s then app s x else V x
  | lift s (T(f,ts)) = T(f, map (lift s) ts);
```

The test $x \in Var(t)$ is implemented as *occurs x t*:

```
(* occurs: vname -> term -> bool *)
fun occurs x (V y)     = x=y
  | occurs x (T(_,ts)) = exists (occurs x) ts;
```

The actual unification code is shown in Fig. 4.5. The functions *solve* and *elim* are defined by mutual recursion and implement the transformation rules of the previous section: $solve([(s_1, t_1), \ldots, (s_n, t_n)], [])$ returns $\vec{T}$, where T is a normal form of $\{s_1 =^? t_1, \ldots, s_n =^? t_n\}$ reached by treating sets like lists and always applying the transformation rules to the head of the list; *elim* implements Eliminate. The only significant departure from the transformation rules is that we have split the unification problem in two: the first argument of *solve* is the actual unification problem still to be solved, the second argument is the substitution already computed. Correctness can easily be established by showing that if $solve(S, \sigma)$ calls (directly or via *elim*) $solve(S', \sigma')$, then $S \cup \sigma \implies S' \cup \sigma'$. The unsolvable system $\perp$ produced by the rules Clash and Occurs-Check is implemented by the exception *UNIFY* that is raised if the system has no solution. The function *unify* is the specialization of *solve* to a single equation.

```
exception UNIFY;

(* solve: (term * term) list * subst -> subst *)
fun solve([], s) = s
  | solve((V x, t) :: S, s) =
        if V x = t then solve(S,s) else elim(x,t,S,s)
  | solve((t, V x) :: S, s) = elim(x,t,S,s)
  | solve((T(f,ts), T(g,us)) :: S, s) =
        if f = g then solve(zip(ts,us) @ S, s) else raise UNIFY

(* elim: vname * term * (term * term) list * subst -> subst *)
and elim(x,t,S,s) =
        if occurs x t then raise UNIFY
        else let val xt = lift [(x,t)]
             in solve(map (fn (t1,t2) => (xt t1, xt t2)) S,
                      (x,t) :: (map (fn (y,u) => (y, xt u)) s))
             end;

(* unify: term * term -> subst *)
fun unify(t1,t2) = solve([(t1,t2)], []);
```

Fig. 4.5. Unification in ML.

This implementation of unification directly inherits the exponential time and space complexity of the transformation rules. Try running Example 4.6.11. Nevertheless *unify* performs well on practical examples.

Although matching can be reduced to unification, this is neither elegant nor efficient. Therefore Fig. 4.6 gives a direct implementation of matching. It follows the same pattern as unification (separate the remaining problem from the substitution computed so far) but implements the transformation rules for matching that are the subject of Exercise 4.19 above: $matchs(S, [])$

returns the solution of the matching problem S or raises exception *UNIFY* if S has no solution; $match(pat, obj)$ solves a single inequation $pat \lesssim^? obj$.

```
(* matchs: (term * term) list * subst -> subst *)
fun matchs([], s) = s
  | matchs((V x, t) :: S, s) =
        if indom x s then if app s x = t then matchs(S,s) else raise UNIFY
        else matchs(S,(x,t)::s)
  | matchs((t, V x) :: S, s) = raise UNIFY
  | matchs((T(f,ts),T(g,us)) :: S, s) =
        if f = g then matchs(zip(ts,us) @ S, s) else raise UNIFY;

(* match: term * term -> subst *)
fun match(pat,obj) = matchs([(pat,obj)],[]);
```

Fig. 4.6. Matching in ML.

Matching must regard all variables on the right-hand sides as constants. Therefore:

1. $x \lesssim^? t$ has the solution $x \mapsto t$ even if $x \in Var(t)$. Therefore there is no *occurs* check.
2. A newly found solution $x \mapsto t$ does not influence solutions for other variables and is not influenced by them. Therefore it suffices to add $x \mapsto t$ to the substitution computed so far. If another pair $x \lesssim^? t'$ is found later on, we only need to check if $t = t'$.

Based on the above implementation of matching, Fig. 4.7 implements term rewriting. The TRS is represented as a list of term pairs.

```
exception NORM;

(* rewrite: (term * term) list -> term -> term *)
fun rewrite [] t = raise NORM
  | rewrite ((l,r)::R) t = lift(match(l,t)) r
                           handle UNIFY => rewrite R t;

(* norm: (term * term) list -> term -> term *)
fun norm R (V x) = V x
  | norm R (T(f,ts)) =
        let val u = T(f, map (norm R) ts)
        in (norm R (rewrite R u)) handle NORM => u end;
```

Fig. 4.7. Term rewriting in ML.

- *rewrite R t* tries to perform a single $\rightarrow_R$ step at the root of t by examining the rules (l,r) of R in order. Each l is matched with t and the resulting substitution is applied to r. If matching fails, the next rule is tried. If no more rules are left, exception *NORM* is raised.

- *norm R t* computes an *R*-normal form of *t* using a bottom-up strategy: after normalizing the subterms of *t*, the resulting term *u* is rewritten once at the root using *rewrite*, and *norm* is applied again. If *rewrite* raises *NORM*, *u* is already in normal form and is returned as the result.

  Note that even if a normal form exists, *norm* may not terminate: if $R = \{a \rightarrow a, f(x) \rightarrow b\}$ then $f(a)$ has the normal form b but *norm R* $(f(a))$ does not terminate.

Exercises

4.21 What is the time and space complexity of *match*?

4.22 Modify the ML implementation of unification to achieve linear space complexity by working with what could be called iterated substitutions. For example, the solution to $\{x =^? f(y), y =^? g(z), z =^? a\}$ should be represented by $[(x,f(y)), (y,g(z)), (z,a)]$. (*Hint:* iterated substitutions should be unfolded lazily, i.e. only so far that either a non-variable term or the end of the instantiation chain is found.)

4.23 Write a top-down version of *norm*.

4.8 Unification of term graphs

The major source of inefficiency of the unification algorithms considered so far is copying. This section presents algorithms on directed acyclic graphs (**dags**) represented as pointer structures. The central idea is never to create new terms but merely to update pointers. The algorithms build an additional pointer structure that links each variable to the term it is instantiated by (if any). The actual substitution can be read off by following those links. This leads to linear space requirements.

In order for this scheme to work, variables have to be shared: there must only be one node for each variable. For example, $f(x,y) =^? f(y,y)$ must be represented by the following dag:

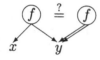

Other subterms may also be shared, but this is not required.

Example 4.8.1 Figure 4.8 shows the equation $t_3(x) =^? s_3(x)$ from Example 4.6.11. The solution is represented by dashed arrows that show how each variable is instantiated. One can clearly see that x_3 becomes the complete binary tree of height 3. Yet it only takes linear space because it is represented as a dag.

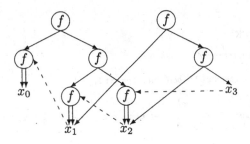

Fig. 4.8. Result of solving $t_3(x) =^? s_3(x)$.

All algorithms in this section are written in Pascal. The type for terms is shown in Fig. 4.9. Remember that if t is a type, then $\hat{\ }t$ is the type of pointers to t.

```
type termP = ^term;
     termsP = ^terms;

     term = record
                case isvar: boolean of
                   true:  (is: termP);
                   false: (fn: string; args: termsP)
            end;

     terms = record t: termP; next: termsP end;
```

Fig. 4.9. Pascal types for terms.

A term $f(t_1, \ldots, t_n)$ is a record with *isvar = false*, *fn* = "f" and *args* a pointer to the linked list of arguments $t_1, \ldots, t_n$. A variable is a record with *isvar = true*. Because variables are shared, they need not carry names (except for input/output, which we ignore). Initially, the *is* field of each variable is **nil**, i.e. the variable is not instantiated. The instantiation of variables is indicated graphically by dashed arrows.

Recall that in Pascal the object addressed by a pointer p is denoted by $p\hat{\ }$, and the field c of a record r is $r.c$. A value is returned from a **function** f by assigning it to f.

The basic operations on terms are instantiating a variable,

```
procedure union(v, t: termP);
begin v^.is := t end;
```

finding the end of an instantiation chain,

```
function find(t: termP): termP;
begin if t^.isvar
      then if t^.is = nil then find := t else find := find(t^.is)
      else find := t
end;
```

and the occurs check:

```
function occurs(v, t: termP): boolean;

   function occs(ts: termsP): boolean; forward;

   function occ(t: termP): boolean;
   begin if t^.isvar then occ := v=t else occ := occs(t^.args) end;

   function occs;
   begin if ts = nil then occs := false
         else if occ(find(ts^.t)) then occs := true
              else occs := occs(ts^.next)
   end;

begin occurs := occ(t) end;
```

The mutually recursive functions (hence **forward**, a Pascal peculiarity) *occ* and *occs* test if a variable x occurs in a term t and a linked list of terms *ts*.

To simplify nested case distinctions we introduce a global array *cases*

```
var cases: array [boolean, boolean] of (FF, FT, TF, TT);
```

which is initialized as follows:

```
cases[false, false] := FF; cases[false, true]  := FT;
cases[true, false]  := TF; cases[true, true]   := TT;
```

The actual unification procedure is shown in Fig. 4.10.

The mutually recursive functions *unify* and *unifys* unify two terms and two linked lists of terms. Unification is realized by a simultaneous depth-first traversal of both term graphs. Whenever a variable is found in one of the two graphs, it is instantiated with the corresponding node in the other graph by updating its *is* field via *union* (provided the variable neither is identical to the other node nor occurs in it). Because variables are shared there is no need to pass a substitution around (as in the ML implementation) to instantiate other occurrences of the same variable. A Boolean value is returned to indicate if unification was successful or not.

A graphical example of the effect of unification is shown in Fig. 4.11.

Although *unify* uses only linear space (because of the stack—it uses no additional heap space), it may still require exponential time. The terms $s_n(.)$ and $t_n(.)$ used in the following two examples were defined in Example 4.6.11.

```
function unify(t1, t2: termP): boolean;

    function unifys(ts1, ts2: termsP): boolean;
    begin case cases[ts1=nil, ts2=nil] of
            TT: unifys := true;
            TF, FT: unifys := false;
            FF: if unify(ts1^.t, ts2^.t) then unifys := unifys(ts1^.next, ts2^.next)
                else unifys := false
        end
    end;

  begin t1 := find(t1); t2 := find(t2);
    if t1 = t2 then unify := true
    else case cases[t1^.isvar, t2^.isvar] of
            TT: begin union(t1, t2); unify := true end;
            TF: if occurs(t1, t2) then unify := false
                else begin union(t1, t2); unify := true end;
            FT: if occurs(t2, t1) then unify := false
                else begin union(t2, t1); unify := true end;
            FF: if t1^.fn = t2^.fn then unify := unifys(t1^.args, t2^.args)
                else unify := false
        end
    end;
```

Fig. 4.10. Unification on dags.

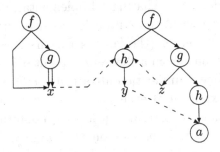

Fig. 4.11. $f(x, g(x, x)) =^? f(h(y), g(z, h(a)))$ after *unify*.

Example 4.8.2 While unifying $s_n(x)$ and $t_n(x)$, the final instantiation of x_n by $T_n := f(x_{n-1}, x_{n-1})$ is preceded by a test if x_n occurs in T_n. However, by this time T_n has already become a complete binary tree of height n, albeit in a space efficient dag representation (omitting *is* links):

$$\textcircled{f} \Rightarrow \textcircled{f} \cdots \textcircled{f} \Rightarrow x_0$$

Function *occurs* takes exponential time to search this dag because it visits shared subgraphs repeatedly.

This is just the result of a naïve implementation of graph searching. The next example reveals a more fundamental problem.

Example 4.8.3 Solving $f(s_n(x), f(s_n(y), x_n)) =^? f(t_n(x), f(t_n(y), y_n))$ proceeds in three stages:

1. Unification of $s_n(x)$ and $t_n(x)$ produces (most *is* pointers omitted)

$$x_n \dashrightarrow \boxed{f} = \boxed{f} \cdots \boxed{f} \Rightarrow x_0$$

2. Unification of $s_n(y)$ and $t_n(y)$ produces (most *is* pointers omitted)

$$y_n \dashrightarrow \boxed{f} = \boxed{f} \cdots \boxed{f} \Rightarrow y_0$$

3. Unifying x_n and y_n leads to an exponential number of calls to *unify* because the same subtrees are unified again and again.

The following subsection addresses both problems.

In spite of its exponential complexity the algorithm of Fig. 4.10 is probably the most popular unification algorithm. The reason is that in practice the exponential behaviour is very rare because most unification problems do not exhibit a high degree of sharing. Implementations of Prolog [54], a programming language whose execution is based on unification, go as far as removing *occurs* altogether (the famous "occurs check") to improve the complexity of unification. From a theoretical point of view this is somewhat pointless: there are linear unification algorithms *with* occurs check and the one above remains exponential even *without* occurs check (see the second example above). What is worse, it can lead to nontermination: check out what happens if the calls to *occurs* are omitted while unifying $f(x, y, x)$ and $f(g(x), g(y), y)$.

4.8.1 A quadratic algorithm

Both sources of exponential behaviour outlined above can be cured with the following type of terms:

```
term = record
         stamp: integer;
         is: termP;
         case isvar: boolean of
            true: ();
            false: (fn: string; args: termsP)
       end;
```

The *stamp* field avoids repeated occurs checks in the same subtree:

```
var time: integer;

function occurs(v, t: termP): boolean;

    function occ(t: termP): boolean;
    begin
      if t^.isvar then occ := v=t
      else if t^.stamp = time then occ := false
           else begin t^.stamp := time; occ := occs(t^.args) end
    end;

begin time := time+1; occurs := occ(t) end;
```

Function *occs* remains unchanged. Both *time* and all *stamp* fields must be initialized to 0.

Instead of a Boolean marker, say *visited*, which needs to be reset after each occurs check, *stamp* records the last time a node was visited and does not need resetting. However, this technique only works well if *integer* is sufficiently large (to avoid overflow) but still of fixed size (to leave the complexity unchanged).

The *is* field is now part of every node. It avoids repeated unification of the same subtrees because it allows sharing not just of variables but also of proper terms. After we have unified two proper terms, the *is* field of one of them is made to point to the other: after all, unification has made them the same. Thus step 3 in Example 4.8.3 can produce the following instantiation in linear time. The vertical arrows are created in the order from right to left.

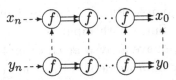

Since every node has an *is* field, which is initialized to **nil**, *find* simply becomes

```
function find(t: termP): termP;
begin while t^.is <> nil do t := t^.is; find := t end;
```

The actual unification procedure is shown in Fig. 4.12. Procedures *union* and *unifys* are unchanged. The only change in *unify* is the insertion of *union(t1, t2)* in front of the call to *unifys*. At first glance this may look a bit premature: after all, *t1* and *t2* have not been unified yet. However, if the term graph is cycle-free, it cannot do any harm to connect *t1* and *t2* already because it cannot influence the unification of their arguments. If the graph contains cycles, it turns out that it is in fact essential to call *union(t1, t2)* before unification of the arguments to avoid infinite recursion.

```
function unify(t1,t2:termP): boolean;

begin t1 := find(t1); t2 := find(t2);
    if t1 = t2 then unify := true
    else case cases[t1^.isvar,t2^.isvar] of
            TT: begin union(t1,t2); unify := true end;
            TF: if occurs(t1,t2) then unify := false
                else begin union(t1,t2); unify := true end;
            FT: if occurs(t2,t1) then unify := false
                else begin union(t2,t1); unify := true end;
            FF: if t1^.fn = t2^.fn
                then begin union(t1,t2); unify := unifys(t1^.args,t2^.args) end
                else unify := false
        end
end;
```

Fig. 4.12. Quadratic unification.

Let m and n be the numbers of edges and nodes in the input dag. The key observation is that $union(t1,t2)$ makes $t1$ unreachable via *find*. This means that each call to *unify*

- either terminates without recursive call,
- or makes one node ($t1$) and k edges (those to the children of $t1$) unreachable and creates k recursive calls to *unify* (via *unifys*).

Therefore the number of recursive calls to *unify* is bounded by m.

Each call of *unify* leads to two calls of *find* and at most one call each of *occurs* and *union*. The complexity of *union*, *find* and *occurs* is $O(1)$, $O(n)$ and $O(m)$, respectively. Since both input terms are connected graphs we have $n \leq m + 2$. Thus we have arrived at an $O(m^2)$ algorithm.

Despite this impressive improvement of the worst case complexity, in situations with a low degree of sharing, internal *is* links do more harm than good. Figure 4.13 shows the result of applying the quadratic algorithm to the problem in Fig. 4.11. None of the internal links is ever used but they have to be created.

4.8.2 An almost linear algorithm

The remaining obstacles are the linearity of *occurs* and *find*. The first of these is dealt with very simply: the occurs check is delayed until the very end. Then it simply consists of a test whether the final dag is cyclic. This test can be done in linear time (see Exercise 4.26).

Improving *find* requires the fast implementation of *Union* and *Find* described in Section 4.4. A sequence of m *Union* and *Find* operations on n

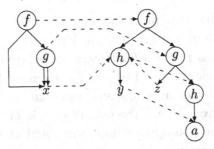

Fig. 4.13. $f(x, g(x, x)) =^? f(h(y), g(z, h(a)))$ after *unify*.

nodes can be executed in time $O(m \, G(n))$ [59], where $G(n)$ is an extremely slowly growing function with the property

$$G(2^{2^{\cdot^{\cdot^{\cdot^2}}}} \Big\} n) = n + 1.$$

Thus in particular $G(2^{65536}) = 5$, i.e. $G(n) \leq 5$ for all practical purposes.

The implementation of *Union* and *Find* is routine. Note that although *Find* replaces *find*, we still need the original version of *union* when unifying a variable and a proper term because the term must not point to the variable—otherwise the information about its subterms would be lost.

```
function unify(t1,t2:termP): boolean;

begin t1 := Find(t1); t2 := Find(t2);
  if t1 = t2 then unify := true
  else case cases[t1^.isvar,t2^.isvar] of
           TT: begin Union(t1,t2); unify := true end;
           TF: begin union(t1,t2); unify := true end;
           FT: begin union(t2,t1); unify := true end;
           FF: if t1^.fn = t2^.fn
                   then begin Union(t1,t2); unify := unifys(t1^.args,t2^.args) end
                   else unify := false
       end
end;

function Unify(t1,t2:termP): boolean;
begin if unify(t1,t2) then Unify := acyclic(t1) else Unify := false end;
```

Fig. 4.14. Almost linear unification.

The new version of *unify* is shown in Fig. 4.14. It is obtained directly from the quadratic version by dropping the occurs check and adjusting the *union* and *find* calls. Note that because of the missing occurs check, instantiation of variables may introduce cycles into the graph, which could lead to nontermination later on. Thus the call of *Union before* the call of *unifys* is now essential because it reduces the number of nodes reachable via *Find* and thus guarantees termination. See also Exercise 4.27.

The main function is now *Unify*. It calls *unify* and checks the result for cycles. For the implementation of *acyclic* see Exercise 4.26.

As in the quadratic version, *unify*, and hence *union*, *Union* and *Find*, are only called $O(m)$ times. Hence the overall cost is $O(m\,G(n))$, i.e. almost linear. The use of the non-optimal *union* can add at most $O(v)$, where v is the number of distinct variables in the terms, to the overall complexity, which is of no consequence.

4.8.3 The complexity of sharing

So far we have ignored the costs of creating term graphs where all occurrences of the same variable are shared (and similarly for constants in the congruence closure algorithm). Assuming we start with a proper tree, where variables carry names, how expensive is this sharing transformation?

The obvious algorithm traverses the tree, building up a table associating variable names with pointers. Upon encountering a pointer p to a variable v, there are two possibilities. If v is not yet in the table, add the pair (v, p) to the table. If v is already associated with some pointer q, replace the reference to p by q. This algorithm has time complexity $O(m\,t(n))$, where $t(n)$ is the time it takes to insert into or search a table with n entries. Using clever data structures, e.g. red-black trees [59], $t(n)$ is $O(\log n)$. Thus the overall running time is $O(m \log n)$.

If we are only allowed to compare variable names, this is the best we can do. It is known [172, p. 78] that detecting duplicates in a list is bounded from below by $\Omega(n \log n)$, and there is a linear-time reduction of the latter problem to our sharing problem: traverse the shared list, marking every element. Then the original list contains duplicates iff at some point you find an element already marked.

There are subtle variations that can improve this result:

1. If we know that the variable names are of a fixed length, i.e. from a finite set, $t(n)$ can be made constant, for example by allocating a large enough array indexed by the names.
2. If we are prepared to use hashing, $t(n)$ is constant on average, although the worst case can be a lot worse.
3. If we have access to the string or bit representation of variable names, we can implement the table as a so-called trie [226], where the lookup time is independent of the number of entries but is linear in the length

of the key. If we now include the size of the variable names in the size of the graph, rather than just counting the number of nodes, we can share variables in linear time.

Exercises

4.24   Modify the exponential version of *unify* to obtain a linear-time matching algorithm that allows variables in both terms.

4.25   Write an imperative analogue of the normalization function *norm* in Section 4.7 using the matching algorithm of the previous exercise.

4.26   Implement almost linear unification. (*Hint* for a linear-time version of *acyclic*: use depth-first search and mark each node as either *untouched* ("white"), or *discovered* ("gray") or *finished* ("black") [59].)

4.27   The almost linear version of *unify* is more powerful than might appear at first sight: it implements unification of **cyclic terms**, i.e. term graphs that may contain cycles. Unify the following two cyclic terms:

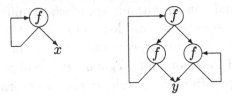

What happens in the above example if, instead of *before unifys*, *Union* is called *afterwards*?

4.9 Bibliographic notes

Decidability and complexity of the word problem in particular algebraic structures are common themes in algebra and logic. Ackermann [1] was the first to show the decidability of $\approx_G$, where G is a finite set of ground identities. (In fact, he considered more general logical problems.) Kozen [146, 147] represented terms by graphs and showed that deciding $\approx_G$ is P-complete. Downey, Sethi and Tarjan [81] present a congruence closure algorithm that runs in worst-case time $O(m(\log m)^2)$ (using trees) and average-case time $O(m \log m)$ (using hash tables). The quadratic congruence closure algorithm in Section 4.4 is due to Nelson and Oppen [184] who report that in their application (theorem proving for program verification) their algorithm performs no worse than the one by Downey, Sethi and Tarjan. However, Nelson and Oppen's proof of the completeness part of Theorem 4.4.3 fails to take into account the inductive nature of congruence closure. An alternative approach to congruence closure is due to Shostak [229, 230, 63]. Basin and Ganzinger [23] generalize the finiteness arguments underlying congruence closure to a whole class of decision problems.

Syntactic unification seems to have appeared first in the work of Herbrand [107] (see [106, p. 540] or [108, p. 148]). The first algorithm accompanied by a proof of correctness and termination is due to Robinson [216]. His exponential algorithm was later independently refined into a quasi-linear one by a number of people [24, 117, 165]. A linear unification algorithm was discovered by Paterson and Wegman [198]. The quadratic algorithm in this book is based on the exposition by Corbin and Bidoit [58].

Dwork, Kanellakis and Mitchell [84] have shown that unification is P-complete. Thus the existence of a fast parallel unification algorithm would contradict the popular belief that P is not contained in NC, the class of problems solvable in polylogarithmic time using polynomially many processors. This is in contrast to matching, which is in NC [84, 85], which provides another argument for implementing matching separately from unification.

An algebraic and non-algorithmic approach to unification is developed by Eder [86] and Lassez, Maher and Marriott [158]. Huet [119] uses a lattice-theoretic duality argument to prove the existence of most general unifiers.

Huet [117] and Paterson and Wegman [198] realized that unification can be seen as a computation on equivalence classes of terms. In fact, unification is dual to congruence closure: in one case equalities are propagated down, in the other case up the tree. This relationship is studied in detail by Kanellakis and Revesz [133].

Almost linear unification algorithms for cyclic terms are given by Huet [117] (essentially our almost linear *unify*) and Martelli and Rossi [166]. Courcelle provides an algebraic treatment of cyclic terms [60].

An account of a computer-checked correctness proof of a unification algorithm is given by Paulson [199].

5

Termination

Termination is an important property of term rewriting systems. For a finite terminating rewrite system, a normal form of a given term can be found by a simple depth-first search. If the system is also confluent, the normal forms are unique, which makes the word problem for the corresponding equational theory decidable. Unfortunately, as shown in the first section of this chapter, termination is an undecidable property of term rewriting systems. This is true even if one allows for only unary function symbols in the rules, or for only one rewrite rule (but then for function symbols of arity greater than 1). In the restricted case of ground rewrite systems, i.e. rewrite systems whose rules must not contain variables, termination becomes decidable, though. In the second section of this chapter, we introduce the notion of a reduction order. These orders are an important tool for proving termination of rewrite systems. The main problem for a given rewrite system is to find an appropriate reduction order that shows its termination. Thus, it is desirable to have a wide range of different possible reduction orders available. In the third and fourth sections of the chapter, we introduce two different ways of defining reduction orders.

5.1 The decision problem

First, we show undecidability of the termination problem for term rewriting systems, and then we consider the decidable subcase of right-ground term rewriting systems (which can be treated by a slight generalization of the well-known proof for ground systems).

5.1.1 Undecidability in the general case

It should be obvious that the termination problem for term rewriting systems is closely connected with the termination problem for programs. This connection is mirrored by the fact that undecidability of termination of rewrite systems can be shown by a reduction of the uniform halting problem for Turing machines (i.e. the problem of whether a given Turing machine halts on all configurations). To be more precise, we first show that any Turing machine can be translated into a finite term rewriting system such that computations of the Turing machine correspond to reduction sequences of the rewrite system. This proves that term rewriting systems provide a computationally complete formalism, but it does not directly imply undecidability of the termination problem for term rewriting systems. The remaining obstacle, which is overcome in the second part of the proof, is that not all terms represent legal Turing machine configurations. Thus, it must be shown that uniform termination of the Turing machine also implies termination of the rewrite system on such "illegal" terms. To make this possible, the reduction is somewhat more complex than might be expected.

Before we start describing the reduction, let us briefly recall the important definitions for Turing machines. Without loss of generality, we use a model with one tape, which is infinite in both directions, and we assume that the input alphabet coincides with the alphabet of tape symbols. In addition, we do not consider distinguished start- and halt-states: the machine terminates if no transition is possible.

Definition 5.1.1 A (nondeterministic) **Turing machine** $\mathcal{M}$ is described by

- a finite **alphabet** $\Gamma := \{s_0, \ldots, s_n\}$ of symbols, where s_0 is considered as the **blank** symbol,
- a finite set $Q = \{q_0, \ldots, q_p\}$ of **states**, and
- a **transition relation** $\Delta \subseteq Q \times \Gamma \times Q \times \Gamma \times \{l, r\}$.

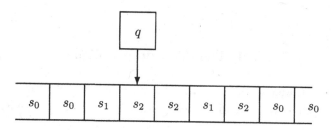

Fig. 5.1. A Turing machine configuration.

The machine works on a tape whose tape squares each contain a symbol of Γ. The tape is infinite in both directions, but it is assumed that there are only finitely many symbols different from the blank symbol s_0 on the tape. In each stage of the computation, the machine is in a state $q \in Q$ and its read-write head scans a particular square of the tape (see Fig. 5.1). If the machine is currently in the state q and a square containing s is scanned, and if a transition (q, s, q', s', d) is contained in Δ, then the machine can make the following computation step: the read-write head replaces s by s', it moves one square to the left (right) if $d = l$ ($d = r$), and the state is changed from q to q'. A computation stage of the machine, called a **configuration** in the following, is thus described by the current state, the current position of the read-write head, and the current content of the tape. We write $K \vdash_{\mathcal{M}} K'$ if configuration K' can be reached from configuration K by one computation step of the Turing machine $\mathcal{M}$.

It is well-known that the following problem, called the **halting problem** for Turing machines, is in general undecidable:

Instance: A Turing machine $\mathcal{M}$ and a configuration K of the machine.
Question: Are all computations starting with K terminating, i.e. is there no infinite computation $K \vdash_{\mathcal{M}} K_1 \vdash_{\mathcal{M}} K_2 \cdots$?

Thus, for the halting problem, both the machine $\mathcal{M}$ and the start configuration K are given as input for the would-be decision procedure, which should answer "yes" if the machine halts given this start configuration, and "no" otherwise. In contrast, for the so-called **uniform halting problem**, only the machine is given as input:

Instance: A Turing machine $\mathcal{M}$.
Question: Are all computations of $\mathcal{M}$ terminating, i.e. is there no configuration K such that K is the starting configuration of an infinite computation $K \vdash_{\mathcal{M}} K_1 \vdash_{\mathcal{M}} K_2 \cdots$?

The uniform halting problem is also known to be undecidable. In fact, it is not even recursively enumerable [109].

In order to reduce the (uniform) halting problem for Turing machines to the termination problem for term rewriting systems, we must simulate computation steps of a given Turing machine $\mathcal{M}$ by rewrite steps of a corresponding term rewriting systems $R_{\mathcal{M}}$. For this purpose, configurations are encoded as terms over an appropriate signature $\Sigma_{\mathcal{M}}$.

Definition 5.1.2 For a Turing machine $\mathcal{M}$, as introduced above, we define

$$\Sigma_{\mathcal{M}} := \{\overrightarrow{s_0}, \ldots, \overrightarrow{s_n}, \overleftarrow{s_0}, \ldots, \overleftarrow{s_n}\} \cup \{q_0, \ldots, q_p\} \cup \{\overrightarrow{l}, \overleftarrow{r}\},$$

where each function symbol in this signature is assumed to be of arity 1.

Let x_0 be a fixed variable. A **configuration term** over $\Sigma_{\mathcal{M}}$ is any term of the form

$$\overrightarrow{l}\,(\overrightarrow{s_{i_k}}(\cdots \overrightarrow{s_{i_1}}(q(\overleftarrow{s_{j_1}}(\cdots \overleftarrow{s_{j_h}}(\overleftarrow{r}(x_0))\cdots)))\cdots)),$$

where $k, h \geq 0$, $\{i_1, \ldots, i_k, j_1, \ldots, j_h\} \subseteq \{0, \ldots, n\}$, and $q \in Q$.

Every configuration term $t = \overrightarrow{l}\,(\overrightarrow{s_{i_k}}(\cdots \overrightarrow{s_{i_1}}(q(\overleftarrow{s_{j_1}}(\cdots \overleftarrow{s_{j_h}}(\overleftarrow{r}(x_0))\cdots)))\cdots))$ describes a unique configuration K_t:

1. the state of the machine in K_t is q,
2. the read-write head scans a square containing s_{j_1}, if $h \geq 1$, and a square containing the blank symbol s_0 if $h = 0$,
3. the squares to the right of the head contain (read from left to right) $s_{j_2}, \ldots, s_{j_h}$ and then infinitely many blanks,
4. the squares to the left of the head contain (read from right to left) $s_{i_1}, \ldots, s_{i_k}$ and then infinitely many blanks.

Conversely, since in every configuration only finitely many tape squares contain symbols different from s_0, every configuration can be represented by infinitely many configuration terms, which differ only in the number of function symbols $\overrightarrow{s_0}$ following $\overrightarrow{l}$ and in the number of function symbols $\overleftarrow{s_0}$ preceding $\overleftarrow{r}$. For example, the following are some of the configuration terms corresponding to the configuration depicted in Fig. 5.1:

$$\overrightarrow{l}\,(\overrightarrow{s_1}(q(\overleftarrow{s_2}(\overleftarrow{s_2}(\overleftarrow{s_1}(\overleftarrow{s_2}(\overleftarrow{r}(x_0))))))))), \quad \overrightarrow{l}\,(\overrightarrow{s_0}(\overrightarrow{s_1}(q(\overleftarrow{s_2}(\overleftarrow{s_2}(\overleftarrow{s_1}(\overleftarrow{s_2}(\overleftarrow{s_0}(\overleftarrow{r}(x_0)))))))))),$$

$$\overrightarrow{l}\,(\overrightarrow{s_0}(\overrightarrow{s_1}(q(\overleftarrow{s_2}(\overleftarrow{s_2}(\overleftarrow{s_1}(\overleftarrow{s_2}(\overleftarrow{r}(x_0)))))))))), \quad \overrightarrow{l}\,(\overrightarrow{s_1}(q(\overleftarrow{s_2}(\overleftarrow{s_2}(\overleftarrow{s_1}(\overleftarrow{s_2}(\overleftarrow{s_0}(\overleftarrow{r}(x_0)))))))))).$$

The symbol $\overrightarrow{l}$ marks the left margin of the tape segment represented in the configuration term, and $\overleftarrow{r}$ marks the right margin of this segment. The intended meaning is that to the left of $\overrightarrow{l}$ and to the right of $\overleftarrow{r}$ there are infinitely many tape squares containing s_0. This explains the special treatment of $\overrightarrow{l}$ and $\overleftarrow{r}$ in the next definition.

The effect that a transition of Δ has on a configuration K_t can easily be expressed by rewrite rules that apply to the corresponding configuration term t.

Definition 5.1.3 The rewrite system $R_{\mathcal{M}}$ consists of the following rewrite rules:

- For each transition $(q, s_i, q', s_j, r) \in \Delta$, $R_{\mathcal{M}}$ contains the rule

$$q(\overleftarrow{s_i}(x)) \to \overrightarrow{s_j}(q'(x)).$$

If $i = 0$, then $R_\mathcal{M}$ contains the additional rule

$$q(\overleftarrow{r}(x)) \to \overrightarrow{s_j}(q'(\overleftarrow{r}(x))).$$

- For each transition $(q, s_i, q', s_j, l) \in \Delta$, $R_\mathcal{M}$ contains the rule

$$\overrightarrow{l}(q(\overleftarrow{s_i}(x))) \to \overrightarrow{l}(q'(\overleftarrow{s_0}(\overleftarrow{s_j}(x)))),$$

and for each $s_k \in \Gamma$ the rule

$$\overrightarrow{s_k}(q(\overleftarrow{s_i}(x))) \to q'(\overleftarrow{s_k}(\overleftarrow{s_j}(x))).$$

If $i = 0$, then $R_\mathcal{M}$ contains the additional rule

$$\overrightarrow{l}(q(\overleftarrow{r}(x))) \to \overrightarrow{l}(q'(\overleftarrow{s_0}(\overleftarrow{s_j}(\overleftarrow{r}(x))))),$$

and for each $s_k \in \Gamma$ the rule

$$\overrightarrow{s_k}(q(\overleftarrow{r}(x))) \to q'(\overleftarrow{s_k}(\overleftarrow{s_j}(\overleftarrow{r}(x)))).$$

The additional rule for the first type of transitions (right move) is necessary because not all the blanks on the tape are contained in the corresponding configuration term. If q immediately precedes $\overleftarrow{r}$, then this means that on the tape the scanned symbol is a blank. Analogously, the additional rules for the left moves can be explained. Obviously, since Δ and Γ are finite, the rewrite system $R_\mathcal{M}$ is finite as well. The next lemma is an immediate consequence of the definition of $R_\mathcal{M}$.

Lemma 5.1.4 *Let $\mathcal{M}$ be a Turing machine and let $R_\mathcal{M}$ be the corresponding rewrite system.*

1. *For any pair t, t' of configuration terms, $t \to_{R_\mathcal{M}} t'$ implies $K_t \vdash_\mathcal{M} K_{t'}$.*
2. *For any pair of configurations K, K' and any configuration term t with $K = K_t$, $K \vdash_\mathcal{M} K'$ implies that there exists a configuration term t' such that $K' = K_{t'}$ and $t \to_{R_\mathcal{M}} t'$.*

Note that we cannot simply state the second part of the lemma as the converse of the first part. Indeed, the configurations K, K' are each described by infinitely many configuration terms, but there are reductions with $R_\mathcal{M}$ only between corresponding pairs of these terms, i.e. pairs where corresponding numbers of blanks on the borders of the non-blank part of the tape are included. The lemma is, however, sufficiently strong to imply that any infinite computation $K_0 \vdash_\mathcal{M} K_1 \vdash_\mathcal{M} K_2 \vdash_\mathcal{M} \cdots$ of $\mathcal{M}$ yields an infinite reduction $t_0 \to_{R_\mathcal{M}} t_1 \to_{R_\mathcal{M}} t_2 \to_{R_\mathcal{M}} \cdots$, and vice versa. Thus, undecidability of the halting problem for Turing machines yields a first undecidability result for termination of term rewriting systems:

Proposition 5.1.5 *The following problem is in general undecidable:*

Instance: *A finite term rewriting system R and a term t.*

Question: *Are all R-reductions starting with t terminating, i.e. is there no infinite reduction $t \to_R t_1 \to_R t_2 \to_R \cdots$?*

This proposition does not imply undecidability of the termination problem since it is only concerned with reductions starting with a particular term t, whereas termination requires that all reductions starting from *all* possible terms are terminating. Neither does the undecidability of the *uniform halting problem* for Turing machines directly yield undecidability of the termination problem: the remaining obstacle is that not all terms over Σ_M are configuration terms. Thus, it is conceivable that all reductions starting with configuration terms terminate (and thus, the Turing machine terminates for all start configurations), but there is a nonterminating reduction starting with a term that is not a configuration term. The next lemma shows, however, that this case cannot occur.

Lemma 5.1.6 *Let t be an arbitrary Σ_M-term. If there is an infinite reduction $t \to_{R_M} t_1 \to_{R_M} t_2 \to_{R_M} \cdots$, then there exist a configuration term t' and an infinite R_M-reduction starting with t'.*

Proof Since the signature Σ_M contains only function symbols of arity 1, we can write a Σ_M-term $t = f_1(f_2(\cdots f_k(x)\cdots))$ simply as $t = w(x)$, where $w := f_1 f_2 \ldots f_k$ is a *word* over the alphabet Σ_M. For $\overrightarrow{\Gamma} := \{\overrightarrow{s_0}, \ldots, \overrightarrow{s_n}\}$ and $\overleftarrow{\Gamma} := \{\overleftarrow{s_0}, \ldots, \overleftarrow{s_n}\}$, we have $\Sigma_M = \overrightarrow{\Gamma} \cup \overleftarrow{\Gamma} \cup Q \cup \{\overleftarrow{r}, \overrightarrow{l}\}$. Any word w over Σ_M can thus be written as

$$w = u_1 v_1 u_2 v_2 \ldots u_q v_q u_{q+1},$$

where the u_is are words over the alphabet $\overrightarrow{\Gamma} \cup \overleftarrow{\Gamma} \cup \{\overleftarrow{r}, \overrightarrow{l}\}$, and the v_is are words in $\overrightarrow{\Gamma}^* Q \overleftarrow{\Gamma}^*$, which are assumed to be maximal, i.e., for $1 \le i \le q$, u_i does not end with a symbol in $\overrightarrow{\Gamma}$, and for $2 \le i \le q+1$, u_i does not begin with a symbol in $\overleftarrow{\Gamma}$. Obviously, one obtains the words v_i of this decomposition by considering all states (i.e. elements of Q) occurring in w, and then going to the left as long as symbols of $\overrightarrow{\Gamma}$ occur and going to the right as long as symbols of $\overleftarrow{\Gamma}$ occur.

Since all the rewrite rules of R_M contain exactly one symbol from Q, any reduction that applies to $w(x)$ in principle takes place inside one of the v_is. More precisely, it is easy to see that the following fact holds:

> **Fact:** *Let $w(x)$ be a Σ_M-term, let $w = u_1 v_1 u_2 v_2 \ldots u_q v_q u_{q+1}$ be the decomposition of w described above, and assume that $w(x) \to_{R_M} w'(x)$.*

Then there exist an index $j, 1 \leq j \leq q$, and a word $v'_j \in \overrightarrow{\Gamma}^* Q \overleftarrow{\Gamma}^*$ such that

- *the corresponding decomposition of w' is*

$$w' = u_1 v_1 u_2 v_2 \ldots u_j v'_j u_{j+1} \ldots u_q v_q u_{q+1},$$

- *and $\overrightarrow{l} v_j \overleftarrow{r}(x_0) \rightarrow_{R_M} \overrightarrow{l} v'_j \overleftarrow{r}(x_0)$.*

Since q is finite, this implies that an infinite reduction starting with $w(x)$ yields an infinite reduction starting with $\overrightarrow{l} v_j \overleftarrow{r}(x_0)$ for some $j, 1 \leq j \leq q$. This proves the lemma since $\overrightarrow{l} v_j \overleftarrow{r}(x_0)$ is a configuration term. $\square$

Note that this lemma only holds because we used different symbols for describing the content of the tape to the left of the read-write head (namely symbols $\overrightarrow{s_i}$) and to the right of the read-write head (namely symbols $\overleftarrow{s_i}$). For Lemma 5.1.4 to hold, it would have been sufficient to use identical symbols.

As an immediate consequence of Lemma 5.1.4, Lemma 5.1.6, and undecidability of the uniform halting problem for Turing machines, we obtain undecidability of the termination problem for term rewriting systems:

Theorem 5.1.7 *The following problem is in general undecidable:*

Instance: *A finite term rewriting system R.*

Question: *Is R terminating, i.e. is there no term t starting an infinite reduction $t \rightarrow_R t_1 \rightarrow_R t_2 \rightarrow_R \cdots$?*

The statement of the theorem could be strengthened as follows: since the uniform halting problem is not even recursively enumerable, the same holds for the termination problem for term rewriting systems.

5.1.2 A decidable subcase

A term rewriting system R is called **right-ground** iff the right-hand sides of rules in R are ground terms, i.e. for all $l \rightarrow r \in R$ we have $Var(r) = \emptyset$. The following lemma can be used to derive an effective test for deciding whether a finite right-ground term rewriting system is terminating or not.

Lemma 5.1.8 *Let R be a finite right-ground term rewriting system. Then the following statements are equivalent:*

1. *R does not terminate.*
2. *There exist a rule $l \rightarrow r \in R$ and a term t such that $r \xrightarrow{+}_R t$ and t contains r as a subterm.*

Proof Obviously, $(2 \Rightarrow 1)$ holds since (2) yields the infinite reduction $r \xrightarrow{+}_R$ $t = t[r]_p \xrightarrow{+}_R t[t]_p = t[t[r]_p]_p \xrightarrow{+}_R \cdots$, where p is a position such that $t|_p = r$.

We show $(1 \Rightarrow 2)$ by induction on the cardinality of R. If R is empty, then 1 is trivially false. Thus, assume that $|R| > 0$, and consider an infinite reduction $t_1 \rightarrow_R t_2 \rightarrow_R t_3 \rightarrow_R \cdots$.

(i) Without loss of generality, we may assume that at least one of these reductions occurs at position ϵ. Otherwise, there exists a (k-ary) function symbol f such that the terms t_i are of the form $t_i = f(t_{i_1}, \ldots, t_{i_k})$ and each reduction step occurs inside one of the subterms t_{i_j}. Since k is finite and the reduction sequence was assumed to be infinite, there exists an index j such that infinitely many reduction steps are applied to the subterm at position j, and thus, t_{1_j} is the first term of an infinite reduction. By iterating this argument, we finally obtain an infinite reduction sequence where at least one step is done at position ϵ.

(ii) This means that there exist an index i, a rule $l \rightarrow r \in R$, and a substitution σ such that $t_i = \sigma(l)$ and $t_{i+1} = \sigma(r) = r$. Consequently, there is an infinite reduction $r \rightarrow_R t_{i+2} \rightarrow_R t_{i+3} \rightarrow_R \cdots$ that starts with r. We distinguish two cases:

- Case a: the rule $l \rightarrow r$ is not used in this reduction. Thus, $R - \{l \rightarrow r\}$ does not terminate, and we can apply the induction hypothesis to this smaller system.
- Case b: the rule $l \rightarrow r$ is used in this reduction. This means that there exists $j \geq 2$ such that r occurs in t_{i+j}, which shows that (2) holds. $\quad\square$

The decision procedure for termination of finite right-ground term rewriting systems derived from this lemma works as follows: consider all right-hand sides $r_1, \ldots, r_n$ of $R = \{l_1 \rightarrow r_1, \ldots, l_n \rightarrow r_n\}$, and simultaneously generate all reduction sequences starting with these right-hand sides. This is done by generating first all reductions of length 1 starting with $r_1, \ldots, r_n$, then all reductions of length 2, etc. If R does not terminate, then this implies (by Lemma 5.1.8) that there are an index i, a term t containing r_i as a subterm, and a finite length $k \geq 1$ such that $r_i \xrightarrow{k}_R t$. Thus, we detect nontermination of R when generating the reductions of length k. If R terminates, then $\rightarrow_R$ is globally finite since it is finitely branching (see Lemma 2.2.4). Thus, the process of generating all reductions starting with $r_1, \ldots, r_n$ terminates, and we detect termination of R after finitely many steps. Thus we have

Theorem 5.1.9 *For finite right-ground term rewriting systems, termination is a decidable property.*

Exercises

5.1 Consider the following modification of the reduction described in Subsection 5.1.1: for a given Turing machine $\mathcal{M}$, let

$$\Sigma'_{\mathcal{M}} := \{s_0, \ldots, s_n\} \cup \{q_0, \ldots, q_p\} \cup \{\overrightarrow{l}, \overleftarrow{r}\},$$

and let $R'_{\mathcal{M}}$ be the rewrite system that is obtained from $R_{\mathcal{M}}$ by replacing both $\overleftarrow{s_i}$ and $\overrightarrow{s_i}$ by s_i. Give an example of a terminating Turing machine $\mathcal{M}$ for which $R'_{\mathcal{M}}$ is not terminating.

5.2 Show (by counterexample) that the following is not a feasible way of testing a given ground term rewriting system $R = \{l_1 \to r_1, \ldots, l_n \to r_n\}$ for termination: Generate all reduction sequences starting with r_1. If one of these sequences yields a term that has r_1 as subterm then conclude that R is not terminating. Otherwise, continue with r_2, etc.

5.3 Prove the analogue of Theorem 5.1.9 for left-ground systems, and explain why this is not an interesting generalization of the theorem for the ground case.

5.4 A term rewriting system R is called **right-reduced** if for all $(l \to r) \in R$, r is R-irreducible. Show that a right-ground term rewriting system that is right-reduced is terminating.

5.2 Reduction orders

In the previous section, we have seen that the termination problem is in general undecidable, i.e. there cannot be a general procedure that, given an arbitrary finite term rewriting system, answers with "yes" if the system terminates, and with "no" otherwise. Nevertheless, it is often necessary to prove for a particular system that it terminates, and it is possible to develop methods that facilitate this task. Ideally, these methods should not just be helpful to a human who tries to prove termination of a given rewrite system by hand. It should be possible to automate them in the sense that, whenever they can indeed be used to prove termination of the rewrite system at hand, they automatically detect this without any human intervention. Of course, undecidability of termination shows that such an automated method cannot succeed for all terminating systems. The methods that we shall introduce below will not all satisfy the requirement that they can be fully automated.

As indicated in Section 2.3, the basic idea when proving termination is to employ a well-founded (i.e. Noetherian, terminating) order. Assume that $R \subseteq T(\Sigma, X) \times T(\Sigma, X)$ is a finite term rewriting system, and that $>$ is a well-founded (strict) order on $T(\Sigma, X)$. Obviously, R is terminating if, for all terms s, t, $s \rightarrow_R t$ implies $s > t$. Instead of deciding $s > t$ for the (infinitely many) pairs s, t with $s \rightarrow_R t$, we should like to check just $l > r$ for the (finitely many) rules $l \rightarrow r \in R$. For this to imply $s > t$ for all s, t with $s \rightarrow_R t$, the order $>$ must satisfy some additional properties. This motivates the definition of reduction orders.

Definition 5.2.1 Let Σ be a signature and V be a (countably infinite) set of variables. A strict order $>$ on $T(\Sigma, V)$ is called a **rewrite order** iff it is

1. **compatible** with Σ-operations: for all $s_1, s_2 \in T(\Sigma, V)$, all $n \geq 0$, and all $f \in \Sigma^{(n)}$, $s_1 > s_2$ implies

$$f(t_1, \ldots, t_{i-1}, s_1, t_{i+1} \ldots, t_n) > f(t_1, \ldots, t_{i-1}, s_2, t_{i+1} \ldots, t_n)$$

   for all $i, 1 \leq i \leq n$, and all $t_1, \ldots, t_{i-1}, t_{i+1} \ldots, t_n \in T(\Sigma, V)$.
2. **closed under substitutions**: for all $s_1, s_2 \in T(\Sigma, V)$ and all substitutions $\sigma \in \mathcal{S}ub(T(\Sigma, V))$, $s_1 > s_2$ implies $\sigma(s_1) > \sigma(s_2)$.

A **reduction order** is a well-founded rewrite order.

We may also call a partial order $\geq$ on terms a reduction order, by which we mean that its strict part $>$ is a well-founded rewrite order. The name "rewrite order" is motivated by the fact that the relations $\xrightarrow{+}_R$ for term rewriting systems R satisfy these two conditions. Note that the first condition implies (and thus is equivalent to) the condition

1'. For all $s_1, s_2, t \in T(\Sigma, V)$ and all $p \in \mathcal{P}os(t)$, $s_1 > s_2$ implies $t[s_1]_p > t[s_2]_p$.

Example 5.2.2 (1) Recall that for a term t, we denote by $|t|$ the size of t. The strict order $>$ on $T(\Sigma, V)$ that is defined by

$$s > t \text{ iff } |s| > |t|$$

is well-founded and compatible with Σ-operations. In general, it is not a reduction order since it need not be closed under substitutions. For example,

$$|f(f(x, x), y)| = 5 > 3 = |f(y, y)|,$$

but for the substitution $\sigma := \{y \mapsto f(x, x)\}$ we have

$$|\sigma(f(f(x, x), y))| = |f(f(x, x), f(x, x))| = 7,$$
$$|\sigma(f(y, y))| = |f(f(x, x), f(x, x))| = 7.$$

(2) The reason why the order defined in (1) is not closed under substitutions is that a variable may occur more often in the smaller term than in the larger. If this is prohibited, we obtain a reduction order. For a term t

and a variable x, we denote by $|t|_x$ the number of occurrences of x in t. The strict order $>$ on $T(\Sigma, V)$ that is defined by

$$s > t \quad \text{iff} \quad |s| > |t| \text{ and, for all } x \in V, |s|_x \geq |t|_x$$

is a reduction order (Exercise 5.5).

Our interest in reduction orders stems from the following termination theorem:

Theorem 5.2.3 *A term rewriting system R terminates iff there exists a reduction order $>$ that satisfies $l > r$ for all $l \to r \in R$.*

Proof (1) Assume that R terminates. In this case, $\xrightarrow{+}_R$ itself is a reduction order, which obviously satisfies $l \xrightarrow{+}_R r$ for all $l \to r \in R$.

(2) Since $>$ is a rewrite order, $l > r$ implies $t[\sigma(l)]_p > t[\sigma(r)]_p$ for all terms t, substitutions σ and positions $p \in Pos(t)$. Thus, $l > r$ for all $l \to r \in R$ implies $s_1 > s_2$ for all terms s_1, s_2 with $s_1 \to_R s_2$. Since $>$ is well-founded, this shows that there cannot be an infinite reduction $s_1 \to_R s_2 \to_R s_3 \cdots$. $\qquad\square$

In some applications, one needs the property that any pair of distinct ground terms is comparable w.r.t. the reduction order employed. We call a reduction order $>$ on $T(\Sigma, V)$ **total on ground terms** iff its restriction to $T(\Sigma, \emptyset)$ is a (strict) linear order.

In the remaining two substantive sections of this chapter, we introduce two different methods for constructing reduction orders on terms. The second method can also be used to construct reduction orders that are total on ground terms.

Exercises

5.5   Show that the strict order $>$ on $T(\Sigma, V)$ that is defined by

$$s > t \quad \text{iff} \quad |s| > |t| \text{ and, for all } x \in V, |s|_x \geq |t|_x$$

is a reduction order.

5.6   Let $>$ be a reduction order on ground terms, i.e. a strict order on $T(\Sigma, \emptyset)$ that is well-founded and satisfies

$$s_1 > s_2 \quad \Rightarrow \quad t[s_1]_p > t[s_2]_p$$

for all $s_1, s_2, t \in T(\Sigma, \emptyset)$ and all $p \in Pos(t)$. Let V be a countably infinite set of variables. We say that a substitution σ is a ground substitution on a finite set $X \subseteq V$ of variables iff $\sigma(x) \in T(\Sigma, \emptyset)$ for all $x \in X$. Show that the relation $\succ \, \subseteq T(\Sigma, V) \times T(\Sigma, V)$ that is defined by

$$s_1 \succ s_2 \quad \text{iff} \quad \text{for all ground substitutions } \sigma \text{ on } Var(s_1) \cup Var(s_2)$$
$$\sigma(s_1) > \sigma(s_2)$$

is the largest reduction order on $T(\Sigma, V)$ that contains $>$.

5.3 The interpretation method

In order to define a reduction order on $T(\Sigma, V)$, this method does not look directly at the terms over Σ. Instead it considers their *interpretation* in a Σ-algebra that is equipped with a well-founded order. Thus, let $\mathcal{A}$ be a Σ-algebra and let $>$ be a well-founded (strict) order on its carrier set A. In principle, we should like to say that a term s is larger than a term t iff the interpretation of s in $\mathcal{A}$ is larger than the interpretation of t in $\mathcal{A}$. Since the interpretation of the variables occurring in these terms is not yet defined, talking about the interpretation of a term with variables only makes sense for a given valuation of the variables. Such a valuation is given by a homomorphism $\pi : \mathcal{T}(\Sigma, V) \to \mathcal{A}$.†

Definition 5.3.1 Let $\mathcal{A}$ be a nonempty Σ-algebra and $>$ be a well-founded (strict) order on its carrier set A. The binary relation $>_{\mathcal{A}}$ on $T(\Sigma, V)$ is defined by

$$s >_{\mathcal{A}} t \quad \text{iff} \quad \pi(s) > \pi(t) \text{ for all homomorphisms } \pi : \mathcal{T}(\Sigma, V) \to \mathcal{A}.$$

Stability under substitutions for $>_{\mathcal{A}}$ is a consequence of the fact that we consider all possible valuations of the variables in this definition. To satisfy compatibility with Σ-operations, we must require that all interpretations of function symbols are monotone in the following sense:

Definition 5.3.2 Let $>$ be a strict order on the set A. A function $F : A^n \to A$ is called **monotone** (w.r.t. $>$) iff

$$a > b \quad \Rightarrow \quad F(a_1, \ldots, a_{i-1}, a, a_{i+1}, \ldots, a_n) > F(a_1, \ldots, a_{i-1}, b, a_{i+1}, \ldots, a_n)$$

holds for all $i, 1 \le i \le n$, and all $a, b, a_1, \ldots, a_{i-1}, a_{i+1}, \ldots, a_n \in A$.

Theorem 5.3.3 *Let $\mathcal{A}$ and $>$ be as in Definition 5.3.1. If the interpretations $f^{\mathcal{A}}$ of all function symbols $f \in \Sigma$ are monotone w.r.t. $>$, then $>_{\mathcal{A}}$ is a reduction order on $T(\Sigma, V)$.*

---

† Recall that this homomorphism is uniquely determined by the images of the variables.

Proof Obviously, the fact that $>$ is a strict order on A implies that $>_A$ is a strict order on $T(\Sigma, V)$. Thus, it remains to be shown that the three conditions of the definition of reduction orders are satisfied.

(1) Assume that there is an infinite chain $s_1 >_A s_2 >_A s_3 >_A \cdots$ in $T(\Sigma, V)$. By definition of $>_A$, this implies $\pi(s_1) > \pi(s_2) > \pi(s_3) > \cdots$ for all homomorphisms $\pi : T(\Sigma, V) \to A$. Thus, if we take an arbitrary such homomorphism, we obtain the infinite chain $\pi(s_1) > \pi(s_2) > \pi(s_3) > \cdots$ in A, which is a contradiction. This shows that $>_A$ must be well-founded.

(2) To prove compatibility with Σ-operations, we must show

$$s_1 >_A s_2 \quad \Rightarrow \quad f(t_1, \ldots, s_1, \ldots, t_n) >_A f(t_1, \ldots, s_2, \ldots, t_n).$$

By definition, $s_1 >_A s_2$ means that $\pi(s_1) > \pi(s_2)$ for all homomorphisms $\pi : T(\Sigma, V) \to A$. Together with monotonicity of f^A, this implies

$$
\begin{aligned}
\pi(f(t_1, \ldots, s_1, \ldots, t_n)) &= f^A(\pi(t_1), \ldots, \pi(s_1), \ldots, \pi(t_n)) \\
&> f^A(\pi(t_1), \ldots, \pi(s_2), \ldots, \pi(t_n)) \\
&= \pi(f(t_1, \ldots, s_2, \ldots, t_n))
\end{aligned}
$$

for all homomorphisms π, i.e. $f(t_1, \ldots, s_1, \ldots, t_n) >_A f(t_1, \ldots, s_2, \ldots, t_n)$.

(3) Assume that $s_1 >_A s_2$, and let σ be a substitution. To obtain $\sigma(s_1) >_A \sigma(s_2)$, we must show that $\pi(\sigma(s_1)) > \pi(\sigma(s_2))$ for all homomorphisms $\pi : T(\Sigma, V) \to A$. This follows immediately from $s_1 >_A s_2$ and the definition of $>_A$ since the composition of π and σ is a homomorphism $\pi' := \pi\sigma : T(\Sigma, V) \to A$. $\square$

Polynomial orders

In the remainder of this section, we introduce a particular class of reduction orders of the form $>_A$, in which function symbols are interpreted as polynomials over the natural numbers.

Definition 5.3.4 Let Σ be a signature. A **polynomial interpretation** of Σ is a Σ-algebra A that satisfies the following properties:

- The carrier set of A is a set of positive integers, i.e. $A \subseteq \mathbb{N} - \{0\}$.
- Every n-ary function symbol $f \in \Sigma$ is associated with a polynomial $P_f(X_1, \ldots, X_n) \in \mathbb{N}[X_1, \ldots, X_n]$, i.e. a polynomial in n indeterminates $X_1, \ldots, X_n$ with coefficients in $\mathbb{N}$. The interpretation of f in A is the valuation function of P_f, i.e. $f^A(a_1, \ldots, a_n) := P_f(a_1, \ldots, a_n)$.

As well-founded order $>$ on A we take the usual order on natural numbers.

The fact that the carrier set A of a Σ-algebra $\mathcal{A}$ is closed under applying Σ-operations implies that the carrier set A of a polynomial interpretation is closed under evaluating the polynomials P_f, i.e. for all $f \in \Sigma$ and $a_1, \ldots, a_n \in A$ we have $P_f(a_1, \ldots, a_n) \in A$. Thus, one cannot simply define a polynomial interpretation by associating each function symbol $f \in \Sigma$ with an appropriate polynomial P_f, and by fixing an arbitrary set A of positive integers as carrier set: one must also make sure that the above closure property is satisfied.

Example 5.3.5 Assume that $\Sigma = \{\oplus, \odot\}$ consists of two binary function symbols, and let $A = \mathbb{N} - \{0, 1\}$. If we associate the polynomial $P_\oplus := 2X + Y + 1$ with $\oplus$ and the polynomial $P_\odot := XY$ with $\odot$, then the corresponding polynomial interpretation $\mathcal{A}$ satisfies $\oplus^{\mathcal{A}}(m, n) = 2m + n + 1$ and $\odot^{\mathcal{A}}(m, n) = mn$ for all $m, n \in \mathbb{N} - \{0, 1\}$. It is easy to see that the closure property is satisfied.

The mapping of function symbols to polynomials can be extended to terms in the obvious way. A term t containing n variables $x_1, \ldots, x_n$ yields a polynomial P_t in n indeterminates $X_1, \ldots, X_n$. For example, the polynomial interpretation from above associates the term $t = x \odot (x \oplus y)$ with the polynomial

$$
\begin{aligned}
P_t &= P_\odot(X, P_\oplus(X, Y)) \\
&= X(2X + Y + 1) \\
&= 2X^2 + XY + X.
\end{aligned}
$$

In general, the interpretations of function symbols in polynomial interpretations need not be monotone for the *strict* order $>$. For example, if we had associated the symbol $\odot$ with the polynomial $P_\odot := X^2$, then we would have had $2 > 1$, but $\odot^{\mathcal{A}}(1, 2) = 1 = \odot^{\mathcal{A}}(1, 1)$. The obvious reason for this problem is that the polynomial $P_\odot(X, Y) = X^2$ does not contain the second indeterminate Y, i.e. it depends only on the first indeterminate X.

Definition 5.3.6 We call a polynomial $P(X_1, \ldots, X_n) \in \mathbb{N}[X_1, \ldots, X_n]$ a **monotone polynomial** iff it depends on all its indeterminates, i.e., for all $i, 1 \leq i \leq n$, it contains a monomial (with non-zero coefficient) in which X_i occurs with an exponent at least 1. A **monotone polynomial interpretation** is a polynomial interpretation in which all function symbols are associated with monotone polynomials.

The polynomial interpretation defined in Example 5.3.5 is monotone.

Lemma 5.3.7 *The functions f^A of a monotone polynomial interpretation are monotone.*

Proof Let f be an n-ary function symbol. For $i \in \{1, \ldots, n\}$ we can write the polynomial $P_f \in \mathbb{N}[X_1, \ldots, X_n] = (\mathbb{N}[X_1, \ldots, X_{i-1}, X_{i+1}, \ldots, X_n])[X_i]$ as a polynomial in the indeterminate X_i with coefficients Q_j in $\mathbb{N}[X_1, \ldots, X_{i-1}, X_{i+1}, \ldots, X_n]$:

$$\begin{aligned} P_f = \ & Q_k(X_1, \ldots, X_{i-1}, X_{i+1}, \ldots, X_n)X_i^k + \cdots + \\ & Q_1(X_1, \ldots, X_{i-1}, X_{i+1}, \ldots, X_n)X_i + \\ & Q_0(X_1, \ldots, X_{i-1}, X_{i+1}, \ldots, X_n). \end{aligned}$$

Since P_f is monotone, it depends on X_i, and thus we can assume that $k > 0$ and that Q_k is not the zero polynomial. Hence, for all $a_1, \ldots, a_{i-1}, a_{i+1}, \ldots, a_n \in A \subseteq \mathbb{N} - \{0\}$, the partially evaluated polynomial $P_f(a_1, \ldots, a_{i-1}, X_i, a_{i+1}, \ldots, a_n)$ is a polynomial of degree $k > 0$ in the indeterminate X_i with coefficients in $\mathbb{N}$. Obviously, this implies

$$a > b \implies P_f(a_1, \ldots, a_{i-1}, a, a_{i+1}, \ldots, a_n) > P_f(a_1, \ldots, a_{i-1}, b, a_{i+1}, \ldots, a_n)$$

for all $a, b \in A \subseteq \mathbb{N} - \{0\}$. $\square$

Together with Theorem 5.3.3, this lemma implies that the relation $>_A$ induced by a monotone polynomial interpretation is a reduction order. We call such a reduction order a **polynomial order**.

Now, we turn to the question of how to determine, for terms l, r, whether $l >_A r$ holds for a given polynomial order $>_A$. For $A \subseteq \mathbb{N} - \{0\}$ and polynomials $P, Q \in \mathbb{N}[X_1, \ldots, X_n]$, we write $P >_A Q$ iff $P(a_1, \ldots, a_n) > Q(a_1, \ldots, a_n)$ for all $a_1, \ldots, a_n$ in A. The following lemma is an immediate consequence of this definition:

Lemma 5.3.8 $l >_A r$ *iff* $P_l >_A P_r$.

In practice, it is often rather convenient to be able to restrict the domain over which the polynomials must be evaluated by choosing an appropriate set A. This is illustrated by the following example.

Example 5.3.9 Consider the term rewriting system

$$R := \{x \odot (y \oplus z) \to (x \odot y) \oplus (x \odot z), (x \oplus y) \oplus z \to x \oplus (y \oplus z)\}.$$

In order to show that R terminates, we take the monotone polynomial interpretation defined in Example 5.3.5.

1. The polynomial P_{l_1} associated with $l_1 := x \odot (y \oplus z)$ is

$$X(2Y + Z + 1) = 2XY + XZ + X,$$

and the polynomial P_{r_1} associated with $r_1 := (x \odot y) \oplus (x \odot z)$ is

$$2XY + XZ + 1.$$

Since all elements of A are greater than 1, we have $P_{l_1} >_A P_{r_1}$, and thus $l_1 >_A r_1$. Note that, for $A' := \mathbb{N} - \{0\}$, we do not have $P_{l_1} >_{A'} P_{r_1}$ since, in this case, X can also be assigned the value 1.

2. The polynomials

$$P_{l_2} = 4X + 2Y + Z + 3$$

associated with $l_2 := (x \oplus y) \oplus z$ and

$$P_{r_2} = 2X + 2Y + Z + 2$$

associated with $r_2 := x \oplus (y \oplus z)$ obviously satisfy $P_{l_2} >_A P_{r_2}$, which implies $l_2 >_A r_2$.

Thus, we have shown termination of R using a polynomial order.

In the example, it was easy to check (by hand) that the chosen polynomial interpretation was such that $P_{l_i} >_A P_{r_i}$ holds for $i = 1, 2$. Unfortunately, it is in general undecidable whether two terms l, r satisfy $P_l >_A P_r$ for a given polynomial interpretation. This is an easy consequence (Exercise 5.8) of the undecidability of **Hilbert's 10th Problem** [69]:

Instance: A polynomial $P \in \mathbb{Z}[X_1, \ldots, X_n]$ in n indeterminates with integer coefficients.

Question: Is there an n-tuple of non-negative integers for which the polynomial P is 0?

Thus, for a given polynomial order, it is in general not possible to decide whether this order is suitable for showing termination of a given finite term rewriting system. Nevertheless, there are automated methods that can (sometimes) be used to show $P >_A Q$ for polynomials $P, Q \in \mathbb{N}[X_1, \ldots, X_n]$ [49]. Another way to obtain a decidable sufficient condition for $P >_A Q$ could be to evaluate the polynomials in the real numbers $\mathbb{R}$ rather than in $\mathbb{N}$. In fact, Tarski's decidability result for the first-order theory of real numbers [239] implies that it is decidable whether $P >_B Q$ holds for a given subset B of $\mathbb{R}$ that is definable in the first-order theory of real numbers (e.g. $B = \{r \in \mathbb{R} \mid r \geq 1\}$ is definable). If $A \subseteq B$, then $P >_B Q$ obviously implies $P >_A Q$.

Another disadvantage of polynomial order is that they cannot show termination of rewrite systems with "very long" reduction chains [115]:

Proposition 5.3.10 *Assume that termination of the finite term rewriting system R can be shown with a polynomial order. Then there exists a constant $c > 0$ in $\mathbb{R}$ such that for all terms t the length of every R-reduction sequence starting with t is bounded by $2^{2^{c|t|}}$.*

Proof Let $\mathcal{A}$ be a polynomial interpretation such that $l >_{\mathcal{A}} r$ holds for all $l \to r \in R$, let a be an arbitrary element of A, and let $\pi_a : \mathcal{T}(\Sigma, V) \to \mathcal{A}$ be the homomorphism that assigns a to all variables. For a reduction sequence $t = t_1 \to_R t_2 \to_R \cdots \to_R t_m$ we have $t = t_1 >_{\mathcal{A}} t_2 >_{\mathcal{A}} \cdots >_{\mathcal{A}} t_m$, and thus also $\pi_a(t) = \pi_a(t_1) > \pi_a(t_2) > \cdots > \pi_a(t_m)$, by definition of $>_{\mathcal{A}}$. This implies that $m \le \pi_a(t)$, which shows that it is sufficient to prove that there exists a constant c such that $\pi_a(t) \le 2^{2^{c|t|}}$ for all terms t.

We choose c such that $c \ge k + \log_2 d$, where k and d are positive integers such that $a \le d$ and

$$P_f(a_1, \ldots, a_m) \le d \cdot \prod_{i=1}^{m} a_i^k$$

for all $m \ge 0$, $f \in \Sigma^{(m)}$ and $a_1, \ldots, a_m \in A$. For a finite collection of polynomials P_f, such numbers k, d obviously exist. If the signature Σ is infinite, we may need to modify the polynomial interpretation first. In fact, only the finitely many polynomials corresponding to function symbols occurring in R must be considered. Assume that a given polynomial interpretation can be used to show termination of R. Then we can modify this interpretation by associating all function symbols g not occurring in R with "small" polynomials (e.g. of the form $X_1 \cdots X_m$ where m is the arity of g). This modified polynomial interpretation still shows termination of R, and there exist appropriate numbers k, d.

We show $\pi_a(t) \le 2^{2^{c|t|}}$ by induction on the size of t. If t is a variable, then $|t| = 1$ and $\pi_a(t) = a \le d \le 2^c < 2^{2^{c|t|}}$. If $t = f(t_1, \ldots, t_m)$, then we have

$$
\begin{aligned}
\pi_a(t) &= P_f(\pi_a(t_1), \ldots, \pi_a(t_m)) \le d \cdot \prod_{i=1}^{m} \pi_a(t_i)^k \\
&\le d \cdot \prod_{i=1}^{m} \left(2^{2^{c|t_i|}}\right)^k \quad \text{(by induction)} \\
&= 2^{\log_2 d} \cdot 2^{k \cdot \Sigma_{i=1}^{m} 2^{c|t_i|}} \le 2^{c \cdot \Sigma_{i=1}^{m} 2^{c|t_i|}} \le 2^{2^c \cdot \Pi_{i=1}^{m} 2^{c|t_i|}} \\
&= 2^{2^{c \cdot \left(1 + \Sigma_{i=1}^{m} |t_i|\right)}} = 2^{2^{c|t|}}. \qquad \square
\end{aligned}
$$

Thus, terminating term rewriting systems that have reduction chains whose length exceeds this doubly-exponential bound cannot be shown to be terminating with the help of a polynomial order. As a simple example, we consider a term rewriting system that computes Ackermann's function, which is well-known not to be primitive recursive:

Example 5.3.11 Let $\Sigma = \{a, s, 0\}$ where a is binary, s is unary, and 0 is a constant symbol. The term rewriting system R_{Ack} consisting of the rules

$$
\begin{aligned}
a(0, y) &\rightarrow s(y), \\
a(s(x), 0) &\rightarrow a(x, s(0)), \\
a(s(x), s(y)) &\rightarrow a(x, a(s(x), y))
\end{aligned}
$$

terminates (see Example 5.4.15 below), but the length of its reduction chains cannot be bounded by a primitive recursive function in the size of the starting term (Exercise 5.10).

Hofbauer and Lautemann [115] also show that their doubly-exponential bound is tight by presenting a term rewriting system that can be shown to be terminating with a polynomial order, and whose reduction chains have a length that may reach the doubly-exponential bound:

Example 5.3.12 Let $\Sigma = \{+, s, d, q, 0\}$ where $+$ is binary, s, d, q are unary, and 0 is a constant symbol. The term rewriting system R consists of the rules

$$
\begin{aligned}
x + 0 &\rightarrow x, & x + s(y) &\rightarrow s(x + y), \\
d(0) &\rightarrow 0, & d(s(x)) &\rightarrow s(s(d(x))), \\
q(0) &\rightarrow 0, & q(s(x)) &\rightarrow q(x) + s(d(x)).
\end{aligned}
$$

Let $A = \mathbb{N} - \{0, 1\}$, and $P_+ = X + 2Y$, $P_s = X + 1$, $P_d = 3X$, $P_q = X^3$, and $P_0 = 2$. It is easy to see that this polynomial interpretation shows termination of R (Exercise 5.11).

Intuitively, R defines the arithmetic functions successor (s), double (d), and square (q) on non-negative integers. Thus, it is easy to see that the term $t_n := q^{n+1}(s^2(0))$ can be reduced to $q(s^{2^{2^n}}(0))$, and the rule $q(s(x)) \rightarrow q(x) + s(d(x))$ alone can generate a sequence of 2^{2^n} reduction steps starting with this term. Consequently, the maximal length of a reduction sequence starting with t_n is at least $2^{2^n} = 2^{2^{|t_n|-4}} \geq 2^{2^{c|t_n|}}$ for $c \leq 1/5$ and $n \geq 1$.

Exercises

5.7 Show that Lemma 5.3.7 would not hold if the carrier A of the polynomial interpretation were allowed to contain 0.

5.8 Show that undecidability of Hilbert's 10th Problem implies that the following problem is undecidable:

Instance: Two polynomials $P, Q \in \mathbb{N}[X_1, \ldots, X_n]$ in n indeterminates with non-negative integer coefficients, and a (decidable) subset A of $\mathbb{N}$.

Question: Does $P >_A Q$ hold, i.e. is the value of P greater than the value of Q for all valuations with elements in A.

Show that this implies that there exists a polynomial interpretation $\mathcal{A}$ for which it is in general undecidable whether two terms l, r satisfy $l >_\mathcal{A} r$ or not.

5.9 Let R be a finite term rewriting system and f be a function symbol. For a term t, let $|t|_f$ denote the number of occurrences of f in t. Show that there exists a positive integer k such that $s \to_R t$ implies $|t|_f \le k(|s|_f + 1)$ for all terms s, t.

5.10 Use the previous exercise and the fact that Ackermann's function is growing faster than any primitive recursive function to show that the length of reduction sequences for the term rewriting system R_{Ack} of Example 5.3.11 cannot be bounded by a primitive recursive function.

5.11 Show that the term rewriting system R of Example 5.3.12 terminates using the polynomial interpretation introduced in the example.

5.12 Use the polynomial interpretation $\mathcal{A}$ with $A := \mathbb{N} - \{0, 1, 2\}$ and $P_f := X^2 + XY$ to show that the term rewriting system

$$\{f(f(x,y), z) \to f(x, f(y,z)), \; f(y, f(x,z)) \to f(x,x)\}$$

terminates.

5.4 Simplification orders

This second method of constructing reduction orders yields classes of orders (e.g. Knuth-Bendix orders and recursive path orders) that can be used in fully automated termination proofs, and that do not impose a doubly-exponential bound on the length of reduction chains. In the following, let Σ be a signature and V be a (countably infinite) set of variables.

Definition 5.4.1 A strict order $>$ on $T(\Sigma, V)$ is called a **simplification order** iff it is a rewrite order and satisfies the following **subterm property**:

For all terms $t \in T(\Sigma, V)$ and all positions $p \in \mathcal{P}os(t) - \{\epsilon\}$, we have $t > t|_p$.

Since $>$ is a rewrite order, the subterm property already follows (Exercise 5.13) from the following simpler property:

For all $n \geq 1$, all function symbols $f \in \Sigma^{(n)}$, all variables $x_1, \ldots, x_n \in V$, and all $i, 1 \leq i \leq n$, we have $f(x_1 \ldots, x_i, \ldots, x_n) > x_i$.

The definition of simplification orders replaces the requirement that $>$ is well-founded in the definition of reduction orders by the subterm property. In order to show that this is a stronger requirement, i.e. that all simplification orders are reduction orders, we introduce the notion of a "homeomorphic embedding" of terms and prove Kruskal's Theorem for this embedding relation.

Definition 5.4.2 Let X be a set of variables. The **homeomorphic embedding** $\unrhd_{emb}$ is a binary relation on $T(\Sigma, X)$ that is defined as follows: $s \unrhd_{emb} t$ iff one of the following conditions holds:

1. $s = x = t$ for a variable $x \in X$.
2. $s = f(s_1, \ldots, s_n)$ and $t = f(t_1, \ldots, t_n)$ for a function symbol $f \in \Sigma^{(n)}$, and $s_1 \unrhd_{emb} t_1, \ldots, s_n \unrhd_{emb} t_n$.
3. $s = f(s_1, \ldots, s_n)$ for a function symbol $f \in \Sigma^{(n)}$, and $s_j \unrhd_{emb} t$ for some $j, 1 \leq j \leq n$.

For example, we have

$$f(f(h(a), h(x)), f(h(x), a)) \unrhd_{emb} f(f(a, x), x).$$

If we look at the tree representation of terms, then $s \unrhd_{emb} t$ means that we can map the nodes of the tree corresponding to t into the nodes of the tree corresponding to s so that the tree order (vertical ordering of the nodes), the argument position, and the labelling of nodes are respected. The mapping that yields the embedding in the above example is depicted in Fig. 5.2. The

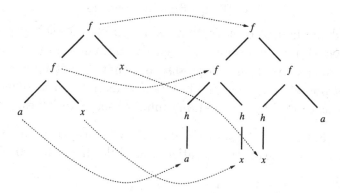

Fig. 5.2. The embedding $f(f(a, x), x) \unlhd_{emb} f(f(h(a), h(x)), f(h(x), a))$.

homeomorphic embedding $\unrhd_{emb}$ could also be defined (Exercise 5.14) as the reduction relation $\xrightarrow{*}_{R_{emb}}$ induced by the rewrite system

$$R_{emb} := \{f(x_1, \ldots, x_n) \to x_i \mid n \geq 1, f \in \Sigma^{(n)}, 1 \leq i \leq n\}.$$

Since R_{emb} is obviously terminating, this shows that $\xrightarrow{*}_{R_{emb}} = \unrhd_{emb}$ is a well-founded partial order. Kruskal's Theorem says that, for finite Σ and X, $\unrhd_{emb}$ satisfies an even stronger property: it is a well-partial-order.

Definition 5.4.3 A partial order $\succeq$ on a set A is a **well-partial-order (wpo)** iff for every infinite sequence $a_1, a_2, a_3, \ldots$ of elements of A there exist indices $i < j$ such that $a_i \preceq a_j$.

We call an infinite sequence $a_1, a_2, a_3, \ldots$ **good** (w.r.t. $\succeq$) iff there exist $i < j$ such that $a_i \preceq a_j$. Otherwise, the sequence is called **bad**. Obviously, an infinite chain $a_1 \succ a_2 \succ a_3 \succ \cdots$ cannot be good, which shows that every wpo is well-founded. The converse need not be true, as can be demonstrated by an infinite anti-chain, i.e. an infinite sequence of pairwise incomparable elements.

The proof of Kruskal's Theorem is facilitated by the following two lemmas.

Lemma 5.4.4 *Let $\succeq$ be a wpo on the set A. Then every infinite sequence $a_1, a_2, a_3, \ldots$ of elements of A has an infinite ascending subsequence, i.e. there exist infinitely many indices $i_1 < i_2 < i_3 < \cdots$ such that $a_{i_1} \preceq a_{i_2} \preceq a_{i_3} \preceq \cdots$.*

Proof Let $a_1, a_2, a_3, \ldots$ be an infinite sequence in A. We call an index $m \geq 1$ *terminal* iff there is no $n > m$ such that $a_m \preceq a_n$. Assume that there are infinitely many terminal indices $m_1 < m_2 < m_3 < \cdots$. Then the sequence $a_{m_1}, a_{m_2}, a_{m_3}, \ldots$ is bad, which contradicts the assumption that $\succeq$ is a wpo. Thus, let $p \geq 1$ be such that all indices $q \geq p$ are not terminal. We define $i_1 := p$. Now, assume that $i_1 < \cdots < i_k$ with $a_{i_1} \preceq \cdots \preceq a_{i_k}$ are already defined. Since $i_k \geq p$ is not terminal, there exists an index $i_{k+1} > i_k$ with $a_{i_k} \preceq a_{i_{k+1}}$. This defines the desired sequence by induction. $\square$

Lemma 5.4.5 *Let $\succeq_1, \ldots, \succeq_n$ be well-partial-orders on the sets $A_1, \ldots, A_n$. Then the relation $\succeq$ that is defined component-wise by*

$$(a_1, \ldots, a_n) \succeq (a_1', \ldots, a_n') \quad \text{iff} \quad a_1 \succeq_1 a_1' \wedge \ldots \wedge a_n \succeq_n a_n'$$

is a wpo on $A_1 \times \ldots \times A_n$.

Proof Obviously, $\succeq$ is a partial order. To show that it is a wpo, let $(a_1^{(1)}, \ldots, a_n^{(1)}), (a_1^{(2)}, \ldots, a_n^{(2)}), \ldots$ be an infinite sequence in $A_1 \times \ldots \times A_n$. By Lemma 5.4.4, there exist infinitely many indices $i_1 < i_2 < i_3 < \cdots$ such that $a_1^{(i_1)} \preceq_1 a_1^{(i_2)} \preceq_1 a_1^{(i_3)} \preceq_1 \cdots$. By induction (on n) we may assume that the component-wise order on $A_2 \times \ldots \times A_n$ is a wpo, and thus there exist indices $k < l$ such that $a_2^{(i_k)} \preceq_2 a_2^{(i_l)} \wedge \ldots \wedge a_n^{(i_k)} \preceq_n a_n^{(i_l)}$. This yields $(a_1^{(i_k)}, \ldots, a_n^{(i_k)}) \preceq (a_1^{(i_l)}, \ldots, a_n^{(i_l)})$. $\square$

Theorem 5.4.6 (Kruskal) *Let Σ be a finite signature and X be a finite set of variables. Then the homeomorphic embedding $\trianglerighteq_{emb}$ on $T(\Sigma, X)$ is a wpo.*

Proof Assume to the contrary that there exists a bad sequence (w.r.t. $\trianglerighteq_{emb}$) in $T(\Sigma, X)$. We construct a *minimal bad sequence* by induction, where the induction step works as follows:

> Assume that terms $t_1, \ldots, t_n$ ($n \geq 0$) are already defined, and that there exists a bad sequence starting with $t_1, \ldots, t_n$. Note that for $n = 0$ this just means that there exists a bad sequence, which we know by assumption. Let $t_{n+1} \in T(\Sigma, X)$ be a minimal term (w.r.t. size) among all terms that occur at position $n+1$ of a bad sequence in $T(\Sigma, X)$ that starts with $t_1, \ldots, t_n$. By our induction hypothesis, there exists at least one such bad sequence. Obviously, the definition of t_{n+1} implies that there exists a bad sequence starting with $t_1, \ldots, t_{n+1}$.

In the limit, this defines an infinite bad sequence $t_1, t_2, t_3, \ldots$.

(1) For $i \geq 1$ we define $S_i := \emptyset$, if t_i is a variable. Otherwise, $t_i = f_i(s_1^{(i)}, \ldots, s_{n_i}^{(i)})$ for a function symbol $f_i \in \Sigma^{(n_i)}$ and terms $s_1^{(i)}, \ldots, s_n^{(i)}$, and we define $S_i := \{s_1^{(i)}, \ldots, s_n^{(i)}\}$. We claim that $\trianglerighteq_{emb}$ is a wpo on $S := \bigcup_{i \geq 1} S_i$.

Assume that $s_1, s_2, s_3, \ldots$ is a bad sequence in S, and let k be such that $s_1 \in S_k$. Because $\trianglerighteq_{emb}$ is reflexive, the sequence can only be bad if all s_i are distinct. Thus, since $U := S_1 \cup \ldots \cup S_{k-1}$ is finite, there exists an $l \geq 1$ such that $s_i \in S - U$ for all $i \geq l$. Because the size of $s_1 \in S_k$ is smaller than the size of t_k, minimality of the sequence $t_1, t_2, t_3, \ldots$ implies that the sequence

$$t_1, \ldots, t_{k-1}, s_1, s_l, s_{l+1}, \ldots$$

is good. Since the sequences $t_1, t_2, t_3, \ldots$ and $s_1, s_2, s_3, \ldots$ are bad, this can only be possible if there exist indices $i \in \{1, \ldots, k-1\}$ and $j \in \{1, l, l+1, \ldots\}$ such that $t_i \trianglelefteq_{emb} s_j$. If $j = 1$, then $s_j = s_1$ is a subterm of t_k, and thus $t_i \trianglelefteq_{emb} s_j = s_1$ yields $t_i \trianglelefteq_{emb} t_k$. Because $i < k$, this implies that $t_1, t_2, t_3, \ldots$ is good, which is a contradiction. Otherwise, let m be such that $s_j \in S_m$. Since $j \geq l$, we know that $s_j \notin U$, which yields $i < k \leq m$. However, $s_j \in S_m$ means that s_j is a subterm of t_m, and thus $t_i \trianglelefteq_{emb} s_j$ implies $t_i \trianglelefteq_{emb} t_m$. Because of $i < m$, this again contradicts the fact that $t_1, t_2, t_3, \ldots$ was constructed as a bad sequence.

(2) Consider the minimal bad sequence $t_1, t_2, t_3, \ldots$ constructed above. Since $\Sigma \cup X$ is finite, there are infinitely many indices $i_1 < i_2 < i_3 < \cdots$ such that the root symbols of the terms $t_{i_1}, t_{i_2}, t_{i_3}, \ldots$ coincide. If this symbol is a variable or a constant, then we have $t_{i_1} = t_{i_2}$, which implies $t_{i_1} \trianglelefteq_{emb} t_{i_2}$. This contradicts the fact that $t_1, t_2, t_3, \ldots$ is bad.

Thus, assume that the root symbol of $t_{i_1}, t_{i_2}, t_{i_3}, \ldots$ is a function symbol $f \in \Sigma^{(n)}$ for $n > 0$, i.e. $t_{i_j} = f(s_1^{(i_j)}, \ldots, s_n^{(i_j)})$. Because of (1) and Lemma 5.4.5, the sequence $(s_1^{(i_1)}, \ldots, s_n^{(i_1)}), (s_1^{(i_2)}, \ldots, s_n^{(i_2)}), \ldots$ is good w.r.t. the component-wise order on $S \times \ldots \times S$, which yields indices $\nu < \mu$ such that $s_1^{(i_\nu)} \trianglelefteq_{emb} s_1^{(i_\mu)} \wedge \ldots \wedge s_n^{(i_\nu)} \trianglelefteq_{emb} s_n^{(i_\mu)}$. This implies $t_{i_\nu} \trianglelefteq_{emb} t_{i_\mu}$. Because $\nu < \mu$ implies $i_\nu < i_\mu$, this contradicts the fact that $t_1, t_2, t_3, \ldots$ is bad.

(3) Summing up, we have shown that our original assumption that there exists a bad sequence in $T(\Sigma, X)$, which we used to construct the minimal bad sequence $t_1, t_2, t_3, \ldots$, leads to a contradiction. $\square$

In the following, we use this theorem to prove that every simplification order is well-founded. As a first step in this direction, we show that every simplification order contains the homeomorphic embedding relation.

Lemma 5.4.7 *Let $>$ be a simplification order on $T(\Sigma, V)$, and let $s, t \in T(\Sigma, V)$ be terms. Then $s \trianglerighteq_{emb} t$ implies $s \geq t$.*

Proof Assume that $s \trianglerighteq_{emb} t$. We consider the three cases in the definition of $\trianglerighteq_{emb}$, and prove $s \geq t$ by induction on $|s|$.

(1) If $s = x = t$ then $s \geq t$ because $\geq$ is reflexive.

(2) Assume that $s = f(s_1, \ldots, s_n)$ and $t = f(t_1, \ldots, t_n)$ for a function symbol $f \in \Sigma^{(n)}$ and $s_1 \trianglerighteq_{emb} t_1, \ldots, s_n \trianglerighteq_{emb} t_n$. By induction, we obtain $s_1 \geq t_1, \ldots, s_n \geq t_n$. Since $>$ is a rewrite order, this implies $f(s_1, \ldots, s_n) \geq f(t_1, \ldots, t_n)$.

(3) Assume that $s = f(s_1, \ldots, s_n)$ for a function symbol $f \in \Sigma^{(n)}$ and $s_j \trianglerighteq_{emb} t$ for some $j, 1 \leq j \leq n$. By induction, we obtain $s_j \geq t$. In addition, the subterm property of $>$ yields $s > s_j$, and thus $s > t$. $\square$

Theorem 5.4.8 *Let Σ be a finite signature. Every simplification order $>$ on $T(\Sigma, V)$ is a reduction order.*

Proof By definition of simplification orders, it remains to be shown that every simplification order is well-founded. Thus, assume that $>$ is a simplification order on $T(\Sigma, V)$, and that $t_1 > t_2 > t_3 > \cdots$ is an infinite chain in $T(\Sigma, V)$.

(1) We show by contradiction that $Var(t_1) \supseteq Var(t_2) \supseteq Var(t_3) \supseteq \cdots$ holds. Assume that $x \in Var(t_{i+1}) - Var(t_i)$. For the substitution $\sigma :=$

$\{x \mapsto t_i\}$ we have, on the one hand, $t_i = \sigma(t_i)$ (since x does not occur in t_i) and $\sigma(t_i) > \sigma(t_{i+1})$ (since $>$ is a rewrite order). On the other hand, t_i is a subterm of $\sigma(t_{i+1})$, and thus the subterm property yields $\sigma(t_{i+1}) \geq t_i$. If we put the two inequalities together, we obtain $t_i > t_i$, which is a contradiction.

(2) The first part of the proof shows that, for the finite set $X := Var(t_1)$, all terms in the sequence $t_1, t_2, t_3, \ldots$ belong to $T(\Sigma, X)$. Since Σ and X are finite, Kruskal's Theorem implies that this sequence is good, i.e. there exist $i < j$ such that $t_i \trianglelefteq_{emb} t_j$. Now, Lemma 5.4.7 yields $t_i \leq t_j$, which is a contradiction since we know that $t_i > t_{i+1} > \cdots > t_j$. $\qquad\square$

The converse of this theorem is not true, i.e. there are reduction orders that are not simplification orders.

Example 5.4.9 Let $\Sigma = \{f, g\}$ consist of two unary function symbols. We consider the term rewriting system

$$R = \{f(f(x)) \to f(g(f(x)))\}.$$

Since R terminates (Exercise 5.17), we know that $\xrightarrow{+}_R$ is a reduction order. It cannot be a simplification order since $f(g(f(x))) \trianglerighteq_{emb} f(f(x))$ would then imply $f(g(f(x))) \xrightarrow{*}_R f(f(x))$, which together with $f(f(x)) \to_R f(g(f(x)))$ contradicts termination of R.

In particular, R is an example of a terminating term rewriting system that cannot be shown to be terminating with the help of a simplification order, since $f(g(f(x))) > f(f(x))$ for any simplification order $>$.

For reduction orders that are total on ground terms, the converse of Theorem 5.4.8 holds in a restricted form.

Proposition 5.4.10 Let $>$ be a reduction order on $T(\Sigma, V)$ that is total on ground terms. Then $>$ satisfies the subterm property for ground terms, i.e., for all $t \in T(\Sigma, \emptyset)$ and all $p \in Pos(t) - \{\epsilon\}$, we have $t > t|_p$.

Proof Let $t \in T(\Sigma, \emptyset)$, $p \in Pos(t) - \{\epsilon\}$, and assume that $t > t|_p$ does not hold. Since $p \neq \epsilon$, we also have $t \neq t|_p$. Thus, totality of $>$ on ground terms implies $t|_p > t$. This contradicts the fact that $>$ is a well-founded rewrite order since it yields the infinite chain

$$t|_p > t = t[t|_p]_p > t[t]_p > t[t[t]_p]_p > \cdots. \qquad\square$$

In the remainder of this section, we introduce three methods for constructing specific simplification orders.

5.4.1 Polynomial simplification orders

In Section 5.3, the restriction to polynomials with coefficients in $\mathbb{N}$ was necessary to ensure well-foundedness of the polynomial orders obtained. Simplification orders offer another way to obtain well-foundedness: the subterm property must be satisfied. Thus, it becomes possible to employ polynomials over the reals, provided that one ensures that they yield a simplification order.

Definition 5.4.11 Let Σ be a finite signature. A **polynomial interpretation over** $\mathbb{R}$ consists of a nonempty domain $A \subseteq \mathbb{R}$, and a mapping of the function symbols $f \in \Sigma^{(n)}$ to polynomials $P_f \in \mathbb{R}[X_1, \ldots, X_n]$ such that the following properties are satisfied:

1. For all $a_1, \ldots, a_n \in A$, we have $P_f(a_1, \ldots, a_n) \in A$.
2. For all $i, 1 \leq i \leq n$, and all $a, b, a_1, \ldots, a_{i-1}, a_{i+1}, \ldots, a_n \in A$,

$$a > b \Rightarrow P_f(a_1, \ldots, a_{i-1}, a, a_{i+1}, \ldots, a_n) > P_f(a_1, \ldots, a_{i-1}, b, a_{i+1}, \ldots, a_n).$$

3. For all $i, 1 \leq i \leq n$, and all $a, a_1, \ldots, a_{i-1}, a_{i+1}, \ldots, a_n \in A$,

$$P_f(a_1, \ldots, a_{i-1}, a, a_{i+1}, \ldots, a_n) > a.$$

The mapping of function symbols to polynomials is extended to terms in the obvious way. For polynomials $P, Q \in \mathbb{R}[X_1, \ldots, X_n]$ we write $P >_A Q$ iff $P(a_1, \ldots, a_n) > Q(a_1, \ldots, a_n)$ for all $a_1, \ldots, a_n \in A$. The **polynomial simplification order** on $T(\Sigma, V)$ induced by such a polynomial interpretation over $\mathbb{R}$ is defined by

$$s > t \quad \text{iff} \quad P_s >_A P_t.$$

It is easy to see that this definition implies that every polynomial simplification order is indeed a simplification order.

If the set A is definable in the first-order theory of real numbers, the conditions 1, 2 and 3 can be checked effectively (using Tarski's decision procedure [239]) for any given mapping of function symbols to polynomials. In addition, for given terms s, t, the question "$P_s >_A P_t$?" is decidable. Thus, it is decidable whether a given polynomial simplification order with definable domain can be used to show termination of a given finite term rewriting system.

It is not even necessary to determine a mapping from function symbols to polynomials by hand. Assume that we have fixed a definable domain A and an upper bound for the degree k of the polynomials that may be employed. Then Tarski's decision procedure can be used to determine whether termination of a given finite term rewriting system can be shown with a polynomial simplification order that has domain A and employs only polynomials whose degree is bounded by k. For this purpose, the coefficients of the polynomials are treated as existentially quantified variables in the decision procedure. The main problem with this approach is, of course, the high complexity of Tarski's decision procedure for the first-order theory of real numbers.

5.4.2 Recursive path orders

The main idea underlying recursive path orders is that two terms are compared by first comparing their root symbols, and then recursively comparing the collections of their immediate subterms. These collections can be seen as unordered multisets (which yields the multiset path order), or as ordered tuples (which yields the lexicographic path order), or one can employ a combination of both (which yields the recursive path order with status). In the following, we consider the lexicographic path order in more detail.

Definition 5.4.12 Let Σ be a *finite signature* and $>$ be a strict order on Σ. The **lexicographic path order** $>_{lpo}$ on $T(\Sigma, V)$ induced by $>$ is defined as follows: $s >_{lpo} t$ iff

(LPO1) $t \in Var(s)$ and $s \neq t$, or

(LPO2) $s = f(s_1, \ldots, s_m)$, $t = g(t_1, \ldots, t_n)$, and

    (LPO2a) there exists $i, 1 \leq i \leq m$, with $s_i \geq_{lpo} t$, or

    (LPO2b) $f > g$ and $s >_{lpo} t_j$ for all $j, 1 \leq j \leq n$, or

    (LPO2c) $f = g$, $s >_{lpo} t_j$ for all $j, 1 \leq j \leq n$, and there exists $i, 1 \leq i \leq m$, such that $s_1 = t_1, \ldots, s_{i-1} = t_{i-1}$ and $s_i >_{lpo} t_i$.

This definition is recursive since in (LPO2a), (LPO2b), and (LPO2c) it refers to the relation $>_{lpo}$ to be defined. Nevertheless, $>_{lpo}$ is well-defined since the definition of $s >_{lpo} t$ only refers to the relation $>_{lpo}$ applied to pairs of terms that are smaller than the pair s, t. In (LPO2a), $\geq_{lpo}$ stands for the reflexive closure of $>_{lpo}$ (and not for the lexicographic path order induced by $\geq$). In (LPO2c), the collections of immediate subterms are compared with respect to $>_{lex}^n$, the n-fold lexicographic product of $>_{lpo}$ with itself, which explains the name *lexicographic* path order. Before showing that $>_{lpo}$ is a simplification order, we consider some examples.

Example 5.4.13 Let $\Sigma = \{f, i, e\}$, where f is binary, i is unary, and e is a constant, and assume that $i > f > e$.

1. $f(x, e) >_{lpo} x$ by (LPO1).
2. $i(e) >_{lpo} e$ by (LPO2a) since we have $e \geq_{lpo} e$.

3. $i(f(x, y)) >_{lpo} f(i(y), i(x))$ by (LPO2b) since $i > f$ and, by (LPO2c),
   $i(f(x, y)) >_{lpo} i(y)$ and $i(f(x, y)) >_{lpo} i(x)$. The preconditions for case
   (LPO2c) are satisfied since we have $i(f(x, y)) >_{lpo} y$, $i(f(x, y)) >_{lpo} x$
   and $f(x, y) >_{lpo} y$, $f(x, y) >_{lpo} x$ by (LPO1).

4. $f(f(x, y), z) >_{lpo} f(x, f(y, z))$ by (LPO2c) with $i = 1$:

   - $f(f(x, y), z) >_{lpo} x$: this holds because of (LPO1).
   - $f(f(x, y), z) >_{lpo} f(y, z)$: again, we have (LPO2c) with $i = 1$:
     - $f(f(x, y), z) >_{lpo} y$ and $f(f(x, y), z) >_{lpo} z$: by (LPO1).
     - $f(x, y) >_{lpo} y$: by (LPO1).
   - $f(x, y) >_{lpo} x$: by (LPO1).

Theorem 5.4.14 *For any strict order $>$ on Σ, the induced lexicographic
path order $>_{lpo}$ is a simplification order on $T(\Sigma, V)$.*

Proof (1) Before we can show transitivity, we need an auxiliary result, which
we prove by induction on $|s| + |t|$:

$$s >_{lpo} t \text{ implies } Var(s) \supseteq Var(t).$$

In (LPO1), $t = x$ is a variable that occurs in s and thus $Var(t) = \{x\} \subseteq
Var(s)$. In (LPO2a), $s_i \geq_{lpo} t$ yields $Var(s) \supseteq Var(s_i) \supseteq Var(t)$ by
induction. In (LPO2b) and (LPO2c), $s >_{lpo} t_j$ for all $j, 1 \leq j \leq n$,
yields $Var(s) \supseteq Var(t_j)$ for all $j, 1 \leq j \leq n$, by induction, and thus
$Var(s) \supseteq \bigcup_{j=1}^{n} Var(t_j) = Var(t)$.

(2) To show *transitivity*, we assume that $r >_{lpo} s$ and $s >_{lpo} t$. We prove
$r >_{lpo} t$ by induction on $|r| + |s| + |t|$. Obviously, $r >_{lpo} s$ implies that r is
not a variable, and $s >_{lpo} t$ implies that s is not a variable.

First, assume that $t = x$ is a variable. To obtain $r >_{lpo} t$ by (LPO1), it is
sufficient to show that the variable x occurs in r. Because of $s >_{lpo} t = x$,
we know that x occurs in s. In addition, as we have shown in (1), $r >_{lpo} s$
implies $Var(r) \supseteq Var(s)$, and thus $x \in Var(r)$.

Now, assume $r = f(r_1, \ldots, r_l)$, $s = g(s_1, \ldots, s_m)$, and $t = h(t_1, \ldots, t_n)$.
First, we consider the two cases where one of the inequalities is due to
(LPO2a):

- $r >_{lpo} s$ is an instance of (LPO2a), i.e. there exists $i, 1 \leq i \leq l$, such
  that $r_i \geq_{lpo} s$. By induction, we obtain $r_i \geq_{lpo} t$, and thus $r >_{lpo} t$
  holds by (LPO2a).
- $s >_{lpo} t$ is an instance of (LPO2a), and $r >_{lpo} s$ is an instance of
  (LPO2b) or (LPO2c). We have $r >_{lpo} s_j$ for all $j, 1 \leq j \leq m$, and
  $s_i \geq_{lpo} t$ for some $i, 1 \leq i \leq m$. By induction, $r >_{lpo} s_i \geq_{lpo} t$ yields
  $r >_{lpo} t$.

Thus, we may assume that both inequalities are due to (LPO2b) or (LPO2c). This implies $f \geq h$ and $s >_{lpo} t_j$ for all $j, 1 \leq j \leq l$. By induction, $r >_{lpo} s >_{lpo} t_j$ yields $r >_{lpo} t_j$ for all $j, 1 \leq j \leq l$. If $f > h$, this is sufficient to obtain $r >_{lpo} t$. Otherwise, we have $f = g = h$, and thus both inequalities are due to (LPO2c). Now, $r >_{lpo} t$ can be shown as in the proof of transitivity of the lexicographic product (where the induction hypothesis yields transitivity for the subterms).

(3) Because we already know that $>_{lpo}$ is transitive, the *subterm property* is proved if we succeed in showing that $f(\ldots, s, \ldots) >_{lpo} s$ for all function symbols f and terms s. If $s = x$ is a variable, then $f(\ldots, s, \ldots) >_{lpo} s$ is an instance of (LPO1). Otherwise, it is an instance of (LPO2a) since $s \geq_{lpo} s$.

(4) *Closure under substitutions*, i.e. $s >_{lpo} t$ implies $\sigma(s) >_{lpo} \sigma(t)$ for all terms s, t and all substitutions σ, is shown by induction on $|s| + |t|$. For (LPO1), $t = x$ is a variable occurring in s and $s \neq t$. Thus, $\sigma(t)$ is a strict subterm of $\sigma(s)$, and we obtain $\sigma(s) >_{lpo} \sigma(t)$ as a consequence of the subterm property. In (LPO2a), $s_i \geq_{lpo} t$ implies $\sigma(s_i) \geq_{lpo} \sigma(t)$ by induction. Similar induction arguments apply in the remaining two cases.

(5) To show *compatibility with Σ-operations*, we assume that $s >_{lpo} t$, $f \in \Sigma^{(n)}$, and $s_1, \ldots, s_{i-1}, s_{i+1}, \ldots, s_n \in T(\Sigma, V)$. Then

$$f(s_1, \ldots, s_{i-1}, s, s_{i+1}, \ldots, s_n) >_{lpo} f(s_1, \ldots, s_{i-1}, t, s_{i+1}, \ldots, s_n)$$

is obtained as an instance of (LPO2c): the subterm property yields

$$f(s_1, \ldots, s_{i-1}, s, s_{i+1}, \ldots, s_n) >_{lpo} s_j$$

for all $j \in \{1, \ldots, i-1, i+1, \ldots, n\}$, and $f(s_1, \ldots, s_{i-1}, s, s_{i+1}, \ldots, s_n) >_{lpo} s$. Together with the assumption $s >_{lpo} t$, this last inequality implies $f(s_1, \ldots, s_{i-1}, s, s_{i+1}, \ldots, s_n) >_{lpo} t$ by transitivity. Finally, $s_1 = s_1, \ldots, s_{i-1} = s_{i-1}$ and $s >_{lpo} t$ are obvious.

(6) In order to show *irreflexivity* of $>_{lpo}$, we assume that there exists a term s such that $s >_{lpo} s$, and try to refute this assumption by induction on the size of s. If $s = x$ is a variable, then the only possible case is (LPO1). However, the condition "$s \neq s$" necessary for this case to apply is obviously not satisfied.

Thus, assume that $s = f(s_1, \ldots, s_n)$. Obviously, (LPO1) and (LPO2b) cannot apply. For (LPO2c), there must exist an $i, 1 \geq i \geq n$, such that $s_i >_{lpo} s_i$. By induction, we know that this is not possible. For (LPO2a), we have on the one hand an index $i, 1 \leq i \leq n$, such that $s_i \geq_{lpo} s$. On the other hand, the subterm property yields $s >_{lpo} s_i$. Transitivity implies $s_i >_{lpo} s_i$, which contradicts our induction hypothesis. $\qquad\square$

One advantage of lexicographic path orders over polynomial orders is that they do not impose a doubly-exponential bound on the length of reduction sequences. In fact, they can even be used to show termination of term rewriting systems with reduction sequences whose length cannot be bounded by a primitive recursive function:

Example 5.4.15 Termination of the term rewriting system R_{Ack} introduced in Example 5.3.11 can be shown using the lexicographic path order that is induced by $a > s$.

A further nice feature of lexicographic path orders is the fact that it is decidable whether termination of a given finite term rewriting system can be shown with the help of such an order.

Proposition 5.4.16 *Let Σ be a finite* signature, $s, t \in T(\Sigma, V)$, *and R a finite term rewriting system over $T(\Sigma, V)$.*

1. *For a given lexicographic path order, $s >_{lpo} t$ can be decided in time polynomial in the size of s, t.*
2. *The question of whether termination of R can be shown using some lexicographic path order on $T(\Sigma, V)$ is an NP-complete problem.*

The first statement of the proposition is an easy consequence of the definition of lexicographic path orders (Exercise 5.25). An NP-algorithm for the problem addressed in the second statement of the proposition simply guesses an order $>$ on Σ, and then uses the polynomial algorithm of the first statement to check whether this guess was correct. NP-hardness of the problem for the multiset path order is shown in [149]. This proof can easily be adapted to the lexicographic path order.

The applicability of this approach for showing termination can be increased by allowing for different ways of comparing the collections of subterms in case (LPO2c) of Definition 5.4.12. Instead of comparing the tuples $(s_1, \ldots, s_m)$ and $(t_1, \ldots, t_m)$ lexicographically from left to right, one can also define an order where they are always compared lexicographically from right to left. More generally, one can associate each function symbol with a fixed permutation of its arguments, and then compare the tuples of immediate subterms lexicographically along this permutation. To obtain the **multiset path order** $>_{mpo}$ induced by a strict order $>$ on Σ, one considers the multisets $\{s_1, \ldots, s_m\}$ and $\{t_1, \ldots, t_m\}$, and compares them with the multiset order induced by $>_{mpo}$. The fact that this yields a well-defined simplification order can be shown by a proof that is similar to the one for $>_{lpo}$ [72]. In the **recursive path order with status**, these different approaches are combined: each function symbol is equipped with a status that determines whether the collections of subterms are compared by the multiset order, or lexicographically with respect to a permutation associated with the function symbol. The following is an example of a rewrite system where only the combination of the multiset and the lexicographic status yields a recursive path order that can show its termination:

Example 5.4.17 Let s be a unary and $+, *$ be binary function symbols. We consider the term rewriting system R that consists of the rules

$$(x + y) + z \;\;\to\;\; x + (y + z),$$
$$x * s(y) \;\;\to\;\; x + (y * x).$$

The first rule can only be oriented in this direction with a recursive path order that assigns lexicographic status (from left to right) to $+$. In order to orient the second rule from left to right, we need $* > +$. In addition, $x * s(y)$ must be larger than $y * x$, which can only be achieved by assigning multiset status to $*$. Note that the additional rule

$$x + s(y) \to s(y + x)$$

would require $+ > s$ and multiset status for $+$, which implies that all three rules together cannot be shown to be terminating with a recursive path order with status.

5.4.3 Recursive path orders in ML

Building on the type of terms (see Section 4.7) and the lexicographic order *lex* already defined, the definition of $>_{lpo}$ is easily turned into ML code:

```
(* (string * string -> order) -> term * term -> order *)
fun lpo ord (s,t) = case (s,t) of
      (s, V x) => if s = t then EQ
                  else if occurs x s then GR (*LPO1*) else NGE
    | (V _, T _) => NGE
    | (T(f,ss), T(g,ts)) => (*LPO2*)
        if forall (fn si => lpo ord (si,t) = NGE) ss
        then case ord(f,g) of
                GR => if forall (fn ti => lpo ord (s,ti) = GR) ts
                      then GR (*LPO2b*) else NGE
              | EQ => if forall (fn ti => lpo ord (s,ti) = GR) ts
                      then lex (lpo ord) (ss,ts) (*LPO2c*)
                      else NGE
              | NGE => NGE
        else GR (*LPO2a*);
```

If *ord* implements the order $>$ on the function symbols, then *lpo ord* implements $>_{lpo}$.

Although we have already indicated the places in the code which correspond to particular clauses in the definition of the lexicographic path order, the following comments should answer any remaining questions.

- The branches returning *NGE* are the result of analysing in which cases neither $s >_{lpo} t$ nor $s = t$ holds. For example, if s is a variable and t is not, then $s >_{lpo} t$ cannot hold because (LPO1) requires t to be a variable and (LPO2) requires s not to be a variable. This justifies the line $(V \_, T \_) \Rightarrow NGE$.

- Case (LPO2a) is slightly disguised because we have replaced the test $\exists 1 \leq i \leq m.\ s_i \geq_{lpo} t$ by $\forall 1 \leq i \leq m.\ s_i \not\geq_{lpo} t$.

- Case (LPO2c) is simplified by appealing to the functional *lex* for comparing the subterms lexicographically. Note that the definition of $>_{lpo}$ avoids the use of $(>_{lpo})_{lex}$ because $(>_{lpo})_{lex}$ is only well-defined if $>_{lpo}$ is a strict order, something we do not yet know while defining $>_{lpo}$.

The precise implementation of the parameter *ord* is not germane to the subject of this book. Suffice it to say that the most straightforward representation is a list of pairs (f, g) meaning $f > g$. There should also be a function to compute the transitive closure of such a list, which obviates the need to supply (f, h) in addition to (f, g) and (g, h).

The recursive path order with status is a generalization of the lexicographic and multiset path orders. At the implementation level it means that *rpo* is an abstraction of *lpo* w.r.t. the functional *lex*:

```
(* rpo: (string -> (term * term -> order) -> term list * term list -> order)
          -> (string * string -> order) -> term * term -> order *)
fun rpo stat ord (s,t) = case (s,t) of
        (s, V x) => if s = t then EQ
                    else if occurs x s then GR else NGE
      | (V _, T _) => NGE
      | (T(f,ss), T(g,ts)) =>
            if forall (fn si => rpo stat ord (si,t) = NGE) ss
            then case ord(f,g) of
                    GR => if forall (fn ti => rpo stat ord (s,ti) = GR) ts
                          then GR else NGE
                  | EQ => if forall (fn ti => rpo stat ord (s,ti) = GR) ts
                          then (stat f) (rpo stat ord) (ss,ts)
                          else NGE
                  | NGE => NGE
            else GR;
```

The additional parameter *stat* maps each function symbol to the appropriate subterm order, e.g. as in (fn "f" => *lex* | "g" => *mul*, ...).

Note that *rpo* is one of the rare examples of a natural third-order function: one of its parameters is a function which itself takes a function as an argument.

5.4.4 Knuth-Bendix orders

Let Σ be a *finite* signature. A Knuth-Bendix order on $T(\Sigma, V)$ is determined by a strict order $>$ on Σ and a **weight function** $w : \Sigma \cup V \to \mathbb{R}_0^+$, where $\mathbb{R}_0^+$ denotes the set of non-negative real numbers. We call such a weight function w **admissible for** $>$ iff it satisfies the following properties:

1. There exists $w_0 \in \mathbb{R}_0^+ - \{0\}$ such that $w(x) = w_0$ for all variables $x \in V$ and $w(c) \geq w_0$ for all constants $c \in \Sigma^{(0)}$.
2. If $f \in \Sigma^{(1)}$ is a unary function symbol of weight $w(f) = 0$, then f is the greatest element in Σ, i.e. $f \geq g$ for all $g \in \Sigma$.

The weight function w can be extended to a function $w : T(\Sigma, V) \to \mathbb{R}_0^+$ as follows:

$$w(t) := \sum_{x \in Var(t)} w(x) \cdot |t|_x + \sum_{f \in \Sigma} w(f) \cdot |t|_f,$$

where $|t|_x$ ($|t|_f$) denotes the number of occurrences of the variable x (function symbol f) in t. Thus, $w(t)$ simply adds up the weights of all occurrences of symbols in t.

Definition 5.4.18 Let Σ be a *finite* signature, $>$ be a strict order on Σ, and $w : \Sigma \cup V \to \mathbb{R}_0^+$ be a weight function. The **Knuth-Bendix order** $>_{kbo}$ on $T(\Sigma, V)$ induced by $>$ and w is defined as follows: for $s, t \in T(\Sigma, V)$, we have $s >_{kbo} t$ iff

(KBO1) $|s|_x \geq |t|_x$ for all $x \in V$ and $w(s) > w(t)$, or

(KBO2) $|s|_x \geq |t|_x$ for all $x \in V$, $w(s) = w(t)$, and one of the following properties holds:

    (KBO2a) There are a unary function symbol f, a variable x, and a positive integer n such that $s = f^n(x)$ and $t = x$.

    (KBO2b) There exist function symbols f, g such that $f > g$ and $s = f(s_1, \ldots, s_m)$, $t = g(t_1, \ldots, t_n)$.

    (KBO2c) There exist a function symbol f and an index $i, 1 \leq i \leq m$, such that $s = f(s_1, \ldots, s_m)$, $t = f(t_1, \ldots, t_m)$, and $s_1 = t_1, \ldots, s_{i-1} = t_{i-1}$ and $s_i >_{kbo} t_i$.

Thus, the Knuth-Bendix order makes a lexicographic comparison, where first the weights of the terms are considered, second their root symbols, and third recursively the collections of the immediate subterms. The order is similar to lexicographic path orders in that it compares the root symbols with respect to a given precedence order $>$, and then recursively the collections of immediate subterms. The main difference between the Knuth-Bendix order and the lexicographic path order is the fact that the former employs a weight function. Because of this use of the weight function, the variable condition "$|s|_x \geq |t|_x$ for all $x \in V$" becomes necessary. Indeed, without this condition the order would not be closed under substitutions (see Example 5.2.2).

Another peculiarity of the Knuth-Bendix order is the treatment of unary function symbols of weight zero. First, note that (KBO2a) can only apply if f has weight 0. Second, admissibility of w for $>$ makes sure that there can be only one such symbol, and that it must be the greatest element in Σ with respect to $>$. The following proposition shows that without this condition, the Knuth-Bendix order would not be a simplification order.

Proposition 5.4.19 *Assume that $f \in \Sigma^{(1)}$, $w(f) = 0$, and that there exists $g \in \Sigma - \{f\}$ such that $f \not> g$. Then the Knuth-Bendix order induced by $>$ and w does not satisfy the subterm property.*

Proof Let $t = g(t_1, \ldots, t_n)$ be an arbitrary term with root symbol g, and define $s := f(t)$. Because of $w(f) = 0$, we have $w(s) = w(t)$. Obviously, (KBO2a) and (KBO2c) cannot apply. In addition, since $f \not> g$, (KBO2b) does not apply. Thus s is not greater than its strict subterm t with respect to the Knuth-Bendix order induced by $>$ and w. $\qquad\square$

One might ask why unary symbols of weight zero are allowed at all. The reason is that otherwise termination of rules like $i(f(x, y)) \rightarrow f(i(y), i(x))$ could not be shown with the help of a Knuth-Bendix order. More generally, it can be shown that the power of Knuth-Bendix orders would be severely restricted when disallowing unary symbols of weight zero (see Example 5.4.25 below and the remark following that example).

Theorem 5.4.20 *Let $>$ be a strict order on Σ, and $w : \Sigma \cup V \rightarrow \mathbb{R}_0^+$ be a weight function that is admissible for $>$. Then the Knuth-Bendix order $>_{kbo}$ on $T(\Sigma, V)$ induced by $>$ and w is a simplification order.*

We split the somewhat lengthy task of proving this theorem into proving four lemmas. The first lemma states some auxiliary results, the second lemma shows that $>_{kbo}$ is a strict order, the third shows that $>_{kbo}$ is compatible with Σ-operations, and the fourth shows that $>_{kbo}$ is closed under substitutions and satisfies the subterm property.

Lemma 5.4.21 *Let w be an admissible weight function for $>$, and let $>_{kbo}$ be the Knuth-Bendix order induced by $>$ and w.*

1. *For all terms t we have $w(t) \geq w_0 > 0$.*
2. *Assume that $w(s) = w(t)$, and that t is a strict subterm of s. Then there exist $f \in \Sigma^{(1)}$ and a positive integer k such that $w(f) = 0$ and $s = f^k(t)$.*
3. *Let x be a variable and s be a term. Then $x >_{kbo} s$ cannot hold.*

4. Let x be a variable and $s \neq x$ be a term that contains x. Then we have $s >_{kbo} x$.

Proof (1) Because w is admissible, we know that $w(c) \geq w_0$ for all constants c, $w(x) = w_0$ for all variables x, and $w_0 > 0$. In addition, any term must contain at least one variable or constant.

(2) We prove the claim by induction on the size of s. Since t is a strict subterm of s, there are an $n \geq 1$ and a function symbol $f \in \Sigma^{(n)}$ such that $s = f(s_1, \ldots, s_n)$ and t is a subterm of s_i for some $i, 1 \leq i \leq n$. First, we show that $n = 1$ and $w(f) = 0$:

- Assume that $n > 1$. We have $w(s) = w(f) + \sum_{j=1}^{n} w(s_j)$, and we know that, for all j, $w(s_j) \geq w_0 > 0$. Thus, $n > 1$ implies $w(s) > w(s_i)$, and since t is a subterm of s_i, $w(s_i) \geq w(t)$. This contradicts our assumption that $w(s) = w(t)$.
- Assume that $w(f) > 0$. Thus, even for $n = 1$, $w(s) = w(f) + \sum_{j=1}^{n} w(s_j)$ yields $w(s) > w(s_i) \geq w(t)$.

This shows that $s = f(s')$ for the unique unary symbol f of weight 0 and a term s' that has t as subterm. For $s' = t$ we are done. Otherwise, we can apply the induction hypothesis since t is a strict subterm of s', $w(s') = w(s) = w(t)$, and $|s'| < |s|$.

(3) We know that $w(s) \geq w_0 = w(x)$. Thus, $x >_{kbo} s$ is only possible if $w(s) = w(x)$, i.e. if (KBO2) applies. However, in all three subcases of (KBO2), the larger term has a function symbol as root symbol.

(4) Since s contains x, we have $w(s) \geq w(x)$, $|s|_x \geq 1 = |x|_x$, and for all variables $y \neq x$, $|s|_y \geq 0 = |x|_y$. If $w(s) > w(x)$, then we are done. If $w(s) = w(x)$, then part 2 of the lemma implies that $s = f^k(x)$ for a unary function symbol f and a positive integer k. Thus, (KBO2a) applies.   □

Lemma 5.4.22 *Let w be an admissible weight function for $>$. Then the Knuth-Bendix order $>_{kbo}$ induced by $>$ and w is a strict order.*

Proof (1) Assume that $>_{kbo}$ is not irreflexive, and let s be a term of minimal size such that $s >_{kbo} s$. Obviously, we have $w(s) = w(s)$, and s has the same root symbol as s. Thus, the only case that could apply is (KBO2c). However, in this case we obtain $s_i >_{kbo} s_i$ for a strict subterm s_i of s, which contradicts minimality of s.

(2) To show transitivity, assume that $r >_{kbo} s$ and $s >_{kbo} t$. We prove $r >_{kbo} t$ by induction on the size of r.

- From $r >_{kbo} s$ and $s >_{kbo} t$ we can deduce that, for all variables x, $|r|_x \geq |s|_x$ and $|s|_x \geq |t|_x$ hold. Thus, we have $|r|_x \geq |t|_x$, which means that the variable condition is satisfied.

- In addition, $r >_{kbo} s$ and $s >_{kbo} t$ yield $w(r) \geq w(s)$ and $w(s) \geq w(t)$, which implies $w(r) \geq w(t)$.

If $w(r) > w(s)$ or $w(s) > w(t)$, then we are done since this yields $w(r) > w(t)$. Thus, we may assume that $w(r) = w(s) = w(t)$, i.e. $r >_{kbo} s$ and $s >_{kbo} t$ are both instances of (KBO2).

For $r >_{kbo} s$, we cannot have (KBO2a) since $s >_{kbo} t$ implies that s is not a variable (see Lemma 5.4.21). Thus, both r and s have a function symbol as root symbol, i.e. $r = f(r_1, \ldots, r_l)$ and $s = g(s_1, \ldots, s_m)$ for function symbols f, g such that $f \geq g$.

If $s >_{kbo} t$ is an instance of (KBO2a), then $t = x$ for a variable x, and $|r|_x \geq |t|_x$ implies that x occurs in r. Since the root symbol of r is a function symbol, we have $r \neq x$, and thus Lemma 5.4.21 yields $r >_{kbo} t$.

It remains to consider the case where $s >_{kbo} t$ is an instance of either (KBO2b) or (KBO2c). In this case, we know that there exists a function symbol h such that $g \geq h$ and $t = h(t_1, \ldots, t_n)$. If $f > g$ or $g > h$, then we have $f > h$, which yields $r >_{kbo} t$ by (KBO2b). Thus, assume that $f = g = h$, i.e. $r >_{kbo} s$ and $s >_{kbo} t$ are instances of (KBO2c): there exist i, j such that $r_1 = s_1, \ldots, r_{i-1} = s_{i-1}$ and $r_i >_{kbo} s_i$, and $s_1 = t_1, \ldots, s_{j-1} = t_{j-1}$, and $s_j >_{kbo} t_j$. By induction, we know that transitivity of $>_{kbo}$ already holds for these subterms, and thus we obtain $r >_{kbo} t$ by (KBO2c). □

Lemma 5.4.23 *Let w be an admissible weight function for $>$. Then the Knuth-Bendix order $>_{kbo}$ that is induced by $>$ and w is compatible with Σ-operations.*

Proof Assume that $s_1 >_{kbo} s_2$, and that $f \in \Sigma^{(n)}$ is an n-ary function symbol. We must show that

$$f(t_1, \ldots, t_{i-1}, s_1, t_{i+1}, \ldots, t_n) >_{kbo} f(t_1, \ldots, t_{i-1}, s_2, t_{i+1}, \ldots, t_n) \quad (*)$$

holds for all $i, 1 \leq i \leq n$, and all terms $t_1, \ldots, t_{i-1}, t_{i+1}, \ldots, t_n$.

From $s_1 >_{kbo} s_2$ we can deduce that s_1 and s_2 satisfy the variable condition in the definition of the Knuth-Bendix order, i.e. $|s_1|_x \geq |s_2|_x$ for all variables x. Obviously, this implies

$$|f(t_1, \ldots, t_{i-1}, s_1, t_{i+1}, \ldots, t_n)|_x \geq |f(t_1, \ldots, t_{i-1}, s_2, t_{i+1}, \ldots, t_n)|_x$$

for all variables x. In addition, if $w(s_1) > w(s_2)$, then

$$w(f(t_1, \ldots, t_{i-1}, s_1, t_{i+1}, \ldots, t_n)) > w(f(t_1, \ldots, t_{i-1}, s_2, t_{i+1}, \ldots, t_n)),$$

which yields $(*)$. Thus, assume that $w(s_1) = w(s_2)$. This implies

$$w(f(t_1, \ldots, t_{i-1}, s_1, t_{i+1}, \ldots, t_n)) = w(f(t_1, \ldots, t_{i-1}, s_2, t_{i+1}, \ldots, t_n)),$$

and since the root symbols of the two terms are identical, $(*)$ holds iff (KBO2c) applies. This is trivial since $t_1 = t_1, \ldots, t_{i-1} = t_{i-1}$, and $s_1 >_{kbo} s_2$. $\qquad \square$

Lemma 5.4.24 *Let w be an admissible weight function for $>$. Then the Knuth-Bendix order $>_{kbo}$ induced by $>$ and w is closed under substitutions and satisfies the subterm property.*

Proof (1) Assume that $s_1 >_{kbo} s_2$, and let σ be a substitution. We show $\sigma(s_1) >_{kbo} \sigma(s_2)$ by induction on the size of s_1.

First, we consider the variable condition. Let $X := \mathcal{V}ar(s_1) \cup \mathcal{V}ar(s_2)$. Because of $s_1 >_{kbo} s_2$, we know that $|s_1|_y \geq |s_2|_y$ for all $y \in X$. For an arbitrary variable x, we have

$$|\sigma(s_1)|_x - |\sigma(s_2)|_x = \sum_{y \in X} |\sigma(y)|_x \cdot (|s_1|_y - |s_2|_y) \geq 0$$

since $|\sigma(y)|_x \geq 0$ for all variables x and $|s_1|_y - |s_2|_y \geq 0$ for all $y \in X$. Thus, the variable condition is satisfied.

A similar computation can done for the weights:

$$w(\sigma(s_1)) - w(\sigma(s_2)) = w(s_1) - w(s_2) + \sum_{y \in X} (|s_1|_y - |s_2|_y) \cdot (w(\sigma(y)) - w_0).$$

We know $|s_1|_y - |s_2|_y \geq 0$ for all $y \in X$, and $w(\sigma(y)) - w_0 \geq 0$ by Lemma 5.4.21. Consequently, $w(s_1) > w(s_2)$ implies $w(\sigma(s_1)) > w(\sigma(s_2))$, which yields $\sigma(s_1) >_{kbo} \sigma(s_2)$.

Thus, assume that $w(s_1) = w(s_2)$, and hence $w(\sigma(s_1)) \geq w(\sigma(s_2))$. If $w(\sigma(s_1)) > w(\sigma(s_2))$, then $\sigma(s_1) >_{kbo} \sigma(s_2)$. Otherwise, we consider the three subcases of (KBO2):

- $s_1 >_{kbo} s_2$ holds by (KBO2a), i.e. $s_1 = f^k(x)$ and $s_2 = x$ for a positive integer k, a unary function symbol f of weight 0, and a variable x. We show $\sigma(s_1) >_{kbo} \sigma(s_2)$ by induction on the size of $\sigma(x)$. If $\sigma(x) =: y$ is a variable, then $\sigma(s_1) = f^k(y) >_{kbo} y = \sigma(s_2)$ holds by (KBO2a). Otherwise, $\sigma(x) = g(t_1, \ldots, t_n)$ for a function symbol $g \in \Sigma^{(n)}$. If $f \neq g$, then admissibility of w w.r.t. $>$ implies $f > g$, and thus $\sigma(s_1) = f^k(g(t_1, \ldots, t_n)) >_{kbo} g(t_1, \ldots, t_n) = \sigma(s_2)$ holds because of (KBO2b). If $f = g$, then we have (KBO2c), and it remains to be shown that $f^k(t_1) >_{kbo} t_1$. If we take a substitution σ' with $\sigma'(x) = t_1$, then the induction hypothesis (for $\sigma'(x)$, which is smaller than $\sigma(x)$) yields $f^k(t_1) = \sigma'(s_1) >_{kbo} \sigma'(s_2) = t_1$.
- $s_1 >_{kbo} s_2$ holds by (KBO2b), i.e. $s_1 = f(s_1^{(1)}, \ldots, s_m^{(1)})$ and $s_2 = g(s_1^{(2)}, \ldots, s_n^{(2)})$ for function symbols f, g with $f > g$. Obviously, $\sigma(s_1)$

has root symbol f and $\sigma(s_2)$ has root symbol g, and thus $\sigma(s_1) >_{kbo}$ $\sigma(s_2)$ by (KBO2b).

- $s_1 >_{kbo} s_2$ holds by (KBO2c), i.e. $s_1 = f(s_1^{(1)}, \ldots, s_m^{(1)})$ and $s_2 = f(s_1^{(2)}, \ldots, s_m^{(2)})$ for a function symbol f, and there exists an $i, 1 \leq i \leq m$, such that $s_1^{(1)} = s_1^{(2)}, \ldots, s_{i-1}^{(1)} = s_{i-1}^{(2)}$, and $s_i^{(1)} >_{kbo} s_i^{(2)}$. This implies $\sigma(s_1^{(1)}) = \sigma(s_1^{(2)}), \ldots, \sigma(s_{i-1}^{(1)}) = \sigma(s_{i-1}^{(2)})$, and by induction $\sigma(s_i^{(1)}) >_{kbo} \sigma(s_i^{(2)})$ (since $s_i^{(1)}$ is smaller than s_1). Thus, $\sigma(s_1) = f(\sigma(s_1^{(1)}), \ldots, \sigma(s_m^{(1)})) >_{kbo} f(\sigma(s_1^{(2)}), \ldots, \sigma(s_m^{(2)})) = \sigma(s_2)$ holds by (KBO2c).

(2) To show the subterm property, we recall that $s >_{kbo} x$ for all variables x and terms $s \neq x$ that contain x (Lemma 5.4.21). This, together with the fact that $>_{kbo}$ is closed under substitutions, obviously implies the subterm property.   □

This completes the proof of Theorem 5.4.20.

As for recursive path orders, one advantage of Knuth-Bendix orders over polynomial orders is that they can be used to show termination of rewrite systems with reduction sequences of more than doubly-exponential length.

Example 5.4.25 For the term rewriting system R consisting of the rules

$$s(x) + (y + z) \rightarrow x + (s(s(y)) + z),$$
$$s(x_1) + (x_2 + (x_3 + x_4)) \rightarrow x_1 + (x_3 + (x_2 + x_4)),$$

the length of its reduction chains cannot be bounded by a primitive recursive function in the size of the starting term [115]. Thus, R cannot be shown to be terminating with the help of a polynomial order. Termination of R can, however, be proved using the Knuth-Bendix order induced by $s > +$ and $w(s) = w(+) = 0, w_0 = 1$.

In this example, it was obviously necessary to use a Knuth-Bendix order that assigns weight 0 to the unary function symbol s. More generally, it can be shown [115] that a Knuth-Bendix order where all unary function symbols have weight greater than 0 yields an exponential upper bound for the length of reduction sequences.

Knuth-Bendix orders also share another nice feature with lexicographic path orders: they are decidable, and it is decidable whether termination of a finite term rewriting system can be shown using such an order.

Proposition 5.4.26 *Let Σ be a finite signature, $s, t \in T(\Sigma, V)$, and R a finite term rewriting system over $T(\Sigma, V)$.*

1. For a given Knuth-Bendix order, $s >_{kbo} t$ can be decided in time polynomial in the size of s, t.

2. The question of whether termination of R can be shown using some Knuth-Bendix order on $T(\Sigma, V)$ is decidable.

The first part of the proposition is an immediate consequence of the definition of Knuth-Bendix orders. The second is shown in [79], where an algorithm for calculating the optimal solutions of a system of linear inequalities over $\mathbb{R}$ is employed to compute appropriate weights for the function symbols.

Exercises

5.13 Let $>$ be a rewrite order. Show that the subterm property follows from the following simpler property:

$$f(\dots, x, \dots) > x \text{ for all } f \in \Sigma \text{ and all } x \in V.$$

5.14 Show that the reduction relation $\xrightarrow{*}_{R_{emb}}$ induced by the rewrite system

$$R_{emb} := \{f(x_1, \dots, x_n) \to x_i \mid n \geq 1, f \in \Sigma^{(n)}, 1 \leq i \leq n\}$$

coincides with the homeomorphic embedding $\trianglerighteq_{emb}$.

5.15 In the proof of Theorem 5.4.8 we have used the fact that the homeomorphic embedding $\trianglerighteq_{emb}$ is a well-partial-order. Why is it not sufficient for the proof just to know that $\trianglerighteq_{emb}$ is a well-founded order?

5.16 Let $\mathcal{A}$ be a monotone polynomial interpretation. For $P, Q \in \mathbb{N}[X_1, \dots, X_n]$, we write $P \geq_A Q$ iff $P(a_1, \dots, a_n) \geq Q(a_1, \dots, a_n)$ holds for all $a_1, \dots, a_n$ in A. Note that $\geq_A$ is not the reflexive closure of $>_A$. Show that $s \trianglerighteq_{emb} t$ implies $P_s \geq_A P_t$. Show that this implies that a polynomial order cannot be used to prove termination of a TRS R if there are terms s, t such that $s \xrightarrow{+}_R t$ and $s \trianglelefteq_{emb} t$.

5.17 Show that the TRS $R := \{f(f(x)) \to f(g(f(x)))\}$ is terminating.

5.18 Show that there exists a reduction order $>$ that cannot be extended to a reduction order that is total on ground terms. (*Hint:* consider the reduction order of Example 5.4.9, and Proposition 5.4.10.)

5.19 Show that every reduction order that is total on ground terms can be extended to a simplification order. (*Hint:* consider Exercise 5.6.)

5.20 Let Σ be a finite signature and let $>$ be a strict *linear* order on Σ.

   (a) Let $>_{lpo}$ be the lexicographic path order induced by $>$. Then $>_{lpo}$ is total on ground terms.

(b) Let w be a weight function that is admissible for $>$, and let $>_{kbo}$ be the Knuth-Bendix order that is induced by w and $>$. Then $>_{kbo}$ is total on ground terms.

5.21 Show that it is not possible to prove termination of the term rewriting system R of Example 5.4.25 with the help of a lexicographic path order.

5.22 Show that it is not possible to prove termination of the term rewriting system $R := \{f(f(x)) \to g(x), g(g(x)) \to f(x)\}$ with the help of a lexicographic path order.

5.23 Show that the condition "$s >_{lpo} t_j$ for all $j, 1 \leq j \leq n$" in (LPO2c) is not necessary when using the multiset order for comparing the collections of subterms. Demonstrate by an example why it cannot be dispensed with for the lexicographic path order.

5.24 Show that the condition "$s >_{lpo} t_j$ for all $j, 1 \leq j \leq n$" in (LPO2c) of the definition of the lexicographic path order can be replaced by "$s >_{lpo} t_j$ for all $j, i < j \leq n$", where i is such that $s_1 = t_1, \ldots, s_{i-1} = t_{i-1}$ and $s_i >_{lpo} t_i$.

5.25 Show that "$s >_{lpo} t$" can be decided in time $O(|s| \cdot |t|)$.

5.26 Prove termination of the term rewriting system R of Example 5.3.11 using a lexicographic path order. Show that it is not possible to prove termination of R using a Knuth-Bendix order.

5.27 Show that termination of the term rewriting system introduced in Exercise 5.12 cannot be shown with a Knuth-Bendix order or a recursive path order with status.

5.28 We have seen that unary function symbols of weight 0 must satisfy a very strong property to be admissible in Knuth-Bendix orders. Why is it not problematic to have weight zero for symbols of arity greater than 1 in the Knuth-Bendix order?

5.5 Bibliographic notes

The undecidability proof presented in Subsection 5.1.1 is due to Huet and Lankford [121]. This proof shows that the termination problem is even undecidable for rewrite systems where all rules contain only unary function symbols. Since the number of rules in $R_{\mathcal{M}}$ depends on the number of transitions in $\mathcal{M}$, the proof does not yield a bound on the number of rules necessary for obtaining undecidability. Dauchet [64, 65] has shown that termination is already undecidable for term rewriting systems consisting of a *single* rewrite rule. However, in his reduction the arities of the function

symbols occurring in this rule depend on the size of the alphabet Γ, the set
of states Q, and the set of transitions Δ of the Turing machine. For term
rewriting systems containing only unary function symbols, termination is
known to be undecidable for systems with *three* rules [171]. For systems
with one or two rules, the problem is open, but there are partial decidability
results for the case of systems with one rule [250, 228]. The decidability
result of Subsection 5.1.2 can be found in [71]. It is the obvious generalization to the right-ground case of Huet and Lankford's result [121] for ground
rewrite systems.

The main ideas underlying the interpretation method were already present in [164], where an interpretation by linear or quadratic polynomials was
proposed. In their general form, polynomial interpretations were introduced
by Lankford [155, 156]. Hofbauer and Lautemann's result [115] that polynomial orders induce a doubly-exponential bound on the length of reduction
chains is complemented by an article by Cichon and Lescanne [52], where it
is shown that termination proofs with polynomial orders induce *polynomial*
bounds on the number-theoretic functions computed by the rewrite systems.
This may seem surprising in the light of Example 5.3.12, where the term
$q^n(s^2(0))$ reduced to the doubly-exponentially larger term $s^{2^{2^n}}(0)$. However,
the number-theoretic function computed by the rewrite system of the example is q, and a term of the form $q(s^m(0))$ reduces to $s^{m^2}(0)$, whose size is
polynomial in the size of $q(s^m(0))$ (see [52] for details).

Simplification orders were first defined by Dershowitz [70]. In this paper,
Dershowitz presents a proof of Kruskal's Theorem, shows that simplification
orders are well-founded, and mentions polynomial simplification orders, as
introduced in Subsection 5.4.1. Rather than Kruskal's original proof [150],
Dershowitz's proof and ours follow the simplified proof of Kruskal's Theorem
presented by Nash-Williams [183]. Another good source for Kruskal's Theorem and other results on well-partial-orders and well-quasi-orders is [218].
We have actually considered a restricted version of the embedding relation
and Kruskal's Theorem: instead of requiring in the second clause of the definition of $\trianglerighteq_{emb}$ that the two terms have the same root symbol, Kruskal's
more general definition just requires that the first term has a root symbol
that is larger than or equivalent to the root symbol of the second with respect
to a given well-quasi-order on the signature. Our embedding is a special
case, since the identity is a well-quasi-order on any *finite* set. By using the
general formulation of Kruskal's Theorem (for a given well-partial-order or
well-quasi-order on the signature), one can extend the results presented in
this chapter to simplification orders on terms over infinite signatures [181].

The original recursive path order defined by Dershowitz [72] was actually what we call multiset path order. The lexicographic path order was introduced by Kamin and Lévy [130], but this paper and the proof that the lexicographic path order is a simplification order were, to the best of our knowledge, never published. Building on the above mentioned more general formulation of Kruskal's Theorem, one can introduce recursive path orders that are induced by well-quasi-orders on (possibly infinite) signatures [73]. The use of well-quasi-orders instead of simply well-partial-orders increases the power of the method: Exercise 5.22 gives an example of a system for which termination cannot be shown using a lexicographic path order induced by a partial order on the function symbols. However, if we use a quasi-order for which f and g are equivalent, then both rules can be ordered appropriately by the wqo-variant of the lexicographic path order (see Definition 19 in [73]).

The Knuth-Bendix order was first introduced in [145] in a slightly more restricted form: the weights were required to be non-negative integers, the precedence order on the function symbols was assumed to be total, and the variable condition in (KBO2) required "$|s|_x = |t|_x$" instead of "$|s|_x \geq |t|_x$". Knuth and Bendix [145] show termination by a direct proof, which makes use of the requirement that weights are non-negative integers. Our more general definition and the proof that Knuth-Bendix orders are simplification orders are derived from the presentation in [79].

6

Confluence

This chapter studies the problem of determining whether a TRS is confluent. After a brief look at the (undecidable) decision problem, the rest of the chapter divides neatly into two parts:

The first part deals with terminating systems, for which confluence turns out to be decidable. This is a key result in our search for decidable equational theories: if E constitutes a terminating TRS, we can decide if it is also confluent, in which case we know by Theorem 4.1.1 that $\approx_E$ is decidable.

The second part deals with those systems not covered by the first part, namely (potentially) nonterminating ones. The emphasis here is not on deciding $\approx_E$ by rewriting, which requires termination, but on the computational content of a TRS. Viewing a TRS as a program, confluence simply means that the program is deterministic. We show that for the class of so-called orthogonal systems, where no two rules interfere with each other, confluence holds irrespective of termination. This result has immediate consequences for the theory and design of functional programming languages.

6.1 The decision problem

Just as for termination and most other interesting properties (of term rewriting systems or otherwise), confluence is in general undecidable:

Theorem 6.1.1 *The following problem is undecidable:*

Instance: *A finite TRS R.*
Question: *Is R confluent?*

Proof Given a set of identities E such that $Var(l) = Var(r)$ and neither l nor r is a variable for all $l \approx r \in E$, we can reduce the ground word problem for E to the confluence problem of a related TRS as follows. Let $R := E \cup E^{-1}$, i.e. orient every equation in both directions. Thus we have

$\rightarrow_R = \leftrightarrow_E$ and therefore R is confluent. By our assumptions on E, R is even a TRS. Given two ground terms s and t and some new constant a, we show below that $R_{st} := R \cup \{a \rightarrow s, a \rightarrow t\}$ is confluent iff $s \approx_E t$. Thus we have reduced the ground word problem for E to the confluence problem for R_{st}. Since there are finite E with undecidable ground word problem satisfying our assumptions on E, e.g. Example 4.1.4, confluence cannot be decidable either. It remains to be shown that R_{st} is confluent iff $s \approx_E t$.

($\Rightarrow$) If R_{st} is confluent, we must have $s \downarrow_{R_{st}} t$, but because neither s nor t contains the new constant a, this implies $s \downarrow_R t$ because the rules $a \rightarrow s$ and $a \rightarrow t$ cannot have been used. Now $s \approx_E t$ follows from $\rightarrow_R = \leftrightarrow_E$.

($\Leftarrow$) Confluence of R_{st} follows because R_{st} is almost symmetric. More precisely, below we show for arbitrary terms u and v that if $u \rightarrow_{R_{st}} v$ then $v^t \xrightarrow{*}_R u^t$, where u^t is the result of replacing all occurrences of a in u by t. Thus, if $u \xrightarrow{*}_{R_{st}} u_i$, $i = 1, 2$, then $u_i \xrightarrow{*}_{R_{st}} u_i^t \xrightarrow{*}_R u^t$ and hence $u_1 \downarrow_{R_{st}} u_2$.

Suppose $u \rightarrow_{R_{st}} v$. We distinguish which rule is used in this step. If $u \rightarrow_R v$, we can safely replace a by t to get $u^t \rightarrow_R v^t$ and thus $v^t \rightarrow_R u^t$ because R is symmetric. If $a \rightarrow s$ is used, then $u|_p = a$ and $v = u[s]_p$ for some position p. From $s \approx_E t$ it follows that $s \leftrightarrow_E t$ and hence $s \xrightarrow{*}_R t$. Thus we have $v \xrightarrow{*}_R u[t]_p$ and therefore also $v^t \xrightarrow{*}_R (u[t]_p)^t = u^t[t^t]_p = u^t[t]_p = u^t$. Finally, if $a \rightarrow t$ is used at position p, then $v^t = (u[t]_p)^t = u^t \xrightarrow{*}_R u^t$. $\square$

Exercises

6.1   Show that confluence is not even decidable if all function symbols are unary. (*Hint:* the above proof almost works, but a is not unary.)

6.2   A TRS over a signature Σ is called **ground confluent** iff it is confluent for all ground terms: $\forall s, t_1, t_2 \in T(\Sigma). \ s \xrightarrow{*} t_1 \wedge s \xrightarrow{*} t_2 \Rightarrow t_1 \downarrow t_2$. Show that every ground TRS is confluent iff it is ground confluent.

6.2 Critical pairs

In this section we show that local confluence is decidable for terminating finite term rewriting systems. Using Newman's Lemma, which says that a terminating reduction is confluent iff it is locally confluent, we obtain as a corollary that confluence is also decidable for such systems.

We can view the study of confluence as a study of nondeterminism. Term rewriting is inherently nondeterministic because a term may contain more than one redex. Nevertheless, the result of normalizing a term w.r.t. a TRS may still be uniquely determined, provided the multiple redexes do not interfere with each other, i.e. if the contraction of one redex does not destroy the others. For example, given $R = \{f(x) \to f'(x),\ g(x) \to g'(x)\}$, the term $f(g(x))$ has a unique normal form, although there are two paths by which it can be reached. In fact, R is confluent. On the other hand, $R = \{f(g(x)) \to r_1,\ g(h(x)) \to r_2\}$ gives rise to interference: $f(g(h(x)))$ rewrites to both $\{x \mapsto h(x)\}(r_1)$ and $f(r_2)$, and it depends very much on the exact form of r_1 and r_2 whether this fork can be joined again.

Let us now look at the general situation when trying to obtain local confluence:

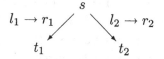

There are rules $l_i \to r_i \in R$, positions $p_i \in \mathcal{P}os(s)$ and substitutions σ_i, such that $s|_{p_i} = \sigma_i l_i$ and $t_i = s[\sigma_i r_i]_{p_i}$, $i = 1, 2$. Now we distinguish several cases, depending on the position of p_1 and p_2 relative to each other.

Case 1. p_1 and p_2 are in separate subtrees, i.e. $p_1 \| p_2$. In this case Fig. 6.1 shows that local confluence always holds.

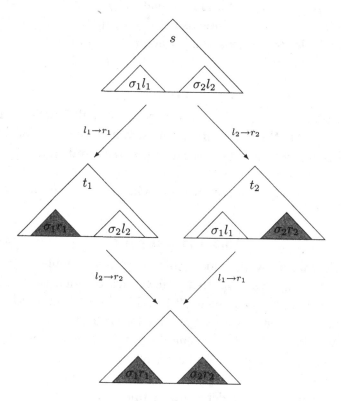

Fig. 6.1. Case 1: no overlap.

Case 2. p_1 is a prefix of p_2, i.e. $p_2 = p_1p$ for some p which could be empty. (The case $p_1 = p_2p$ is dual.) Then s has the following form:

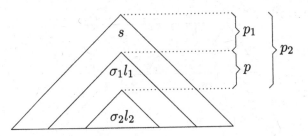

We can now restrict our attention to the subterm $s|_{p_1} = \sigma_1 l_1$ because

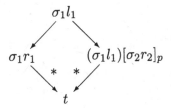

implies $t_1 = s[\sigma_1 r_1]_{p_1} \overset{*}{\to} s[t]_{p_1} \overset{*}{\leftarrow} s[(\sigma_1 l_1)[\sigma_2 r_2]_p]_{p_1} = s[\sigma_2 r_2]_{p_2} = t_2$ by compatibility of $\to$ with the context $s[.]_{p_1}$.

Now we must distinguish how far apart the two redexes are.

Case 2.1. The redex $\sigma_2 l_2$ does not overlap with l_1 itself but is contained in σ_1, i.e. $p = q_1 q_2$ such that q_1 is a variable position of l_1. Then $\sigma_1 l_1$ has the following form:

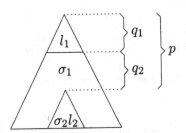

We call this a **non-critical overlap** of two redexes. Local confluence holds in this situation as well, but the analysis is complicated by the fact that $x := l_1|_{q_1}$ can occur repeatedly in both l_1 and r_1. Fig. 6.2 shows how local confluence is achieved in a prototypical situation where x occurs three times in l_1 and twice in r_1. In general, the rule $l_2 \to r_2$ needs to be applied n times to t_1 and $m-1$ times to t_2, where x occurs m times in l_1 and n times in r_1.

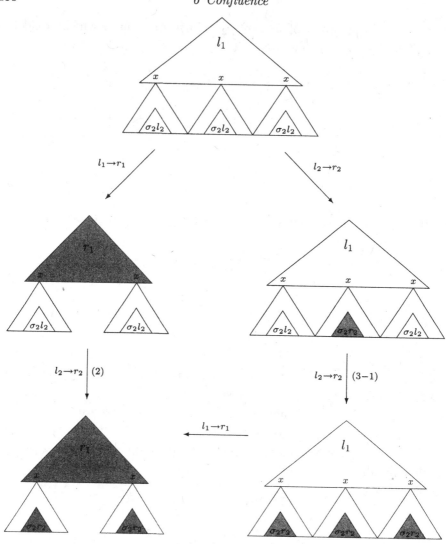

Fig. 6.2. Case 2.1: non-critical overlap.

Case 2.2. The two left-hand sides l_1 and l_2 overlap, i.e. $p \in \mathcal{P}os(l_1)$, $l_1|_p$ is not a variable, and $\sigma_1(l_1|_p) = \sigma_2 l_2$. Then $\sigma_1 l_1$ has the following form:

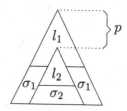

This is called a **critical overlap** of two redexes. We will now show that this situation is an instance of a so-called *critical pair*. Informally, a critical pair is the result of unifying the lhs of one rule with a non-variable subterm of the lhs of another (or possibly the same) rule, and reducing the resulting term using both rules.

We interrupt our analysis of Case 2.2 for the formal definition of critical pairs.

Definition 6.2.1 Let $l_i \to r_i$, $i = 1, 2$, be two rules whose variables have been renamed such that $Var(l_1, r_1) \cap Var(l_2, r_2) = \emptyset$. Let $p \in Pos(l_1)$ be such that $l_1|_p$ is not a variable and let θ be an mgu of $l_1|_p =^? l_2$. This determines a **critical pair** $\langle \theta r_1, (\theta l_1)[\theta r_2]_p \rangle$:

$$\theta l_1$$

$$\theta r_1 \qquad\qquad (\theta l_1)[\theta r_2]_p$$

If two rules give rise to a critical pair, we say that they **overlap**.

The critical pairs of a TRS R are the critical pairs between any two of its (renamed) rules and are denoted by $CP(R)$. This includes overlaps of a rule with a renamed variant of itself, except at the root, i.e. if $p = \epsilon$. In the latter case the overlap is of the form $r \leftarrow l \to r$ and can be ignored safely.

Note that by definition $u_1 \approx_R u_2$ for any critical pair $\langle u_1, u_2 \rangle$ of R: critical pairs of R are equational consequences of R.

Example 6.2.2 Consider the rules

$$(1) \quad f(f(x, y), z) \quad \to \quad f(x, f(y, z)),$$
$$(2) \quad f(i(x_1), x_1) \quad \to \quad e,$$

which give rise to a critical pair by unifying the non-variable subterm $f(x, y)$ of the lhs of rule (1) and the lhs $f(i(x_1), x_1)$ of rule (2). An mgu is $\{x \mapsto i(x_1), y \mapsto x_1\}$ and the corresponding fork is

$$f(f(i(x_1), x_1), z)$$

$$f(i(x_1), f(x_1, z)) \qquad\qquad f(e, z)$$

Let us now return to our analysis of Case 2.2 and our claim that it is an instance of a critical pair. To simplify technicalities, we assume that the two rules have been renamed such that they use disjoint sets of variables, i.e. $Var(l_1, r_1) \cap Var(l_2, r_2) = \emptyset$. This does not change the induced rewrite relation, but it means that we can assume $Dom(\sigma_1)$ and $Dom(\sigma_2)$ are disjoint and hence that $\sigma := \sigma_1 \cup \sigma_2$ is well-defined. But now we find that

$\sigma(l_1|_p) = \sigma_1(l_1|_p) = \sigma_2 l_2 = \sigma l_2$, i.e. σ is a unifier of $l_1|_p$ and l_2. Thus σ is an instance of every mgu θ of $l_1|_p$ and l_2, which in turn means that the pair $\langle \sigma_1 r_1, (\sigma_1 l_1)[\sigma_2 r_2]_p \rangle = \langle \sigma r_1, (\sigma l_1)[\sigma r_2]_p \rangle$ is an instance of the critical pair $\langle \theta r_1, (\theta l_1)[\theta r_2]_p \rangle$. The case $p = \epsilon$ and $\rho(l_1 \to r_1) = (l_2 \to r_2)$ for some renaming ρ does not count as a critical pair but it means that $\sigma_1 x = \sigma_2 \rho x$ holds for all $x \in Var(l_1) \supseteq Var(r_1)$ and hence $t_1 = \sigma_1 r_1 = \sigma_2 \rho r_1 = \sigma_2 r_2 = t_2$.

This concludes Case 2.2. Calling p_1 p (because Case 2 is symmetric in p_1 and p_2, and we only picked out the case $p_1 \leq p_2$) we can summarize our analysis as follows:

Lemma 6.2.3 *If $s \to_R t_i$, $i = 1, 2$, then $t_1 \downarrow_R t_2$ or $t_i = s[u_i]_p$, $i = 1, 2$, where $\langle u_1, u_2 \rangle$ or $\langle u_2, u_1 \rangle$ is an instance of a critical pair of R.*

This is called the **Critical Pair Lemma** and brings us to the **Critical Pair Theorem**:

Theorem 6.2.4 *A TRS is locally confluent iff all its critical pairs are joinable.*

Proof The $\Leftarrow$-direction follows directly from the Critical Pair Lemma: given $t_i = s[u_i]_p$, $i = 1, 2$, where (w.l.o.g.) $\langle u_1, u_2 \rangle$ is an instance of some critical pair $\langle v_1, v_2 \rangle$, i.e. $u_i = \delta v_i$, then $v_i \xrightarrow{*} t$ for some term t implies $u_i \xrightarrow{*} \delta t$ and hence also $t_i \xrightarrow{*} s[\delta t]_p$, $i = 1, 2$. The $\Rightarrow$-direction is a consequence of the fact that every critical pair is the product of a fork $\theta r_1 \leftarrow \theta l_1 \to (\theta l_1)[\theta r_2]_p$. Hence joinability follows from local confluence. □

Using Newman's Lemma we immediately obtain

Corollary 6.2.5 *A terminating TRS is confluent iff all its critical pairs are joinable.*

Because a finite TRS has only finitely many critical pairs, this yields

Corollary 6.2.6 *Confluence of a finite and terminating TRS R is decidable.*

Proof For every pair of rules $l_1 \to r_1$ and $l_2 \to r_2$ (there are $|R|^2$ of them) and for every $p \in \mathcal{P}os(l_1)$ such that $l_1|_p$ is not a variable (there are at most $|l_1|$ of them) try to generate a critical pair by unifying variable-disjoint variants of $l_1|_p$ and l_2. For each of these finitely many critical pairs $\langle u_1, u_2 \rangle$ reduce u_i to some R-normal form $\hat{u}_i$, $i = 1, 2$. We claim that R is confluent iff $\hat{u}_1 = \hat{u}_2$ for all critical pairs. If always $\hat{u}_1 = \hat{u}_2$ then all critical pairs are joinable and hence R is confluent by Corollary 6.2.5. On the other hand, if there is some critical pair with $\hat{u}_1 \neq \hat{u}_2$ then the definition of a critical pair implies the following non-confluent situation: $\hat{u}_1 \xleftarrow{*} u_1 \leftarrow u \to u_2 \xrightarrow{*} \hat{u}_2$. □

Example 6.2.7 Consider the one-rule TRS $R := \{f(f(x)) \to g(x)\}$ which has exactly one critical pair as a result of overlapping the rule with a renamed variant $f(f(y)) \to g(y)$ of itself. The lhs $f(f(x))$ unifies with the subterm $f(y)$ of the renamed lhs producing the mgu $\{y \mapsto f(x)\}$. Thus we obtain the critical pair

$$f(f(f(x)))$$

$$g(f(x)) \qquad\qquad f(g(x))$$

Clearly R is not confluent because the critical pair is already in normal form and hence not joinable.

This example demonstrates the necessity for two conditions in the definition of the critical pairs of a TRS:

- Rules need to be renamed. In the example, $f(f(x))$ and $f(x)$ are not unifiable and would not give rise to a critical pair.
- The critical pairs between a rule and (a renamed copy of) itself need to be taken into account. Otherwise all one-rule systems would appear to be locally confluent, which is clearly not the case.

The example also demonstrates that critical pairs can be helpful lemmas: $g(f(x)) \approx_R f(g(x))$ is an interesting consequence of $f(f(x)) \to_R g(x)$ which may not be apparent at first sight. Even more, we can turn R into a convergent system R' by adding the rule $f(g(x)) \to g(f(x))$. Termination of R' can be shown with the lexicographic path order induced by $f > g$. Confluence follows because R' has only one additional critical pair $g(g(x)) \leftarrow_{R'} f(f(g(x))) \to_{R'} f(g(f(x)))$ which is easily seen to be joinable: $f(g(f(x))) \to_{R'} g(f(f(x))) \to_{R'} g(g(x))$.

Because critical pairs are equational consequences, adding a critical pair as a new rewrite rule does not change the induced equality, i.e. $\approx_R = \approx_{R'}$. This idea of adding critical pairs as new rewrite rules is known as "completion" and is the subject of Chapter 7.

Exercises

6.3   Find r_1 and r_2 such that $\{f(g(x)) \to r_1, \; g(h(x)) \to r_2\}$ is confluent.

6.4   Is $R := \{f(g(f(x))) \to g(x)\}$ confluent? Find a convergent R' such that $\approx_R = \approx_{R'}$.

6.5   Compute all critical pairs for each of the following systems:

     (a) $f(g(f(x))) \;\to\; x, \qquad f(g(x)) \;\to\; g(f(x));$

(b) $\quad 0 + y \quad \rightarrow \quad y, \qquad s(x) + y \quad \rightarrow \quad s(x+y),$
$\qquad\quad x + 0 \quad \rightarrow \quad x, \qquad x + s(y) \quad \rightarrow \quad s(x+y);$

(c) $\quad f(x,x) \quad \rightarrow \quad a, \qquad f(x, g(x)) \quad \rightarrow \quad b;$

(d) $\quad f(f(x,y),z) \quad \rightarrow \quad f(x, f(y,z)), \qquad f(x,1) \quad \rightarrow \quad x;$

(e) $\quad f(f(x,y),z) \quad \rightarrow \quad f(x, f(y,z)), \qquad f(1,x) \quad \rightarrow \quad x;$

(f) $\qquad\qquad f(x, f(y,z)) \quad \rightarrow \quad f(f(x,y), f(x,z)),$
$\qquad\qquad f(f(x,y),z) \quad \rightarrow \quad f(f(x,z), f(y,z)),$
$\qquad f(f(x,y), f(y,z)) \quad \rightarrow \quad y.$

Which systems are locally confluent? Which ones are convergent?

6.6 Show that the following system is convergent:

$$f(f(x)) \quad \rightarrow \quad f(x), \qquad f(g(x)) \quad \rightarrow \quad g(x),$$
$$g(g(x)) \quad \rightarrow \quad f(x), \qquad g(f(x)) \quad \rightarrow \quad g(x).$$

Can you determine the normal form of a term as a function of the numbers of fs and gs in it?

6.7 Call R **left-reduced** if for all $(l \rightarrow r) \in R$, l is in normal form w.r.t. $R - \{l \rightarrow r\}$.

(a) Show that every left-reduced and terminating ground TRS is confluent.

(b) Let G be a finite set of ground identities over Σ and let $>$ be a reduction order which is total on ground terms over Σ. Describe an algorithm which turns E into a finite left-reduced TRS R such that $\approx_R = \approx_E$ and $R \subseteq >$.

(c) Conclude from the above that the word problem is decidable for a finite set of ground identities.

6.8 Our proof of local confluence in Case 2.1 relies entirely on pictures. For an algebraic proof define the substitution σ_1' by $\sigma_1' x := (\sigma_1 x)[\sigma_2 r_2]_{q_2}$ and $\sigma_1' y := \sigma_1 y$ for all $y \neq x$. Using the lemma below (which you should also prove) show formally that $\sigma_1 r_1 \overset{*}{\rightarrow} \sigma_1' r_1 \overset{*}{\leftarrow} (\sigma_1 l_1)[\sigma_2 l_2]_{q_1}$.

Lemma *Let x be some fixed variable and let σ and σ' be substitutions such that $\sigma x \rightarrow \sigma' x$ and $\sigma y = \sigma' y$ for all $y \neq x$. If $\{o_1, \ldots, o_n\}$ is the set of positions in some term t such that $t|_{o_i} = x$, then $t_i \overset{n-i}{\rightarrow} \sigma' t$, where $t_0 := \sigma t$ and $t_{i+1} := t_i[\sigma' x]_{o_i}$.*

6.9 What is the difficulty if you try to put a complexity bound in terms of the size of R on the running time of the decision procedure outlined in the proof of Corollary 6.2.6?

6.10 Consider the system $\{f(x) \rightarrow g(x,y)\}$. Does it have any critical pairs? Is the induced rewrite relation confluent? What is going wrong here?

Critical pairs in ML

We start with the mundane issue of renaming terms. Because the datatype *term* (see Section 4.7) provides indexed variables (type *vname*), renaming can be reduced to incrementing indices:

```
(* rename: int -> term -> term *)
fun rename n (V(x,i))  = V(x,i+n)
  | rename n (T(f,ts)) = T(f, map (rename n) ts);
```

Renaming a term t away from a term u is now simply a matter of incrementing t's indices beyond those of u. Thus we need to compute the maximum index in a term. To simplify matters we make the reasonable assumption that all variables have non-negative indices. This justifies the base case of *maxs*, which computes the maximum of a list of natural numbers:

```
fun max(i,j:int) = if i > j then i else j;
```

```
(* maxs: int list -> int *)
fun maxs (i::is) = max(i, maxs is)
  | maxs []      = 0;
```

```
(* maxindex: term -> int *)
fun maxindex (V(x,i))  = i
  | maxindex (T(_,ts)) = maxs(map maxindex ts);
```

Now we can turn to the actual computation of critical pairs shown in Fig. 6.3. Remember that term rewriting systems are implemented as lists of term pairs. The main functions are easily characterized:

CriticalPairs R computes a list of all critical pairs of R (including the trivial ones obtained by overlapping a rule with itself at the root).

CriticalPairs2 R_1 R_2 computes a list of all critical pairs formed by unifying a lhs of R_1 with a subterm of a lhs of R_2.

CPs R (l,r) computes a list of all critical pairs formed by unifying a lhs of R with a subterm of l.

The core of the computation takes place in *CPs R (l,r)*. It traverses l (by means of *cps* and *innercps*) and tries to unify (in *CP*) each subterm with all left-hand sides of R. In order to keep track of the context while descending into l, the context is implemented as a function which performs subterm replacement: the context at position p of l is a function C of type *term -> term* such that $C(s) = l[s]_p$ for all terms s. If in addition $t = l|_p$ then we can specify the functions *CP*, *cps* and *innercps* as follows:

CP C (t,r) (l_2,r_2) computes individual critical pairs. It returns the singleton list $[(\sigma r, \sigma(l[r_2]_p))]$ if σ is an mgu of $l|_p =^? l_2$, and returns $[]$ if $l|_p =^? l_2$ has no solution. Note that $\langle \sigma r, \sigma(l[r_2]_p) \rangle$ is the desired critical pair because $\sigma(l[r_2]_p) = (\sigma l)[\sigma r_2]_p$.

```
(* CP: (term -> term) -> term * term -> term * term -> (term * term) list *)
fun CP C (t,r) (l2,r2) = let val sigma = lift(unify(t,l2))
                         in [(sigma r, sigma(C r2))] end
                         handle UNIFY => [];

(* CPs: (term * term) list -> term * term -> (term * term) list *)
fun CPs R (l,r) =

    let fun cps C (V _, _) = []
          | cps C (T(f,ts),r) =
                concat(map (CP C (T(f,ts),r)) R) @ (innercps C (f,[],ts,r))

        and innercps _ (_, _, [], _) = []
          | innercps C (f, ts0, t::ts1, r) =
                let fun Cf s = C(T(f, ts0 @ [s] @ ts1))
                in (cps Cf (t,r)) @ (innercps C (f, ts0 @ [t], ts1, r)) end

        val m = maxs(map (fn (l,r) => max(maxindex l, maxindex r)) R) + 1

    in cps (fn t => t) (rename m l, rename m r) end;

fun CriticalPairs2 R1 R2 = concat(map (CPs R1) R2);

fun CriticalPairs R = CriticalPairs2 R R;
```

Fig. 6.3. Computing Critical Pairs in ML.

cps C (t,r) returns a list of all critical pairs formed by unifying a lhs of R with some non-variable subterm of $l|_p$.

cps C $(f, [t_1, \ldots, t_{i-1}], [t_i, \ldots t_n], r)$, where $l|_p = f(t_1, \ldots, t_n)$, returns a list of all critical pairs formed by unifying a lhs of R with some non-variable subterm of $l|_{pi}$.

Looking at the initial call of *cps*, it is easy to verify that $C(s) = l[s]_p$ and $t = l_p$ trivially hold because C is the identity, i.e. the empty context, and thus $p = \epsilon$.

Of course *CPs* renames (l,r) first by incrementing its indices by m, the maximum index in R plus 1. Thus the indices in the renamed rule and R are disjoint.

Exercise

6.11   The functional implementation of contexts comes with certain performance penalties which can be avoided by the representation

```
type context = (string * term list * term list) list;

(* replace: context -> term -> term *)
fun replace [] t = t
  | replace ((f,ts,us)::Cs) t = replace Cs (T(f, ts @ [t] @ us));
```

Convert the computation of critical pairs to use *context* and *replace*.

6.3 Orthogonality

How do we determine confluence of nonterminating systems? Because confluence is undecidable in general but decidable for terminating systems, it cannot be decidable for nonterminating ones as well. Hence all we can hope for are sufficient conditions which cover large classes of nonterminating systems. These classes will be defined by restrictions both on the rules and on the way in which critical pairs must be joinable.

Definition 6.3.1 A rewrite rule $l \to r$ is called **left-linear** (resp. **right-linear**) if no variable occurs twice in l (resp. r); it is called **linear** if it is both left- and right-linear. A TRS is called left-linear (resp. right-linear, resp. linear) if all of its rules are left-linear (resp. right-linear, resp. linear).

Since our analysis of forks in the proof of the Critical Pair Lemma is independent of termination, we can reuse it in the current section, which does not assume termination. Hence we keep on referring to the cases 1, 2.1 and 2.2 distinguished there. Linearity restrictions will help to simplify case 2.1.

Linearity by itself is not enough to guarantee confluence. Hence we also need to restrict the kinds of critical pairs that may arise. We start with a simple restriction related to strong confluence.

Definition 6.3.2 Two terms s_1 and s_2 are called **strongly joinable** (w.r.t. $\to$) if there are terms t_1 and t_2 such that $s_1 \xrightarrow{=} t_1 \xleftarrow{*} s_2$ and $s_1 \xrightarrow{*} t_2 \xleftarrow{=} s_2$.

This brings us to the **Strong Confluence Lemma**:

Lemma 6.3.3 *If R is linear and every critical pair of R is strongly joinable, then R is strongly confluent.*

Proof Let us follow the redex analysis in the proof of the Critical Pair Lemma.

Case 1 is unchanged and we obtain not just strong confluence but even the diamond property.

Case 2.1 is simplified by the linearity restriction. The diagram, which is an instance of strong confluence, is shown in Fig. 6.4. Note that $l_1 \to r_1$ erases x (and the subterm below it) if $x \notin \mathcal{V}ar(r_1)$, which explains the lower left $\xrightarrow{=}$.

Case 2.2, the instance of a critical pair, is strongly joinable because all critical pairs are strongly joinable, which their instances inherit.   □

Since any strongly confluent relation is confluent (Lemma 2.7.4) we have in fact proved that if R is linear and every critical pair of R is strongly joinable, then R is confluent.

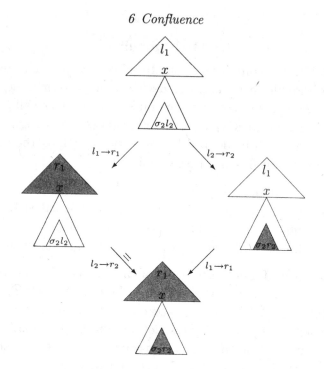

Fig. 6.4. Case 2.1 for linear term rewriting systems.

Example 6.3.4 The following TRS is linear and nonterminating

$$s(x) + y \;\to\; s(x+y),$$
$$x + s(y) \;\to\; s(x+y),$$
$$x + y \;\to\; y + x,$$

and its three critical pairs (of which we show two) are strongly joinable:

$$
\begin{array}{ccc}
 & s(s(x)+y) & \\
 \nearrow & \downarrow & \\
s(x)+s(y) & s(s(x+y)) & \\
 \searrow & \uparrow & \\
 & s(x+s(y)) &
\end{array}
\qquad
\begin{array}{ccc}
 & s(x+y) & \\
 \nearrow & \downarrow & \\
s(x)+y & s(y+x) & \\
 \searrow & \uparrow & \\
 & y+s(x) &
\end{array}
$$

Unfortunately, the applicability of the Strong Confluence Lemma is limited by its requirement of right-linearity. As we indicated in the introduction to this chapter, (potentially) nonterminating TRS are functional programs, but right-linear functional programs are so cumbersome as to be practically useless. Neither can we simply drop right-linearity, as the following example shows:

Example 6.3.5 (J.J. Lévy) All critical pairs of the following left-linear TRS are strongly joinable:

$$
\begin{array}{rclcrcl}
f(a,a) & \to & g(b,b), & \qquad & g(b,b) & \to & f(a,a), \\
a & \to & a', & & b & \to & b', \\
f(a',x) & \to & f(x,x), & & g(b',x) & \to & g(x,x), \\
f(x,a') & \to & f(x,x), & & g(x,b') & \to & g(x,x);
\end{array}
$$

but it is not confluent:

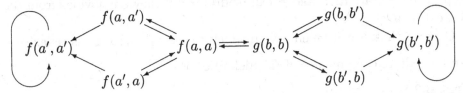

Left-linearity is equally essential, as Example 6.3.12 below demonstrates.

However, we can trade right-linearity for a further restriction on the critical pairs. We first show that left-linearity suffices, if there are no critical pairs, and later strengthen this result by allowing critical pairs to be joined in a special way. Although the latter result is more general, the proof of the weaker version exhibits the underlying principles more clearly.

Definition 6.3.6 A TRS is called **orthogonal** if it is left-linear and has no critical pairs.

A naive confluence proof for orthogonal systems runs into the following problem: the lack of right-linearity means that joining the fork in Case 2.1 may need more than one application of $l_2 \to r_2$, and hence all we can deduce is local confluence. The key idea now is to use a different rewrite relation which not only is confluent but even has the diamond property. The latter is advantageous because we only need to analyse one-step forks and yet obtain confluence instead of just local confluence.

Looking at Case 2.1 we see that the remaining obstacle on the road to the diamond property is the repeated reduction $l_2 \to r_2$ in parallel subtrees. Linearity is a rather drastic restriction and only achieves strong confluence. A more ingenious idea is to consider parallel reduction of redexes in separate subtrees as suggested by the following picture:

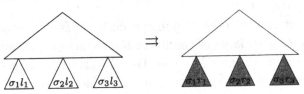

Definition 6.3.7 We say that a set of positions is **parallel** if $p \| q$ or $p = q$ for all $p, q \in P$. Let $P = \{p_1, \ldots, p_n\} \subseteq \mathcal{P}os(s)$ be a set of parallel positions. Given a term t_p for each $p \in P$, we define the notation

$$s[t_p]_{p \in P} := s[t_{p_1}]_{p_1} \cdots [t_{p_n}]_{p_n}.$$

Because the p_i are parallel to each other, their order is irrelevant.

If for each $p \in P$ we are given a rule $l_p \to r_p \in R$ and a substitution σ_p such that $s|_p = \sigma_p l_p$, we write $s \Rrightarrow^P_R s[\sigma_p r_p]_{p \in P}$ and call it a **parallel reduction** step. The decorations P and R can be dropped if they are obvious from the context or irrelevant.

Observe that P can be empty, in which case $s \Rrightarrow^P s$, i.e. $\Rrightarrow$ is reflexive.

An immediate consequence of this definition is

Fact 6.3.8 $\to \subseteq \Rrightarrow \subseteq \xrightarrow{*}$.

The proof of the following easy lemma is left as an exercise:

Lemma 6.3.9 *If R has no critical pairs then $s \to^p_R t_1$ and $s \to^p_R t_2$ imply $t_1 = t_2$.*

And now, the main theorem about orthogonal systems:

Theorem 6.3.10 *If R is orthogonal then $\Rrightarrow_R$ has the diamond property.*

In the sequel, we frequently use a little coding trick: the mapping $i \mapsto 1 - i$ swaps 0 and 1: $1 - 0 = 1$ and $1 - 1 = 0$.

Proof Assume $s \Rrightarrow^{P_i} t_i$, $i = 0, 1$. We partition P_i into $A_i \cup B_i \cup C$ where

$$
\begin{aligned}
A_i &:= \{p \in P_i \mid \nexists q \in P_{1-i}.\ q \le p\}, \\
B_i &:= \{p \in P_i \mid \exists q \in P_{1-i}.\ q < p\}, \\
C &:= P_0 \cap P_1.
\end{aligned}
$$

Thus A_i contains those positions contracted in $s \Rrightarrow t_i$ that are not below some position contracted in $s \Rrightarrow t_{1-i}$, B_i contains those positions contracted in $s \Rrightarrow t_i$ that are strictly below some position contracted in $s \Rrightarrow t_{1-i}$, and C is the set of positions contracted in both steps. Fig. 6.5 traces the reduction of the different positions by looking at one example from each set.

The elements of C are unproblematic: from Lemma 6.3.9 it follows that $t_0|_c = t_1|_c$ for all $c \in C$.

Because there are no critical pairs, each $b_i \in B_i$ lies inside a subterm corresponding to a variable of the lhs of the reduction rule applied at a_{1-i}. The reduction $s \Rrightarrow t_{1-i}$ merely copies the subterm $s|_{b_i}$. This copying is the reason why we need parallel reductions to achieve the diamond property.

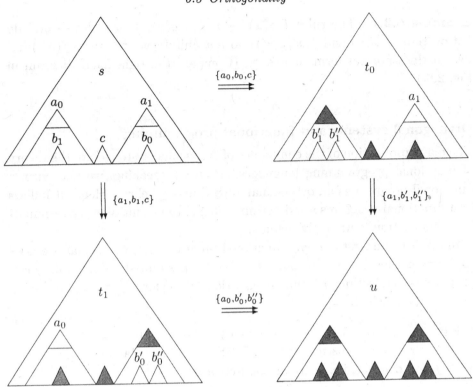

Fig. 6.5. The diamond property of orthogonal reductions.

The reduction $t_{1-i} \Rrightarrow u$ uses the same rules at copies of positions in B_i (called b'_i and b''_i in the figure) that are used at the original positions in B_i in the reduction $s \Rrightarrow t_i$.

A redex at position $a_i \in A_i$ cannot be destroyed by a reduction at some $b_{1-i} \in B_{1-i}$ because they do not overlap critically and because R is left-linear: otherwise the applicability of a rule with lhs $f(x, x)$ could be lost by a reduction in one of the arguments of f. Therefore the reduction $t_{1-i} \Rrightarrow u$ uses the same rules at positions in A_i as the reduction $s \Rrightarrow t_i$. □

The above pictorial argument is designed to convey the essential intuition. For a formal proof, see Section 6.4 below.

Because $\Rrightarrow$ is in between $\to$ and $\xrightarrow{*}$, and because the diamond property implies strong confluence, we can now use Corollary 2.7.7 to establish

Corollary 6.3.11 *Every orthogonal TRS is confluent.*

Note that left-linearity is essential:

Example 6.3.12 The rules $f(x,x) \to a$, $f(x,g(x)) \to b$ and $c \to g(c)$ do not overlap ($f(x,x)$ and $f(x',g(x'))$ do *not* unify!), yet the term $f(c,c)$ has two distinct normal forms a and b. (Compare the right-hand diagram in Fig. 2.6.)

Orthogonal systems and functional programming

The main application of the confluence of orthogonal systems is to the theory of functional programming languages. Roughly speaking, we may view a functional program as an orthogonal TRS (but see below). Hence it follows that functional programs are deterministic, i.e. the result of every terminating computation is uniquely defined.

In order to understand why functional programs are orthogonal, we need to consider their syntax in more detail. In the simplest case, a functional program is a collection of recursion equations of the form $f_i(x_1, \ldots, x_{k_i}) = t_i$, $i = 1, \ldots, n$, such that

- $Var(t_i) \subseteq \{x_1, \ldots, x_{k_i}\}$, i.e. the equations form a TRS,
- all $x_1, \ldots, x_{k_i}$ are distinct, i.e. the TRS is left-linear, and
- all f_i are distinct, i.e. there are no overlaps.

This is the syntax of languages like LISP. More recent languages like ML are more liberal and allow complex patterns on the lhs as well, with certain restrictions.

Definition 6.3.13 A TRS over a signature Σ is a **constructor TRS** if Σ can be partitioned into two sets of **constructors** Σ_c and **defined** functions Σ_d such that the lhs of every rule has the form $f(\overline{s_n})$ with $f \in \Sigma_d$ and $s_1, \ldots, s_n \in T(\Sigma_c, V)$.

For example, $\{f(0) \to r_0, \ f(s(x)) \to r_1\}$ is a constructor TRS, whereas $f(f(x)) \to r$ cannot be part of any constructor TRS.

Now we can describe an ML-like functional program as a left-linear constructor TRS where the (renamed) left-hand sides of two distinct rules do not unify. In a constructor TRS, the last requirement amounts to saying that no two rules overlap. Thus an ML-like functional program is an orthogonal constructor TRS.

The constructor aspect has nothing to do with confluence. It simply means that critical pairs can only arise as root overlaps. Orthogonality, however, is almost forced upon us if the language is to be deterministic. Hence one has to be very careful if one tampers with orthogonality: even dropping left-linearity is not advisable (see Example 6.3.12 above).

Unfortunately, functional programming and term rewriting are further apart than we pretended above. There are many differences, both minor (e.g. in a functional program, clauses may overlap because the order of clauses ensures that only one of them matches a given term) and major (functional programs allow higher-order functions and partial application), which can be resolved only at the expense of complicating matters considerably. A rigorous treatment of functional programs is beyond the scope of this book but our techniques, if not our results, carry over to that area.

Exercises

6.12 Can you use the Strong Confluence Lemma as the basis of a decision procedure for confluence of linear term rewriting systems?

6.13 Is the following TRS confluent?

$$
\begin{aligned}
h(f(x,y)) &\rightarrow f(h(r(x)),y), \\
f(x,k(y,z)) &\rightarrow g(p(y),q(z,x)), \\
h(q(x,y)) &\rightarrow q(x,h(r(y))), \\
q(x,h(r(y))) &\rightarrow h(q(x,y)), \\
h(g(x,y)) &\rightarrow g(x,h(y)).
\end{aligned}
$$

6.14 Show that the rewrite rules of combinatory logic (Example 4.1.3) are confluent.

6.15 Prove Lemma 6.3.9.

6.16 Is $\{f(x,x) \rightarrow a, \ c \rightarrow g(c), \ g(x) \rightarrow f(x,g(x))\}$ a confluent TRS?

6.4 Beyond orthogonality

Although orthogonality captures the current state of functional programming languages, there is scope for extensions. The prototypical example is "parallel or":

$$
\begin{aligned}
or(true,x) &\rightarrow true, \\
or(x,true) &\rightarrow true.
\end{aligned}
$$

Most functional languages let you write the above two rules. What they implement, however, is the following orthogonal specialization:

$$
\begin{aligned}
or(true,x) &\rightarrow true, \\
or(false,true) &\rightarrow true.
\end{aligned}
$$

Consequently, the term $or(u, true)$, where u has no normal form, rewrites to *true* in the first system but has no normal form in the second one. (Of course the above rules are assumed to be part of a larger TRS/program which need not terminate as a whole. Therefore a critical pair analysis can only yield local confluence.) The reason for this transformation is performance: the first TRS requires quasi-parallel evaluation of the arguments of or, whereas the second one allows sequential evaluation. Going beyond orthogonality increases expressiveness but does not come for free.

This section can be seen either as an attempt to relax the orthogonality requirement imposed by functional programming languages without sacrificing their determinacy, or as a purely abstract study of confluence for nonterminating rewrite systems. It requires some subtle arguments which go beyond pictures. Hence we first develop the basis for formal proofs.

The following three propositions are obvious enough that we can leave it to the reader to draw the pictures corresponding to their proofs:

Lemma 6.4.1 *Let $P \subseteq \mathcal{P}os(s)$ be a set of parallel positions. If $s_p \rightrightarrows t_p$ for all $p \in P$, then $s[s_p]_{p \in P} \rightrightarrows s[t_p]_{p \in P}$.*

Lemma 6.4.2 *If $\sigma x \rightrightarrows \sigma' x$ for all $x \in Var(s)$, then $\sigma s \rightrightarrows \sigma' s$.*

Lemma 6.4.3 *If $s \rightrightarrows^P t$ and $\forall p \in P \, \exists a \in A. \, a \leq p$, then $t = s[t|_a]_{a \in A}$.*

At the heart of many proofs about orthogonal systems we have the so-called **Parallel Moves Lemma**:

Lemma 6.4.4 *Let R be a TRS and $l \rightarrow r \in R$ a left-linear rule. If $\sigma l \rightrightarrows_R^P t$ and all elements of P are below some variable position of l, then there exists a substitution σ' such that $\sigma r \rightrightarrows_R \sigma' r \leftarrow_R t$.*

Proof For every $x \in Var(l)$ there is a unique (because l is linear) $q_x \in \mathcal{P}os(l)$ such that $l|_{q_x} = x$. Let P_x be the redex positions below q_x: $P_x := \{p \in \mathcal{P}os(\sigma x) \mid q_x p \in P\}$. Thus, for each $p \in P_x$ there are a rule $l_p \rightarrow r_p \in R$ and a substitution σ_p such that $(\sigma x)|_p = \sigma_p l_p$. Now define the substitution σ' by $\sigma' x := (\sigma x)[\sigma_p r_p]_{p \in P_x}$ for every $x \in Var(l)$. By definition we have $\sigma x \rightrightarrows \sigma' x$. Therefore Lemma 6.4.2 yields $\sigma r \rightrightarrows \sigma' r$. It is easy to see that because l is linear, t can be written as $\sigma' l$. Thus it also follows that $t \rightarrow \sigma' r$. The whole construction is shown in Fig. 6.6. $\qquad\qquad\square$

We can now give a formal proof that for orthogonal systems $\rightrightarrows$ has the diamond property (Theorem 6.3.10 above). Suppose $s \rightrightarrows^{P_i} t_i$, $i = 0, 1$, define A_i and C as in the proof of Theorem 6.3.10, and let $A := A_0 \cup A_1$. By Lemma 6.4.3 we can write t_i as $s[t_i|_p]_{p \in A \cup C}$. Hence it suffices to construct, for each $p \in A \cup C$, a term u_p such that $t_i|_p \rightrightarrows u_p$ because Lemma 6.4.1 then implies $t_i \rightrightarrows s[u_p]_{p \in A \cup C}$. If $p \in C$, Lemma 6.3.9 implies $t_0|_p = t_1|_p$ and hence we set $u_p := t_i|_p$. If $p \in A$, we assume w.l.o.g. $p \in P_1$. Hence there are a rule $l \rightarrow r$ and a substitution σ such that $s|_p = \sigma l$ and $t_1|_p = \sigma r$. Define

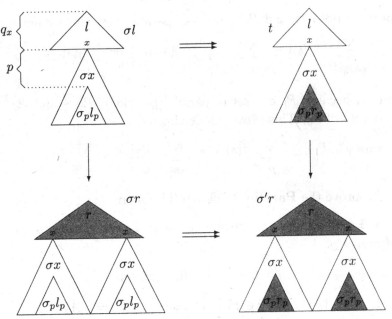

Fig. 6.6. Parallel Moves Lemma.

$B_p := \{q \mid pq \in P_0\}$. Hence $s|_p \Rrightarrow^{B_p} t_0|_p$. Because there are no critical pairs, each $q \in B_p$ must be below some variable position of l. Therefore the Parallel Moves Lemma implies that there exists a substitution σ' such that $t_1|_p \Rrightarrow \sigma'r \leftarrow t_0|_p$ and we set $u_p := \sigma'r$.

However, we can do better:

Definition 6.4.5 A TRS is called **parallel closed** if $u_2 \Rrightarrow u_1$ for all critical pairs $\langle u_1, u_2 \rangle$.

Note the asymmetry in this definition: critical pairs are ordered. The proof below that left-linear parallel closed systems are confluent relies on the fixed direction $u_2 \Rrightarrow u_1$. It is greatly facilitated by the following notation.

Definition 6.4.6 Let P and Q be sets of positions and $\lessgtr$ some relation on positions. Then we define $P^{\lessgtr Q} := \{p \in P \mid \exists q \in Q. \ p \lessgtr q\}$.

The complexity of a fork $s \Rrightarrow^{P_i} t_i$, $i = 0, 1$, can be measured by the amount of overlap between the redexes in P_0 and P_1:

$$m(s, P_0, P_1) \quad := \sum_{b \in P_0^{\geq P_1}} |(s|_b)| + \sum_{b \in P_1^{\geq P_0}} |(s|_b)|.$$

Lemma 6.4.7 $\qquad m(s, P_0, P_1) \leq \sum_{p \in P_0} |(s|_p)|.$

Proof Because both P_0 and P_1 are sets of parallel positions we have

$$\sum_{b \in P_1^{\geq P_0}} |(s|_b)| = \sum_{a \in P_0^{\leq P_1}} \sum_{b \in P_1^{\geq \{a\}}} |(s|_b)| \leq \sum_{a \in P_0^{\leq P_1}} |(s|_a)|.$$

Furthermore, because P_1 is a set of parallel positions, $P_0^{\leq P_1}$ and $P_0^{\geq P_1}$ are disjoint subsets of P_0. This proves the claim:

$$m(s, P_0, P_1) \leq \sum_{b \in P_0^{\geq P_1}} |(s|_b)| + \sum_{a \in P_0^{\leq P_1}} |(s|_a)| \leq \sum_{p \in P_0} |(s|_p)|. \qquad \square$$

Now we can prove the **Parallel Closure Theorem**:

Theorem 6.4.8 *If R is left-linear and parallel closed, then $\Rrightarrow_R$ has the diamond property.*

Proof Suppose $s \Rrightarrow^{P_i} t_i$, $i = 0, 1$, and define the sets

$$A_i := \{p \in P_i \mid \nexists q \in P_{1-i}.\ q < p\}, \qquad A := A_0 \cup A_1.$$

A is the set of redex positions not strictly below some other redex position.

By induction on $m(s, P_0, P_1)$ we now construct u such that $t_i \Rrightarrow u$.

By Lemma 6.4.3 we can write t_i as $s[t_i|_p]_{p \in A}$. Hence it suffices to construct, for each $p \in A$, a term u_p such that $t_i|_p \Rrightarrow u_p$ because Lemma 6.4.1 then implies $t_i \Rrightarrow s[u_p]_{p \in A} =: u$ as claimed above.

Suppose $p \in A$. Assume w.l.o.g. $p \in P_1$. Thus there are a rule $l \to r \in R$ and a substitution σ such that $s|_p = \sigma l$ and $t_1|_p = \sigma r$. Define $B_p := \{q \mid pq \in P_0\}$, the set of redex positions below p. We distinguish two cases.

Case 1. There is no critical overlap, i.e. all elements of B_p are below variable positions of l. Therefore the Parallel Moves Lemma implies there exists a substitution σ' such that $t_1|_p \Rrightarrow \sigma' r \leftarrow t_0|_p$ and we set $u_p := \sigma' r$.

Case 2. There is a critical overlap, i.e. some $q_0 \in B_p$, a rule $l_0 \to r_0 \in R$, and a substitution σ_0 such that

- $s|_{pq_0} = \sigma_0 l_0$ and $t_0|_{pq_0} = \sigma_0 r_0$,
- $q_0 \in Pos(l)$ and $l|_{q_0}$ is not a variable,
- there exist a critical pair $\langle u_1, u_2 \rangle$ (between $l \to r$ and $l_0 \to r_0$) and a substitution δ such that $t_1|_p = \delta u_1$ and $t := (s|_p)[\sigma_0 r_0]_{q_0} = \delta u_2$.

This situation is illustrated in Fig. 6.7. Because R is parallel closed, there is a set of positions Q_1 such that $u_2 \Rrightarrow^{Q_1} u_1$. Because $\Rrightarrow$ is closed under substitution this implies $t \Rrightarrow^{Q_1} t_1|_p$. On the other hand we can also contract the remaining redex positions $Q_0 := B_p - \{q_0\}$: $t \Rrightarrow^{Q_0} t_0|_p$. Thus we have created a new fork $t \Rrightarrow^{Q_i} t_i|_p$. Lemma 6.4.7 tells us something about its

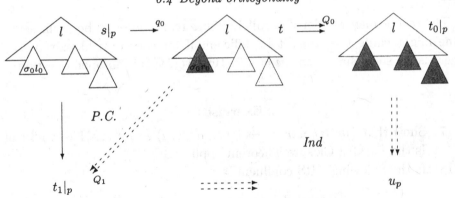

Fig. 6.7. Case 2.

complexity: $m(t, Q_0, Q_1) \leq \sum_{q \in Q_0} |(t|_q)| =: n$. Because $t|_q = s|_{pq}$ for all $q \in Q_0$, and because $pq \in P_0^{\geq P_1}$ for all $q \in B_p$, we conclude that

$$n = \sum_{q \in Q_0} |(s|_{pq})| < \sum_{q \in B_p} |(s|_{pq})| \leq \sum_{b \in P_0^{\geq P_1}} |(s|_b)| \leq m(s, P_0, P_1).$$

Because $m(t, Q_0, Q_1) < m(s, P_0, P_1)$ we can use the induction hypothesis that there exists a term u such that $t_i|_p \Rrightarrow u$. Now simply set $u_p := u$. $\qquad\square$

As in the case of orthogonal systems we can derive

Corollary 6.4.9 *Every left-linear parallel closed TRS is confluent.*

Example 6.4.10 Consider the following unusual reduction rules for propositional logic:

$$or(x, false) \rightarrow or(x, x),$$
$$or(false, y) \rightarrow or(y, y).$$

This system is left-linear and parallel closed because there is only one, trivial, critical pair $\langle or(false, false), or(false, false) \rangle$.

The example deserves a few remarks:

- Although the system is strongly joinable, it is not right-linear. Therefore we cannot apply the Strong Confluence Lemma.
- Left-linear systems where all critical pairs are trivial, i.e. of the form $\langle u, u \rangle$, are often called **weakly orthogonal**. Because weakly orthogonal systems are trivially parallel closed, it follows that they are confluent.
- Overlapping two rules at the root produces two symmetric critical pairs $\langle u_1, u_2 \rangle$ and $\langle u_2, u_1 \rangle$. Parallel closure requires both $u_2 \Rrightarrow u_1$ and $u_1 \Rrightarrow u_2$. Exercise 6.19 shows that this can be relaxed slightly.

The reader may wonder if parallel closure really needs to be asymmetric. One might conjecture that it is sufficient if for each critical pair $\langle u_1, u_2 \rangle$ there is a t such that $u_i \Rightarrow t$, $i = 1, 2$. However, this is an open question.

Exercises

6.17 Show that $\{or(true, true) \rightarrow true, \ or(x, y) \rightarrow or(y, x)\}$ is confluent. Is the Parallel Closure Theorem applicable?

6.18 Is the following TRS confluent?

$$
\begin{aligned}
f(g(x, a, b)) &\rightarrow x, & p(a) &\rightarrow c, \\
g(f(h(c, d)), x, y) &\rightarrow h(p(x), q(x)), & q(b) &\rightarrow d.
\end{aligned}
$$

6.19 The Parallel Closure Theorem can be generalized slightly by distinguishing root critical pairs, i.e. critical pairs of the form $\sigma r_1 \leftarrow \sigma l_1 = \sigma l_2 \rightarrow \sigma r_2$, from the remaining critical pairs.

(a) Prove the following theorem:

If R is left-linear, all root critical pairs are strongly joinable w.r.t. $\Rightarrow_R$, and $u_2 \Rightarrow_R u_1$ for all other critical pairs $\langle u_1, u_2 \rangle$ of R, then $\Rightarrow_R$ is strongly confluent.

(Hint: modify the proof of the Parallel Closure Theorem.)

(b) Show confluence of the TRS

$$
\begin{aligned}
or(true, x) &\rightarrow or(x, not(x)), \\
or(x, true) &\rightarrow or(not(x), x), \\
or(x, y) &\rightarrow or(y, x)
\end{aligned}
$$

and explain why the Parallel Closure Theorem does not apply.

6.20 Find a TRS R such that for every critical pair $\langle u_1, u_2 \rangle$ there is a term t with $u_i \Rightarrow_R t$, but $\Rightarrow_R$ does not have the diamond property.

6.21 Show that $\Rightarrow$ is strongly confluent iff $t_1 \leftarrow s \Rightarrow t_2 \Rightarrow \exists t. \ t_1 \Rightarrow t \stackrel{*}{\leftarrow} t_2$.

6.22 The Parallel Closure Theorem relies on an ingenious induction to reduce multiple overlaps to critical pairs. This induction can be avoided by using so-called parallel critical pairs. For example, the rules $f(a, b) \rightarrow c$, $a \rightarrow a'$ and $b \rightarrow b'$ give rise to the parallel critical pair $c \leftarrow f(a, b) \Rightarrow f(a', b')$, in addition to the ordinary critical pairs. Formally, a renamed rule $l \rightarrow r$, a set of parallel positions $P \subseteq Pos(l)$ such that $l|_p \notin Var(l)$ for all $p \in P$, a renamed rule $l_p \rightarrow r_p$ for each $p \in P$, and an mgu σ of the unification problem $\{l|_p =^? l_p \mid p \in P\}$ determine a **parallel critical pair** $\langle \sigma r, (\sigma l)[\sigma r_p]_{p \in P} \rangle$.

Show that $\Rightarrow_R$ is strongly confluent if R is left-linear and the following conditions hold:

(a) $(\sigma l_1)[\sigma r_2]_p \Rightarrow_R \cdot \overset{*}{\leftarrow}_R \sigma r_1$ for all critical pairs $\langle \sigma r_1, (\sigma l_1)[\sigma r_2]_p \rangle$ and

(b) $(\sigma l)[\sigma r_p]_{p \in P} \overset{*}{\to}_R \sigma r$ for all parallel critical pairs where $\epsilon \notin P$.

(*Hint:* combine Exercise 6.21 with an exhaustive case analysis.)

6.5 Bibliographic notes

Although confluence is undecidable in general, it is decidable for finite ground TRS. This was first shown by Dauchet and Tison using a special algorithm [67] and later generalized to a whole class of properties of finite ground TRS [68] and also to finite left-linear right-ground TRS [66].

The theory of critical pairs is due to Knuth and Bendix [145], who proved Corollaries 6.2.5 and 6.2.6. The definitive version of the theory is due to Huet [119], whose article is the basis for most of the material in this chapter. Huet's article extends the theory to confluence modulo an equational theory (see Section 11.1).

The study of (almost) orthogonal term rewriting systems started with Rosen [217] but was again generalized and put into its definitive form by Huet [119]. His Parallel Closure Theorem was later extended by Toyama [244, Corollary 3.2] (see Exercise 6.19) and van Oostrom [196]. An alternative and incomparable approach based on parallel critical pairs is due to Toyama [241]. Exercise 6.22 is based on the work of Gramlich [99] who rediscovered a slightly restricted version of Toyama's main theorem.

It is still an open problem whether certain modifications of parallel closure, e.g. replacing $u_2 \Rightarrow u_1$ by $u_1 \Rightarrow u_2$, also guarantee confluence [75, Problem 13].

7

Completion

This chapter is concerned with the question of how to construct a decision procedure for the word problem for a given finite set of identities E. Because the word problem is in general undecidable, any such method is necessarily incomplete, that is, it cannot succeed for all finite sets E. Theorem 4.1.1, which says that the word problem for E is decidable if $\rightarrow_E$ is convergent, suggests a first approach, which is, however, not very likely to succeed:

Show termination: Try to find a reduction order $>$ such that $s > t$ holds for all identities $(s \approx t) \in E$. If this succeeds, consider the term rewriting system $R := \{s \rightarrow t \mid (s \approx t) \in E\}$, and continue with this system in the next step; otherwise fail.

Show confluence: Decide confluence of the TRS R, which is known to be terminating, by computing all critical pairs between rules in R and testing whether they are joinable (see Corollary 6.2.6). If this step succeeds, the rewrite relation $\rightarrow_R$ yields a decision procedure for the word problem for E; otherwise fail.

Example 7.0.1 Let $E := \{x+0 \approx x,\ x+s(y) \approx s(x+y)\}$. In the first step, *termination* of the rewrite system $R := \{x + 0 \rightarrow x,\ x + s(y) \rightarrow s(x + y)\}$ can be shown using the lexicographic path order $>_{lpo}$ that is induced by a precedence order $>$ satisfying $+ > s$. *Confluence* of R follows because there are no critical pairs.

Consequently, R is canonical and can thus be used to decide the word problem for E. On the one hand, we can now deduce that, for example, $s(s(0)) + s(0) \approx_E s(0) + s(s(0))$ holds because these two terms reduce to the same normal form $s(s(s(0)))$ with respect to R. On the other hand, we can use R to show that a certain identity is not a consequence of E: for example, $x + y \approx_E y + x$ does not hold because the two terms are R-irreducible and distinct.

One reason for this simple method to fail is that some identity $s \approx t$ needs to be turned into $t \to s$ rather than $s \to t$. For example, $x \approx x + 0$ would yield a nonterminating rewrite rule $x \to x + 0$, whereas $x + 0 \to x$ is terminating. Thus, a more sensible first step would be one that tries to order the input identities in an appropriate way:

Show termination: Let $E = \{s_1 \approx t_1, \ldots, s_n \approx t_n\}$. Try to find a reduction order $>$ such that, for all $i, 1 \leq i \leq n$, there exist terms l_i, r_i satisfying $\{l_i, r_i\} = \{s_i, t_i\}$ and $l_i > r_i$. If this succeeds, consider the term rewriting system $R := \{l_1 \to r_1, \ldots, l_n \to r_n\}$ in the next step; otherwise fail.

Of course, this modified first step may still fail fairly often. This can be the case either because one of the identities is inherently nonterminating, such as the identity $x + y \approx y + x$, or because we do not succeed in finding an appropriate reduction order even though such an order exists (recall that the termination problem for term rewriting systems is not recursively enumerable).

Even if the first step is successful, the method might still fail because the resulting terminating rewrite system is not confluent.

Example 7.0.2 Let $E := \{x + 0 \approx x, \, x + s(y) \approx s(x + y)\}$ as in the previous example, but assume that in the first step we use the Knuth-Bendix order $>_{kbo}$ that is induced by a precedence order $>$ satisfying $s > +$, and a weight function w satisfying $w_0 = 1 = w(+) = w(s) = w(0)$. This yields the terminating rewrite system $R' := \{x + 0 \to x, \, s(x + y) \to x + s(y)\}$.

The left-hand side $x + 0$ of the first rule unifies with the subterm $u + v$ of the left-hand side of the renamed second rule $s(u + v) \to u + s(v)$ with mgu $\{u \mapsto x, v \mapsto 0\}$. This yields the critical pair $\langle x + s(0), s(x) \rangle$. The terms in this pair are R'-irreducible and distinct, which shows that R' is not confluent.

Instead of stopping with failure in this situation, completion uses the computed critical pairs to extend the rewrite system, with the goal of generating an equivalent confluent system. For example, if we add the (terminating) rule $x + s(0) \to s(x)$ to R', the critical pair $\langle x + s(0), s(x) \rangle$ is obviously joinable in the resulting system R''. It is important to note that adding this new rule does not change the equational theory generated since $x + s(0) \approx_{R'} s(x)$ implies $\approx_{R'} = \approx_{R''}$. However, since R'' contains an additional rule, new critical pairs must be computed and tested for joinability. The computation of critical pairs is iterated until no more non-joinable critical pairs are found. This describes the main idea underlying the basic completion procedure.

7.1 The basic completion procedure

This procedure, which is described in Fig. 7.1, starts with a finite set of
identities E and tries to find a convergent term rewriting system R that is
equivalent to E, i.e. a system that satisfies $\approx_E = \approx_R$. We assume that the
reduction order needed in the termination test is provided as an input for
the procedure.

Input:
> A finite set E of Σ-identities and a reduction order $>$ on $T(\Sigma, V)$.

Output:
> A finite convergent TRS R that is equivalent to E, if the procedure
> terminates successfully;
> "**Fail**", if the procedure terminates unsuccessfully.

Initialization:
> If there exists $(s \approx t) \in E$ such that $s \neq t$, $s \not> t$ and $t \not> s$,
> then terminate with output **Fail**.
> Otherwise, $i := 0$ and $R_0 := \{l \to r \mid (l \approx r) \in E \cup E^{-1} \wedge l > r\}$.

repeat $R_{i+1} := R_i$;

> **for all** $\langle s, t \rangle \in CP(R_i)$ **do**

> **(a)** Reduce s, t to some R_i-normal forms $\hat{s}, \hat{t}$;
> **(b)** If $\hat{s} \neq \hat{t}$ and neither $\hat{s} > \hat{t}$ nor $\hat{t} > \hat{s}$, then terminate with output
> **Fail**;
> **(c)** If $\hat{s} > \hat{t}$, then $R_{i+1} := R_{i+1} \cup \{\hat{s} \to \hat{t}\}$;
> **(d)** If $\hat{t} > \hat{s}$, then $R_{i+1} := R_{i+1} \cup \{\hat{t} \to \hat{s}\}$;
> **od**

> $i := i + 1$;

until $R_i = R_{i-1}$;
output R_i;

Fig. 7.1. The basic completion procedure.

In the initialization phase, the basic completion procedure removes trivial
identities of the form $s = s$, and tries to orient the remaining nontrivial
identities. If this succeeds, then it computes all critical pairs of the rewrite
system obtained. The terms in each critical pair $\langle s, t \rangle$ are reduced to their
normal forms $\hat{s}$ and $\hat{t}$. If the normal forms are identical, then this critical pair
is joinable, and nothing needs to be done for it. Otherwise, the procedure
tries to orient the terms $\hat{s}$ and $\hat{t}$ into a rewrite rule whose termination can be
shown using $>$. If this succeeds, then the new rule is added to the current
rewrite system. This process is iterated until failure occurs or the rewrite

system is not changed during a step of the iteration, that is, the system does not have non-joinable critical pairs.

Thus, the basic completion procedure may show three different types of behaviour, depending on the particular input E and $>$:

1. It may terminate with failure because one of the nontrivial input identities cannot be ordered using $>$, or the normal forms of the terms in one of the critical pairs are distinct and cannot be ordered using $>$. In this case, not much is gained. One could, however, try to run the procedure again, using another reduction order.
2. It may terminate successfully with output R_n because in the nth step of the iteration all critical pairs are joinable.
3. It may run for ever since infinitely many new rules are generated.

Before proving that the basic completion procedure is correct, we consider one example for each of the three different types of behaviour of the procedure.

Example 7.1.1 Consider the theory $E := \{(x * y) * (y * z) \approx y\}$ defining so-called *central groupoids*, and let $>$ be an arbitrary simplification order. Because of the subterm property of $>$, we have $(x*y)*(y*z) > y$, and thus $R_0 = \{(x * y) * (y * z) \to y\}$.

Overlapping $(x*y)*(y*z) \to y$ with its renamed copy $(x'*y')*(y'*z') \to y'$ yields two critical pairs:

- $x*y$ unifies with $(x' * y') * (y' * z')$ with mgu $\{x \mapsto x' * y', y \mapsto y' * z'\}$:

$$((x' * y') * (y' * z')) * ((y' * z') * z)$$

$$y' * z' \quad < \quad y' * ((y' * z') * z)$$

- $y*z$ unifies with $(x' * y') * (y' * z')$ with mgu $\{y \mapsto x' * y', z \mapsto y' * z'\}$:

$$(x * (x' * y')) * ((x' * y') * (y' * z'))$$

$$x' * y' \quad < \quad (x * (x' * y')) * y'$$

Since the terms in these critical pairs are R_0-irreducible and can be ordered (as indicated in the figures) we obtain (after some renaming) the new rewrite system R_1:

$$\{(x * y) * (y * z) \to y, \; x * ((x * y) * z) \to x * y, \; (x * (y * z)) * z \to y * z\}.$$

In the next iteration, all the critical pairs of R_1 turn out to be joinable (Exercise 7.2), and thus the procedure terminates successfully with output R_1.

Example 7.1.2 Consider the theory

$$E := \{x * (y + z) \approx (x * y) + (x * z), \; (u + v) * w \approx (u * w) + (v * w)\},$$

which expresses (left and right) distributivity of $*$ over $+$. If we take as reduction order the lexicographic path order $>_{lpo}$ induced by a precedence satisfying $* > +$, then the identities are ordered from left to right, i.e.

$$R_0 = \{x * (y + z) \to (x * y) + (x * z), \; (u + v) * w \to (u * w) + (v * w)\}.$$

Overlapping the first rule with the second at the root yields the following critical pair and corresponding normal forms:

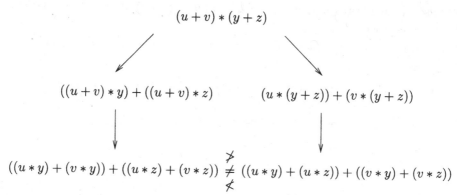

$$(u + v) * (y + z)$$

$$((u + v) * y) + ((u + v) * z) \qquad (u * (y + z)) + (v * (y + z))$$

$$((u * y) + (v * y)) + ((u * z) + (v * z)) \; \not\approx \; ((u * y) + (u * z)) + ((v * y) + (v * z))$$

These normal forms are distinct, and they cannot be ordered using any reduction order since their instances under the substitution $\sigma := \{u \mapsto x, \; v \mapsto x, \; y \mapsto x, \; z \mapsto x\}$ are identical. For this reason, the completion procedure fails.

Example 7.1.3 To obtain an example for nontermination of the basic completion procedure, we return to Example 7.0.2, where we have seen that in the first iteration there is a non-joinable critical pair, which is already in normal form. This pair can be ordered using the reduction order of Example 7.0.2, which yields the new system

$$R_1 := \{x + 0 \to x, \; s(x + y) \to x + s(y), \; x + s(0) \to s(x)\}.$$

An overlap between the second and the third rules yields the critical pair $\langle x + s(s(0)), s(s(x)) \rangle$, which is in normal form and thus not joinable. This yields the new system $R_2 := R_1 \cup \{x + s(s(0)) \rightarrow s(s(x))\}$. It is easy to see that in each step of the iteration a new rule of the form $x + s^n(0) \rightarrow s^n(x)$ is generated.

Theorem 7.1.4 *Let E be a finite set of identities and $>$ be a reduction order.*

1. *If the basic completion procedure applied to $(E, >)$ terminates successfully with output R_n, then R_n is a finite convergent TRS that is equivalent to E. In this case, R_n yields a decision procedure for the word problem for E.*
2. *If the basic completion procedure applied to $(E, >)$ does not terminate, then $R_\infty := \bigcup_{i \geq 0} R_i$ is an infinite convergent TRS that is equivalent to E. In this case, the completion procedure can be used as a semidecision procedure for $\approx_E$.*

Proof (1) The system R_n is finite since it is obtained after finitely many iterations, and in each iteration only finitely many rules are added (for a finite system R_i, the set $CP(R_i)$ is always finite). Obviously, R_n is terminating by construction since all rules $l \rightarrow r \in R_n$ satisfy $l > r$ for the reduction order $>$. It is also confluent since the procedure terminates successfully with output R_n only if all critical pairs of R_n are joinable.

To show that $\approx_{R_n} = \approx_E$, we note that $\approx_E \subseteq \approx_{R_n}$ follows from the fact that $\approx_{R_0} = \approx_E$ and $R_0 \subseteq R_1 \subseteq \ldots \subseteq R_n$. For the other direction, we show by induction on i that $\approx_{R_i} \subseteq \approx_E$. The base case is trivial. For the induction step, we use the fact that $s \approx_{R_i} t$ holds for each critical pair $\langle s, t \rangle$ of R_i, and that the R_i-normal forms $\widehat{s}, \widehat{t}$ of s, t satisfy $s \approx_{R_i} \widehat{s}$ and $t \approx_{R_i} \widehat{t}$. Thus, we have $\widehat{s} \approx_{R_i} \widehat{t}$, which implies $\widehat{s} \approx_E \widehat{t}$ by the induction hypothesis.

Finally, because R_n is a finite convergent TRS, we know that $\approx_{R_n} = \approx_E$ is decidable by Theorem 4.1.1.

(2) The system R_∞ is infinite since in each iteration of the procedure at least one rule is added. Equivalence of R_∞ and E, and termination of R_∞, can be shown as in the first part of the proof.

We prove confluence of R_∞ by showing that all critical pairs between rules in R_∞ are joinable. Assume that $\langle s, t \rangle$ is a critical pair between the rules $l \rightarrow r, g \rightarrow d \in R_\infty$. Because $R_\infty = \bigcup_{i \geq 0} R_i$ and $R_0 \subseteq R_1 \subseteq \ldots$, this means that there exists an $n \geq 0$ such that $l \rightarrow r, g \rightarrow d \in R_n$, which implies that $\langle s, t \rangle \in CP(R_n)$. Now, either $\langle s, t \rangle$ is already joinable in R_n, or it is joinable in R_{n+1} since an appropriate rule has been added. In both cases, $\langle s, t \rangle$ is joinable in the larger system R_∞.

The semidecision procedure for $\approx_E$ works as follows: given terms s and t, it tests after each step of the iteration whether these terms are joinable with respect to the current rewrite system R_n. This test can be computed in finite time since R_n is finite and terminating, and thus $\to_{R_n}$ is globally finite by Lemma 2.2.4. If, for some n, s and t turn out to be joinable, then obviously $s \approx_E t$ holds.

Conversely, assume that $s \approx_E t$ holds. Because R_∞ is a convergent TRS that is equivalent to E, this implies that s and t are joinable with respect to R_∞. The corresponding reduction chains use only finitely many different rewrite rules of R_∞. Since $R_\infty = \bigcup_{i \geq 0} R_i$ and $R_0 \subseteq R_1 \subseteq \ldots$, there exists an n such that all these rules are already contained in R_n. Thus, s and t are joinable with respect to R_n. $\qquad\qquad\qquad\qquad\qquad\qquad\qquad\square$

Exercises

7.1   Consider the following sets of identities:

$$E_1 := \{f(g(f(x))) \approx x\} \quad \text{and} \quad E_2 := \{f(g(f(x))) \approx f(g(x))\}.$$

Choose an appropriate reduction order $>$ and apply the basic completion procedure to the input $(E_i, >)$ $(i = 1, 2)$.

7.2   Show that the TRS

$$\{(x * y) * (y * z) \to y,\ x * ((x * y) * z) \to x * y,\ (x * (y * z)) * z \to y * z\}$$

is confluent.

7.2 An improved completion procedure

In practice, the basic completion procedure described above usually generates a huge number of rules. Since all of them must be taken into account when computing critical pairs, both the run time of and the space requirements for the completion process are often unacceptably high. For this reason, all implementations of completion "simplify" rules by reducing them with the help of other rules. If both sides of a rule reduce to the same term, the whole rule can be removed. Even though this appears to be very natural, it has turned out to be surprisingly hard to show that simplification does not destroy correctness of the completion procedure.

In the following, we present an improved completion method that extends basic completion by simplification of rules. Following Bachmair [14], this method is described by a set of inference rules that covers a wide range of different specific completion procedures. Consequently, our proof of correctness applies to a whole class of completion procedures. A specific completion procedure is obtained from this set of rules by fixing a strategy for rule application, that is, a method that determines in each situation which rule to apply next. It should be noted that such a strategy may also decide not to apply any rule (and thus cause the completion procedure to terminate) even though there are applicable rules.

The inference rules, which are given in Fig. 7.2, work on pairs (E, R) where E is a finite set of identities and R is a finite set of rewrite rules. Intuitively, E contains input identities or critical pairs that have not yet been transformed into rules, whereas R is a terminating set of rewrite rules. As with basic completion, termination of R is ensured by a reduction order $>$ that is given as an input to the completion procedure. The goal is to transform an initial pair $(E_0, \emptyset)$ into a pair $(\emptyset, R)$ such that R is convergent and equivalent to E_0. A completion procedure using these rules may achieve this goal after finitely many inference steps, it may fail (either after finitely many steps or "in the limit"), or it may achieve the goal "in the limit".

DEDUCE	$\dfrac{E, R}{E \cup \{s \approx t\}, R}$	if $s \leftarrow_R u \rightarrow_R t$
ORIENT	$\dfrac{E \cup \{s \doteq t\}, R}{E, R \cup \{s \rightarrow t\}}$	if $s > t$
DELETE	$\dfrac{E \cup \{s \approx s\}, R}{E, R}$	
SIMPLIFY-IDENTITY	$\dfrac{E \cup \{s \doteq t\}, R}{E \cup \{u \approx t\}, R}$	if $s \rightarrow_R u$
R-SIMPLIFY-RULE	$\dfrac{E, R \cup \{s \rightarrow t\}}{E, R \cup \{s \rightarrow u\}}$	if $t \rightarrow_R u$
L-SIMPLIFY-RULE	$\dfrac{E, R \cup \{s \rightarrow t\}}{E \cup \{u \approx t\}, R}$	if $s \overset{\sqsupset}{\rightarrow}_R u$

Fig. 7.2. The inference rules for completion.

The rule DEDUCE derives an identity that is a direct consequence of rules in R, and adds this identity to E. A special case of applying this rule is adding a critical pair of R to E. Most completion procedures use the rule DEDUCE only in this way. An advantage of the more general formulation is that the correctness result applies to a larger class of completion procedures, while its proof does not become more complex.

ORIENT takes an identity that can be ordered with the help of $>$, and adds the corresponding rule to R. Note that the dot in $s \mathbin{\dot\approx} t$ is meant to indicate that this identity should be seen as an unordered pair, i.e. $s \mathbin{\dot\approx} t \in E$ means that $s \approx t \in E$ or $t \approx s \in E$. This notation avoids the need for two versions of ORIENT, one where the left-hand side is larger, and one where the right-hand side is larger.

DELETE removes a trivial identity, and SIMPLIFY-IDENTITY uses R to reduce identities. By applying SIMPLIFY-IDENTITY to a given identity as long as possible one can reduce the terms occurring in the identity to their R-normal forms. Again, the notation $s \mathbin{\dot\approx} t$ is employed to avoid writing two versions of the rule. Taken together, SIMPLIFY-IDENTITY and DELETE can be used to remove joinable critical pairs.

R-SIMPLIFY-RULE reduces the right-hand side of a rule. Since, by assumption, termination of R can be shown using $>$, we know that $s \to_R t \to_R u$ implies $s > t > u$. For this reason, $s \to u$ can be kept as a rule. In contrast, when reducing the left-hand side of a rule $s \to t$ to u, it is not clear whether $u > t$ is satisfied. For this reason, L-SIMPLIFY-RULE adds $u \approx t$ as an identity. The notation $s \xrightarrow{\sqsupset}_R u$ is used to express that s is reduced by a rule $l \to r \in R$ such that l cannot be reduced by $s \to t$. The symbol $\sqsupset$ stands for the strict part of the **encompassment** quasi-order $\mathbin{\raise2pt\hbox{$\sqsupseteq$}\kern-6pt\lower2pt\hbox{$\sim$}}$, which is defined as $s \mathbin{\raise2pt\hbox{$\sqsupseteq$}\kern-6pt\lower2pt\hbox{$\sim$}} l$ iff some subterm of s is an instance of l. Obviously, $s \mathbin{\raise2pt\hbox{$\sqsupseteq$}\kern-6pt\lower2pt\hbox{$\sim$}} l$ means that s is reducible with any rule that has l as its left-hand side. If $s \sqsupset l$, that is, $s \mathbin{\raise2pt\hbox{$\sqsupseteq$}\kern-6pt\lower2pt\hbox{$\sim$}} l$ but $l \mathbin{\not{\raise2pt\hbox{$\sqsupseteq$}\kern-6pt\lower2pt\hbox{$\sim$}}} s$, then no rule with left-hand side s can reduce l. For example, $f(x,x) \mathbin{\raise2pt\hbox{$\sqsupseteq$}\kern-6pt\lower2pt\hbox{$\sim$}} f(x,y)$ since $f(x,x)$ is a subterm of itself, and $f(x,x) = \sigma(f(x,y))$ for the substitution $\sigma := \{y \mapsto x\}$. Since no subterm of $f(x,y)$ is an instance of $f(x,x)$, we have $f(x,x) \sqsupset f(x,y)$. Thus, if $R := \{f(x,x) \to x,\ f(x,y) \to x\}$, then L-SIMPLIFY-RULE can be applied to $f(x,x) \to x$. If $R := \{f(x,y) \to x,\ f(x,y) \to y\}$, then L-SIMPLIFY-RULE cannot be applied. From a proof-technical point of view, the need for such a restriction of the applicability of L-SIMPLIFY-RULE will become clear in the proof of Lemma 7.3.4. Example 7.2.9 will illustrate what may go wrong if this restriction is removed.

We write $(E,R) \vdash_C (E',R')$ to indicate that (E,R) can be transformed to (E',R') by applying one of the inference rules of Fig. 7.2.

The inference rules generate terminating rewrite systems since all rules are oriented with the help of the reduction order $>$:

Lemma 7.2.1 *If $R \subseteq >$ and $(E,R) \vdash_C (E',R')$, then $R' \subseteq >$.*

It is an obvious consequence of this lemma that the rewrite system R in the pair (E, R) is terminating if this pair has been obtained from an initial pair of the form $(E_0, \emptyset)$ by application of the inference rules.

Next, we show that the inference rules are **sound** in the sense that they do not change the equational theory generated.

Lemma 7.2.2 $(E_1, R_1) \vdash_C (E_2, R_2)$ *implies* $\approx_{E_1 \cup R_1} = \approx_{E_2 \cup R_2}$.

Proof This is trivial for the first three rules. For SIMPLIFY-IDENTITY, $E_1 = E \cup \{s \doteq t\}$, $E_2 = E \cup \{u \approx t\}$, $R_1 = R = R_2$, and $s \to_R u$. Thus, we have $u \approx_{E_1 \cup R_1} t$, which shows that $\approx_{E_2 \cup R_2} \subseteq \approx_{E_1 \cup R_1}$. Conversely, $u \approx t \in E_2$, $s \to_R u$, and $R = R_2$ imply $s \approx_{E_2 \cup R_2} t$, and hence $\approx_{E_1 \cup R_1} \subseteq \approx_{E_2 \cup R_2}$.

For R-SIMPLIFY-RULE, we have $E_1 = E = E_2$, $R_1 = R \cup \{s \to t\}$, $R_2 = R \cup \{s \to u\}$, and $t \to_R u$. Obviously, $s \to t \in R_1$, $t \to_R u$, and $R \subseteq R_1$ imply $s \approx_{E_1 \cup R_1} u$, and $s \to u \in R_2$, $t \to_R u$, and $R \subseteq R_2$ imply $s \approx_{E_2 \cup R_2} t$. This shows that $\approx_{E_1 \cup R_1} = \approx_{E_2 \cup R_2}$.

L-SIMPLIFY-RULE can be treated similarly. $\qquad\square$

As mentioned above, a specific completion procedure is obtained from the inference rules of Fig. 7.2 by fixing a strategy for rule application. This is formalized in the next definition.

Definition 7.2.3 A **completion procedure** is a program that accepts as input a finite set of identities E_0 and a reduction order $>$, and uses the rules of Fig. 7.2 to generate a (finite or infinite) sequence

$$(E_0, R_0) \vdash_C (E_1, R_1) \vdash_C (E_2, R_2) \vdash_C (E_3, R_3) \vdash_C \cdots,$$

where $R_0 := \emptyset$. This sequence is called a **run** of the completion procedure on input E_0 and $>$.

By Lemma 7.2.1, all R_i are contained in the reduction order $>$. In order to be able to treat finite and infinite runs simultaneously, we extend every finite run $(E_0, R_0) \vdash_C \cdots \vdash_C (E_n, R_n)$ to an infinite one by setting $(E_{n+i}, R_{n+i}) := (E_n, R_n)$ for all $i \geq 1$. The set E_ω of **persistent identities** and the set R_ω of **persistent rules** of a run $(E_0, R_0) \vdash_C (E_1, R_1) \vdash_C \cdots$ are defined as

$$E_\omega := \bigcup_{i \geq 0} \bigcap_{j \geq i} E_j \quad \text{and} \quad R_\omega := \bigcup_{i \geq 0} \bigcap_{j \geq i} R_j.$$

For a finite run $(E_0, R_0) \vdash_C \cdots \vdash_C (E_n, R_n)$, which has been extended as described above, the set of persistent identities (rules) is just the set E_n (R_n). For an infinite run, persistent identities (rules) are identities (rules) that belong to some E_i (R_i) and are never removed in later inference steps.

The basic completion procedure described in Section 7.1 can be considered as a completion procedure in the sense of the above definition: as noted above, DEDUCE can be used to compute critical pairs, SIMPLIFY-IDENTITY reduces them to normal form, ORIENT turns them into rules if the normal forms can be ordered by $>$, and DELETE removes joinable critical pairs. The rules R-SIMPLIFY-RULE and L-SIMPLIFY-RULE are not used by the basic completion procedure.

Example 7.2.4 As in Example 7.1.1, we take the theory $E_0 := \{(x*y)*(y* z) \approx y\}$ and an arbitrary simplification order $>$ as input of the completion procedure. An application of ORIENT yields

$$(E_0, \emptyset) \vdash_C (\emptyset, \{(x * y) * (y * z) \to y\}).$$

Two applications of DEDUCE allow us to derive the pair

$$\left(\left\{ \begin{array}{l} x * ((x * y) * z) \approx x * y, \\ (x * (y * z)) * z \approx y * z \end{array} \right\}, \quad \{(x * y) * (y * z) \to y\} \right),$$

which, by two applications of ORIENT, can be turned into the pair (E_1, R_1):

$$\left(\emptyset, \left\{ \begin{array}{l} (x * y) * (y * z) \to y, \\ x * ((x * y) * z) \to x * y, \\ (x * (y * z)) * z \to y * z \end{array} \right\} \right).$$

By applying DEDUCE, the critical pairs between these rules can be put into the first component of the pair (E_1, R_1), and SIMPLIFY-IDENTITY can be used to reduce these critical pairs to trivial identities, which can then be removed using DELETE. After this, the basic completion procedure terminates with success, which means that no more inference rules are applied. As described above, the finite run thus obtained is extended to an infinite one. This yields $E_\omega = E_1 = \emptyset$ and $R_\omega = R_1$.

More generally, it is easy to see that, for a non-failing run of the basic completion procedure, that is, a run that terminates successfully or does not terminate, $E_\omega = \emptyset$ (since all identities are turned into rules) and $R_\omega = \bigcup_{i \geq 0} R_i = R_\infty$ (since rules are never simplified). If the basic completion procedure terminates with output `Fail`, then $E_\omega \neq \emptyset$: the non-orientable identity that causes the failure (during an attempt to apply ORIENT to it) is contained in the current set of identities, and thus in all subsequent sets of identities in the infinite extension of the finite run. This motivates the following definition for arbitrary completion procedures.

Definition 7.2.5 A run on input E_0 of a completion procedure is said to **succeed** iff $E_\omega = \emptyset$ and R_ω is convergent and equivalent to E_0. The run

fails iff $E_\omega \neq \emptyset$. A completion procedure is **correct** iff every run that does not fail succeeds.

For the basic completion procedure, this notion of failure coincides with the one introduced in Section 7.1, where failure occurs if an input identity cannot be oriented or the normal forms of a critical pair are distinct (i.e. cannot be removed using DELETE) and cannot be oriented using > (i.e. cannot be transformed from an identity into a rule). In this case, the basic completion procedure terminates, that is, failing runs of basic completion are finite. The next example shows that an arbitrary completion procedure may also have *infinite* failing runs.

Example 7.2.6 First, consider the behaviour of basic completion on the input $(E_0, >_{lpo})$, where

$$E_0 := \{h(x,y) \approx f(x), \; h(x,y) \approx f(y), \; g(x,y) \approx h(x,y), \; g(x,y) \approx a\}$$

and $>_{lpo}$ is the lexicographic path order induced by the precedence $g > h > f > a$. The basic completion procedure uses ORIENT to generate the rules

$$R_1 := \{h(x,y) \to f(x), \; h(x,y) \to f(y), \; g(x,y) \to h(x,y), \; g(x,y) \to a\},$$

and then DEDUCE to compute the critical pairs $f(x) \approx f(y)$ and $h(x,y) \approx a$. It then tries to simplify and orient these critical pairs. Obviously, the terms in $f(x) \approx f(y)$ are R_1-irreducible, and they cannot be compared with any reduction order. Thus, basic completion fails on this input. However, the second critical pair $h(x,y) \approx a$ could have been oriented into the rule $h(x,y) \to a$. Using this rule to compute critical pairs would have provided us with the identity $f(x) \approx a$ and, since this identity can be oriented from left to right, with the rule $f(x) \to a$. Finally, this rule could have been used to reduce $f(x) \approx f(y)$ to the trivial identity $a \approx a$.

This shows that it makes sense not to terminate with failure if a reduced and non-orientable identity is encountered. Instead, one simply defers the orientation of this identity until new rules are obtained. If the new set of rules allows one to simplify the identity to an orientable or trivial one, then one can apply ORIENT or DELETE. Otherwise, the treatment of this identity is again deferred. For the input $(E_0, >_{lpo})$ from above, this strategy would yield a finite successful run of the completion procedure. However, this strategy may lead to infinite failing runs. For example, for the input $(E'_0, >_{lpo})$ with

$$E'_0 := \{h(x,y) \approx f(x), \; h(x,y) \approx f(y), \; f(g(f(x))) \approx f(g(x))\},$$

it generates an infinite run such that $E_\omega = \{f(x) \approx f(y)\}$ and

$$R_\omega = \{h(x,y) \to f(x),\ h(x,y) \to f(y)\} \cup \{fg^n f(x) \to fg^n(x) \mid n \geq 1\}.$$

Theorem 7.1.4 shows that basic completion is correct in the sense of Definition 7.2.5. Without an additional fairness assumption, an arbitrary completion procedure need not be correct. Obviously, a necessary condition for correctness is that all the relevant critical pairs are computed.

Definition 7.2.7 A run of a completion procedure is called **fair** iff

$$CP(R_\omega) \subseteq \bigcup_{i \geq 0} E_i.$$

A completion procedure is **fair** iff every non-failing run is fair.

In the next section, we shall prove that this condition is also sufficient for correctness:

Theorem 7.2.8 *Every fair completion procedure is correct.*

It should be noted that correctness is not the only criterion for evaluating the quality of a completion procedure. Another criterion is how often the procedure fails. For basic completion, failure occurs only if a non-orientable identity or critical pair is encountered. An arbitrary completion procedure may, for example, fail because it simply chooses to ignore some of the critical pairs (i.e. it never applies SIMPLIFY-IDENTITY or ORIENT to them, even though this would be possible). In particular, a completion procedure that always fails is correct in the sense of Definition 7.2.5.

We conclude this section with an example that demonstrates that the encompassment condition in L-SIMPLIFY-RULE cannot be dispensed with.

Example 7.2.9 Consider the set $E_0 := \{f(g(f(x))) \approx f(g(x)),\ g(g(x)) \approx g(x)\}$ and the lexicographic path order $>_{lpo}$ induced by $f > g$, and assume that, in the formulation of L-SIMPLIFY-RULE, "$s \stackrel{\sqsupset}{\to}_R u$" is replaced by "$s \to_R u$". We will construct a non-failing and fair run on input $(E_0, >_{lpo})$ (using the modified rule L-SIMPLIFY-RULE) such that the set R_ω of persistent rules is not equivalent to E_0. The main idea underlying this construction is to generate infinitely many rules $l_n \to r_n$ with identical left-hand sides $l_n = fgf(x)$, but different right-hand sides $r_n = fg^{2^n}(x)$. For all $n \geq 1$, the rule $l_n \to r_n$ is then simplified by $l_{n+1} \to r_{n+1}$ using the modified rule L-SIMPLIFY-RULE. Consequently, none of the rules $l_n \to r_n$ will be persistent.

Starting with $(E_0, \emptyset)$, two applications of ORIENT yield the pair

$$(\emptyset,\ \{fgf(x) \to fg(x),\ gg(x) \to g(x)\}).$$

First, DEDUCE adds the trivial identity $gg(x) \approx gg(x)$, which is obtained by overlapping the second rule with itself. Obviously, this identity can be removed with the help of DELETE. Second, DEDUCE adds the critical pair $fggf(x) \approx fgfg(x)$, which is obtained by overlapping the first rule with itself. Two applications of SIMPLIFY-IDENTITY can be used to reduce this identity to the form $fgf(x) \approx fgg(x)$. Finally, ORIENT turns this identity into a rule. Note that we have not applied SIMPLIFY-IDENTITY exhaustively. Even though this may not be a good strategy for rule application, it does not cause failure (since the identity can be oriented even though it is not completely reduced). To sum up, we have reached the pair

$$(\emptyset, \ \{fgf(x) \to fg(x), \ fgf(x) \to fgg(x), \ gg(x) \to g(x)\}) \, .$$

The modified rule L-SIMPLIFY-RULE reduces the first rule to the identity $fgg(x) \approx fg(x)$, and SIMPLIFY-IDENTITY reduces this identity to the trivial identity $fg(x) \approx fg(x)$, which is removed by DELETE. Thus we have generated the pair $(\emptyset, \ \{fgf(x) \to fgg(x), \ gg(x) \to g(x)\})$.

Now, assume that we have already generated the pair

$$\left(\emptyset, \ \{fgf(x) \to fg^{2^n}(x), \ gg(x) \to g(x)\}\right)$$

for some $n \geq 1$. Using the same strategy as above, we can first generate the pair

$$\left(\emptyset, \ \{fgf(x) \to fg^{2^n}(x), \ fgf(x) \to fg^{2^{n+1}}(x), \ gg(x) \to g(x)\}\right),$$

and then with the help of L-SIMPLIFY-RULE, SIMPLIFY-IDENTITY, and DELETE the pair

$$\left(\emptyset, \ \{fgf(x) \to fg^{2^{n+1}}(x), \ gg(x) \to g(x)\}\right) \, .$$

It is easy to see that this way we generate a fair and non-failing run. However, $R_\omega = \{gg(x) \to g(x)\}$ is not equivalent to E_0.

Exercises

7.3 Show that the encompassment relation $\trianglerighteq$ is a quasi-order, and that its strict part $\sqsupset$ is a well-founded strict partial order.

7.4 Let $\equiv$ denote the equivalence relation that is induced by $\trianglerighteq$, i.e. $s \equiv t$ iff $s \trianglerighteq t$ and $t \trianglerighteq s$. Show that $s \equiv t$ holds iff s and t are equal up to renaming. Show that, for a given term s, there exist up to $\equiv$ only finitely many terms t such that $s \trianglerighteq t$.

7.3 Proof orders

Proof orders are a convenient tool for showing correctness of an arbitrary fair completion procedure. The presence of the inference rules L-SIMPLIFY-RULE and R-SIMPLIFY-RULE makes this proof considerably harder than for basic completion (in particular for infinite runs): Of course, in a non-failing and fair run, all relevant critical pairs are computed (because $CP(R_\omega) \subseteq \bigcup_{i \geq 0} E_i$), and these critical pairs are joinable with respect to the set $\bigcup_{i \geq 0} R_i$ of all computed rules (because $E_\omega = \emptyset$). It is, however, not at all obvious that the critical pairs are also joinable with respect to the set R_ω of persistent rules. Similarly, even though all sets $E_i \cup R_i$ are equivalent to E_0, it is not clear why R_ω is equivalent to E_0.

In the following, we assume that

$$(E_0, \emptyset) \vdash_C (E_1, R_1) \vdash_C (E_2, R_2) \vdash_C (E_3, R_3) \vdash_C \cdots$$

is an arbitrary but fixed non-failing and fair run of a completion procedure. We define $R_\infty := \bigcup_{i \geq 1} R_i$ and $E_\infty := \bigcup_{i \geq 0} E_i$.

Definition 7.3.1　A **proof** of an identity $s \approx t$ in $E_\infty \cup R_\infty$ is a finite sequence $(s_0, \ldots, s_n)$ of length $n + 1 > 0$ such that $s_0 = s$, $s_n = t$, and for all $i, 1 \leq i \leq n$,

1. $s_{i-1} \leftrightarrow_{E_\infty} s_i$, or
2. $s_{i-1} \to_{R_\infty} s_i$, or
3. $s_i \to_{R_\infty} s_{i-1}$.

For $i = 1, \ldots, n$, the pairs (s_{i-1}, s_i) are called **proof steps**. Two proofs in $E_\infty \cup R_\infty$ are called **equivalent** iff they prove the same identity. A proof $(s_0, \ldots, s_n)$ in $E_\infty \cup R_\infty$ is called a **rewrite proof** in R_ω iff there exists $k, 0 \leq k \leq n$, such that $s_{i-1} \to_{R_\omega} s_i$ for all $i, 1 \leq i \leq k$, and $s_i \leftarrow_{R_\omega} s_{i+1}$ for all $i, k \leq i < n$.

Obviously, the identity $s \approx t$ has a proof in $E_\infty \cup R_\infty$ iff $s \approx_{E_\infty \cup R_\infty} t$ holds. The difference between a proof and a rewrite proof of an identity is illustrated in Fig. 7.3.

Our goal is to show that every proof in $E_\infty \cup R_\infty$ is equivalent to a rewrite proof in R_ω. Theorem 7.2.8, which says that every fair completion procedure is correct, can be obtained as an immediate consequence of this fact. We will prove the goal by well-founded induction. For this purpose, we define a well-founded order $\succ_C$ on proofs (a so-called **proof order**), and show that for every proof that is not a rewrite proof there exists an equivalent proof that is smaller with respect to $\succ_C$.

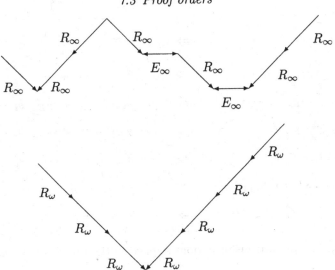

Fig. 7.3. An arbitrary proof (upper part) and a rewrite proof (lower part).

Definition 7.3.2 For a given proof $P = (s_0, \ldots, s_n)$, the "cost" $c(s_{i-1}, s_i)$ of a proof step (s_{i-1}, s_i) is a triple that is defined as follows:

1. If $s_{i-1} \leftrightarrow_{E_\infty} s_i$, then $c(s_{i-1}, s_i) := (\{s_{i-1}, s_i\}, -, -)$, where the first component is a multiset of terms, and the other components are irrelevant, i.e. "$-$" stands for an arbitrary term.
2. If $s_{i-1} \rightarrow_{R_\infty} s_i$ with $l \rightarrow r \in R_\infty$, then $c(s_{i-1}, s_i) := (\{s_{i-1}\}, l, s_i)$.
3. If $s_i \rightarrow_{R_\infty} s_{i-1}$ with $l \rightarrow r \in R_\infty$, then $c(s_{i-1}, s_i) := (\{s_i\}, l, s_{i-1})$.

The overall cost of the proof P is the multiset $c(P)$ of the costs of all its proof steps.

Proof steps are compared using the lexicographic product of

1. the multiset extension of the reduction order $>$ in the first component,
2. the strict part $\sqsupset$ of the encompassment quasi-order in the second component, and
3. the reduction order $>$ in the third component,

and proofs are compared using the multiset extension of this lexicographic product. This defines the relation $\succ_C$ on proofs.

Lemma 7.3.3 *The relation $\succ_C$ is a well-founded order.*

Proof The reduction order $>$ and its multiset extension are obviously well-founded orders, and we have seen in Exercise 7.3 that $\sqsupset$ is a well-founded order. Thus, their lexicographic product and the multiset extension of this product are also well-founded orders. □

$$\cdots \; s_{i-1} \leftrightarrow_{E_\infty} s_i \; \cdots \qquad\qquad \Longrightarrow \qquad \begin{array}{l} \cdots \; s_{i-1} \rightarrow_{R_\infty} s_i \; \cdots \\ \cdots \; s_{i-1} \leftarrow_{R_\infty} s_i \; \cdots \end{array} \qquad (1.1)$$

$$\cdots \; s_{i-1} \leftrightarrow_{E_\infty} s_{i-1} \; \cdots \qquad\qquad \Longrightarrow \qquad \cdots \; s_{i-1} \; \cdots \qquad\qquad\qquad (1.2)$$

$$\cdots \; s_{i-1} \leftrightarrow_{E_\infty} s_i \; \cdots \qquad\qquad \Longrightarrow \qquad \cdots \; s_{i-1} \rightarrow_{R_\infty} s' \leftrightarrow_{E_\infty} s_i \; \cdots \qquad (1.3)$$

$$\cdots \; s_{i-1} \rightarrow_{R_\infty} s_i \; \cdots \qquad\qquad \Longrightarrow \qquad \cdots \; s_{i-1} \rightarrow_{R_\infty} s' \leftarrow_{R_\infty} s_i \; \cdots \qquad (2.1)$$

$$\cdots \; s_{i-1} \rightarrow_{R_\infty} s_i \; \cdots \qquad\qquad \Longrightarrow \qquad \cdots \; s_{i-1} \rightarrow_{R_\infty} s' \leftrightarrow_{E_\infty} s_i \; \cdots \qquad (2.2)$$

$$\cdots \; s_{i-1} \leftarrow_{R_\omega} s_i \rightarrow_{R_\omega} s_{i+1} \; \cdots \qquad \Longrightarrow \qquad \cdots \; s_{i-1} \downarrow_{R_\omega} s_{i+1} \; \cdots \qquad (3.1)$$

$$\cdots \; s_{i-1} \leftarrow_{R_\omega} s_i \rightarrow_{R_\omega} s_{i+1} \; \cdots \qquad \Longrightarrow \qquad \cdots \; s_{i-1} \leftrightarrow_{E_\infty} s_{i+1} \; \cdots \qquad (3.2)$$

Fig. 7.4. The proof transformations applied in the proof of Lemma 7.3.4.

Lemma 7.3.4 *Let P be a proof in $E_\infty \cup R_\infty$ that is not a rewrite proof in R_ω. Then there exists a proof P' in $E_\infty \cup R_\infty$ such that P' is equivalent to P and $P \succ_C P'$.*

Proof If $P = (s_0, \ldots, s_n)$ is not a rewrite proof in R_ω, then there are three possible reasons:

1. P contains a proof step that is in E_∞.
2. P contains a proof step that is in $R_\infty - R_\omega$.
3. P contains an R_ω-peak, i.e. a subproof of the form

$$s_{i-1} \leftarrow_{R_\omega} s_i \rightarrow_{R_\omega} s_{i+1}.$$

In the following, we consider each of these three cases separately. (Fig. 7.4 summarizes the transformations that are applied to subproofs in each of the subcases considered below.)

(1) Assume that $s_{i-1} \leftrightarrow_{E_\infty} s_i$ with an identity $s \doteq t \in E_\infty$. The cost of this proof step is $c(s_{i-1}, s_i) = (\{s_{i-1}, s_i\}, -, -)$. Since $E_\omega = \emptyset$, the identity $s \doteq t$ is removed from the set of identities at some stage of the inference process using ORIENT, DELETE, or SIMPLIFY-IDENTITY.

(1.1) Assume that ORIENT has replaced the identity $s \doteq t$ by the rule $s \rightarrow t$. Then $s \rightarrow t \in R_\infty$, and we can replace the proof step $s_{i-1} \leftrightarrow_{E_\infty} s_i$ in P by either $s_{i-1} \rightarrow_{R_\infty} s_i$ or $s_{i-1} \leftarrow_{R_\infty} s_i$. The cost of this new proof step is of the form $(\{s_{i-1}\}, \ldots)$ or $(\{s_i\}, \ldots)$, and thus smaller than $(\{s_{i-1}, s_i\}, -, -)$. This shows that the new proof P' obtained in this way satisfies $P \succ_C P'$.

(1.2) Assume that DELETE has removed the identity $s \doteq t$ because $s = t$. Thus $s_{i-1} = s_i$, which shows that $P' := (s_0, \ldots, s_{i-1}, s_{i+1}, \ldots, s_n)$ is also a proof of $s_0 \approx s_n$. Obviously, $P \succ_C P'$ is satisfied.

(1.3) Assume that SIMPLIFY-IDENTITY has been applied to $s \doteq t$ because $s \rightarrow_{R_k} u$. Thus, we have $u \approx t \in E_\infty$ and $s \rightarrow_{R_\infty} u$. Assume (without loss of generality) that $s_{i-1}|_p = \sigma(s)$ and $s_i = s_{i-1}[\sigma(t)]_p$. If we define $s' := s_{i-1}[\sigma(u)]_p$, then $s_{i-1} \rightarrow_{R_\infty} s'$ and $s' \leftrightarrow_{E_\infty} s_i$ are valid proof steps in $E_\infty \cup R_\infty$. Let P' be the proof that is obtained from P by replacing the step (s_{i-1}, s_i) by the two steps (s_{i-1}, s') and (s', s_i). The cost $c(s_{i-1}, s') = (\{s_{i-1}\}, \ldots)$ of the first (rewrite) step is obviously smaller than $c(s_{i-1}, s_i) = (\{s_{i-1}, s_i\}, \ldots)$. The cost $c(s', s_i) = (\{s', s_i\}, \ldots)$ of the second (equational) step is smaller than $c(s_{i-1}, s_i)$ since $s' < s_{i-1}$. Thus, we have $P \succ_C P'$ because the triple $c(s_{i-1}, s_i)$ is replaced by the two smaller triples $c(s_{i-1}, s')$ and $c(s', s_i)$ when going from $c(P)$ to $c(P')$.

(2) Assume (without loss of generality) that $s_{i-1} \rightarrow_{R_\infty} s_i$ with a rule $s \rightarrow t \in R_\infty - R_\omega$ at position p in s_{i-1} with substitution σ, i.e. $s_{i-1}|_p = \sigma(s)$ and $s_i = s_{i-1}[\sigma(t)]_p$. The cost of this proof step is $c(s_{i-1}, s_i) = (\{s_{i-1}\}, s, s_i)$. Since $s \rightarrow t \notin R_\omega$, the rule $s \rightarrow t$ is removed from the set of rules at some stage of the inference process using R-SIMPLIFY-RULE or L-SIMPLIFY-RULE.

(2.1) Assume that R-SIMPLIFY-RULE has replaced $s \rightarrow t$ by $s \rightarrow u$ because $t \rightarrow_{R_k} u$. Thus, we have $s \rightarrow u \in R_\infty$ and $t \rightarrow_{R_\infty} u$. If we define $s' := s_{i-1}[\sigma(u)]$, then $s_{i-1} \rightarrow_{R_\infty} s'$ and $s' \leftarrow_{R_\infty} s_i$ are valid proof steps in $E_\infty \cup R_\infty$. Let P' be the proof that is obtained from P by replacing the step (s_{i-1}, s_i) by the two steps (s_{i-1}, s') and (s', s_i). The cost $c(s_{i-1}, s') = (\{s_{i-1}\}, s, s')$ of the first step is smaller than $c(s_{i-1}, s_i) = (\{s_{i-1}\}, s, s_i)$ since $s' < s_i$. The cost $c(s', s_i) = (\{s_i\}, \ldots)$ of the second step is smaller than $c(s_{i-1}, s_i)$ since $s_i < s_{i-1}$.

(2.2) Assume that L-SIMPLIFY-RULE has replaced the rule $s \rightarrow t$ by the identity $u \approx t$ because $s \xrightarrow{\sqsupset}_{R_k} u$ with a rule $l \rightarrow r \in R_k$ such that $s \sqsupset l$. Thus, we have $u \approx t \in E_\infty$ and $s \rightarrow_{R_\infty} u$. If we define $s' := s_{i-1}[\sigma(u)]$, then $s_{i-1} \rightarrow_{R_\infty} s'$ and $s' \leftrightarrow_{E_\infty} s_i$ are valid proof steps in $E_\infty \cup R_\infty$. Let P' be the proof that is obtained from P by replacing the step (s_{i-1}, s_i) by the two steps (s_{i-1}, s') and (s', s_i). The cost $c(s_{i-1}, s') = (\{s_{i-1}\}, l, s')$ of the first step is smaller than $c(s_{i-1}, s_i) = (\{s_{i-1}\}, s, s_i)$ since $s \sqsupset l$. The cost $c(s', s_i) = (\{s', s_i\}, \ldots)$ of the second step is smaller than $c(s_{i-1}, s_i)$ since $s' < s_{i-1}$ and $s_i < s_{i-1}$.

(3) Assume that $s_i \rightarrow_{R_\omega} s_{i-1}$ with a rule $l \rightarrow r \in R_\omega$ at position p, and that $s_i \rightarrow_{R_\omega} s_{i+1}$ with a rule $g \rightarrow d \in R_\omega$ at position q.

(3.1) If there is no overlap between the two redexes (i.e. $p \| q$) or the overlap is non-critical, then $s_{i-1} \downarrow_{R_\omega} s_{i+1}$, as shown in Section 6.2. Thus, there exist terms $u_1, \ldots, u_m, v_1, \ldots, v_{n-1}$ such that

$$s_{i-1} \rightarrow_{R_\omega} u_1 \rightarrow_{R_\omega} \cdots \rightarrow_{R_\omega} u_m \leftarrow_{R_\omega} v_{n-1} \leftarrow_{R_\omega} \cdots \leftarrow_{R_\omega} v_1 \leftarrow_{R_\omega} s_{i+1}$$

is a valid sequence of proof steps in $E_\infty \cup R_\infty$. Let P' be the proof that is obtained from P by replacing the two steps $s_{i-1} \leftarrow_{R_\omega} s_i \rightarrow_{R_\omega} s_{i+1}$ by this sequence. It is easy to see that the cost of each proof step in this sequence is smaller than the cost $c(s_i, s_{i+1}) = (\{s_i\}, \ldots)$ of $s_i \rightarrow_{R_\omega} s_{i+1}$, since $s_i > s_{i-1} > u_1 > \cdots > u_m$ and $s_i > s_{i+1} > v_1 > \cdots > v_{n-1}$.

(3.2) Assume that the peak $s_{i-1} \leftarrow_{R_\omega} s_i \rightarrow_{R_\omega} s_{i+1}$ is due to a critical overlap of the rules $l \rightarrow r$ and $g \rightarrow d$. By the Critical Pair Lemma, there is a critical pair $\langle s, t \rangle \in CP(R_\omega)$ such that s_{i-1} can be rewritten to s_{i+1} using the identity $s \doteq t$. Because of the fairness assumption, we know that $s \approx t \in E_\infty$. Thus, $s_{i-1} \leftrightarrow_{E_\infty} s_{i+1}$ is a valid proof step in $E_\infty \cup R_\infty$. Let P' be the proof that is obtained from P by replacing the two steps $s_{i-1} \leftarrow_{R_\omega} s_i \rightarrow_{R_\omega} s_{i+1}$ by $s_{i-1} \leftrightarrow_{E_\infty} s_{i+1}$. The cost $c(s_{i-1}, s_{i+1}) = (\{s_{i-1}, s_{i+1}\}, \ldots)$ of this step is smaller than the cost $c(s_i, s_{i+1}) = (\{s_i\}, \ldots)$ of $s_i \rightarrow_{R_\omega} s_{i+1}$ since $s_{i-1} < s_i$ and $s_{i+1} < s_i$. $\qquad\square$

The treatment of L-SIMPLIFY-RULE in the above proof shows that, instead of the strict encompassment order, an arbitrary well-founded strict order on the left-hand sides of the rules in R_∞ could have been employed to restrict the applicability of this inference rule. The reason for using encompassment is that one wants to keep the restriction as weak as possible: if s can be reduced with the rule $l \rightarrow r$, then one already knows $s \sqsupseteq l$. An even less restricted applicability condition can be obtained by using a well-founded order that extends $\sqsupseteq$; for example, $s \succ l$ iff $s \sqsupset l$ or $s \sqsupseteq l$ and the rule $l \rightarrow r$ has been generated before $s \rightarrow t$ during the run of the completion procedure.

We sum up the results of this section in a theorem. As an obvious consequence, we obtain that every fair completion procedure is correct. This completes the proof of Theorem 7.2.8.

Theorem 7.3.5 *Let $(E_0, \emptyset) \vdash_C (E_1, R_1) \vdash_C (E_2, R_2) \vdash_C (E_3, R_3) \vdash_C \cdots$ be a non-failing and fair run of a completion procedure.*

1. *Every proof in $E_\infty \cup R_\infty$ is equivalent to a rewrite proof in R_ω.*
2. *R_ω is equivalent to the set of input identities E_0.*
3. *R_ω is convergent.*
4. *If R_ω is finite, then the word problem for E_0 is decidable. Otherwise, the run yields a semidecision procedure for $\approx_{E_0}$.*

Proof (1) The first part of the theorem is proved by well-founded induction on the well-founded proof order $\succ_C$. Let P be a proof in $E_\infty \cup R_\infty$. If P is itself a rewrite proof in R_ω, then we are done. Otherwise, Lemma 7.3.4

yields an equivalent proof P' such that $P \succ_C P'$. By induction, P' (and thus also P) is equivalent to a rewrite proof in R_ω.

(2) The inclusion $\approx_{R_\omega} \subseteq \approx_{E_0}$ is an easy consequence of Lemma 7.2.2. The other direction follows from (1) since every proof in $E_0 \subseteq E_\infty \cup R_\infty$ is equivalent to a proof in R_ω.

(3) Termination of R_ω is an easy consequence of Lemma 7.2.1. Confluence of R_ω again follows from (1) since every proof in $R_\omega \subseteq E_\infty \cup R_\infty$ is equivalent to a rewrite proof in R_ω.

(4) By Theorem 4.1.1, a finite convergent term rewriting system that is equivalent to E_0 yields a decision procedure for the word problem for E_0.

The semidecision procedure for $\approx_{E_0}$ works similarly to the one obtained from basic completion: Given terms s and t, it tests after each inference step whether these terms are joinable with respect to the current rewrite system R_n. If, for some n, s and t turn out to be joinable, then obviously $s \approx_E t$ holds.

Conversely, assume that $s \approx_{E_0} t$ holds. Because R_ω is a convergent TRS that is equivalent to E_0, this implies that s and t are joinable with respect to R_ω. The corresponding reduction chains use only finitely many different rewrite rules of R_ω. Consequently, there exists an n such that all these (persistent) rules are already contained in R_n. Thus, s and t are joinable with respect to R_n. $\qquad\square$

Exercise

7.5 The simple semidecision procedure described in the proof of Theorem 7.3.5 is rather inefficient because after each inference step it tests whether s and t are joinable by computing *all* normal forms of s and t with respect to the (possibly non-confluent) TRS R_n. Show that the following procedure is also a semidecision procedure for $\approx_E$: Let $s_0 := s$ and $t_0 := t$. After the first inference step, the procedure computes arbitrary R_1-normal forms s_1 and t_1 of s_0 and t_0. After the second inference step, it computes arbitrary R_2-normal forms s_2 and t_2 of s_1 and t_1, after the third step arbitrary R_3-normal forms s_3 and t_3 of s_2 and t_2, etc. It answers with "yes" (that is, $s \approx_{E_0} t$) if $s_n = t_n$ for some $n \geq 0$. (*Hint:* show the following:

- $s \approx_{E_0} s_n$ and $t \approx_{E_0} t_n$ for all $n \geq 0$.
- Since R_∞ is terminating, there is an $n \geq 0$ such that $s_n = s_m$ and $t_n = t_m$ for all $m \geq n$.)

7.4 Huet's completion procedure

Huet was the first to give a complete proof of correctness of a completion procedure that allows for simplification of rules [120]. Compared to the proof method used above, Huet's proof is rather complex, and its applicability is restricted to one specific completion procedure. In this section, we present Huet's procedure as a concrete example of a correct completion procedure (see Fig. 7.5). We will see that correctness of this procedure is not an immediate consequence of Theorem 7.2.8 since the procedure is not fair in the sense of Definition 7.2.7. However, it satisfies a slightly weaker fairness condition, which turns out to be sufficient for Lemma 7.3.4 to hold.

Like the inference rules for completion, Huet's procedure works on a set E of identities and a terminating set R of rewrite rules. In order to keep track of whether a rule has already been used for computing critical pairs, rules may be *marked* or not.

The following series of lemmas shows that Huet's procedure is a correct completion procedure, provided that it employs an appropriate strategy for computing critical pairs. In addition, a run of this procedure fails (in the sense of Definition 7.2.5) iff the procedure terminates with output `Fail`.

Lemma 7.4.1 *Huet's completion procedure is a completion procedure in the sense of Definition 7.2.3.*

Proof The computation of critical pairs in the outer while-loop can be realized using DEDUCE. Step (b) of the inner while-loop can be achieved using SIMPLIFY-IDENTITY, and (c) corresponds to DELETE. Step (e) can be achieved using ORIENT, R-SIMPLIFY-RULE, and L-SIMPLIFY-RULE. This is trivial for the orientation step. In order to show that R-SIMPLIFY-RULE can be used to generate the rules $g \to \widehat{d} \in R_{i+1}$, one must prove that the simultaneous reductions $d \xrightarrow{*}_{R_i} \widehat{d}$, which are all done with the original system R_i, can be realized by a sequence of R-SIMPLIFY-RULE steps, in which the already partially modified TRS must be used in each simplification step. This is an immediate consequence of Exercise 7.6 below. Finally, note that the strict encompassment condition of L-SIMPLIFY-RULE is satisfied when reducing the left-hand side of a rule $g \to d \in R_i$ with $l \to r$ since l is in R_i-normal form, and thus $l \sqsupuppt. g$ is not possible for a rule $g \to d \in R_i$. $\qquad \square$

Lemma 7.4.2 *A run of Huet's completion procedure fails iff the procedure terminates with output* `Fail`.

Proof If Huet's procedure terminates with output `Fail`, then there is an identity that cannot be turned into a rule by simplification and orientation. Thus, $E_\omega \neq \emptyset$. To show the converse, assume that Huet's procedure does not

Input:
> A finite set E of Σ-identities and a reduction order $>$ on $T(\Sigma, V)$.

Output:
> A finite convergent TRS R_i that is equivalent to E, if the procedure terminates successfully; "**Fail**", if the procedure terminates unsuccessfully. If the procedure does not terminate, it generates an infinite limit system R_ω that is convergent and equivalent to E.

Initialization:
> $R_0 := \emptyset;\ \ E_0 := E;\ \ i := 0;$

while $E_i \neq \emptyset$ or there is an unmarked rule in R_i **do**

> **while** $E_i \neq \emptyset$ **do**
> (a) Choose an identity $s \approx t \in E_i$;
> (b) Reduce s, t to some R_i-normal forms $\hat{s}, \hat{t}$;
> (c) If $\hat{s} = \hat{t}$, then
>> $R_{i+1} := R_i;$
>> $E_{i+1} := E_i - \{s \approx t\};$
>> $i := i + 1;$
>
> (d) Otherwise, if $\hat{s} \not> \hat{t}$ and $\hat{t} \not> \hat{s}$, then terminate with output **Fail**;
> (e) Otherwise, let l, r be such that $\{l, r\} = \{\hat{s}, \hat{t}\}$ and $l > r$;

$$R_{i+1} := \{g \to \hat{d} \mid g \to d \in R_i,\ g \text{ cannot be reduced}$$
$$\text{with } l \to r, \text{ and } \hat{d} \text{ is a normal}$$
$$\text{form of } d \text{ w.r.t. } R_i \cup \{l \to r\}\}$$
$$\cup \{l \to r\};$$
$$(*\ g \to \hat{d} \text{ inherits the marker of } g \to d\ *)$$
$$(*\ l \to r \text{ is not marked } *)$$
$$E_{i+1} := (E_i - \{s \approx t\}) \cup$$
$$\{g' \approx d \mid g \to d \in R_i \text{ and } g \text{ can be}$$
$$\text{reduced to } g' \text{ with } l \to r\};$$
$$i := i + 1;$$

> **od** (* end of inner while-loop *)
> If there is an unmarked rule in R_i, then let $l \to r$ be such a rule.

$$R_{i+1} := R_i;$$
$$E_{i+1} := \{s \approx t \mid \langle s, t \rangle \text{ is a critical pair of } l \to r \text{ with}$$
$$\text{itself or a marked rule in } R_i\};$$
$$i := i + 1;$$
$$\text{Mark } l \to r;$$

od (* end of outer while-loop *)
output R_i;

Fig. 7.5. Huet's completion procedure.

---

terminate with output **Fail**. In order to prove that $E_\omega = \emptyset$, i.e. that there are no persistent identities, it is sufficient to show that the inner while-loop always terminates. For this purpose, we associate with each iteration of the loop a multiset of pairs that is defined as follows:

$$K_i := \{(\{s,t\},1) \mid s \approx t \in E_i\} \cup \{(\{l,r\},0) \mid l \to r \in R_i\}.$$

The first components of the pairs are ordered using the multiset order induced by the reduction order $>$, the second components are ordered $1 > 0$, and the pairs are ordered using the lexicographic product of these two orders. Finally, the multisets K_i are ordered using the multiset extension of this order on pairs. The order $\succ$ obtained is obviously well-founded, and it is easy to show that $K_i \succ K_{i+1}$ holds in each iteration of the inner while-loop.

□

Obviously, the procedure can only be correct if choosing an unmarked rule for computing critical pairs is realized in a "fair" manner, i.e. if there is no unmarked persistent rule. This can, for example, be realized by always choosing the oldest unmarked rule. Nevertheless, this does not yield a completion procedure that is fair in the sense of Definition 7.2.7. The reason is that new rules that are obtained by simplifying the right-hand sides of existing rules inherit the marker of the corresponding old rule. Thus, if the old rule has already been chosen for computing critical pairs, the new rule is not chosen again. Consequently, the fairness condition $CP(R_\omega) \subseteq E_\infty$ need not be satisfied if the simplified rule turns out to be persistent. The next lemma shows, however, that the critical pairs computed for the old rules also serve their purpose for the new simplified rules (see Theorem 7.4.4 below).

Lemma 7.4.3 *Consider a run of Huet's procedure and assume that there are no unmarked persistent rules. If a peak $s_{i-1} \leftarrow_{R_\omega} s_i \to_{R_\omega} s_{i+1}$ is due to a critical overlap, then there exist terms s'_{i-1} and s'_{i+1} such that $s_i \to_{R_\infty} s'_{i-1} \xrightarrow{*}_{R_\infty} s_{i-1}$, $s_i \to_{R_\infty} s'_{i+1} \xrightarrow{*}_{R_\infty} s_{i+1}$, and $s'_{i-1} \leftrightarrow_{E_\infty} s'_{i+1}$.*

Proof The situation is illustrated in the following figure:

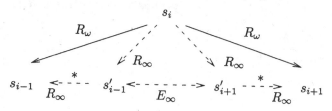

Assume that the peak is due to a critical overlap of the rules $l \to r, g \to d \in R_\omega$. Since there are no unmarked persistent rules, we know that there exist rules $l \to r_1, g \to d_1 \in R_\infty$ such that

1. $l \to r$ has been obtained from $l \to r_1$ and $g \to d$ has been obtained from $g \to d_1$ by repeated application of R-SIMPLIFY-RULE. Thus, we have $r_1 \xrightarrow{*}_{R_\infty} r$ and $d_1 \xrightarrow{*}_{R_\infty} d$.

2. Both $l \to r_1$ and $g \to d_1$ have been chosen to compute critical pairs.

If $l \to r_1$ and $g \to d_1$ are the same rule, then this rule was overlapped with itself when computing critical pairs for it, and thus all critical pairs between $l \to r_1$ and $g \to d_1$ are contained in E_∞. Otherwise, assume (without loss of generality) that $l \to r_1$ was chosen before $g \to d_1$. Thus, when critical pairs for $g \to d_1$ were computed, the set of rules contained a *marked* rule $l \to r_2$ that was obtained from $l \to r_1$ by repeated application of R-SIMPLIFY-RULE, and that was simplified afterwards to $l \to r$. Consequently, all critical pairs between $l \to r_2$ and $g \to d_1$ are contained in E_∞, and $r_2 \xrightarrow{*}_{R_\infty} r$.

To sum up, we have seen that there exist rules $l \to r', g \to d' \in R_\infty$ such that $r' \xrightarrow{*}_{R_\infty} r$, $d' \xrightarrow{*}_{R_\infty} d$, and all critical pairs between $l \to r'$ and $g \to d'$ are contained in E_∞. Using the same critical overlap between l and g as in the peak $s_{i-1} \leftarrow_{R_\omega} s_i \to_{R_\omega} s_{i+1}$, but applying the rules $l \to r', g \to d'$ instead of $l \to r, g \to d$, thus yields a peak $s'_{i-1} \leftarrow_{R_\infty} s_i \to_{R_\infty} s'_{i+1}$. Now, $s'_{i-1} \leftrightarrow_{E_\infty} s'_{i+1}$ follows because the critical pair corresponding to this peak is in E_∞. In addition, $r' \xrightarrow{*}_{R_\infty} r$ and $d' \xrightarrow{*}_{R_\infty} d$ imply $s'_{i-1} \xrightarrow{*}_{R_\infty} s_{i-1}$ and $s'_{i+1} \xrightarrow{*}_{R_\infty} s_{i+1}$. $\qquad\square$

Theorem 7.4.4 *Assume that Huet's procedure uses a strategy for choosing unmarked rules to compute critical pairs that guarantees that there are no unmarked persistent rules. Then it is a correct completion procedure.*

Proof If one again considers the correctness proof of the previous section, then one observes that the only place where the fairness assumption $CP(R_\omega) \subseteq E_\infty$ comes into play is the last case in the proof of Lemma 7.3.4, where two proof steps $s_{i-1} \leftarrow_{R_\omega} s_i \to_{R_\omega} s_{i+1}$ that form a critical peak are replaced by the smaller step $s_{i-1} \leftrightarrow_{E_\infty} s_{i+1}$. Lemma 7.4.3 yields terms s'_{i-1} and s'_{i+1} such that $s_{i-1} \xleftarrow{*}_{R_\infty} s'_{i-1} \leftrightarrow_{E_\infty} s'_{i+1} \xrightarrow{*}_{R_\infty} s_{i+1}$ is a valid proof in $E_\infty \cup R_\infty$. Since $s_i > s'_{i-1}$ and $s_i > s'_{i+1}$, it is easy to see that the cost of each proof step in this proof is lower than the cost of $s_i \to_{R_\omega} s_{i+1}$. Thus, replacing the peak $s_{i-1} \leftarrow_{R_\omega} s_i \to_{R_\omega} s_{i+1}$ by $s_{i-1} \xleftarrow{*}_{R_\infty} s'_{i-1} \leftrightarrow_{E_\infty} s'_{i+1} \xrightarrow{*}_{R_\infty} s_{i+1}$ yields a smaller proof. $\qquad\square$

Exercises

7.6 Let R be a finite and *terminating* TRS, and assume that, for all $g \to d \in R$, $\hat{d}$ is a term such that $d \xrightarrow{*}_R \hat{d}$. Show that there exists an enumeration $g_1 \to d_1, \ldots, g_n \to d_n$ of all rules in R such that, for all $i = 1, \ldots, n$ and $R_i := \{g_{i+1} \to d_{i+1}, \ldots, g_n \to d_n\}$, we have $d_i \xrightarrow{*}_{R_i} \hat{d}_i$. (*Hint:* define the relation $\succ$ on R by $g \to d \succ g' \to d'$ iff $g \to d$ is used in the reduction $d' \xrightarrow{*}_R \hat{d}'$, and show that the transitive closure of $\succ$ is acyclic.)

7.7   Consider the following set of identities E:

$$\{f(f(x,y), z) \approx f(x, f(y, z)), \ f(x, x) \approx x, \ f(f(x, y), x) \approx x\}.$$

Choose an appropriate reduction order $>$ and apply Huet's completion procedure to the input $(E, >)$.

7.8   Consider the set of identities

$$E := \{f(x, y) \approx h(x, c), \ f(x, y) \approx h(c, y), \ h(c, c) \approx c\},$$

and the lexicographic path order $>_{lpo}$ that is induced by $f > h > c$. Apply Huet's completion procedure to the input $(E, >_{lpo})$.

7.9   Consider the TRS

$$R := \{f(x, y) \to c, \ h(c, y) \to c, \ h(x, c) \to c\}.$$

Show that R is confluent and equivalent to the set E of the previous example, and that the order $>_{lpo}$ of the previous example can be used to prove that R is terminating.

7.10   A TRS R is called **interreduced** iff the right-hand side r of each rule $l \to r \in R$ is R-irreducible and the left-hand side l is irreducible w.r.t. $R - \{l \to r\}$. Show that the system R_ω generated by a non-failing run of Huet's completion procedure is interreduced.

7.11   Let G be a finite set of ground identities over Σ and let $>$ be a reduction order that is total on ground terms over Σ. Show that Huet's completion procedure terminates successfully if applied to the input $(G, >)$. Compare this result with Exercise 6.7.

7.5 Huet's completion procedure in ML

This section brings together much of the functionality implemented in earlier chapters: normalization w.r.t. a TRS (*norm*), critical pair computations (*CriticalPairs2*), and orders. The ML-implementation of Huet's completion procedure follows the imperative algorithm in Fig. 7.5 quite closely. Hence there is no need for detailed comments. The only real difference is that instead of having marked and unmarked rules, two separate lists of rules are maintained.

The outer **while**-loop is realized by the function *compl*

```
type ids = (term * term) list;

(* complete: (term * term -> order) -> ids -> ids *)
fun complete ord E =
   let fun compl(E,S,R) = case orient ord (E,S,R) of
              ([],R') => R'
            | (S',R') => let val (rl,S") = choose S'
                             val cps = CriticalPairs2 [rl] R' @
                                       CriticalPairs2 R' [rl] @
                                       CriticalPairs2 [rl] [rl]
                         in compl(cps,S",rl::R') end
   in compl(E,[],[]) end;
```

(R contains the marked, S the unmarked rules) and the inner **while**-loop by
the function *orient*

```
(* orient: (term * term -> order) -> ids * ids * ids -> ids * ids *)
fun orient ord =
   let fun ori([],S,R) = (S,R)
         | ori((s,t)::E,S,R) =
              let val s' = norm (R@S) s
                  val t' = norm (R@S) t
              in if s' = t' then ori(E,S,R) else
                 if ord(s',t')=GR then ori(addRule(s',t',E,S,R)) else
                 if ord(t',s')=GR then ori(addRule(t',s',E,S,R)) else raise FAIL
              end
   in ori end;
```

which orients each identity and raises

```
exception FAIL;
```

upon encountering a non-orientable identity. Function *addRule* performs
step (e) of the imperative algorithm. It adds a new rule to the set of unmarked rules and uses it to simplify all other rules:

```
(* addRule: term * term * ids * ids * ids -> ids * ids * ids *)
fun addRule(l,r,E,S,R) =
   let fun simpl([],E',R') = (E',R')
         | simpl((g,d)::U,E',U') =
              let val g' = norm [(l,r)] g
              in if g' = g then let val d' = norm ((l,r)::R@S) d
                                in simpl(U, E', (g,d')::U') end
                 else simpl(U, (g',d)::E, U')
              end
       val (E',S') = simpl(S,E,[])
       val (E",R') = simpl(R,E',[])
   in (E", (l,r)::S', R') end;
```

The choice of the next unmarked rule in *compl* is guided by the heuristic
that smaller rules are more helpful than larger ones because they have more
simplifying power. The size of a term is computed by *size*

```
(* size: term -> int *)
fun size(V _) = 1
  | size(T(_,ts)) = sizes ts + 1
and sizes [] = 0
  | sizes(t::ts) = size t + sizes ts;
```

and *minRule* splits a set of rules into one of least size and the remaining rules:

```
(* minRule: (term * term) * int * ids * ids -> (term * term) * ids *)
fun minRule(rl,n,[],        R') = (rl,R')
  | minRule(rl,n,(l,r)::R,R') =
      let val m = size l + size r
      in if m < n then minRule((l,r),m,R,rl::R')
                  else minRule(rl,n,R,(l,r)::R')
      end;
```

The definition of *choose*, which is never called with an empty list, is obvious:

```
fun choose((l,r)::R) = minRule((l,r), size l + size r, R, []);
```

This selection strategy is fair in the sense of Theorem 7.4.4 (see Exercise 7.13).

Exercises

7.12 Apply *complete* to the following three axioms of group theory:

$$E := \{(x * y) * z \approx x * (y * z),\ i(x) * x \approx 1,\ 1 * x \approx x\}.$$

Find a suitable reduction order *ord* which leads to the following convergent system:

$$
\begin{aligned}
(x * y) * z &\rightarrow x * (y * z), & i(1) &\rightarrow 1, \\
1 * x &\rightarrow x, & i(i(x)) &\rightarrow x, \\
x * 1 &\rightarrow x, & i(x * y) &\rightarrow i(y) * i(x), \\
x * i(x) &\rightarrow 1, & x * (i(x) * y) &\rightarrow y, \\
i(x) * x &\rightarrow 1, & i(x) * (x * y) &\rightarrow y.
\end{aligned}
$$

What happens if you start with

$$E' := \{(x * y) * z \approx x * (y * z),\ x * i(x) \approx 1,\ 1 * x \approx x\}?$$

7.13 Show that choosing an unmarked rule of least size guarantees that there are no unmarked persistent rules.

7.6 Bibliographic notes

Completion was introduced by Knuth and Bendix [145] as a tool for deciding word problems in equational theories that are of interest in abstract algebra. For this reason, completion as described in this chapter is often called *Knuth-Bendix completion* in the literature. The first complete proof of correctness of a completion procedure that allows for simplification of rules was given by Huet [120]. The description of completion procedures using inference rules, and the use of proof orders as a convenient tool for showing their correctness, were introduced by Bachmair, Dershowitz, and Hsiang in [17], and investigated in more detail by Bachmair in [14].

If applied to a finite set of ground identities together with a reduction order that is total on ground terms, completion always terminates successfully. In this case, the computation of critical pairs just amounts to reducing the left-hand side of one rule by another rule (see Exercise 6.7). Efficient algorithms for computing a finite convergent TRS that is equivalent to a given finite set of ground identities are described in [93, 235].

We have seen that Huet's procedure is not fair in the strict sense that all critical pairs between persistent rules are computed. In the proof of its correctness we have used the fact that it is sufficient to know that each of these critical pairs has a proof that is smaller than the corresponding critical peak. This observation can be used to prove correctness for more general "critical pair criteria", that is, criteria that describe which critical pairs are redundant, and thus need not be computed [249, 151, 16, 251, 14].

Exercise 7.8 together with Exercise 7.9 demonstrates that a correct completion procedure (here Huet's procedure) may fail for an input $(E, >)$ even though there exists a finite convergent TRS that is contained in $>$ and equivalent to E. This phenomenon is more thoroughly investigated in [77], where it is also shown that there exist equational theories with decidable word problem such that there does not exist an equivalent finite convergent TRS.

If it does not fail on input $(E, >)$, Huet's procedure yields a convergent TRS R_ω that is contained in $>$, equivalent to E, and interreduced (see Exercise 7.10). Métivier [174] shows that interreduced convergent systems are unique up to E and $>$, that is, if R_1 and R_2 are interreduced convergent systems such that $\approx_{R_i} = \approx_E$ and $R_i \subseteq >$ (for $i = 1, 2$), then R_1 and R_2 are equal up to variable renaming. This fact can be used to show that Huet's procedure terminates (successfully or with failure) on input $(E, >)$ if there exists a finite convergent system that is contained in $>$ and equivalent to E [77].

The completion procedures we have described above are parameterized by a reduction order $>$, and they use this order throughout the completion process. Failure of the procedure on input $(E, >)$ may in some cases simply be due to the fact that $>$ is the wrong order. One might think that it is admissible to change the order during completion, provided that the new order contains the current set of rules. In [221] it is shown, however, that this destroys correctness of completion, even in cases where the procedure terminates without failure.

There are two extensions of rewriting and completion that try to cope with the problem of non-orientable identities (see Chapter 11 for more details). On the one hand, ordered rewriting and unfailing completion [18, 252] depend on a reduction order that is total on ground terms. Non-orientable identities do not lead to failure of the procedure. Like oriented rules, they are used for computing critical pairs, but in both directions. On the other hand, rewriting modulo equational theories takes some of the identities completely out of the rewriting process. Conceptually, these identities define a congruence relation on terms, and the remaining identities are used to rewrite the congruence classes [203, 127]. Proof orders can also be employed to show correctness of these extended completion procedures [14].

8

Gröbner Bases and Buchberger's Algorithm

We have seen in the previous chapter that in some cases completion generates a convergent term rewriting system for a given equational theory, and that such a system can then be used to decide the word problem for this equational theory. A very similar approach has independently been developed in the area of computer algebra, where *Gröbner bases* are used to decide the ideal congruence and the ideal membership problem in polynomial rings. The close connection to rewriting is given by the fact that Gröbner bases define convergent reduction relations on polynomials, and that the ideal congruence problem can be seen as a word problem. In addition, Buchberger's algorithm, which is very similar to the basic completion procedure presented above, can be used to compute Gröbner bases. In contrast to the situation for term rewriting, however, termination of the reduction relation can always be guaranteed, and Buchberger's algorithm always terminates with success. The purpose of this chapter is, on the one hand, to provide another example for the usefulness of the rewriting and completion approach introduced above. On the other hand, the basic definitions and results from the area of Gröbner bases are presented using the notations and results for abstract reduction systems introduced in Chapter 2.

8.1 The ideal membership problem

Let us first introduce the basic algorithmic problems that can be solved with the help of Gröbner bases. We assume that the reader is familiar with the elementary notions and definitions for polynomials. For this reason, they will be presented in a rather informal way (strictly formal definition can, for example, be found in [124]).

We consider the **ring** $K[X_1, \ldots, X_n]$ **of** n-**variate polynomials** over K, where n is a positive integer and K is an arbitrary field. The elements of

$K[X_1, \ldots, X_n]$ are thus polynomials in the indeterminates $X_1, \ldots, X_n$ with coefficients in K. For example, if $n = 2$ and $K = \mathbb{Q}$, the field of rational numbers, then $f := 2X_1^2 X_2 - X_1 X_2^2 + 5X_1 + 17$ is an element of $K[X_1, X_2]$. Addition "+"and multiplication "·" of polynomials are defined in the usual way. We will often omit "·" when writing the multiplication of polynomials or field elements.

Monomials in $K[X_1, \ldots, X_n]$ are of the form $X_1^{k_1} \cdots X_n^{k_n}$, where $k_1, \ldots, k_n$ are non-negative integers. If $k_i = 0$, then the indeterminate X_i is usually just left out. The monomial $X_1^0 \cdots X_n^0$ is denoted by 1. The **degree** of the monomial $X_1^{k_1} \cdots X_n^{k_n}$ is the sum of its exponents, i.e. $deg(X_1^{k_1} \cdots X_n^{k_n}) := k_1 + \cdots + k_n$. The **coefficient** of a monomial in a polynomial f is the element of K that "stands in front of this monomial" in the representation of f. In a given polynomial, all but finitely many monomials have coefficient 0. Monomials with coefficient 0 are usual omitted when writing f. For this reason, we say that a monomial **occurs** in f iff it has a non-zero coefficient in f. For example, the monomials $X_1^2 X_2, X_1 X_2^2, X_1, 1$ are all the monomials occurring in the polynomial $f := 2X_1^2 X_2 - X_1 X_2^2 + 5X_1 + 17$. The monomial $X_1 X_2^2$ has coefficient -1, and the monomial 1 has coefficient 17.

One should note that this representation of polynomials as sums of monomials with coefficients assumes that after each operation (like addition, multiplication) there is an implicit normalization step. Also, the indeterminates should not be confused with variables in terms. In the context of Gröbner bases, they rather play the rôle of constant symbols. Thus, polynomials are like ground terms, but considered modulo the ring axioms, which are used to transform the polynomials into their representation as sums of monomials with coefficients.

Definition 8.1.1 A *nonempty* set $J \subseteq K[X_1, \ldots, X_n]$ is an **ideal** of the ring $K[X_1, \ldots, X_n]$ iff it is closed under addition and under multiplication with ring elements, i.e. it satisfies

1. $f, g \in J$ implies $f + g \in J$,
2. $f \in J$ and $g \in K[X_1, \ldots, X_n]$ implies $f \cdot g \in J$.

The **ideal generated by** $f_1, \ldots, f_k \in K[X_1, \ldots, X_n]$ is the set

$$\langle f_1, \ldots, f_k \rangle := \{f_1 \cdot g_1 + \cdots + f_k \cdot g_k \mid g_1, \ldots, g_k \in K[X_1, \ldots, X_n]\}.$$

The **ideal congruence** $\equiv_J$ induced by an ideal J is defined by $f \equiv_J g$ iff $f - g \in J$.

It follows from this definition that any ideal contains the zero polynomial 0, and that the relation $\equiv_J$ is a congruence relation on $K[X_1, \ldots, X_n]$. It is easy to see that the set $\langle f_1, \ldots, f_k \rangle$ is in fact an ideal of $K[X_1, \ldots, X_n]$, namely the smallest ideal of $K[X_1, \ldots, X_n]$ that contains $f_1, \ldots, f_k$.

The **ideal membership problem** is concerned with the following question:

Instance: $f, f_1, \ldots, f_k \in K[X_1, \ldots, X_n]$
Question: Is $f \in \langle f_1, \ldots, f_k \rangle$ satisfied?

Lemma 8.1.2 *The ideal membership problem for $J := \langle f_1, \ldots, f_k \rangle$ is decidable iff the ideal congruence $\equiv_J$ is decidable.*

Proof The direction from left to right is an immediate consequence of the definition of $\equiv_J$. The other direction follows from the fact that $f \in J$ iff $f \equiv_J 0$. $\square$

The question "$f \equiv_J g$?" corresponds to the word problem for equational theories. It will be solved with the help of a convergent reduction relation on polynomials.

Exercises

8.1   Let J be an ideal of $K[X_1, \ldots, X_n]$. Show that J contains the zero polynomial, and that $\equiv_J$ is a congruence relation on $K[X_1, \ldots, X_n]$.

8.2   Let $f_1, \ldots, f_k \in K[X_1, \ldots, X_n]$. Show that $\langle f_1, \ldots, f_k \rangle$ is the smallest ideal of $K[X_1, \ldots, X_n]$ that contains $f_1, \ldots, f_k$.

8.2 Polynomial reduction

Our goal is to introduce a reduction relation on polynomials that is induced by the polynomials $f_1, \ldots, f_k$ that generate the ideal $J := \langle f_1, \ldots, f_k \rangle$. How can a polynomial be used as a rewrite rule? The idea is to take the "largest" monomial of the polynomial as the left-hand side, and the (negated) remainder of the polynomial as the right-hand side of the rule.

Example 8.2.1 Consider the polynomial $f := X_1^2 X_2 + X_1 X_2 - 17$. The monomial $X_1^2 X_2$ is a "natural candidate" for the largest monomial since it has the largest degree of all monomials occurring in f. Thus, f gives rise to the rewrite rule $X_1^2 X_2 \to -X_1 X_2 + 17$. Assume that we want to apply this rule to the polynomial $g := X_1^2 X_2^2 + X_1 X_2^2 - 3$. The monomial $X_1^2 X_2^2$ is a multiple of the left-hand side $X_1^2 X_2$ of the rule: $X_1^2 X_2^2 = (X_1^2 X_2) \cdot X_2$. The rule $X_1^2 X_2 \to -X_1 X_2 + 17$ is applied to g by replacing $X_1^2 X_2^2$ by the corresponding multiple of the right-hand side. This yields the polynomial

$(-X_1X_2^2 + 17X_2) + X_1X_2^2 - 3 = 17X_2 - 3$. Obviously, this rule application corresponds to adding the multiple $f \cdot (-X_2)$ of f to g.

Before we can define the reduction relation induced by a polynomial in the general case, we must clarify with respect to which order the largest monomial is chosen.

Definition 8.2.2 Let $M_n := \{X_1^{k_1} \cdots X_n^{k_n} \mid (k_1, \ldots, k_n) \in \mathbb{N}^n\}$ denote the set of all monomials in $K[X_1, \ldots, X_n]$. A *total* order $\succ$ on M_n is called **admissible** iff it satisfies

1. $m_1 \mid m_2$ implies $m_1 \preceq m_2$,
2. $m_1 \prec m_2$ implies $m \cdot m_1 \prec m \cdot m_2$.

The notation "$m_1 \mid m_2$" stands for "m_1 divides m_2", i.e. there exists a monomial m such that $m_1 \cdot m = m_2$. Obviously, $m_1 := X_1^{k_1} \cdots X_n^{k_n}$ is a divisor of $m_2 := X_1^{l_1} \cdots X_n^{l_n}$ iff the exponent tuples satisfy $(k_1, \ldots, k_n) \leq (l_1, \ldots, l_n)$, where $\leq$ denotes the component-wise order on n-tuples of natural numbers, i.e. $(k_1, \ldots, k_n) \leq (l_1, \ldots, l_n)$ iff $k_1 \leq l_1 \wedge \ldots \wedge k_n \leq l_n$.

Lemma 8.2.3 *Any admissible order $\succ$ on M_n is well-founded.*

Proof The order $\geq$ on natural numbers is obviously a well-partial-order, and thus its component-wise extension to $\mathbb{N}^n$ is also a well-partial-order, by Lemma 5.4.5. Consequently, any order on M_n that satisfies (1) of Definition 8.2.2 is well-founded, since it is an extension of a well-partial-order. $\square$

Example 8.2.4 It is easy to see that the order $\succ$ defined by $X_1^{k_1} \cdots X_n^{k_n} \succ X_1^{l_1} \cdots X_n^{l_n}$ iff

1. $\sum_{i=1}^n k_i > \sum_{i=1}^n l_i$, or
2. $\sum_{i=1}^n k_i = \sum_{i=1}^n l_i$ and $(k_1, \ldots, k_n) >_{lex}^n (l_1, \ldots, l_n)$

is an admissible total order on M_n.

In the following, we assume that $\succ$ is an arbitrary, but fixed, admissible total order on M_n. Let $f \in K[X_1, \ldots, X_n]$ be a polynomial. The largest monomial (with respect to $\succ$) occurring in f is denoted by $H(f)$ (**head monomial**), its coefficient is denoted by $HC(f)$ (**head coefficient**), and the **remainder** of the polynomial is $R(f) := f - HC(f) \cdot H(f)$.

When defining the reduction relation induced by a polynomial f, we may (without loss of generality) restrict our attention to polynomials f with $HC(f) = 1$. In fact, if $f_1, \ldots, f_k$ are non-zero polynomials, then we have $\langle f_1, \ldots, f_k \rangle = \langle HC(f_1)^{-1} \cdot f_1, \ldots, HC(f_1)^{-1} \cdot f_k \rangle$. In addition, the zero polynomial can be removed from a given generating set without changing the ideal, unless all polynomials in the generating set are zero. Since the ideal membership problem and the ideal congruence are trivially decidable for the trivial ideal $\{0\}$, the degenerate case that all generating polynomials are zero need not be considered here.

Definition 8.2.5 Let f be a polynomial with head coefficient 1, i.e. $f = H(f) + R(f)$. Then f induces the following **reduction relation** on polynomials: $g \to_f g'$ iff

1. g contains a monomial m with coefficient $a \neq 0$,
2. there exists a monomial m' such that $m = H(f) \cdot m'$, and
3. $g' = g - am' \cdot f$.

If $F := \{f_1, \ldots, f_k\}$ is a finite set of polynomials with head coefficients 1, then the reduction relation $\to_F$ induced by F is defined as follows:

$$\to_F := \bigcup_{i=1}^{k} \to_{f_i}.$$

Before we can show that $\overset{*}{\leftrightarrow}_F$ coincides with the ideal congruence $\equiv_J$ for $J := \langle F \rangle$, we need a technical lemma.

Lemma 8.2.6 *Let f, g, g', h be polynomials, m'' a monomial, and $b \in K - \{0\}$, and assume that f has head coefficient 1.*

1. *$f \to_f 0$.*
2. *$g \to_f g'$ implies $bm'' \cdot g \to_f bm'' \cdot g'$.*
3. *$g \to_f g'$ implies $h + g \downarrow_f h + g'$.*

Proof (1) The polynomial f can reduce its own head monomial $m := H(f)$. The coefficient of m in f is 1, and $m = H(f) \cdot 1$. Thus, this reduction yields the polynomial $f - 1 \cdot f = 0$.

(2) From the assumption $g \to_f g'$ we can infer that g contains a monomial m with coefficient $a \neq 0$, $m = H(f) \cdot m'$ for a monomial m', and $g' = g - am' \cdot f$. Consequently, $bm'' \cdot g$ contains the monomial $m \cdot m''$ with coefficient $a \cdot b \neq 0$, $m \cdot m'' = H(f) \cdot (m' \cdot m'')$, and $bm'' \cdot g' = bm'' \cdot g - (a \cdot b)(m' \cdot m'') \cdot f$, which shows that $bm'' \cdot g \to_f bm'' \cdot g'$.

(3) Assume that $g \to_f g'$, and that the reduction is applied to a monomial m with coefficient $a \neq 0$ in g. Let m' be such that $m = H(f) \cdot m'$. By assumption, $g' = g - am' \cdot f$. We distinguish three cases, depending on the coefficient b of m in h.

Case 1: $b = 0$. In this case, $h + g \to_f h + g'$ obviously holds.

Case 2: $a + b = 0$, and thus $b = -a$. In this case, $h + g' \to_f h + g$ holds because $h + g' - bm' \cdot f = h + g - am' \cdot f - bm' \cdot f = h + g$. Note that the coefficient of m in $h + g'$ is b since the coefficient of m in g' is 0. In the first equation we have used the fact that $g' = g - am' \cdot f$ and in the second that $b = -a$.

Case 3: $a + b \neq 0$ and $b \neq 0$. In this case,

$$h + g \rightarrow_f (h + g) - (a + b)m' \cdot f \leftarrow_f h + g'.$$

Note that the coefficient of m in $h + g$ is $a + b$, and the coefficient of m in $h + g'$ is b.   □

Theorem 8.2.7 *If* $F := \{f_1, \ldots, f_k\}$ *is a finite set of polynomials with head coefficients 1, and* $J := \langle f_1, \ldots, f_k \rangle$, *then* $\equiv_J = \overset{*}{\leftrightarrow}_F$.

Proof ($\supseteq$) It is sufficient to show that $\rightarrow_F \subseteq \equiv_J$. Thus, assume that $g \rightarrow_{f_i} g'$ for some $i, 1 \leq i \leq k$. By definition, this means that there exist $a \in K$ and a monomial m' such that $g' = g - am' \cdot f_i$. Consequently, $g - g' = am' \cdot f_i \in J$, which shows that $g \equiv_J g'$.

($\subseteq$) Assume that $f \equiv_J g$, that is, $f - g \in J$. Because $J = \langle f_1, \ldots, f_k \rangle$, this means that there exist polynomials $g_1, \ldots, g_k \in K[X_1, \ldots, X_n]$ such that $f - g = \sum_{i=1}^{k} g_i \cdot f_i$. If we decompose the polynomials g_i into the sums of their monomials and then apply the distributivity law, we obtain $a_1, \ldots, a_l \in K$, $m_1, \ldots, m_l \in M_n$, and a mapping $s : \{1, \ldots, l\} \to \{1, \ldots, k\}$ such that

$$f = g + \sum_{j=1}^{l} a_j m_j \cdot f_{s(j)}.$$

We prove $f \overset{*}{\leftrightarrow}_F g$ by induction on l.

The induction base ($l = 0$) is trivial since $f = g$ obviously implies $f \overset{*}{\leftrightarrow}_F g$.

In the induction step, we define $f' := g + \sum_{j=1}^{l-1} a_j m_j \cdot f_{s(j)}$, and assume that $f' \overset{*}{\leftrightarrow}_F g$ is already proved. By (1) and (2) of Lemma 8.2.6, we have $a_l m_l \cdot f_{s(l)} \rightarrow_{f_{s(l)}} 0$, and thus (3) of Lemma 8.2.6 yields $f = f' + a_l m_l \cdot f_{s(l)} \downarrow_{f_{s(l)}} f'$. Together with $f' \overset{*}{\leftrightarrow}_F g$, this implies $f \overset{*}{\leftrightarrow}_F g$.   □

Corollary 8.2.8 *Let* $F := \{f_1, \ldots, f_k\}$ *be a finite set of polynomials with head coefficients 1, and* $J := \langle f_1, \ldots, f_k \rangle$. *If* $\rightarrow_F$ *is confluent and terminating, then* $\equiv_J$ *is decidable.*

Proof Analogous to the proof of Theorem 4.1.1.   □

The reduction relation $\rightarrow_F$ is always terminating, but it need not be confluent.

Proposition 8.2.9 *Let* F *be a finite set of polynomials whose head coefficients are equal to 1. Then* $\rightarrow_F$ *is a terminating reduction relation.*

Proof With each polynomial $f \in K[X_1, \ldots, X_n]$ we associate the set $M(f)$ of monomials occurring in f, and we compare these sets with the multiset order $\succ_{mul}$ induced by the admissible order $\succ$ on M_n. Since $\succ$ is well-founded, $\succ_{mul}$ is also well-founded. Thus, it is sufficient to show that $g \to_F g'$ implies $M(g) \succ_{mul} M(g')$.

Assume that $g \to_f g'$ for a polynomial $f = H(f) + R(f) \in F$. Thus, the polynomial g contains a monomial m with coefficient $a \neq 0$, there exists a monomial m' such that $m = H(f) \cdot m'$, and $g' = g - am' \cdot f$. Since $\succ$ is admissible and $H(f)$ is the largest monomial in f, all monomials in $am' \cdot R(f)$ are smaller than $m = H(f) \cdot m'$. Thus, $M(g')$ is obtained from $M(g)$ by replacing the monomial m by smaller monomials, which implies that $M(g) \succ_{mul} M(g')$. $\qquad\square$

Example 8.2.10 Let $F := \{X_1^2 X_2 - X_1^2, X_1 X_2^2 - X_2^2\}$, and $\succ$ be the admissible order introduced in Example 8.2.4. The head monomial of $f_1 := X_1^2 X_2 - X_1^2$ is $X_1^2 X_2$ and the head monomial of $f_2 := X_1 X_2^2 - X_2^2$ is $X_1 X_2^2$. It is easy to see that $X_1^2 \leftarrow_{f_1} X_1^2 X_2 \leftarrow_{f_1} X_1^2 X_2^2 \to_{f_2} X_1 X_2^2 \to_{f_2} X_2^2$. Since $X_1^2 \neq X_2^2$ and both polynomials are $\to_F$ irreducible, this shows that $\to_F$ is not confluent.

Exercises

8.3   Let $\succ$ be a *well-founded* total order on M_n. Show that under this assumption (2) of Definition 8.2.2 implies (1).

8.4   Show that the binary relation on M_n introduced in Example 8.2.4 is a total admissible order on M_n.

8.3 Gröbner bases

Corollary 8.2.8 and Proposition 8.2.9 show that the ideal congruence problem for a given ideal J is decidable, if J is generated by a finite set G of polynomials that induces a confluent reduction relation $\to_G$. This motivates the following definition.

Definition 8.3.1 Let $G := \{f_1, \ldots, f_k\}$ be a finite set of polynomials with head coefficients 1. Then G is a **Gröbner basis** of the ideal J iff $J = \langle f_1, \ldots, f_k \rangle$ and $\to_G$ is confluent.

We have seen in Example 8.2.10 that not every finite generating set of an ideal is a Gröbner basis of that ideal. Similarly as in the case of term rewriting systems, confluence of polynomial reductions can be decided by considering finitely many "critical situations". For polynomial reductions, these critical situations give rise to *S-polynomials*:

Definition 8.3.2 Let $f_i = H(f_i) + R(f_i)$ and $f_j = H(f_j) + R(f_j)$ be polynomials with head coefficients 1, let $m := lcm(H(f_i), H(f_j))$ be the least common multiple of the head monomials of f_i and f_j, and let m_i, m_j be monomials such that $m_i \cdot H(f_i) = m = m_j \cdot H(f_j)$. The **S-polynomial** induced by the polynomials f_i, f_j is defined as $S(f_i, f_j) := m_i \cdot f_i - m_j \cdot f_j$.

Note that, for monomials $m_1 := X_1^{k_1} \cdots X_n^{k_n}$ and $m_2 := X_1^{l_1} \cdots X_n^{l_n}$, the least common multiple is $lcm(m_1, m_2) = X_1^{r_1} \cdots X_n^{r_n}$, where $r_i := max(k_i, l_i)$ (for $i = 1, \ldots, n$).

For example, the polynomials $X_1^2 X_2 - X_1^2, X_1 X_2^2 - X_2^2$ of Example 8.2.10 induce the S-polynomial $X_1 X_2^2 - X_1^2 X_2$.

The S-polynomial $S(f_i, f_j)$ corresponds to the following critical overlap between an application of $\rightarrow_{f_i}$ and one of $\rightarrow_{f_j}$:

$$m - m_i \cdot f_i \leftarrow_{f_i} m \rightarrow_{f_j} m - m_j \cdot f_j.$$

Thus, instead of considering the "critical pair" $\langle m - m_i \cdot f_i, m - m_j \cdot f_j \rangle$, we consider the difference between the two polynomials in this pair: $S(f_i, f_j) = m - m_j \cdot f_j - (m - m_i \cdot f_i)$. If an S-polynomial reduces to 0, then the corresponding critical situation is confluent. This is an immediate consequence of the next lemma.

Lemma 8.3.3 $f - g \xrightarrow{*}_F 0$ *implies* $f \downarrow_F g$.

Proof by induction on the length of the reduction sequence. If $f - g = 0$, then $f = g$ and $f \downarrow_F g$ trivially holds. For the induction step, assume that $f - g \rightarrow_{f_i} h \xrightarrow{*}_F 0$ for a polynomial $f_i \in F$. Assume that the reduction is applied to the monomial m in $f - g$, let m' be such that $m = H(f_i) \cdot m'$, and let a be the coefficient of m in f and b the coefficient of m in g. Thus, $a - b \neq 0$ since it is the coefficient of m in $f - g$, and $h = (f - g) - (a - b)m' \cdot f_i$.

Depending on whether a, b are zero or not, we have the following zero- or one-step reductions:

$$f \xrightarrow{=}_{f_i} f - am' \cdot f_i \quad \text{and} \quad g \xrightarrow{=}_{f_i} g - bm' \cdot f_i.$$

Since $h = (f - am' \cdot f_i) - (g - bm' \cdot f_i)$, the induction hypothesis yields $f - am' \cdot f_i \downarrow_F g - bm' \cdot f_i$. $\qquad\square$

The following theorem states that the S-polynomials really capture all the critical overlaps.

Theorem 8.3.4 *Let* $G := \{f_1, \ldots, f_k\}$ *be a finite set of polynomials with head coefficients 1. Then* G *is a Gröbner basis of* $\langle f_1, \ldots, f_k \rangle$ *iff all S-polynomials induced by the polynomials in* G *reduce to 0.*

Proof To show the $\Rightarrow$-direction, assume that $\rightarrow_G$ is confluent, and thus also Church-Rosser by Theorem 2.1.5. Obviously, the definition of the S-polynomial $f := S(f_i, f_j)$ implies that $f \in J$, and thus $f \equiv_J 0$. Since $\equiv_J = \overset{*}{\leftrightarrow}_G$ and $\rightarrow_G$ is Church-Rosser, this implies that $f \downarrow_G 0$. Because 0 is obviously $\rightarrow_G$-irreducible, $f \downarrow_G 0$ yields $f \overset{*}{\rightarrow}_G 0$.

Since $\rightarrow_G$ is terminating, the $\Leftarrow$-direction of the theorem can be shown by proving that $\rightarrow_G$ is locally confluent. For this purpose we look at the following critical situation:

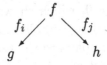

Case 1: the reductions are applied to different monomials in f. Assume that $\rightarrow_{f_i}$ is applied to the monomial m_1 with coefficient a in f, and that $\rightarrow_{f_j}$ is applied to the monomial m_2 with coefficient b in f, where $m_1 \neq m_2$. Thus, we have the following situation:

- $f = f_1 + am_1 + bm_2$, where f_1 is a polynomial in which neither m_1 nor m_2 occurs.
- There exist monomials m_i, m_j such that $m_1 = H(f_i) \cdot m_i$ and $m_2 = H(f_j) \cdot m_j$.
- $g = f - am_i \cdot f_i = f_1 - am_i \cdot R(f_i) + bm_2$, and
- $h = f - bm_j \cdot f_j = f_1 + am_1 - bm_j \cdot R(f_j)$.

Without loss of generality, we assume that $m_1 \succ m_2$. Thus $m_1 \succ m_2 = H(f_j) \cdot m_j$ implies that m_1 is larger than all the monomials occurring in $bm_j \cdot R(f_j)$. For this reason, the polynomial h contains the monomial m_1 with coefficient a, which shows that the reduction $h \rightarrow_{f_i} h - am_i \cdot f_i$ is possible. In addition, $f \rightarrow_G h$ yields

$$g = f + (-am_i \cdot f_i) \downarrow_F h + (-am_i \cdot f_i) = h - am_i \cdot f_i,$$

by Lemma 8.2.6. Thus, we have shown that g and h are joinable.

Case 2: the reductions are applied to the same monomial in f. Thus, we have the following situation:

- $f = f_1 + am_1$, where f_1 is a polynomial in which m_1 does not occur.
- There exist monomials m_i, m_j such that $H(f_i) \cdot m_i = m_1 = H(f_j) \cdot m_j$.
- $g = f - am_i \cdot f_i$ and $h = f - am_j \cdot f_j$.

Since both $H(f_i)$ and $H(f_j)$ divide m_1, their least common multiple $m :=$ $\mathrm{lcm}(H(f_i), H(f_j))$ divides m_1 as well. Thus, there exists a monomial m' such that $m_1 = m \cdot m'$. If m_i', m_j' denote the monomials such that $H(f_i) \cdot m_i' = m = H(f_j) \cdot m_j'$, then $S(f_i, f_j) = m_i' \cdot f_i - m_j' \cdot f_j$. Note that $H(f_i) \cdot m_i = m_1 = m \cdot m' = H(f_i) \cdot m_i' \cdot m'$ implies that $m_i = m_i' \cdot m'$. The equality $m_j = m_j' \cdot m'$ can be shown similarly.

By assumption, $S(f_i, f_j) \xrightarrow{*}_G 0$, which implies $am' \cdot S(f_i, f_j) \xrightarrow{*}_G 0$ by Lemma 8.2.6. Since $am' \cdot S(f_i, f_j) = am' \cdot m_i' \cdot f_i - am' \cdot m_j' \cdot f_j = am_i \cdot f_i - am_j \cdot f_j = h - g$, we thus know that $h - g \xrightarrow{*}_G 0$. By applying Lemma 8.3.3, we finally obtain $h \downarrow_G g$. $\qquad\square$

In Example 8.2.10, the S-polynomial $X_1 X_2^2 - X_1^2 X_2$ reduces to the irreducible polynomial $X_2^2 - X_1^2 \neq 0$, which shows that F is not a Gröbner basis. Similar to the idea underlying completion, namely adding appropriately oriented non-confluent critical pairs to the term rewriting system, Buchberger's algorithm extends the set of polynomials by those S-polynomials that do not reduce to 0. For example, if $X_2^2 - X_1^2$ is added to F, then the S-polynomial $X_1 X_2^2 - X_1^2 X_2$ reduces to 0. However, one must now compute new S-polynomials between the polynomials in F and the new polynomial.

8.4 Buchberger's algorithm

The goal of this algorithm, which is described in Fig. 8.1, is to transform a finite generating set $F := \{f_1, \ldots, f_k\}$ of an ideal J into a Gröbner basis for J. As mentioned above, this is achieved by computing S-polynomials and by extending F by those S-polynomials that do not reduce to 0 (more precisely, F is extended by the corresponding irreducible polynomials). Since $S(f, f) = 0$ by definition, it is not necessary to compute an S-polynomial between a polynomial and itself. In addition, $S(f, g) = -S(g, f)$ implies that $S(f, g)$ reduces to 0 iff $S(g, f)$ reduces to 0. Thus, it is sufficient to compute only one of the two S-polynomials.

Theorem 8.4.1 *Buchberger's algorithm terminates for every finite input set* $F := \{f_1, \ldots, f_k\}$, *and it yields a Gröbner basis of* $J := \langle f_1, \ldots, f_k \rangle$ *as output.*

Proof First, note that in every step of the algorithm $\langle G_i \rangle = J$ is satisfied. This is an easy consequence of the following two facts:

- If $f_i, f_j \in J$, then $S(f_i, f_j) \in J$.
- If $S(f_i, f_j) \in J = \langle G_i \rangle$ and $S(f_i, f_j) \xrightarrow{*}_{G_i} h$, then $HC(h)^{-1} \cdot h \in J$.

Input:
>   A finite set $F := \{f_1, \ldots, f_k\}$ of polynomials in $K[X_1, \ldots, X_n]$ with
>   head coefficients 1 and an admissible order $\succ$ on M_n.

Output:
>   A finite set G_i of polynomials in $K[X_1, \ldots, X_n]$ that is a Gröbner basis
>   of $J := \langle f_1, \ldots, f_k \rangle$.

Initialization:
> $i := 0;\ G_0 := F$;
> $B_0 := \{(f_i, f_j) \mid 1 \le i < j \le k\}$;

`while` $B_i \ne \emptyset$ `do`
>   (a) Choose a pair $(f_l, f_r) \in B_i$;
>   (b) Compute the S-polynomial $S(f_l, f_r)$;
>   (c) Compute a $\rightarrow_{G_i}$-normal form h of $S(f_l, f_r)$;
>   (d) If $h \ne 0$, then
> $\quad B_{i+1} := (B_i - \{(f_l, f_r)\}) \cup \{(f, HC(h)^{-1} \cdot h) \mid f \in G_i\}$;
> $\quad G_{i+1} := G_i \cup \{HC(h)^{-1} \cdot h\}$;
> $\quad i := i + 1$;
>   (e) Otherwise, $B_{i+1} := B_i - \{(f_l, f_r)\};\ G_{i+1} := G_i;\ i := i + 1$;

`od`

Output G_i;

Fig. 8.1. Buchberger's algorithm.

Thus, if the algorithm terminates with output G_i, then $J = \langle G_i \rangle$.

The output set G_i is a Gröbner basis since all its S-polynomials reduce to 0. In fact, if $f, g \in G_i$, then at some step j of the computation one of the S-polynomials $S(f, g)$ or $S(g, f)$ was computed. Assume without loss of generality that $S(f, g)$ was computed. If $S(f, g) \xrightarrow{*}_{G_j} 0$, then $S(f, g) \xrightarrow{*}_{G_i} 0$ since $G_j \subseteq G_i$. Otherwise, $S(f, g) \xrightarrow{*}_{G_j} h$ and $HC(h)^{-1} \cdot h \in G_{j+1}$. Since $HC(h)^{-1} \cdot h$ can be used to reduce h to 0 in one step, this implies $S(f, g) \xrightarrow{*}_{G_{j+1}} 0$, and thus $S(f, g) \xrightarrow{*}_{G_i} 0$.

In order to show termination of the algorithm, assume to the contrary that it does not terminate. It is easy to see that this implies that infinitely many new polynomials are added in (d). Let $h_1, h_2, h_3, \ldots$ be the list of these polynomials, in the order in which they are added. Consider the sequence $H(h_1), H(h_2), H(h_3), \ldots$ of their head monomials. Since the divisibility relation on monomials coincides with the component-wise order on their exponent tuples, and since this component-wise order on tuples of natural numbers is a well-partial-order (see proof of Lemma 8.2.3), there exist indices $1 \le i < j$ such that $H(h_i) \mid H(h_j)$. Consequently, h_i can be used to reduce h_j. This is a contradiction, since the polynomials added in step (d) of the algorithm are irreducible with respect to the polynomials that are contained in the current set of polynomials, and this set contains h_i. $\square$

For the sake of simplicity, we have presented a version of Buchberger's algorithm that is very similar to the basic completion procedure described in Section 7.1. As with completion, the efficiency of Buchberger's algorithm can be improved by simplifying old polynomials with the help of the newly generated ones. In addition, the use of appropriate "critical pair criteria" that avoid the computation of redundant S-polynomials is important. We have shown that Buchberger's algorithm terminates for all finite input sets F and admissible orders $\succ$, but the run time of the algorithm strongly depends on which admissible order is used. Thus, appropriate criteria for choosing the "right" admissible order are also important.

Exercises

8.5   Let G be a finite set of polynomials with head coefficients 1, and let $J := \langle G \rangle$ be the ideal generated by G. Show the following:

- If $f, g \in G$, then $S(f,g) \in J$.
- If $f \in J$ and $f \xrightarrow{*}_G h$, then $h \in J$.

8.6   Apply Buchberger's algorithm to $F := \{X_1^2 X_2 - X_1^2, X_1 X_2^2 - X_2^2\}$.

8.5 Bibliographic notes

Gröbner bases and an algorithm for computing them were developed in 1965 in B. Buchberger's Ph.D. thesis [36, 37], but were then almost forgotten for more than a decade. In 1976, research on this topic was resumed by Buchberger and many others, leading to a more thorough analysis of the method (see e.g., [39, 38, 15]), several generalizations (e.g. to polynomials over certain rings [131, 238]), and applications in various areas of mathematics and computer algebra (see [40, 43] for an overview of the results and applications). In [39], Buchberger introduced the name "Gröbner basis" in honour of his thesis adviser W. Gröbner, who stimulated his research on this topic, and had some initial ideas on how to attack the problem [101]. Later on, it turned out that Gröbner bases had already been introduced under the name "standard bases" by H. Hironaka [114], but their existence for an arbitrary finitely generated ideal was proved in a non-constructive way, that is, [114] does not describe an algorithm for computing standard bases.

The connection between Buchberger's algorithm and the critical pair/completion approach in term rewriting was first observed in [161, 44], and more closely analysed in [41, 42]. This connection has, for example, been used to translate criteria for avoiding the computation of redundant S-polynomials into critical pair criteria for completion of term rewriting systems [249, 151]. There are several works that describe completion of term rewriting systems and Buchberger's algorithm in a common framework, or try to present Buchberger's algorithm as a special case of completion of generalized term rewriting systems [248, 48, 132, 45, 19].

The proofs of some of the technical lemmas in this chapter have been derived from [39, 15]. Two recent books on the topic are [247, 2].

9

Combination Problems

We have seen that properties like termination and confluence are in general undecidable and require sophisticated technology to solve interesting subclasses. Because the likelihood that a given TRS can be treated with a particular method decreases with the size of the TRS, it is desirable to modularize tests for confluence and termination. For example, the system $R := \{f(x, x) \to x, \ a \to g(a)\}$ cannot be shown to be confluent by any of the methods of Chapter 6 because R is neither left-linear nor terminating. However, $R_0 := \{f(x, x) \to x\}$ is terminating, has no critical pairs and is therefore confluent. Similarly, $R_1 := \{a \to g(a)\}$ is orthogonal and thus also confluent. Wouldn't it be nice if we could conclude that $R = R_0 \cup R_1$ must therefore also be confluent? A famous theorem by Toyama, which started the whole field of combination problems for term rewriting systems, asserts that this is the case because R_0 and R_1 do not share function symbols. This chapter studies under what conditions we can transfer confluence and/or termination from individual systems to their union.

Computer scientists want to combine not just properties but also algorithms. Hence the final substantive section in this chapter is devoted to one particularly well-behaved instance, that of combining decision procedures for the word problem: given decision procedures for $\approx_{E_0}$ and $\approx_{E_1}$, how can we decide $\approx_{E_0 \cup E_1}$? Of course, for arbitrary E_0 and E_1 this is not possible, but if they do not share function symbols, it is.

9.1 Basic notions

It is obvious that the less interaction there is between two term rewriting systems R_0 and R_1, the easier combination problems become. Although most of the time we restrict ourselves to the case where R_0 and R_1 do not share function symbols, the problems are still far from trivial.

Definition 9.1.1 A property P of term rewriting systems is **modular** if

$$P(R_0 \cup R_1) \Leftrightarrow P(R_0) \wedge P(R_1)$$

holds for all R_0 and R_1 over disjoint signatures Σ_0 and Σ_1. If Σ_0 and Σ_1 are disjoint, $R_0 \cup R_1$ is called the **disjoint union** of R_0 and R_1.

In the sequel let R_0 and R_1 be two arbitrary but fixed term rewriting systems over the signatures Σ_0 and Σ_1. Unless stated otherwise, we assume that Σ_0 and Σ_1 are disjoint. Furthermore we define $R := R_0 \cup R_1$, $\Sigma := \Sigma_0 \cup \Sigma_1$, $\rightarrow := \rightarrow_R$ and $\rightarrow_k := \rightarrow_{R_k}$ $(k = 0, 1)$. Note that $1 - k$ is the "complement" of k if $k \in \{0, 1\}$.

Of course modularity can be iterated: if P is modular then

$$P(R_0 \cup \ldots \cup R_n) \Leftrightarrow P(R_0) \wedge \ldots \wedge P(R_n)$$

holds for all $R_0, \ldots, R_n$ over pairwise disjoint signatures $\Sigma_0, \ldots, \Sigma_n$.

In order to talk about terms consisting of a mixture of function symbols from different signatures, it helps to introduce a suggestive notation for separating such terms into homogeneous layers.

Definition 9.1.2 Let $\square$ be a new symbol which does not yet occur in $\Sigma_k \cup V$. A Σ_k-**context** is a term $t \in T(\Sigma_k, V \cup \{\square\})$ and can be seen as a term with "holes", represented by $\square$, in it. Contexts are denoted by C. If $\{p_1, \ldots, p_n\} = \{p \in \mathcal{P}os(C) \mid C|_p = \square\}$, where p_i is to the left of p_{i+1} in the tree representation of C, then $C(t_1, \ldots, t_n) := C[t_1]_{p_1} \ldots [t_n]_{p_n}$.

Unless stated otherwise, a term will be an element of $T(\Sigma, V)$. A term s is called **pure** if $s \in T(\Sigma_k, V)$ for some k. The root symbol of a term s is abbreviated by $root(s)$.

Given a term s, we write $s = C[s_1, \ldots, s_n]$ if $s = C(s_1, \ldots, s_n)$ and

1. $C \neq \square$ is a Σ_k-context for some k, and
2. $root(s_i) \in \Sigma_{1-k}$ for $i = 1, \ldots, n$.

Note that C and the s_i are uniquely determined by s. The s_i are called the **alien subterms** of s.

The **rank** of a term is the maximal number of signature changes along any of its branches:

$$rank(t) := \begin{cases} 0 & \text{if } t \text{ is pure,} \\ 1 + max\{rank(s_1), \ldots, rank(s_n)\} & \text{if } t = C[s_1, \ldots, s_n], n \geq 1. \end{cases}$$

For compactness we also write $C(\overline{t_n})$ and $C[\overline{s_n}]$. Note that $C(t_1, \ldots, t_n)$ and $C[s_1, \ldots, s_n]$ allows for $n = 0$, in which case the degenerate context C is simply an element of $T(\Sigma_k, V)$.

9.2 Termination

We start with a simple exercise in modularity. Recall that a reduction relation is normalizing if every element has a normal form. Let us call this the normalization property. The following diagrammatic example indicates that the normalization property is modular because the normal form of a term can be found by a bottom-up strategy:

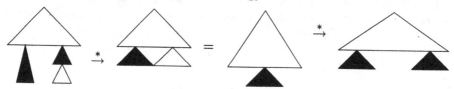

The black and white triangles represent pure terms over different signatures. In the first step, the three small triangles are normalized. The black one on the left merely changes it shape, whereas the black one on the right disappears, which means that some rule of the form $l \to x$ must have been used. In the resulting term, the small black and white triangles are in normal form. Because the small and the big white triangles are of the same signature, they can be combined into a single white term with a single black subterm, which is still in normal form. This is not a rewrite step but merely adjusts the layout. The final step represents the normalization of the white top layer of the term. The key point here is that the black subterm can be duplicated but it cannot change its shape, i.e. it remains in normal form.

Theorem 9.2.1 *The normalization property is modular.*

Proof First assume that R is normalizing. To see that the R-normal form of a Σ_k-term is also an R_k-normal form we look at an R-reduction sequence starting with a Σ_k-term:

1. Only R_k-rules are applicable to a Σ_k-term because Σ_0 and Σ_1 are disjoint and the lhs of a rewrite rule cannot be a variable.
2. Hence all intermediate terms in the sequence must also be Σ_k-terms and all rules used in the reduction must be R_k-rules.

Therefore R_0 and R_1 are normalizing as well.

Now assume that R_0 and R_1 are normalizing and let s be a Σ-term. We show by induction on the rank of s that s has an R-normal form. Let $s = C[\overline{s_m}]$ where C is a Σ_k-context. By induction hypothesis each s_i has an R-normal form t_i. Let $C(\overline{t_m}) = C'[\overline{u_n}]$ for suitable C' and u_i. Let $\{x_1, \ldots, x_n\}$ be a set of new variables such that $x_i = x_j \Leftrightarrow u_i = u_j$. Since R_k is normalizing, $C'(\overline{x_n})$ has an R_k-normal form t, which is also an R-normal form. Thus we have $s \xrightarrow{*} C(\overline{t_m}) = \sigma(C'(\overline{x_n})) \xrightarrow{*} \sigma t$ where $\sigma =$

$\{x_1 \mapsto u_1, \ldots\}$. It is easy to see that σt is in R-normal because t and the σx_i are in R-normal form, $x_i = x_j \Leftrightarrow \sigma x_i = \sigma x_j$, and because $t \in T(\Sigma_k, V)$ but $root(u_i) \in \Sigma_{1-k}$. $\qquad\square$

It is very tempting to assume the same is true for termination. However ...

Example 9.2.2 (Toyama [242]) Termination is not modular.

$$
\begin{aligned}
R_0 &:= \{f(0, 1, x) \rightarrow f(x, x, x)\}, \\
R_1 &:= \{g(x, y) \rightarrow x, \; g(x, y) \rightarrow y\}.
\end{aligned}
$$

Both R_0 and R_1 terminate, but R does not:

$$
s_0 := f(g(0, 1), g(0, 1), g(0, 1)) \xrightarrow{2} f(0, 1, g(0, 1)) \rightarrow s_0 \rightarrow \cdots.
$$

Termination of R_1 is obvious, termination of R_0 can be established with the following measure function into multisets of natural numbers:

$$
\varphi(t) := \{\, max\{\text{length of } q \mid q \in \mathcal{P}os(t|_p)\} \mid p \in \mathcal{P}os(t) \wedge \exists s.\, t|_p = f(0, 1, s)\}.
$$

It turns out that this counterexample is typical in the sense that one system contains a duplicating, the other a collapsing rule:

Definition 9.2.3 A rule $l \rightarrow r$ is **collapsing** if r is a variable and **duplicating** if some variable occurs more often in r than in l.

The main theorem provides three sufficient conditions for the preservation of termination:

Theorem 9.2.4 *The disjoint union of two terminating systems terminates if*

- *neither system contains collapsing rules, or*
- *neither system contains duplicating rules, or*
- *one of the systems contains neither collapsing nor duplicating rules.*

Its proof is a beautiful demonstration of the standard tools for combination problems, some of which still need to be introduced:

Definition 9.2.5 A reduction $s \rightarrow t$ is called **inner**, and we write $s \blacktriangleright t$, if it takes place in one of the alien subterms of s; otherwise it is called an **outer** reduction and we write $s \triangleright t$. Obviously, pure terms give rise only to outer reductions.

A step $s \rightarrow t$ is called **collapsing at level**

$$
\begin{cases}
0 & \text{if } root(s) \in \Sigma_k \text{ but } root(t) \notin \Sigma_k, \\
i+1 & \text{if } s = C[s_1, \ldots, s_j, \ldots, s_n],\, t = C[s_1, \ldots, t_j, \ldots, s_n] \text{ for some } j, \\
& \text{and } s_j \rightarrow t_j \text{ is collapsing at level } i.
\end{cases}
$$

Note that by definition any step $s \to x$ is collapsing at level 0. Note further that not every application of a collapsing rule gives rise to a collapsing step. For example, if $R_0 = \{f(x) \to x\}$ then $f(f(x)) \to_0 f(x)$ is not a collapsing step. In contrast, we call a step **duplicating** if it uses a duplicating rule.

Lemma 9.2.6 $s \to t \Rightarrow rank(s) \geq rank(t)$.

Proof by induction on the rank of s. Let $s = C[s_1, \ldots, s_n]$. If $s \blacktriangleright t$ then $rank(s) \geq rank(t)$ follows by induction hypothesis. If $s \rhd t$ then either $t = s_i$ for some i, and hence $rank(s) > rank(t)$, or $t = C'[u_1, \ldots, u_m]$ such that $\{\overline{u_m}\} \subseteq \{\overline{s_n}\}$, and hence $rank(s) \geq rank(t)$. $\square$

For multiset-order purposes we define

$$S(C[s_1, \ldots, s_n]) := \{s_1, \ldots, s_n\},$$

the *multiset* of alien subterms of a term. The following two lemmas are easy to prove:

Lemma 9.2.7 *If $s \rhd t$ is neither collapsing nor duplicating then $S(s) \supseteq S(t)$.*

Lemma 9.2.8 *If $s = C[s_1, \ldots, s_j, \ldots, s_n] \blacktriangleright C(s_1, \ldots, t_j, \ldots, s_n) = t$ is collapsing at level 1, then $S(t) = (S(s) - \{s_j\}) \cup S(t_j)$.*

The following lemma is the key to a compact proof of our main theorem:

Lemma 9.2.9 (Ohlebusch [193]) *If R_0 and R_1 are terminating but R is not, then there is an infinite R-reduction which contains*

1. *no collapsing step at level 0,*
2. *an infinite number of outer steps,*
3. *an infinite number of collapsing steps at level 1, and*
4. *an infinite number of outer duplicating steps.*

Proof Define the rank of an infinite reduction sequence $s_0 \to s_1 \to \cdots$ as the minimal rank of all the s_i. Let M be the set of all infinite sequences $s_0 \to s_1 \to \cdots$ of minimal rank (i.e. there is no infinite reduction sequence of smaller rank) such that $rank(s_i) = rank(s_{i+1})$ for all i. To see that M is nonempty, take an arbitrary infinite reduction sequence of minimal rank and observe that by Lemma 9.2.6 the rank of its elements cannot increase. Since the rank is bounded below by 0, it must become constant from some point on. Therefore the suffix starting at that point is an element of M.

  (0) Observe that any suffix of a sequence in M is also in M. If we can show that each $D \in M$ contains an occurrence of a particular step, then so

does each suffix of D, in which case each D must contain an infinite number of such steps.

Now let D be some arbitrary sequence $s_0 \to s_1 \to \cdots$ in M. We prove that D fulfils conditions 1–4 above.

(1) Since $rank(s_i)$ is constant, there can be no collapsing step at level 0.

For the remaining three conditions note that observation (0) above reduces our obligations to showing that there is one step of each kind. In each case the proof is by contradiction.

(2) Suppose there is no outer step in D. Hence D is of the form $C[\overline{t_n}] \blacktriangleright C(\overline{u_n}) \blacktriangleright C(\ldots) \blacktriangleright \cdots$ where $t_i \overset{=}{\to} u_i \overset{=}{\to} \cdots$ for $i = 1, \ldots, n$. This gives rise to an infinite reduction starting with some t_i. But this reduction sequence is of smaller rank than D, a contradiction.

(3) Suppose D contains no collapsing step at level 1. Then all steps in D are either of the form $C[\ldots] \blacktriangleright C[\ldots]$, or of the form $C[\ldots] \rhd C'[\ldots]$ such that $C[x, \ldots, x] \to_k C'[x, \ldots, x]$. Note that replacing all alien subterms of $C[\ldots]$ by the same variable x cannot disable the rule used in the step $C[\ldots] \rhd C'[\ldots]$. And because all variables on the rhs of a rewrite rule must also occur on the lhs, the alien subterms of $C'[\ldots]$ must be a subset of those of $C[\ldots]$, which is why we may also replace $C'[\ldots]$ by $C'[x, \ldots, x]$.

Because there are infinitely many outer steps, this gives rise to an infinite R_k-reduction sequence $C[x, \ldots, x] \to_k C'[x, \ldots, x] \to_k C''[x, \ldots, x] \to_k \cdots$, contradicting termination of R_k.

(4) Suppose D contains no outer duplicating step. Define the complexity of a term t as the *multiset*

$$K(t) := \{rank(s) \mid s \in S(t)\}$$

and recall that $\geq_{mul}$ is the reflexive closure of $>_{mul}$, where in the current context $>$ has its usual interpretation on $\mathbb{N}$. We analyse how $K(s_i)$ develops, depending on the form of the step $s_i \to s_{i+1}$:

Outer: Then $S(s_i) \supseteq S(s_{i+1})$ by Lemma 9.2.7 because outer steps are neither collapsing nor duplicating. This implies $K(s_i) \geq_{mul} K(s_{i+1})$.

Inner, non-collapsing at level 1: $s_i = C[t_1, \ldots, t_j, \ldots, t_n]$, $t_j \to t'_j$ and $s_{i+1} = C[t_1, \ldots, t'_j, \ldots, t_n]$. Then $rank(t_j) \geq rank(t'_j)$ and hence $K(s_i) \geq_{mul} K(s_{i+1})$.

Inner, collapsing at level 1: $s_i = C[t_1, \ldots, t_j, \ldots, t_n]$, $t_j \to t'_j$ and $s_{i+1} = C(t_1, \ldots, t'_j, \ldots, t_n)$. Then Lemma 9.2.8 implies $S(s_{i+1}) = (S(s_i) - \{t_j\}) \cup S(t'_j)$. Because $rank(t_j) > rank(u)$ for every $u \in S(t'_j)$ we obtain $K(s_i) >_{mul} K(s_{i+1})$.

Because $>_{mul}$ is well-founded, there can only be finitely many steps in D which are collapsing at level 1, a contradiction to (3).   □

Now note that because the infinite R-reduction has no outer collapsing steps, all outer steps are R_k-steps and all steps at level 1 are R_{1-k}-steps for a fixed k. Hence R_k is duplicating and R_{1-k} collapsing:

Corollary 9.2.10 *If the disjoint union of two terminating systems fails to terminate, then one of the two systems must contain a collapsing and the other one a duplicating rule.*

Because this corollary is the contrapositive of Theorem 9.2.4, we have also proved the latter.

Although it may seem that we have completely characterized the cases where termination is modular, this is not quite true: the union of a duplicating with a collapsing system may but need not result in nontermination. For example, both $R_0 := \{f_1(x) \to f_2(x, x)\}$ and $R_1 := \{g(x, y) \to x,\ g(x, y) \to y\}$ are terminating, and so is $R_0 \cup R_1$ (exercise: why?). This shows that when combining two terminating systems, one duplicating and the other one collapsing, proving termination of the union can be nontrivial. This is hardly surprising in view of the fact that termination of the disjoint union of terminating systems is undecidable [176].

For the benefit of those readers who are still a bit bemused by the non-modularity of termination, it should be mentioned that termination is modular for graph-based non-copying implementations of rewriting where multiple occurrences of the same variable on the rhs of a rule are shared. Under this interpretation, the standard counterexample 9.2.2 vanishes into thin air:

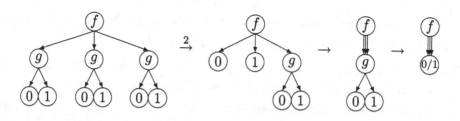

The intuitive reason is quite simple: non-copying reduction essentially means that there are no duplicating rules, in which case we know that termination is modular. This phenomenon was discovered by Plump [206] and refined by Kurihara and Ohuchi [153], who also proved that termination is modular for systems whose termination can be shown by a simplification order [152].

Exercise

9.1   Show directly, i.e. without appealing to any of the theorems above, that if R is a non-duplicating TRS over the signature Σ, then R is terminating iff $R \cup \{g(x,y) \to x, \ g(x,y) \to y\}$, where $g \notin \Sigma$, is terminating (Gramlich [98]).

9.3 Confluence

The detailed treatment of modularity of confluence for disjoint unions is beyond the scope of this book. Hence the following subsection merely states the important results and refers the interested reader to the literature for proofs. The subsequent subsection replaces the disjointness requirement by orthogonality. Although the resulting theorems are just as useful, their proofs are far simpler.

9.3.1 The disjoint case

Theorem 9.3.1 (Toyama [243, 143]) *Confluence is a modular property.*

One particularly simple consequence of this theorem is that a confluent TRS over a signature Σ_0 is confluent not just for $T(\Sigma_0, V)$ but also for $T(\Sigma', V)$ for every $\Sigma' \supseteq \Sigma_0$. (Why?)

Looking back at Example 9.2.2, the counterexample to modularity of termination, and noticing that R_1 is not confluent, it is tempting to conjecture that convergence could be modular. However, this is not true either:

Example 9.3.2 (Drosten [82])

$$
\begin{aligned}
R_0 &:= \ \{f(0,1,x) \to f(x,x,x), \ f(x,y,z) \to 2, \ 0 \to 2, \ 1 \to 2\}, \\
R_1 &:= \ \{g(x,y,y) \to x, \ g(x,x,y) \to y\}.
\end{aligned}
$$

Both R_0 and R_1 are convergent, but R does not terminate: if $t = g(0,1,1)$ then

$$
f(t,t,t) \to f(0,t,t) \xrightarrow{2} f(0, g(2,2,1), t) \to f(0,1,t) \to f(t,t,t) \to \cdots.
$$

If we also require left-linearity, we finally arrive at

Theorem 9.3.3 *Convergence is modular for left-linear systems.*

This was first proved by Toyama, Klop and Barendregt [245]. A much simplified proof is due to Schmidt-Schauß, Marchiori and Panitz [225].

9.3.2 The orthogonal case

In this subsection the key property in the study of modularity of confluence is commutation (see Subsection 2.7.1). Recall the Commutative Union Lemma, which, when translated to term rewriting, says that

$$R_0 \cup R_1 \text{ is confluent if } R_0 \text{ and } R_1 \text{ are confluent and commute.}$$

Note that there are no disjointness requirements. Hence Σ_0 and Σ_1 can be arbitrary signatures in the remainder of this section. We now concentrate our efforts on commutation, obtaining confluence as a corollary.

Definition 9.3.4 We call R_0 and R_1 **mutually orthogonal** if they are left-linear and no rule of R_0 overlaps with a rule of R_1.

Remember that "overlaps" is a symmetric notion.

The remainder of this section is concerned with proving

Theorem 9.3.5 *Mutually orthogonal term rewriting systems commute.*

Using the Commutative Union Lemma we immediately obtain

Corollary 9.3.6 *If R_0 and R_1 are confluent and mutually orthogonal, then $R_0 \cup R_1$ is confluent.*

Example 9.3.7 Suppose $R_0 := \{f(f(x,y),z) \to f(x,f(y,z))\}$ and $R_1 := \{g(x) \to f(x,g(x))\}$. Both systems are confluent (R_0 is terminating and its critical pair is joinable, R_1 is orthogonal) and they are mutually orthogonal. Hence $R_0 \cup R_1$ is confluent.

However, none of the theorems in the confluence chapter can deal with $R_0 \cup R_1$: it is not terminating (hence the Critical Pair Theorem does not apply), not linear (hence the Strong Confluence Lemma does not apply) and not parallel closed.

Now we develop an elementary proof of Theorem 9.3.5 which relies not on positions or contexts but merely on the inductive nature of terms. The main idea of this proof is the same as in our previous encounter with orthogonality: parallel reduction. This time, however, we use the following inductive definition:

Definition 9.3.8 Let R be a TRS. The relation $\Rrightarrow_R$ is the smallest relation which satisfies the following rules:

$$s \Rrightarrow s \quad (A) \qquad \frac{(l \to r) \in R}{\sigma l \Rrightarrow_R \sigma r} \ (B) \qquad \frac{s_1 \Rrightarrow_R t_1 \quad \cdots \quad s_n \Rrightarrow_R t_n}{f(s_1,\ldots,s_n) \Rrightarrow_R f(t_1,\ldots,t_n)} \ (C)$$

The relation $\Rrightarrow_R$ extends to substitutions in the pointwise way: if W is a set of variables, $\sigma \Rrightarrow_R^W \sigma'$ means $\sigma x \Rrightarrow_R \sigma' x$ for all $x \in W$.

It is easy to see that this definition of $\Rightarrow_R$ is equivalent to the original one.

The following lemma can easily be proved by induction on t:

Lemma 9.3.9 *If* $\sigma \Rightarrow_R^W \sigma'$ *and* $Var(t) \subseteq W$ *then* $\sigma t \Rightarrow_R \sigma' t$.

The next lemma is quite simple, although a bit technical. It generalizes the Parallel Moves Lemma:

Lemma 9.3.10 *Let l be a linear term such that no non-variable subterm of l unifies with a renamed lhs of a rule in R. Then $\sigma l \Rightarrow_R s$ implies that there is a σ' such that $\sigma \Rightarrow_R^{Var(l)} \sigma'$, $s = \sigma' l$ and $Dom(\sigma') \subseteq Var(l)$:*

Proof by induction on l. The base case $l \in V$ is trivial: $\sigma' := \{l \mapsto s\}$. For the induction step we assume $l = f(\overline{l_n})$ and distinguish according to which rule was used in the last step of the derivation of $\sigma l \Rightarrow_R s$:

(A) Because $s = \sigma l$, $\sigma' := \{x \mapsto \sigma x \mid x \in Var(l)\}$ does the job.

(B) By assumption, the case $\sigma l = \sigma_2 l_2$ for some $(l_2 \to r_2) \in R$ cannot arise because it would mean that l and a renamed version of l_2 are unifiable.

(C) In this case $\sigma l = f(\overline{\sigma l_n})$, $s = f(\overline{s_n})$ and $\sigma l_i \Rightarrow_R s_i$. Because each l_i is a subterm of l, it satisfies the assumptions about l. Therefore the induction hypothesis applies and there are σ_i such that $\sigma \Rightarrow_R^{Var(l_i)} \sigma_i$, $\sigma_i l_i = s_i$ and $Dom(\sigma_i) \subseteq Var(l_i)$. Define $\sigma' := \bigcup_{i=1}^n \sigma_i$. Because l is linear, the variables in the different subterms l_i are disjoint and hence σ' is well-defined. In particular we have $\sigma \Rightarrow_R^{Var(l)} \sigma'$, $\sigma' l = f(\overline{\sigma_n l_n}) = f(\overline{s_n}) = s$ and $Dom(\sigma) \subseteq Var(l)$. $\square$

Now we can give an inductive proof of the counterpart of Theorem 6.3.10:

Theorem 9.3.11 *If R_0 and R_1 are mutually orthogonal, then $\Rightarrow_{R_0}$ and $\Rightarrow_{R_1}$ have the commuting diamond property.*

Proof Abbreviate $\Rightarrow_{R_k}$ by $\Rightarrow_k$. Suppose $s \Rightarrow_k t_k$, $k = 0, 1$. We show by induction on the derivation of $s \Rightarrow_0 t_0$ that there is a u such that $t_k \Rightarrow_{1-k} u$, $k = 0, 1$. If $s \Rightarrow_0 t_0$ or $s \Rightarrow_1 t_1$ by rule (A), i.e. $t_k = s$ for $k = 0$ or $k = 1$, simply set $u := t_{1-k}$ and recall that $\Rightarrow$ is reflexive: $t_{1-k} \Rightarrow_k u \Leftarrow_{1-k} t_k$. Now consider the remaining cases (see Fig. 9.1):

(B) In this case $s = \sigma l$ and $t_0 = \sigma r$ for some $(l \to r) \in R_0$. We distinguish according to which rule was used in the last step of the derivation of $s \Rightarrow_1 t_1$:

$$\begin{array}{ccc} f(s_1,\ldots) & = & \sigma l \ \Rrightarrow_0 \ \sigma r \\ \Downarrow_1 & & \Downarrow_1 \\ f(t_{11},\ldots) & = & \sigma'l \ \Rrightarrow_0 \ \sigma'r \end{array} \qquad \begin{array}{ccc} f(s_1,\ldots) & \Rrightarrow_0 & f(t_{01},\ldots) \\ \Downarrow_1 & & \Downarrow_1 \\ f(t_{11},\ldots) & \Rrightarrow_0 & f(u_1,\ldots) \end{array}$$

Fig. 9.1. Cases (B)-(C) and (C)-(C).

(B) Because of mutual orthogonality, the case $s = \sigma_1 l_1$ and $t_1 = \sigma_1 r_1$ for some $(l_1 \to r_1) \in R_1$ cannot arise, as it would indicate a critical pair between R_0 and R_1.

(C) In this case $s = f(\overline{s_n})$, $t_1 = f(\overline{t_{1n}})$ and $s_i \Rrightarrow_1 t_{1i}$, $i = 1,\ldots,n$. Because l is not a variable it is of the form $f(\overline{l_n})$. Therefore $\sigma l_i \Rrightarrow_1 t_{1i}$. Since l is the lhs of a rule in R_0, and R_0 and R_1 are mutually orthogonal, each l_i fulfils the assumptions of Lemma 9.3.10. Hence there are σ_i such that $\sigma \Rrightarrow_1^{Var(l_i)} \sigma_i$, $\sigma_i l_i = t_{1i}$ and $\mathcal{D}om(\sigma_i) \subseteq Var(l_i)$. Let $\sigma' := \bigcup_{i=1}^n \sigma_i$, which is well-defined because l is linear. Thus we have $\sigma \Rrightarrow_1^{Var(l)} \sigma'$ and, because $Var(r) \subseteq Var(l)$, Lemma 9.3.9 implies $t_0 = \sigma r \Rrightarrow_1 \sigma'r$. Since we also have $t_1 = f(\overline{t_{1n}}) = f(\overline{\sigma_n l_n}) = \sigma'(f(\overline{l_n})) = \sigma'l \Rrightarrow_0 \sigma'r$ it follows that $u := \sigma'r$ works.

(C) In this case $s = f(\overline{s_n})$, $t_0 = f(\overline{t_{0n}})$ and $s_i \Rrightarrow_0 t_{0i}$. We again distinguish according to which rule was used in the last step of the derivation of $s \Rrightarrow_1 t_1$:

(B) This case is dual to the nested case (C) above.

(C) In this case $t_1 = f(\overline{t_{1n}})$ and $s_i \Rrightarrow_1 t_{1i}$. By induction hypothesis there are u_i such that $t_{ki} \Rrightarrow_{1-k} u_i$ for all k and i. Hence $t_k \Rrightarrow_{1-k} f(\overline{u_n}) =: u$ by rule (C). $\qquad \square$

Because two reductions are strongly commuting if they have the commuting diamond property, it now follows from the Commutation Lemma that $\Rrightarrow_{R_0}$ and $\Rrightarrow_{R_1}$ commute. Because $\overset{*}{\Rrightarrow} = \overset{*}{\to}$, this proves Theorem 9.3.5.

What is the relationship between orthogonality and mutual orthogonality? In Subsection 2.7.1 we saw an example of how commutation generalizes confluence: the Commutation Lemma implies Lemma 2.7.4. It is tempting to think the same is true in this subsection, namely that Theorem 9.3.5 ("Mutually orthogonal systems commute") subsumes Corollary 6.3.11 ("Orthogonal systems are confluent"). This would indeed be the case if "R is orthogonal" implied "R and R are mutually orthogonal". However, there is a subtlety here: "R is orthogonal" means that R has no critical pairs, which, by definition, allows trivial overlaps of a rule with itself at the root. On the other hand, mutual orthogonality rules out *all* overlaps, even trivial ones. Therefore "R and R are mutually orthogonal" is true only if $R = \emptyset$.

Nevertheless, it is possible to generalize Theorem 9.3.5 so that it subsumes Corollary 6.3.11. Call R_0 and R_1 **mutually weakly orthogonal** if they are left-linear and all critical pairs between a rule of R_0 and a rule of R_1 are of the form $\langle u, u \rangle$. A result by Toyama [244, Thm. 3.1] implies that mutually weakly orthogonal systems commute. Because R and R are mutually weakly orthogonal if R is weakly orthogonal, this implies that weakly orthogonal systems are confluent.

Exercises

9.2 Show that the following system is confluent:

$$g(x) + y \;\to\; f(x + h(y)), \qquad h(a) + g(y) \;\to\; f(h(y) + g(y)),$$
$$h(x) + g(a) \;\to\; f(h(x) + g(x)), \qquad x + h(y) \;\to\; f(g(x) + y).$$

9.3 Prove that confluence is modular for terminating systems.

9.4 Prove the following theorem for arbitrary R_0 and R_1 and reflect on its usefulness.

If R_0 and R_1 are confluent, all critical pairs between a rule of R_0 and a rule of R_1 are joinable w.r.t. $R_0 \cup R_1$, and $R_0 \cup R_1$ terminates, then $R_0 \cup R_1$ is confluent.

9.5 Prove directly, i.e. without using Toyama's Theorem, that

  (a) if the disjoint union $R_0 \cup R_1$ is confluent on $T(\Sigma_0 \cup \Sigma_1, V)$, then each R_k is confluent on $T(\Sigma_k, V)$,

  (b) if R_0 is confluent on $T(\Sigma_0, V)$, then R_0 is confluent on $T(\Sigma', V)$ for every $\Sigma' \supseteq \Sigma_0$.

9.6 Prove convergence of R_0 in Example 9.3.2.

9.7 Prove that the original definition of $\Rightarrow$ and the one given in Definition 9.3.8 are equivalent.

9.8 Prove Toyama's theorem for left-linear systems using Theorem 9.3.5.

9.9 Let R_0 and R_1 be mutually orthogonal. Does confluence of $R_0 \cup R_1$ imply confluence of both R_0 and R_1? Give a proof or counterexample.

9.4 Combining word problems

We are now back from the world of term rewriting to that of equational reasoning. Given decision procedures for a collection of equational theories $\approx_{E_k}$, can they be combined into a decision procedure for $\approx_E$, where E is the union of the E_k? Of course this cannot work in general: it is easy to find decidable equational theories whose union is undecidable (see Exercise 9.10). Hence we assume that the individual theories do not share function symbols. Nevertheless the problem remains nontrivial. Therefore we have structured our approach as follows: An example-based subsection explains the key ideas ("how"). It is followed by two subsections which formalize the intuitive ideas and prove that they work ("why"). Finally we present a realization in ML.

9.4.1 The key ideas

We start with just two theories:

$$\Sigma_1 := \{+\}, \; E_1 := \{x + y \approx y + x\}, \quad \Sigma_2 := \{1, \cdot\}, \; E_2 := \{1 \cdot x \approx x \cdot 1\}.$$

In the sequel $\approx_k$ abbreviates $\approx_{E_k}$ and E is the union of all E_k.

Given a word problem $s \approx_E t$, where s and t may contain function symbols of all signatures involved, we cannot apply the decision procedures for any of the $\approx_k$ because they require pure terms. This obstacle can be overcome quite easily by "abstracting" alien subterms:

> Replace all alien subterms in $s \approx_E t$ by new variables, replacing equivalent subterms by the same variable.

For example, in the mixed problem $(x \cdot 1) + y \approx_E y + (1 \cdot x)$ the two alien subterms $x \cdot 1$ and $1 \cdot x$ are equivalent modulo $\approx_2$. Therefore they are replaced by the same new variable v, which yields the pure problem $v + y \approx_1 y + v$, which is valid.

In general, the abstraction process is recursive. For example, abstracting

$$(1 \cdot (x + y)) + z \;\approx_E\; z + ((y + x) \cdot 1) \tag{9.1}$$

requires us to check the identity

$$1 \cdot (x + y) \;\approx_E\; (y + x) \cdot 1 \tag{9.2}$$

which in turn requires us to check the pure identity

$$x + y \;\approx_1\; y + x.$$

Since this identity is valid, identity (9.2) becomes

$$1 \cdot v \;\approx_2\; v \cdot 1$$

which is also valid, and identity (9.1) becomes

$$v + z \;\approx_1\; z + v$$

which is also valid, thus implying validity of the original identity (9.1).

Based on this abstraction process we define an approximation $\cong$ of $\approx_E$:

> $s \cong t$ iff the root symbols of s and t come from the same signature Σ_k and abstracting $s \approx_E t$ as explained above (where alien subterms are recursively compared w.r.t. $\cong$) yields a valid identity $s' \approx_k t'$.

If each E_k is **collapse-free**, i.e. does not contain an identity $s \approx x$ or $x \approx s$, it turns out that $\cong$ coincides with $\approx_E$. Otherwise $\cong$ is too weak, i.e. does not identify all $\approx_E$-equivalent terms. For example, let us add a third theory

$$\Sigma_3 := \{h\}, \quad E_3 := \{h(x, x) \approx x\},$$

and consider the identity

$$h(x + y, h(y, y) + x) \ \approx_E \ y + x. \tag{9.3}$$

Because the root symbols h and $+$ come from distinct theories, the two terms are not equivalent modulo $\cong$. However, the identity is valid because the terms can be collapsed to two $\cong$-equivalent terms. This collapsing process is the second key component in the combination procedure.

Collapsing is a bottom-up process. We go through identity (9.3) but ignore subterms with root symbol $+$ because E_1 is collapse-free. Hence we start with the subterm $h(y, y)$ which collapses to y because the identity $h(y, y) \approx_3 y$ holds (which can be checked using the decision procedure for $\approx_3$). In order to collapse the resulting lhs $h(x + y, y + x)$ further, we need to go through the same abstraction process as above. Because $x + y \cong y + x$, both alien subterms are abstracted by the same new variable v, which yields $h(v, v)$. Because $h(v, v) \approx_3 v$ holds, the whole lhs collapses to either $x + y$ or $y + x$, it does not matter which. Now we can safely use $\cong$ to decide the collapsed identity $x + y \approx_E y + x$ (or $y + x \approx_E y + x$).

In general, the collapsing process works like this:

> To collapse a term r with root symbol in Σ_k, first collapse all alien subterms of r resulting in a new term s. Now abstract all alien subterms of s w.r.t. $\cong$, resulting in a pure term t. If $t \approx_k v$ for some $v \in Var(t)$, then t collapses to the term u abstracted by v, or to v if v is not the result of an abstraction. Otherwise t collapses no further.

Remarks:

1. The test $t \approx_k v$ is effective because $\approx_k$ is decidable.
2. If E_k is nontrivial, there is at most one $v \in Var(t)$ such that $t \approx_k v$, because $t \approx_k x$ and $t \approx_k y$ implies $x \approx_k y$, which implies every identity if $x \neq y$.

To decide $s \approx_E t$, it suffices to test $s' \cong t'$, where s' and t' are the result of collapsing s and t. The remainder of this section is dedicated to formalizing and proving this statement. All examples in the following subsections refer to the theories $\approx_1$, $\approx_2$ and $\approx_3$ as defined above.

9.4.2 The formal solution

We are given an index set K and for each $k \in K$ a set of identities $E_k \subseteq T(\Sigma_k, V) \times T(\Sigma_k, V)$ such that $s \approx_k t$ is decidable for all $s, t \in T(\Sigma_k, W)$ where W can be an arbitrary set disjoint from Σ_k. The signatures Σ_k are pairwise disjoint. We abbreviate $\bigcup_{k \in K} \Sigma_k$ by Σ.

We assume that each E_k is nontrivial, i.e. $x \approx_k y$ does not hold. This is no restriction: if E_k is trivial, so is E, and trivial theories are trivially decidable. On the other hand we can now prove the following nice consequence:

Lemma 9.4.1 $t \approx_k x \Rightarrow x \in Var(t)$.

Proof If $t \approx_k x$ but $x \notin Var(t)$ then we could instantiate $t \approx_k x$ to $t = \{x \mapsto y\}(t) \approx_k \{x \mapsto y\}(x) = y$ which would lead to $x \approx_k t \approx_k y$, thus contradicting the nontriviality of E_k.   □

To simplify matters a little, we work with ground terms, i.e. elements of $T(\Sigma)$, unless stated otherwise. This is no restriction, because variables can be treated as yet another theory, say 0, such that $\Sigma_0 = V$ and $E_0 = \emptyset$. For any ground term t we define $theory(t) := k$ if $root(t) \in \Sigma_k$. The letters F, G and H range over ground contexts, i.e. $\bigcup_{k \in K} T(\Sigma_k, \{\Box\})$. Note that any term $s \in T(\Sigma)$ can be written uniquely as $F[\overline{s_n}]$ for suitable $F \neq \Box$ and $\overline{s_n}$. In case $s \in T(\Sigma_k)$ we get $F = s$ and $n = 0$.

Let $\equiv$ be an equivalence relation on $T(\Sigma)$. Abstracting the alien subterms of a term w.r.t. $\equiv$ is defined as follows:

$$[F[\overline{s_n}]]^k_\equiv := \begin{cases} F([s_1]_\equiv, \ldots, [s_n]_\equiv) & \text{if } F \in T(\Sigma_k, \{\Box\}), \\ [F[\overline{s_n}]]_\equiv & \text{otherwise.} \end{cases}$$

For example, $[(x \cdot 1) + y]^1_{\approx_2} = [x \cdot 1]_{\approx_2} + [y]_{\approx_2} = \{x \cdot 1, 1 \cdot x\} + \{y\}$ and $[(x \cdot 1) + y]^2_{\approx_2} = [(x \cdot 1) + y]_{\approx_2} = \{(x \cdot 1) + y, (1 \cdot x) + y\}$.

It its easy to see that $[f(\overline{s_n})]^k_\equiv = f([s_1]^k_\equiv, \ldots, [s_n]^k_\equiv)$ if $f \in \Sigma_k$.

Note that $[s]^k_\equiv$ is an element of $T(\Sigma_k, T(\Sigma)/\equiv)$, which we now take a closer look at. Although $T(\Sigma)/\equiv$ is not called V and its elements are not called x, y and z, they play exactly the rôle of variables in the formation of $T(\Sigma_k, T(\Sigma)/\equiv)$ because Σ_k and $T(\Sigma)/\equiv$ are disjoint. In particular, identities over terms in $T(\Sigma_k, T(\Sigma)/_{\equiv})$ are stable under substitutions acting on equivalence classes. Summing up this discussion, $[.]^k_{\approx_E}$ is precisely the abstraction operation informally described in the previous subsection.

With respect to computability, note that it is neither necessary nor in general feasible to compute the set-theoretic representation of the equivalence classes: in order to decide that $[x \cdot 1]_{\approx_2} + [y]_{\approx_2} \approx_1 [y]_{\approx_2} + [1 \cdot x]_{\approx_2}$ holds, it does not matter which (potentially infinite) sets $[x \cdot 1]_{\approx_2}$ and $[1 \cdot x]_{\approx_2}$ expand to, but merely that they are identical, which can be tested by comparing the representatives, i.e. checking that $x \cdot 1 \approx_2 1 \cdot x$. More generally, this means that $[s]^k_{\cong} \approx_k [t]^k_{\cong}$ is decidable if $\equiv$ is. Thus we define $\cong$ as follows:

$$s \cong t :\Leftrightarrow \exists k. \; k = theory(s) = theory(t) \wedge [s]^k_{\cong} \approx_k [t]^k_{\cong}.$$

This constitutes a definition of $\cong$ by recursion on the rank of s and t: if $k = theory(s) = theory(t)$ then all abstracted subterms in $[s]^k_{\cong}$ and $[t]^k_{\cong}$ are of the form $[u]_{\cong}$ where u is an alien subterm of s or t. This explains why the above definition of $\cong$ constitutes a total recursive function for computing $\cong$. The following recasting of example (9.1) should make things clearer:

$$
\begin{aligned}
(1 \cdot (x + y)) + z \;\; &\cong \;\; z + ((y + x) \cdot 1) \\
\Leftarrow \quad [1 \cdot (x + y)]_{\cong} + [z]_{\cong} \;\; &\approx_1 \;\; [z]_{\cong} + [(y + x) \cdot 1]_{\cong} \\
\Leftarrow \quad 1 \cdot [x + y]_{\cong} \;\; &\approx_2 \;\; [y + x]_{\cong} \cdot 1 \\
\Leftarrow \quad [x]_{\cong} + [y]_{\cong} \;\; &\approx_1 \;\; [y]_{\cong} + [x]_{\cong}.
\end{aligned}
$$

Note that by assumption the variables x, y and z are part of a theory k such that $x \approx_k y \Leftrightarrow x = y$ and hence also $x \cong y \Leftrightarrow x = y$.

Next we formalize the collapsing process. We say that s **collapses** to t if t is an alien subterm of s and $[s]^k_{\cong} \approx_k [t]_{\cong}$, where $k := theory(s)$.

For every $f \in \Sigma_k^{(n)}$ we define an n-ary function $f^{\Downarrow}$ on terms:

$$f^{\Downarrow}(s_1, \ldots, s_n) := \text{if } f(\overline{s_n}) \text{ collapses to } t \text{ then } t \text{ else } f(\overline{s_n}).$$

Obviously $f^{\Downarrow}$ is not uniquely defined because $f(\overline{s_n})$ could collapse to more than one t (we will see that all such t are equivalent w.r.t. $\cong$). In this case $f^{\Downarrow}$ returns an arbitrary but fixed such t: $f^{\Downarrow}$ is still a function, albeit an underspecified one. The collapsing process extends homomorphically to a function $\Downarrow$ on terms:

$$f(s_1, \ldots, s_n)\Downarrow := f^{\Downarrow}(s_1\Downarrow, \ldots, s_n\Downarrow).$$

We leave it to the reader to verify that $h(x+y, h(y,y)+x)\Downarrow \in \{x+y, y+x\}$, as claimed in the informal solution to example (9.3).

Observe that there is a gap between the informal explanation of collapsing in the previous subsection and $\Downarrow$: the latter is less "efficient" but simpler to work with because it descends into the term one function symbol at a time, whereas the former descends to the alien subterms in one step. We will see that the two methods are equivalent (modulo $\cong$).

Correctness of the decision procedure for $\approx_E$ outlined earlier amounts to

Theorem 9.4.2 $s \approx_E t \Leftrightarrow s\!\Downarrow \cong t\!\Downarrow$.

The proof of this theorem is the subject of the next subsection.

Clearly $\approx_E$ is decidable if $\cong$ and $\Downarrow$ are decidable/computable. This in turn is implied if each $\approx_k$ is decidable, *theory* is computable and there exists a computable mapping from each k to $\approx_k$. The latter two conditions are easily satisfied if K and each Σ_k are finite.

Corollary 9.4.3 *Let K and each Σ_k be finite. If each $\approx_k$ is decidable, so is $\approx_E$.*

An ML implementation of the decision procedure for $\approx_E$ is presented in Subsection 9.4.4.

9.4.3 Correctness

We start by deriving two useful lemmas for reasoning with equivalence classes. The first one needs some more notation:

Definition 9.4.4 The set of alien subterms of s is denoted by $\mathcal{A}liens(s)$. Now define $\mathcal{A}liens_k(s) :=$ if $theory(s) = k$ then $\mathcal{A}liens(s)$ else $\{s\}$.

Recall now that equivalence classes act like variables.

Lemma 9.4.5 *If $\equiv_1$ and $\equiv_2$ are equivalences on $T(\Sigma)$ such that $u \equiv_1 v \Rightarrow u \equiv_2 v$ for all $u, v \in \mathcal{A}liens_k(s) \cup \mathcal{A}liens_k(t)$ then $[s]^k_{\equiv_1} \approx_E [t]^k_{\equiv_1}$ implies $[s]^k_{\equiv_2} \approx_E [t]^k_{\equiv_2}$.*

Proof The substitution $\sigma := \{[u]_{\equiv_1} \mapsto [u]_{\equiv_2} \mid u \in \mathcal{A}liens_k(s) \cup \mathcal{A}liens_k(t)\}$ is by assumption well-defined. Because $\approx_E$ is closed under instantiation, $[s]^k_{\equiv_1} \approx_E [t]^k_{\equiv_1}$ implies $[s]^k_{\equiv_2} = \sigma([s]^k_{\equiv_1}) \approx_E \sigma([t]^k_{\equiv_1}) = [t]^k_{\equiv_2}$. $\square$

In a similar vein we have

Lemma 9.4.6 $[s]^k_{\approx_E} \approx_E [t]^k_{\approx_E} \Rightarrow s \approx_E t$.

Proof Let $\pi : T(\Sigma)/_{\approx_E} \to T(\Sigma)$ be some function mapping each equivalence class to some representative, i.e. $\pi([u]_{\approx_E}) \approx_E u$. Because $\approx_E$ is closed under instantiation, it is in particular closed under the homomorphic extension of π to $T(\Sigma_k, T(\Sigma)/_{\approx_E})$ and we obtain $s \approx_E \pi([s]^k_{\approx_E}) \approx_E \pi([t]^k_{\approx_E}) \approx_E t$. $\square$

We will now examine the basic properties of $\cong$.

Lemma 9.4.7 $s \cong t \implies [s]^k_{\cong} \approx_k [t]^k_{\cong}$.

Proof Assume $s \cong t$. By definition this means $theory(s) = theory(t)$. If $theory(s) = k$ then $[s]^k_{\cong} \approx_k [t]^k_{\cong}$ follows by definition of $\cong$. Otherwise $[s]^k_{\cong} = [s]_{\cong} = [t]_{\cong} = [t]^k_{\cong}$. □

More interestingly, we have

Lemma 9.4.8 *The relation $\cong$ is a congruence on $T(\Sigma)$.*

Proof It is easy to see that $\cong$ is an equivalence because each $\approx_k$ is one. To see that it is a congruence, let $f \in \Sigma^{(n)}_k$ and $s_i \cong t_i$, $i = 1, \ldots, n$. Lemma 9.4.7 implies $[s_i]^k_{\cong} \approx_k [t_i]^k_{\cong}$. Because $\approx_k$ is a congruence, this means $[f(\overline{s_n})]^k_{\cong} = f([\overline{s_n}]^k_{\cong}) \approx_k f([\overline{t_n}]^k_{\cong}) = [f(\overline{t_n})]^k_{\cong}$ and thus $f(\overline{s_n}) \cong f(\overline{t_n})$. □

Observe that the notation $[\overline{s_n}]_{\cong}$ is short for $[s_1]_{\cong}, \ldots, [s_n]_{\cong}$.

Finally we can show soundness of $\cong$ w.r.t. $\approx_E$. This lemma is so basic we seldom refer to it explicitly in the sequel.

Lemma 9.4.9 $s \cong t \implies s \approx_E t$.

Proof by induction on the rank of $s = F[\overline{s_m}]$ and $t = G[\overline{t_n}]$. Assume the lemma holds for all $s', t' \in \{s_1, \ldots, s_m, t_1, \ldots, t_n\}$.

$$
\begin{aligned}
s \cong t \implies\;& F([\overline{s_m}]_{\cong}) \approx_k G([\overline{t_n}]_{\cong}) \\
\implies\;& F([\overline{s_m}]_{\cong}) \approx_E G([\overline{t_n}]_{\cong}) \\
\implies\;& F([\overline{s_m}]_{\approx_E}) \approx_E G([\overline{t_n}]_{\approx_E}) \quad \text{by ind. hyp. and Lemma 9.4.5} \\
\implies\;& F(\overline{s_m}) \approx_E G(\overline{t_n}) \qquad\qquad\;\; \text{by Lemma 9.4.6.} \qquad\qquad \square
\end{aligned}
$$

These lemmas are all we need to know about $\cong$. Let us now turn to $\Downarrow$. We start by showing that $f^{\Downarrow}$ is uniquely determined modulo $\cong$:

Lemma 9.4.10 *If $f(\overline{s_n})$ collapses to t then $f^{\Downarrow}(\overline{s_n}) \cong t$.*

Proof If $f(\overline{s_n})$ collapses to t then $f^{\Downarrow}(\overline{s_n}) = t'$ for some t' that $f(\overline{s_n})$ collapses to. But then $[f(\overline{s_n})]^k_{\cong} \approx_k [t]_{\cong}$ and $[f(\overline{s_n})]^k_{\cong} \approx_k [t']_{\cong}$ imply $[t]_{\cong} \approx_k [t']_{\cong}$ and hence, because E_k is nontrivial, $[t]_{\cong} = [t']_{\cong}$, i.e. $t \cong t'$. □

Now we can prove that $\Downarrow$ is sound w.r.t. $\approx_E$:

Lemma 9.4.11 $s\Downarrow \approx_E s$.

Proof by induction on $s = f(\overline{s_n})$ where $f \in \Sigma^{(n)}_k$. From the induction hypothesis $s_i\Downarrow \approx_E s_i$, $i = 1, \ldots, n$, we obtain $s' := f(\overline{s_n\Downarrow}) \approx_E f(\overline{s_n}) = s$. Now we analyse $s\Downarrow = f^{\Downarrow}(\overline{s_n\Downarrow})$.

If s' collapses to t, then $s\Downarrow \cong t$ (by Lemma 9.4.10) and $[s']^k_{\cong} \approx_k [t]_{\cong} = [t]^k_{\cong}$. The latter implies $[s']^k_{\cong} \approx_E [t]^k_{\cong}$ and therefore, by Lemma 9.4.5, $[s']^k_{\approx_E} \approx_E$

$[t]_{\approx_E}^k$, which in turn, by Lemma 9.4.6, implies $s' \approx_E t$. Putting this all together we get $s\Downarrow \cong t \approx_E s' \approx_E s$.

If s' does not collapse, we have $s\Downarrow = f^{\Downarrow}(\overline{s_n}\Downarrow) = s' \approx_E s$. □

Combining Lemmas 9.4.9 and 9.4.11 we obtain $s\Downarrow \cong t\Downarrow \Rightarrow s \approx_E s\Downarrow \approx_E t\Downarrow \approx_E t$, the soundness direction of Theorem 9.4.2.

We now start to work on completeness. As a warming-up exercise we show that $\Downarrow$ is idempotent:

Lemma 9.4.12 *No subterm of $s\Downarrow$ collapses.*

Proof by induction on $s = f(\overline{s_n})$ where $f \in \Sigma_k^{(n)}$.

If $f(\overline{s_n}\Downarrow)$ collapses, then $s\Downarrow$ is an alien subterm of $f(\overline{s_n}\Downarrow)$ and therefore a subterm of some $s_i\Downarrow$, in which case the induction hypothesis applies.

If $f(\overline{s_n}\Downarrow)$ does not collapse, $s\Downarrow = f(\overline{s_n}\Downarrow)$. Therefore $s\Downarrow$ does not collapse and by induction hypothesis its proper subterms don't either. □

Recall that every term is its own subterm. Hence $s\Downarrow$ does not collapse either.

Now we concentrate on the interaction between $\cong$ and $\Downarrow$. For a start we show that $\cong$ preserves collapse:

Lemma 9.4.13 *If $s_1 \cong s_2$ and s_1 collapses to t_1, then s_2 collapses to some t_2 such that $t_1 \cong t_2$.*

Proof Assume $s_1 \cong s_2$ and $[s_1]_{\cong}^k \approx_k [t_1]_{\cong}$ for some $t_1 \in \mathcal{A}liens(s_1)$. Lemma 9.4.7 implies $[s_2]_{\cong}^k \approx_k [s_1]_{\cong}^k$ and hence $[s_2]_{\cong}^k \approx_k [t_1]_{\cong}$. By Lemma 9.4.1 it follows that $[t_1]_{\cong} \in \mathcal{V}ar([s_2]_{\cong}^k)$. Therefore there is some $t_2 \in \mathcal{A}liens(s_2)$ such that $t_1 \cong t_2$ and hence s_2 collapses to t_2. □

Now we can easily show that $\cong$ is compatible with every $f^{\Downarrow}$:

Lemma 9.4.14 *If $f \in \Sigma_k^{(n)}$ and $s_i \cong t_i$, $i = 1, \ldots, n$, then $f^{\Downarrow}(\overline{s_n}) \cong f^{\Downarrow}(\overline{t_n})$.*

Proof Because $\cong$ is a congruence, $s_i \cong t_i$ implies $f(\overline{s_n}) \cong f(\overline{t_n})$. By Lemma 9.4.13 there are exactly two cases. Either $f(\overline{s_n})$ collapses to some s, $f(\overline{t_n})$ collapses to some t and $s \cong t$, in which case Lemma 9.4.10 implies $f^{\Downarrow}(\overline{s_n}) \cong s \cong t \cong f^{\Downarrow}(\overline{t_n})$. Or neither $f(\overline{s_n})$ nor $f(\overline{t_n})$ collapses, in which case $f^{\Downarrow}(\overline{s_n}) = f(\overline{s_n}) \cong f(\overline{t_n}) = f^{\Downarrow}(\overline{t_n})$. □

We now bridge the gap between the recursion pattern for $\cong$ and $\Downarrow$: while $\Downarrow$ is defined by recursion on the structure of terms, $\cong$ is defined by recursion on their rank. The following lemma shows that $\Downarrow$ can be extended to recursion on the rank.

Notation: in the sequel we extend $\Downarrow$ to substitutions in the obvious way: $\sigma^{\Downarrow}x := (\sigma x)\Downarrow$.

Lemma 9.4.15 *If $s \in T(\Sigma_k, V)$ then*

$$(\sigma s){\Downarrow} \cong \begin{cases} t & \text{if } \sigma^{\Downarrow}s \text{ collapses to } t, \\ \sigma^{\Downarrow}s & \text{otherwise.} \end{cases}$$

Proof by induction on s. Call the rhs of the claim $\sigma^{\Downarrow}\langle s\rangle$. We need to prove $(\sigma s){\Downarrow} \cong \sigma^{\Downarrow}\langle s\rangle$. If s is a variable, then $(\sigma s){\Downarrow} = \sigma^{\Downarrow}s$. Lemma 9.4.12 tells us that $\sigma^{\Downarrow}s$ cannot collapse and hence $(\sigma s){\Downarrow} = \sigma^{\Downarrow}s = \sigma^{\Downarrow}\langle s\rangle$.

If $s = f(\overline{s_n})$, then $(\sigma s){\Downarrow} = f^{\Downarrow}(\overline{\sigma s_n}{\Downarrow})$. Note that because $s_i \in T(\Sigma_k, V)$ either $[\sigma^{\Downarrow}\langle s_i\rangle]_{\cong}^k = [\sigma^{\Downarrow}\langle s_i\rangle]_{\cong} \approx_k [\sigma^{\Downarrow}s_i]_{\cong}^k$ (if $\sigma^{\Downarrow}s_i$ collapses, which excludes $s_i \in V$ because of Lemma 9.4.12) or $\sigma^{\Downarrow}\langle s_i\rangle = \sigma^{\Downarrow}s_i$ (otherwise) and hence $[\sigma^{\Downarrow}\langle s_i\rangle]_{\cong}^k \approx_k [\sigma^{\Downarrow}s_i]_{\cong}^k$ in both cases. By Lemma 9.4.7, the induction hypotheses and the observation just made, we get $[(\sigma s_i){\Downarrow}]_{\cong}^k \approx_k [\sigma^{\Downarrow}\langle s_i\rangle]_{\cong}^k \approx_k [\sigma^{\Downarrow}s_i]_{\cong}^k$ and hence $[f(\overline{\sigma s_n}{\Downarrow})]_{\cong}^k \approx_k [f(\sigma^{\Downarrow}\overline{s_n})]_{\cong}^k$, which implies $f(\overline{\sigma s_n}{\Downarrow}) \cong f(\sigma^{\Downarrow}\overline{s_n}) = \sigma^{\Downarrow}s$. Lemma 9.4.13 tells us there are exactly two cases. Either $f(\overline{\sigma s_n}{\Downarrow})$ collapses to some t, $\sigma^{\Downarrow}s$ collapses to some t' and $t \cong t'$, in which case $(\sigma s){\Downarrow} \cong t \cong t' \cong \sigma^{\Downarrow}\langle s\rangle$. Or $f(\overline{\sigma s_n}{\Downarrow})$ and $\sigma^{\Downarrow}s$ do not collapse, in which case $(\sigma s){\Downarrow} = f(\overline{\sigma s_n}{\Downarrow}) \cong \sigma^{\Downarrow}s = \sigma^{\Downarrow}\langle s\rangle$. $\qquad\Box$

Lemma 9.4.16 *If $l \approx r \in E_k$ then $(\sigma l){\Downarrow} \cong (\sigma r){\Downarrow}$.*

Proof First we consider the case where $theory(\sigma^{\Downarrow}l) = theory(\sigma^{\Downarrow}r) = k$. Observe that $[\sigma^{\Downarrow}l]_{\cong}^k = \sigma'l \approx_k \sigma'r = [\sigma^{\Downarrow}r]_{\cong}^k$, where $\sigma'x := [\sigma^{\Downarrow}x]_{\cong}^k$, and hence that $\sigma^{\Downarrow}l \cong \sigma^{\Downarrow}r$. By Lemma 9.4.13 there are two cases.

Either $\sigma^{\Downarrow}l$ collapses to some s and $\sigma^{\Downarrow}r$ collapses to some t such that $t \cong s$. Then Lemma 9.4.15 implies $(\sigma l){\Downarrow} \cong s \cong t \cong (\sigma r){\Downarrow}$. Or neither $\sigma^{\Downarrow}l$ nor $\sigma^{\Downarrow}r$ collapses, in which case $(\sigma l){\Downarrow} = \sigma^{\Downarrow}l \cong \sigma^{\Downarrow}r = (\sigma r){\Downarrow}$.

Now we look at the case where either $theory(\sigma^{\Downarrow}l) \neq k$ or $theory(\sigma^{\Downarrow}r) \neq k$. For concreteness, assume $theory(\sigma^{\Downarrow}l) \neq k$ and hence $l \in V$, in which case Lemma 9.4.1 implies $l \in Var(r)$. The case $theory(\sigma^{\Downarrow}r) \neq k$ is trivial because it implies $r \in V$ and hence $l = r$. Because $\sigma^{\Downarrow}l$ does not collapse (Lemma 9.4.12) and because $\sigma^{\Downarrow}r$ collapses to $\sigma^{\Downarrow}l$ ($theory(\sigma^{\Downarrow}r) = k$), Lemma 9.4.15 yields $(\sigma l){\Downarrow} = \sigma^{\Downarrow}l \cong (\sigma r){\Downarrow}$. $\qquad\Box$

Now we can establish the completeness direction of Theorem 9.4.2:

Lemma 9.4.17 $\qquad s \approx_E t \Rightarrow s{\Downarrow} \cong t{\Downarrow}.$

Proof Because $\approx_E = \overset{*}{\leftrightarrow}_E$ and $\cong$ is transitive and symmetric, it suffices to show that $s \rightarrow_E t$ implies $s{\Downarrow} \cong t{\Downarrow}$. Suppose $s \rightarrow_E t$, i.e. there are $(l \approx r) \in E_k$, $p \in \mathcal{P}os(s)$ and σ such that $s|_p = \sigma l$ and $t = s[\sigma r]_p$. Lemma 9.4.16 implies $(\sigma l){\Downarrow} \cong (\sigma r){\Downarrow}$. Using Lemma 9.4.14, a simple inductive argument on the length of p shows $s{\Downarrow} = (s[\sigma l]_p){\Downarrow} \cong (s[\sigma r]_p){\Downarrow} = t{\Downarrow}$. $\qquad\Box$

9.4.4 The implementation in ML

The ML implementation follows the above mathematical treatment quite closely. The main question is how to deal with subterm abstraction, for example in the test $[s]_{\cong}^k \approx_k [t]_{\cong}^k$? Instead of doing the abstraction before calling the decision procedure for $\approx_k$, say eq_k, we let eq_k do the abstraction itself by passing it a decision procedure for $\cong$. This could be called lazy subterm abstraction. This distinction can be made more precise by introducing a type abbreviation:

```
type eqf = term * term -> bool
```

Eager subterm abstraction would mean that each eq_k has type *eqf*; lazy subterm abstraction means it has type *eqf -> eqf* because it is passed the decision procedure for equality of its alien subterms as an argument. The index set K is implemented by *int*. Hence we assume there is a function *eq* of type *int -> eqf -> eqf* such that *eq k* is the decision procedure for $\approx_k$. We also assume there is a function *theory* of type *term -> int*.

Lazy subterm abstraction may seem to defeat modularity: we now require a decision procedure for $\approx_k$ to expect terms containing alien subterms which need to be compared with the help of an additional argument function. Fortunately, this is not a real restriction: every black-box decision procedure of type *eqf* can be turned into one of type *eqf -> eqf* as follows:

```
(* mkLazy: eqf -> (eqf -> eqf) *)
fun mkLazy eagerEq subEq (s,t) =
    let val (s',t') = Abstract alien subterms of s and t modulo subEq by new variables
    in eagerEq (s',t') end;
```

However, unless the decision procedure is really given as a black box, it is usually trivial to modify its code to expect alien subterms. In particular, the result is much more efficient than wrapping the unmodified procedure up in *mkLazy*.

Due to lazy subterm abstraction, the implementation of $\cong$, called *cfeq* ("collapse-free equality") of type *eqf*, is trivial:

```
fun cfeq (s,t) = (theory s = theory t) andalso (eq (theory s) cfeq (s,t));
```

The implementation of $\Downarrow$ (see Fig. 9.2) follows the strategy inherent in Lemma 9.4.15: first collapse all alien subterms, then collapse the top layer in one step: *collAliens k* collapses all k-alien subterms and *coll* collapses the whole term. The latter is achieved by *trying* to equate the term t with one alien subterm u after the other. $Aliens_k(t)$ is computed by *aliens k t*.

Now we can define the combined decision procedure of type *eqf*:

```
fun eqE (s,t) = cfeq (collapse s, collapse t);
```

```
(* collapse: term -> term *)
fun collapse t =
  let fun collAliens k t = (case t of
            V _ => t
          | T(f, ts) => if theory(t) <> k then coll t
                        else T(f, map (collAliens k) ts))
      and coll s =
          let val k = theory s
              val t = collAliens k s
              fun try [] = t
                | try (u::us) = if eq k cfeq (t,u) then u else try us
          in try(aliens k t) end
  in coll t end;


(* aliens: int -> term -> term list *)
fun aliens k t = if theory(t) <> k then [t]
                 else case t of V _    => []
                     | T(_,ts) => concat(map (aliens k) ts);
```

Fig. 9.2. ⇓ in ML.

If *eq k* implements $\approx_k$ then *eqE* implements $\approx_E$.

Strictly speaking, the above functions should be parameterized over *eq* and *theory* to make them truly generic. We have avoided this merely to keep matters as simple as possible.

So much for the combination aspect. Let us now look at a sample instantiation. Here we have four theories, where 0 represents variables:

```
fun theory(V _) = 0
  | theory(T(f,_)) = case f of "f" => 1 | "g" => 2 | "h" => 3;
```

Each index is mapped by *eq* to a decision procedure of type *eqf -> eqf*:

```
fun eq 0 = varEq
  | eq 1 = commEq
  | eq 2 = assocEq
  | eq 3 = idempEq;
```

Equality on variables is identity:

```
fun varEq _ (x,y) = x=y;
```

To see how lazy subterm abstraction works, we look at *assocEq*

```
fun assocEq eq (s,t) =
  let fun fringe(T("g",[s,t])) = (fringe s) @ (fringe t)
        | fringe(t) = [t];
      val fs = fringe s;
      val ft = fringe t
  in (length fs = length ft) andalso forall eq (zip(fs,ft)) end;
```

which implements equality modulo associativity: *fringe* "flattens" the term, i.e. it accumulates (from left to right) the alien subterms in a list. This list is a normal form of the term under associativity and hence two such terms can be compared by comparing their fringes. For example, both $g(g(x, y), z)$ and $g(x, g(y, z))$ have the fringe $[x, y, z]$. Subterm abstraction enters the picture when two fringes are compared: the equality test used is the argument function *eq*.

The same pattern repeats itself in the other two decision procedures *commEq* and *idempEq*: alien subterms are compared with the help of the extra argument of type *eqf*. We leave it as an exercise to implement these two functions.

Exercises

9.10 Find two sets of identities E_1 and E_2 such that the word problem is decidable for E_1 and E_2 but not for $E_1 \cup E_2$. (*Hint:* use Example 4.1.4).

9.11 Find two sets of identities E_1 and E_2 over disjoint signatures such that the ground word problem is decidable for E_1 and E_2 but not for $E_1 \cup E_2$ (*Hint:* use Exercise 4.1).

9.12 Implement the missing ML functions *commEq* and *idempEq* for commutative and idempotent ($h(x, x) \approx x$) equality.

9.5 Bibliographic notes

Research on modularity of termination started with Toyama's counterexamples [242]. The first two conditions in Theorem 9.2.4 were first proved by Rusinowitch [220], the last one by Middeldorp [175, 176]. Further sufficient conditions are due to Gramlich [98] and Ohlebusch [194].

Subsection 9.3.2 deals only with orthogonal combinations. Theorem 9.3.5 goes back to Raoult and Vuillemin [214]. A direct generalization of Huet's Parallel Closure Theorem to commutation is also possible. Toyama [244] even goes a little further by considering root overlaps separately.

Sketches of the combination of decision procedures for the word problem are due to Tidén [240] and Schmidt-Schauß [223]. The above treatment is due to Nipkow [186, 188]. An alternative proof idea based on unfailing completion goes back to [32]. The combination procedures underlying these approaches are all based on collapsing and abstracting alien subterms in a fixed order. Baader and Tinelli [13] present a combination method which is based on transformation rules that can be applied in any order. Their correctness proof is purely algebraic.

10

Equational Unification

Equational unification is concerned with the satisfiability problem w.r.t. a fixed set of identities E: given terms s and t, find a substitution σ such that $\sigma(s) \approx_E \sigma(t)$. This substitution is called an E-unifier of s and t. Syntactic unification, as considered in Section 4.5, is the special case where $E = \emptyset$. Equational unification thus generalizes syntactic unification by taking into account semantic properties of function symbols (axiomatized by the identities in E). For example, assume that E implies that the binary function symbol f is commutative (i.e. $f(x, y) \approx_E f(y, x)$ holds for arbitrary variables x and y). Given the (syntactic) unification problem $S := \{f(x, y) =^? f(a, b)\}$, where x, y are variables and a, b are constants, the algorithm for syntactic unification described in Section 4.5 returns the most general unifier $\sigma := \{x \mapsto a, y \mapsto b\}$. The substitution $\tau := \{x \mapsto b, y \mapsto a\}$ is not a syntactic unifier of S since $\sigma(f(x, y)) = f(b, a) \neq f(a, b) = \sigma(f(a, b))$. It is, however, an E-unifier since $f(b, a) \approx_E f(a, b)$.

On the one hand, our interest in equational unification comes from the fact that it can be seen as a dual problem to the word problem: whereas the word problem for E asks whether the *universal* formula $\forall \overline{x}.\ s \approx t$ holds in all models of E, the unification problem is concerned with whether the *existential* formula $\exists \overline{x}.\ s \approx t$ holds in all nonempty models of E (see the remark at the beginning of Chapter 4). On the other hand, equational unification is a very useful tool in term rewriting, theorem proving, and logic programming. In rewriting modulo an equational theory $\approx_E$ (see Section 11.1), the computation of critical pairs depends on an E-unification algorithm. In theorem proving, it was initially shown by Plotkin and then extended by others that certain equational axioms can be handled in a more efficient way by a resolution-based theorem prover if they are removed from the set of input clauses and instead built into an equational unification procedure. In logic programming with equality, logic programs extended by a set of identities E also require E-unification in place of syntactic unification in SLD-resolution.

In the following, we extend the definitions introduced in Section 4.5 for syntactic unification (such as instantiation quasi-order, unification problem, mgu, etc.) to the case of equational unification. Subsequently, we investigate the unification properties of three specific equational theories more closely, namely, commutativity, associativity and commutativity, and the theory of Boolean rings. Whereas the unification algorithm for commutativity is quite similar to the one for syntactic unification, the algorithms for the other two theories depend on semantics rather than on syntax.

10.1 Basic definitions and results

In the following, let E be a fixed set of identities. We let $Sig(E)$ denote the signature of E, i.e. the set of all function symbols occurring in E. Let Σ be a signature that contains $Sig(E)$.

Definition 10.1.1 An **E-unification problem** over Σ is a finite set of equations $S = \{s_1 \approx_E^? t_1, \ldots, s_n \approx_E^? t_n\}$ between Σ-terms with variables in V. An **E-unifier** or **E-solution** of S is a substitution σ such that $\sigma(s_i) \approx_E \sigma(t_i)$ for $i = 1, \ldots, n$. The set of all E-unifiers of S is denoted by $\mathcal{U}_E(S)$, and S is called **E-unifiable** if $\mathcal{U}_E(S) \neq \emptyset$.

If an E-unification problem consists of a single equation $s \approx_E^? t$, then we will often omit the set brackets and call $s \approx_E^? t$ the unification problem.

For a given E-unification problem over Σ, the signature Σ determines which function symbols may occur in the terms to be unified and in the unifiers. The next definition classifies E-unification problems according to which symbols may occur in $\Sigma - Sig(E)$.

Definition 10.1.2 Let S be an E-unification problem over Σ.

- S is an **elementary** E-unification problem iff $Sig(E) = \Sigma$.
- S is an E-unification problem **with constants** iff $\Sigma - Sig(E)$ consists of constant symbols.
- In a **general** E-unification problem, $\Sigma - Sig(E)$ may contain arbitrary function symbols.

In the following, we will often dispense with specifying Σ explicitly. In this case we assume by default that Σ consists of the function symbols occurring in E or S.

For syntactic unification, i.e. the case where $E = \emptyset$, elementary unification problems consist of equations between variables, and unification problems with constants consist of equations between variables and constants. Thus, in this case the only interesting type of unification is general $\emptyset$-unification. The distinction between these three types of problems is important since an equational theory may have different unification properties depending on which type of unification is considered. Many applications of equational. unification give rise to general unification problems. For example, assume that we want to solve the word problem for the theory of Abelian groups with the help of a convergent TRS. Since the group operation f is commutative, and commutativity cannot be oriented into a terminating rewrite rule, this problem requires rewriting modulo an equational theory. In this case, the appropriate theory turns out to be AC, which axiomatizes associativity and commutativity of f (see Section 10.3 below). Now, the terms considered when computing critical pairs modulo $\approx_{AC}$ may contain an additional unary function symbol, the inverse operation in Abelian groups, and an additional constant symbol, the unit element in Abelian groups.

The set of all E-unifiers of a given E-unification problem S is usually infinite. In the case of syntactic unification, it is possible to represent this possibly infinite set as the instances of a single most general unifier. For equational unification, a single E-unifier is not always sufficient to represent all unifiers. In this case, the rôle that the *most general unifier* plays for syntactic unification is taken on by a *minimal complete set of unifiers*. Before we can define this notion formally, we must adapt the definition of the instantiation quasi-order (Definition 4.5.1) to the case of E-unification.

Definition 10.1.3 Let X be a set of variables. A substitution σ is **more general** modulo $\approx_E$ than a substitution σ' on X if there is a substitution δ such that $\sigma'(x) \approx_E \delta(\sigma(x))$ for all $x \in X$. In this case we write $\sigma \lesssim_E^X \sigma'$. We also say that σ' is an E-**instance** of σ on X.

It is easy to see that the relation $\lesssim_E^X$ defined in this way is again a quasi-order. This definition differs from Definition 4.5.1 in two respects: syntactic equality is replaced by equality modulo $\approx_E$, and the substitutions need not be equal on all variables, but only on the variables contained in the set X. In the following, X will always be the set of variables occurring in the E-unification problem S under consideration. We denote this set by $Var(S)$. The above definition of the E-instantiation quasi-order is justified by the fact that any E-instance on $Var(S)$ of an E-unifier of S is again an E-unifier of S, which is the property needed in applications. With a more restrictive definition (which requires syntactic equality or E-equality on all variables), fewer substitutions could be compared with the instantiation quasi-order, and thus the minimal complete sets of E-unifiers (see below) might become unnecessarily large.

Definition 10.1.4 Let S be an E-unification problem over Σ and let $X :=$ $Var(S)$. A **complete set of E-unifiers** of S is a set of substitutions $\mathcal{C}$ that satisfies

- each $\sigma \in \mathcal{C}$ is an E-unifier of S,
- for all $\theta \in \mathcal{U}_E(S)$ there exists $\sigma \in \mathcal{C}$ such that $\sigma \lesssim_E^X \theta$.

A **minimal complete set of E-unifiers** is a complete set of E-unifiers $\mathcal{M}$ that satisfies the additional condition

- for all $\sigma, \sigma' \in \mathcal{M}$, $\sigma \lesssim_E^X \sigma'$ implies $\sigma = \sigma'$.

The substitution σ is a **most general E-unifier** (mgu) of S iff $\{\sigma\}$ is a minimal complete set of E-unifiers of S.

Example 10.1.5 Let $C := \{f(x,y) \approx f(y,x)\}$ be the theory that axiomatizes commutativity of the binary function symbol f, and let $S := \{f(x,y) \approx_C^? f(a,b)\}$ where a and b are constant symbols. It is easy to see that any C-unifier of S must either map x to a and y to b, or map x to b and y to a. Consequently, the set $\{\sigma_1, \sigma_2\}$, where

$$\sigma_1 := \{x \mapsto a,\ y \mapsto b\} \quad \text{and} \quad \sigma_2 := \{x \mapsto b,\ y \mapsto a\},$$

is a complete set of C-unifiers of S. This set is also minimal since these two substitutions are obviously incomparable with respect to $\lesssim_C^{\{x,y\}}$.

Minimal complete sets of E-unifiers need not always exist (since completeness and minimality may contradict each other), but if they exist, they are unique up to the equivalence $\sim_E^X$ associated with $\lesssim_E^X$:

$$\sigma \sim_E^X \sigma' \quad \text{iff} \quad \sigma \lesssim_E^X \sigma' \text{ and } \sigma' \lesssim_E^X \sigma.$$

Lemma 10.1.6 *Assume that $\mathcal{M}_1$ and $\mathcal{M}_2$ are minimal complete sets of E-unifiers of S. Then there exists a bijective mapping $B : \mathcal{M}_1 \to \mathcal{M}_2$ such that $\sigma_1 \sim_E^X B(\sigma_1)$ holds for all $\sigma_1 \in \mathcal{M}_1$.*

Proof Since $\mathcal{M}_1$ is a set of E-unifiers of S and $\mathcal{M}_2$ is a complete set of E-unifiers of S, we know that for every $\sigma_1 \in \mathcal{M}_1$ there exists $\sigma_2 \in \mathcal{M}_2$ such that $\sigma_2 \lesssim_E^X \sigma_1$. This shows that we can define a mapping $B : \mathcal{M}_1 \to \mathcal{M}_2$ such that $B(\sigma_1) \lesssim_E^X \sigma_1$ for all $\sigma_1 \in \mathcal{M}_1$. By exchanging the rôles of $\mathcal{M}_1$ and $\mathcal{M}_2$ in the above argument, we can also show that there exists a mapping $B' : \mathcal{M}_2 \to \mathcal{M}_1$ such that $B'(\sigma_2) \lesssim_E^X \sigma_2$ for all $\sigma_2 \in \mathcal{M}_2$.

Because $B'(B(\sigma_1)) \lesssim_E^X B(\sigma_1) \lesssim_E^X \sigma_1$, minimality of $\mathcal{M}_1$ implies that $B'(B(\sigma_1)) = \sigma_1$ for all $\sigma_1 \in \mathcal{M}_1$. Symmetrically, $B(B'(\sigma_2)) = \sigma_2$ for all

$\sigma_2 \in \mathcal{M}_2$. Consequently, B and B' are bijections that are inverse to each other. Finally, we have (for all $\sigma_1 \in \mathcal{M}_1$) $\sigma_1 = B'(B(\sigma_1)) \lesssim_E^X B(\sigma_1) \lesssim_E^X \sigma_1$, which shows $B(\sigma_1) \sim_E^X \sigma_1$. $\qquad\qquad\square$

In particular, this lemma tells us that all minimal complete sets of E-unifiers of a given problem S have the same cardinality. For this reason, we can define the *unification type* of an equational theory $\approx_E$ with respect to the existence and cardinality of minimal complete sets of E-unifiers.

Definition 10.1.7 The set of identities E (or, equivalently, the equational theory $\approx_E$) is of **unification type**

unitary iff a minimal complete set of E-unifiers exists for all E-unification problems S, and it always has cardinality ≤ 1.

finitary iff a minimal complete set of E-unifiers exists for all E-unification problems S, and it always has finite cardinality.

infinitary iff a minimal complete set of E-unifiers exists for all E-unification problems S, and there exists an E-unification problem for which this set is infinite.

zero iff there exists an E-unification problem that does not have a minimal complete set of E-unifiers.

Thus, E is *unitary* iff every solvable E-unification problem has a most general E-unifier (mgu). The empty set of identities $\emptyset$, which defines syntactic equality, is unitary. If E is *finitary*, then the set of all E-unifiers of a given E-unification problem can always be represented as E-instances of finitely many unifiers. Commutativity C yields an example of a finitary theory that is not unitary (see Section 10.2).

A finite representation of all E-unifiers via E-instantiation is not always possible for theories having one of the other two types. *Infinitary theories* always allow for a non-redundant (albeit possibly infinite) representation of all unifiers. Associativity $A := \{f(x, f(y, z)) \approx f(f(x, y), z)\}$ defines such a theory (see Exercise 10.3). For theories of *type zero*, a non-redundant representation of all unifiers need not exist. It is easy to see that a finite complete set of E-unifiers can always be turned into a minimal one by removing redundant elements. Thus, a unification problem that does not allow for a non-redundant representation of all unifiers cannot have a finite complete set of unifiers. The equational theory induced by $AI := A \cup \{f(x, x) = x\}$ is of type zero [8, 222].

The definition of unification type allows for arbitrary (i.e. general) E-unification problems. If we restrict the definition to elementary E-unification problems (E-unification problems with constants), we may obtain different unification types. For example, the theory $AC1 := \{f(x, f(y, z)) \approx f(f(x, y), z), f(x, y) \approx f(y, x), f(x, 1) \approx x\}$ is unitary for elementary unification, but only finitary for unification with constants and for general unification (see Section 10.3).

Given a set of identities E, unification theory tries to answer the following questions:

- Is solvability of E-unification problems decidable? What is the complexity of this decision problem?
- What is the unification type of E? How can (minimal) complete sets of E-unifiers be computed? How large are these sets, depending on the size of the unification problem, and what is the complexity of computing them?

As pointed out above, the answers to these questions may differ, depending on which kind of unification problems (elementary, with constants, or general) are considered. Algorithms that are able to decide solvability of E-unification problems are called **decision procedures** for E-unification. For finitary theories, algorithms that compute (finite) minimal complete sets of E-unifiers are called **E-unification algorithms**. Algorithms that enumerate (possibly infinite) complete sets of E-unifiers are called **E-unification procedures**.

Exercises

10.1 Show that, for a set of identities E with an undecidable word problem, E-unification with constants is undecidable.

10.2 Show that for every E-unification problem S there exists a general E-unification problem S' such that $|S'| = 1$ and $\mathcal{U}_E(S) = \mathcal{U}_E(S')$.

10.3 Let $A := \{f(x, f(y, z)) \approx f(f(x, y), z)\}$, and consider the unification problem $S := \{f(a, x) \approx_A^? f(x, a)\}$. For $n \geq 1$, we define substitutions σ_n inductively as follows:

$$\sigma_1 := \{x \mapsto a\} \quad \text{and} \quad \sigma_{n+1} := \{x \mapsto f(a, \sigma_n(x))\}.$$

Show that for all A-unifiers θ of S_1 there exists an $n \geq 1$ such that $\theta(x) \approx_A \sigma_n(x)$, and that this implies that $\{\sigma_n \mid n \geq 1\}$ is a minimal complete set of A-unifiers of S.

10.4 Show that the A-unification problem $\{f(a, x) \approx_A^? f(x, b)\}$ does not have a solution.

10.5 Let E be a set of identities, σ a substitution, and X a finite set of variables. Show that there exists a substitution τ such that $\sigma \sim^X_E \tau$ and τ is idempotent on X (i.e. $\tau\tau(x) = \tau(x)$ for all $x \in X$).

10.6 The purpose of this exercise is to show that Lemma 4.5.3, which says that two substitutions are instances of each other iff they are equal up to a renaming, need not hold for E-instantiation, even if we use "equal modulo $\approx_E$" in place of "equal": Consider the set of identities $I := \{f(x,x) \approx x\}$, and the substitutions $\sigma := \{x \mapsto y\}$ and $\tau := \{x \mapsto f(y,z)\}$. Show that $\sigma \sim^{\{x\}}_I \tau$, but there does not exist a renaming ρ such that $\sigma(x) \approx_I \rho\tau(x)$

10.7 Let E be a set of identities such that, for every term t, the $\approx_E$-class of t is finite. Show that in this case Lemma 4.5.3 also holds for E-instantiation:

$$\sigma \sim^X_E \sigma' \Leftrightarrow \exists \text{renaming } \rho.\ \sigma(x) \approx_E \rho\sigma'(x) \text{ for all } x \in X,$$

where X is a finite set of variables. (*Hint:* Show that finiteness of the $\approx_E$-classes implies that E is **regular**, i.e. $s \approx_E t$ implies $Var(s) = Var(t)$. Then, use the fact that the $\approx_E$-classes are finite to reduce the above claim to Lemma 4.5.3.)

10.8 The matching problem can be generalized to E-**matching** as follows: Given terms l and s, determine if there is a substitution σ such that $\sigma(l) \approx_E s$. This substitution is called an E-**matcher** of l and s. Now, let E be a set of identities such that, for every term t, the $\approx_E$-class of t is finite. Show that in this case E-matching is decidable, and that there is an algorithm for computing E-matchers. (*Hint:* compare with Exercise 4.2.)

10.9 This exercise is meant to clarify the definition of the unification type of an equational theory by considering complete and minimal complete sets in an abstract order-theoretic setting. To keep things simple, we consider partial orders instead of quasi-orders. Thus, let $(U, \geq)$ be a partially ordered set. A subset C of U is called **complete** iff for all u in U there exists $c \in C$ such that $c \leq u$. A subset M of U is **minimal complete** iff it is complete and for all $m, m' \in M$, $m \leq m'$ implies $m = m'$.

   (a) Show that U can have at most one minimal complete set.

   (b) Show that U has a minimal complete set iff the set of minimal elements of U is complete.

   (c) Give an example of a partially ordered set U that does not have a minimal complete set.

(d) Show that a partially ordered set U that does not have a minimal complete set must have an infinitely descending chain. (*Hint:* Zorn's lemma.)

(e) Give an example of a partially ordered set that has an infinitely descending chain, but also has a minimal complete set.

10.2 Commutative functions

Commutativity of the binary function symbol g can be defined by the identity $C_g := \{g(x, y) \approx g(y, x)\}$. In the following, we consider signatures containing finitely many commutative symbols together with finitely many free symbols. To be more precise, let $\Sigma := \Sigma_C \cup \Sigma_F$ be the disjoint union of a finite set of binary function symbols Σ_C (the **commutative** symbols) and an arbitrary finite signature Σ_F (consisting of the **free** symbols). The set of identities $C := \bigcup_{g \in \Sigma_C} C_g$ axiomatizes commutativity of the symbols in Σ_C.

The following lemma states some useful properties of $\approx_C$.

Lemma 10.2.1 *Let $s, t \in T(\Sigma, V)$ for a set of variables V.*

1. *$s \approx_C t$ implies that $|s| = |t|$, $Var(s) = Var(t)$, and the root symbols of s and t agree.*
2. *For all $n \geq 0$ and $f \in \Sigma_F^{(n)}$, $f(s_1, \ldots, s_n) \approx_C f(t_1, \ldots, t_n)$ iff $s_i \approx_C t_i$ for $i = 1, \ldots, n$.*
3. *For all $g \in \Sigma_C$,*

$$g(s_1, s_2) \approx_C g(t_1, t_2) \quad \text{iff} \quad s_1 \approx_C t_1 \wedge s_2 \approx_C t_2 \ \text{or}$$
$$s_1 \approx_C t_2 \wedge s_2 \approx_C t_1.$$

Proof The $\Leftarrow$-directions of statements (2) and (3) are trivial. For (1) and the $\Rightarrow$-directions of (2) and (3), one can use the fact that $s \approx_C t$ implies that there exists an $n \geq 0$ such that $s \overset{n}{\leftrightarrow}_C t$. It is now easy to prove the claims by induction on n. $\square$

10.2.1 A unification algorithm

The above lemma shows that in many respects $\approx_C$ behaves similarly to syntactic equality. For this reason, one can design a C-unification algorithm by simply extending the transformation-based algorithm for syntactic unification with a rule that treats commutative function symbols according to (3) of Lemma 10.2.1: an equation $g(s_1, s_2) \approx_C^? g(t_1, t_2)$ for $g \in \Sigma_C$ can be decomposed in two different ways. It is replaced either by the equations

$s_1 \approx_C^? t_1$ and $s_2 \approx_C^? t_2$, or by $s_1 \approx_C^? t_2$ and $s_2 \approx_C^? t_1$. This means that a given C-unification problem is transformed into two new problems, with the intended meaning that the original problem is solvable if one of the new problems is solvable. Consequently, we must work with finite sets of C-unification problems.

Definition 10.2.2 An **extended C-unification problem** is a finite (possibly empty) set $\mathcal{M}$ of C-unification problems. The set of all C-unifiers of $\mathcal{M}$ is defined as

$$\mathcal{U}_C(\mathcal{M}) := \bigcup_{S \in \mathcal{M}} \mathcal{U}_C(S),$$

that is, σ is a C-unifier of $\mathcal{M}$ iff it is a C-unifier of an element S of $\mathcal{M}$.

As in the case of syntactic unification, our goal is to transform a given (extended) C-unification problem into solved form. Recall from syntactic unification that a $(C\text{-})$ unification problem S is in solved form iff it is of the form $S = \{x_1 \approx_C^? t_1, \ldots, x_n \approx_C^? t_n\}$ for pairwise distinct variables x_i, none of which occurs in any of the t_j (Definition 4.6.1).

Definition 10.2.3 The extended C-unification problem $\mathcal{M}$ is in **solved form** iff all $S \in \mathcal{M}$ are in solved form (w.r.t. Definition 4.6.1).

Note that, according to this definition, the empty set $\mathcal{M} = \emptyset$ is an extended C-unification problem in solved form. By Definition 10.2.2, the set of all C-unifiers of $\mathcal{M} = \emptyset$ is empty. Thus, $\mathcal{M} = \emptyset$ can be used as the "solved" form of unsolvable (extended) C-unification problems. This situation should not be confused with the case where $\emptyset \in \mathcal{M}$, i.e. where $\mathcal{M}$ contains an empty C-unification problem, which has the identity substitution as solution.

As in the syntactic case, a C-unification problem in solved form $S := \{x_1 \approx_C^? t_1, \ldots, x_n \approx_C^? t_n\}$ defines a substitution $\vec{S} := \{x_1 \mapsto t_1, \ldots, x_n \mapsto t_n\}$. Since $\vec{S}$ is a syntactic unifier of S, it is also a C-unifier.

Lemma 10.2.4 *Let S be a C-unification problem and $\mathcal{M}$ an extended C-unification problem.*

1. *If S is in solved form then $\vec{S}$ is a most general C-unifier of S.*
2. *If $\mathcal{M}$ is in solved form then $\{\vec{S} \mid S \in \mathcal{M}\}$ is a complete set of C-unifiers of $\mathcal{M}$.*

Proof The proof of (1) is very similar to the proof of Lemma 4.6.3, and (2) is an immediate consequence of (1). $\square$

For a given C-unification problem S, our transformation-based C-unification algorithm first builds the extended C-unification problem $\{S\}$, and then applies the rules of syntactic unification Delete, Orient, and Eliminate, as well as Decompose (to free symbols f) and C-Decompose (to commutative symbols g).

C-Decompose

$$\{g(s_1, s_2) \approx_C^? g(t_1, t_2)\} \uplus T \quad \Longrightarrow \quad \begin{matrix} \{s_1 \approx_C^? t_1, s_2 \approx_C^? t_2\} \cup T \\ \{s_1 \approx_C^? t_2, s_2 \approx_C^? t_1\} \cup T \end{matrix}$$

Application of such a rule to an extended C-unification problem $\mathcal{M}$ means that an element S of $\mathcal{M}$ is chosen to which the rule applies, and then S is replaced in $\mathcal{M}$ by

- the problem S' obtained by applying one of the rules Delete, Orient, Eliminate, Decompose (for free symbols f) to S, or
- the problems S' and S'' obtained by applying C-Decompose (for commutative symbols g) to S.

In addition, if one of the rules Clash and Occurs-Check applies to a problem S in $\mathcal{M}$, then we can simply remove the (unsolvable) problem S from $\mathcal{M}$. We write $\mathcal{M} \Longrightarrow \mathcal{M}'$ to indicate that $\mathcal{M}'$ can be obtained from the extended C-unification problem $\mathcal{M}$ by application of one of the rules Delete, Orient, Eliminate, Decompose (for free symbols f), C-Decompose (for commutative symbols g), Clash, and Occurs-Check.

Lemma 10.2.5 *Let $\mathcal{M}$ be in normal form w.r.t. $\Longrightarrow$. Then $\mathcal{M}$ is in solved form.*

Proof Similar to the syntactic case. □

The transformation-based C-unification algorithm can now be described as follows:

$$CUnify(S) =$$
$$\quad \mathcal{M} := \{S\};$$
$$\quad \texttt{while there is some } \mathcal{M}' \texttt{ such that } \mathcal{M} \Longrightarrow \mathcal{M}' \texttt{ do } \mathcal{M} := \mathcal{M}';$$
$$\quad \texttt{return } \{\vec{T} \mid T \in \mathcal{M}\}.$$

If the extended C-unification problem in solved form obtained by applying the transformation rules is empty, then the algorithm yields the empty set of substitutions as output. Thus, it is not necessary to treat non-unifiability of S by a separate failure case.

Before proving that the algorithm always computes a finite complete set of C-unifiers of the input problem S, we illustrate it by an example.

Example 10.2.6 Let $g \in \Sigma_C$, and $a, b \in \Sigma_F^{(0)}$. Fig. 10.1 shows a sequence of transformations that starts with the input problem $\{g(g(a, x), z) \approx_C^? g(g(y, b), g(a, b))\}$, and yields the two solved forms $\{y \approx_C^? a,\ x \approx_C^? b,\ z \approx_C^? g(a, b)\}$ and $\{x \approx_C^? b,\ z \approx_C^? g(y, b)\}$. The corresponding output of *CUnify* is the set $\{\sigma, \tau\}$ where $\sigma := \{y \mapsto a,\ x \mapsto b,\ z \mapsto g(a, b)\}$ and $\tau := \{x \mapsto b,\ z \mapsto g(y, b)\}$. Note that σ is a C-instance of τ on $Var(S)$, i.e. the complete set of C-unifiers computed by *CUnify* is not minimal.

$$\{\{g(g(a, x), z) \approx_C^? g(g(y, b), g(a, b))\}\} \quad \Longrightarrow \text{C-Decompose}$$

$$\left\{ \begin{array}{l} \{g(a, x) \approx_C^? g(y, b),\ z \approx_C^? g(a, b)\}, \\ \{g(a, x) \approx_C^? g(a, b),\ z \approx_C^? g(y, b)\} \end{array} \right\} \quad \Longrightarrow \text{C-Decompose}$$

$$\left\{ \begin{array}{l} \{a \approx_C^? y,\ x \approx_C^? b,\ z \approx_C^? g(a, b)\}, \\ \{a \approx_C^? b,\ x \approx_C^? y,\ z \approx_C^? g(a, b)\}, \\ \{g(a, x) \approx_C^? g(a, b),\ z \approx_C^? g(y, b)\} \end{array} \right\} \quad \Longrightarrow \text{Clash}$$

$$\left\{ \begin{array}{l} \{a \approx_C^? y,\ x \approx_C^? b,\ z \approx_C^? g(a, b)\}, \\ \{g(a, x) \approx_C^? g(a, b),\ z \approx_C^? g(y, b)\} \end{array} \right\} \quad \Longrightarrow \text{C-Decompose}$$

$$\left\{ \begin{array}{l} \{a \approx_C^? y,\ x \approx_C^? b,\ z \approx_C^? g(a, b)\}, \\ \{a \approx_C^? a,\ x \approx_C^? b,\ z \approx_C^? g(y, b)\}, \\ \{a \approx_C^? b,\ x \approx_C^? a,\ z \approx_C^? g(y, b)\} \end{array} \right\} \quad \Longrightarrow \text{Clash}$$

$$\left\{ \begin{array}{l} \{a \approx_C^? y,\ x \approx_C^? b,\ z \approx_C^? g(a, b)\}, \\ \{a \approx_C^? a,\ x \approx_C^? b,\ z \approx_C^? g(y, b)\} \end{array} \right\} \quad \Longrightarrow \text{Orient} \circ \Longrightarrow \text{Decompose}$$

$$\left\{ \begin{array}{l} \{y \approx_C^? a,\ x \approx_C^? b,\ z \approx_C^? g(a, b)\}, \\ \{x \approx_C^? b,\ z \approx_C^? g(y, b)\} \end{array} \right\}$$

Fig. 10.1. An example for *CUnify*.

Lemma 10.2.7 *CUnify terminates for all inputs.*

Proof We associate each C-unification problem S with the same triple of natural numbers as in the proof of Lemma 4.6.5. An extended C-unification problem $\mathcal{M}$ is associated with the multiset of the triples corresponding to its elements. These multisets are ordered with the multiset order induced by the lexicographic order on the triples. It is easy to see that each transformation step decreases the multisets with respect to this order. $\square$

Lemma 10.2.8 *Let M and M' be extended C-unification problems. If $M \Longrightarrow M'$, then $U_C(M) = U_C(M')$.*

Proof This is an easy consequence of Lemma 10.2.1. □

Together with Lemma 10.2.4 and 10.2.5, the last two lemmas show that the algorithm *CUnify* is correct.

Theorem 10.2.9 *Applied to a given C-unification problem S, CUnify always terminates and computes a complete set of C-unifiers of S.*

As Example 10.2.6 demonstrates, this complete set need not be minimal. By removing redundant elements (in the example the substitution σ), the finite complete set obtained in this way can be transformed into a minimal complete set. It is, however, not clear how to design a C-unification algorithm that computes such a minimal complete set "directly".

Corollary 10.2.10 *C is finitary (w.r.t. general unification), but not unitary (even w.r.t. elementary unification).*

Example 10.1.5 shows that C is not unitary for C-unification with constants. Exercise 10.12 yields an example of an elementary C-unification problem whose minimal complete set of C-unifiers has cardinality > 1.

10.2.2 The decision problem

By Theorem 10.2.9, *CUnify* yields a decision procedure for C-unification: the input problem S is solvable iff the complete set computed by *CUnify* is nonempty. If we are only interested in the decision problem, it is not necessary to compute the whole complete set (which may be exponentially large in the size of S). It is sufficient to design a nondeterministic algorithm that guesses how to find one of the elements of the nonempty complete set.

Theorem 10.2.11 *The decision problem for C-unification is NP-complete, provided that $\Sigma_C \neq \emptyset$ and Σ_F contains at least two constant symbols.*

Proof Let us first show that the problem is in NP, i.e. there is a nondeterministic polynomial decision procedure for (general) C-unification. This nondeterministic procedure works on C-unification problems (instead of extended C-unification problems) since it uses a nondeterministic version of C-Decompose, which chooses just one of the two problems generated by its deterministic counterpart. Consequently, each search path of the nondeterministic procedure is very similar to a run of the transformation-based algorithm for syntactic unification. As we have seen in the syntactic case, the transformation process may need exponential space and time. It is, however, easy to show that the methods used to derive an almost linear algorithm for syntactic unification can be used to obtain a nondeterministic almost linear decision procedure for C-unification.

NP-hardness of the decision problem for C-unification (with constants) can be shown by a reduction from positive 1-in-3-SAT, which is known to be an NP-complete problem [95]. An instance of positive 1-in-3-SAT is given by a finite set $C = \{C_1, \ldots, C_n\}$ of clauses of the form $C_i = p_i \vee q_i \vee r_i$, where p_i, q_i, r_i are propositional variables. A solution of C is a propositional valuation that makes exactly one propositional variable true in each clause C_i of C.

The positive 1-in-3-SAT instance C is transformed into a C-unification problem S_C as follows: Let $g \in \Sigma_C$, and let $a, b \in \Sigma_F$ be distinct constant symbols. For each propositional variable p in C we introduce a variable x_p, and for each clause C_i a variable y_i. Replacing x_p by a (b) will be interpreted as evaluating p by true (false). The clause $C_i = p_i \vee q_i \vee r_i$ is translated into the equation

$$g(g(g(x_{p_i}, x_{q_i}), x_{r_i}), y_i) \approx^?_C g(g(g(b, b), a), g(g(b, a), b)). \qquad (*)$$

The C-unification problem S_C is the set of all these equations (for $i = 1, \ldots, n$). We claim that a substitution σ is a C-unifier of $(*)$ iff it replaces exactly one of the variables x_{p_i}, x_{q_i}, and x_{r_i} by a, and the other two by b. Obviously, this implies that S_C has a C-unifier iff C has a solution.

It is easy to see that any substitution that replaces exactly one of the variables x_{p_i}, x_{q_i}, and x_{r_i} by a, and the other two by b, can be turned into a C-unifier of $(*)$ by choosing an appropriate image for y_i. To prove the other direction of the claim, assume that σ is a C-unifier of $(*)$. By Lemma 10.2.1, there are two cases: either (1) $\sigma(g(g(x_{p_i}, x_{q_i}), x_{r_i})) \approx_C g(g(b, b), a)$ or (2) $\sigma(g(g(x_{p_i}, x_{q_i}), x_{r_i})) \approx_C g(g(b, a), b)$.

In case (1), we have either (1.1) $\sigma(g(x_{p_i}, x_{q_i})) \approx_C g(b, b)$ and $\sigma(x_{r_i}) \approx_C a$, or (1.2) $\sigma(g(x_{p_i}, x_{q_i})) \approx_C a$ and $\sigma(x_{r_i}) \approx_C g(b, b)$. Obviously, (1.1) implies that $\sigma(x_{p_i}) = \sigma(x_{q_i}) = b$ and $\sigma(x_{r_i}) = a$. Case (1.2) is not possible since $g(s, t) \not\approx_C a$ for all terms s, t.

In case (2), we have either (2.1) $\sigma(g(x_{p_i}, x_{q_i})) \approx_C g(b, a)$ and $\sigma(x_{r_i}) \approx_C b$, or (2.2) $\sigma(g(x_{p_i}, x_{q_i})) \approx_C b$ and $\sigma(x_{r_i}) \approx_C g(b, a)$. Case (2.2) is again impossible, and Case (2.1) yields two subcases: (2.1.1) $\sigma(x_{p_i}) = \sigma(x_{r_i}) = b$ and $\sigma(x_{q_i}) = a$, or (2.1.2) $\sigma(x_{q_i}) = \sigma(x_{r_i}) = b$ and $\sigma(x_{p_i}) = a$. $\qquad \square$

Exercises

10.10 Show that for every $t \in T(\Sigma, V)$, the $\approx_C$-class of t is finite.

10.11 Let X be a finite set of variables. Show that the C-instantiation relation on substitutions, $\lesssim_C^X$, is decidable. (*Hint:* use the above exercise and compare with Exercise 10.8.)

10.12 Let $g \in \Sigma_C$. Show that the C-unification problem

$$\{g(x, y) \approx_C^? g(z, g(z, z))\}$$

has a minimal complete set of C-unifiers of cardinality 2.

10.13 Let $s, t \in T(\Sigma, V)$. By Exercise 10.10 we know that the $\approx_C$-classes of these terms are finite. Let $\{s_1, \ldots, s_m\}$ be the $\approx_C$-class of s, and $\{t_1, \ldots, t_n\}$ the $\approx_C$-class of t. Show that

$$\mathcal{U}_C(\{s \approx_C^? t\}) = \bigcup_{\substack{1 \le i \le m \\ 1 \le j \le n}} \mathcal{U}_\emptyset(\{s_i =^? t_j\}),$$

and that $\{\sigma \mid \sigma \text{ is mgu of } s_i =^? t_j \text{ for some } i, j, 1 \le i \le m, 1 \le j \le n\}$ is a complete set of C-unifiers of $s \approx_C^? t$.

10.3 Associative and commutative functions

The equational theory induced by the set of identities

$$AC := \{(x * y) * z \approx x * (y * z),\ x * y \approx y * x\},$$

which axiomatizes associativity and commutativity of a (single) binary function symbol $*$, is one of the theories most frequently used in rewriting modulo equational theories and in theorem proving with built-in theories. One reason is that, on the one hand, associativity and commutativity are properties satisfied by many common binary operations (such as addition and multiplication in rings, conjunction and disjunction in logics). On the other hand, commutativity cannot be handled appropriately by the rewriting approach introduced in this book since the identity $x * y \approx y * x$ would lead to a nonterminating rule. In addition, modulo commutativity, associativity can no longer be turned into a terminating rule (see Exercise 10.14).

In the following, we restrict our attention to elementary AC-unification, which can be reduced to solving homogeneous linear diophantine equations in the non-negative integers. AC-unification with constants can in principle be treated by the same approach; it leads to both homogeneous and inhomogeneous linear diophantine equations, which complicates the description of the technical details, without providing new insights.

It is more convenient to start with unification modulo the theory induced by $AC1 := AC \cup \{x * 1 \approx x\}$, and then go from there to AC-unification. In the following, let $\Sigma := \{*\}$ for a binary symbol $*$, and $\Sigma_1 := \Sigma \cup \{1\}$ for a constant symbol 1. All terms considered in this section will be elements of $T(\Sigma_1, V)$ for a countably infinite set of variables $V := \{x_1, x_2, x_3, \ldots\}$. Before we consider unification modulo $\approx_{AC}$ and $\approx_{AC1}$, we show that the congruence classes of these theories can be characterized with the help of vectors of non-negative integers.

10.3.1 Terms as vectors and substitutions as matrices

Since $*$ is associative, we can dispense with all parentheses. Following the usual conventions in mathematics, we will also drop the multiplication symbol $*$ (e.g., use xy in place of $x * y$), and express iterated multiplication by exponentiation (e.g., write x^3 instead of $x * x * x$). The exponent 0 yields the unit 1 (e.g., x^0 stands for 1). Commutativity of $*$ means that we can group identical variables together (e.g., write $x^3 y^2$ instead of $xyxyx$). This observation leads to the following characterization of the congruence classes of $\approx_{AC1}$. Recall that the number of occurrences of the variable x in the term t is denoted by $|t|_x$.

Lemma 10.3.1 *Let* $s, t \in T(\Sigma_1, V)$.

$$s \approx_{AC1} t \quad \textit{iff} \quad |s|_x = |t|_x \textit{ for all } x \in V.$$

Proof The $\Rightarrow$-direction can easily be shown by induction on the number of rewrite steps necessary to transform s into t. To prove the $\Leftarrow$-direction, let $x_1, \ldots, x_n \in V$ be such that $Var(s) \cup Var(t) \subseteq \{x_1, \ldots, x_n\}$, and let $k_i := |s|_{x_i}$ and $\ell_i := |t|_{x_i}$ $(i = 1, \ldots, n)$. Obviously, $s \approx_{AC1} x_1^{k_1} \cdots x_n^{k_n}$ and $t \approx_{AC1} x_1^{\ell_1} \cdots x_n^{\ell_n}$. Thus, $k_i = \ell_i$ for $i = 1, \ldots, n$ implies $s \approx_{AC1} t$. $\square$

Given a finite set $X_n := \{x_1, \ldots, x_n\}$ of variables, the $\approx_{AC1}$-class of a term $s \in T(\Sigma_1, X_n)$ is thus uniquely determined by the vector $\vec{v}_n(s) := (|s|_{x_1}, \ldots, |s|_{x_n}) \in \mathbb{N}^n$. Obviously, $s \approx_{AC1} 1$ iff $\vec{v}_n(s) = \vec{0} := (0, \ldots, 0)$, and every term $s \in T(\Sigma_1, X_n)$ that is not $\approx_{AC1}$-congruent to 1 is congruent to a term in $T(\Sigma, X_n)$.

Lemma 10.3.2 *Let* $s, t \in T(\Sigma, X_n)$.

1. $s \approx_{AC1} t$ *iff* $\vec{v}_n(s) = \vec{v}_n(t)$ *iff* $s \approx_{AC} t$.
2. $\vec{v}_n(s) \in \mathbb{N}^n - \vec{0}$.

Proof (2) is trivial. The implication "$s \approx_{AC1} t \Rightarrow \vec{v}_n(s) = \vec{v}_n(t)$" is an immediate consequence of Lemma 10.3.1, and "$s \approx_{AC} t \Rightarrow s \approx_{AC1} t$" is trivial.

Finally, "$\vec{v}_n(s) = \vec{v}_n(t) \Rightarrow s \approx_{AC} t$" can be shown as in the proof of the $\Leftarrow$-direction of Lemma 10.3.1.   □

Let $n, m \geq 0$, $s \in T(\Sigma_1, X_n)$, and σ be a substitution such that $\mathcal{D}om(\sigma) \subseteq X_n$ and $\sigma(x_i) \in T(\Sigma_1, X_m)$ for all $x_i \in X_n$. Given $\vec{v}_n(s)$ and $\vec{v}_m(\sigma(x_i))$ for all $x_i \in X_n$, it is easy to compute $\vec{v}_m(\sigma(s))$:

$$|\sigma(s)|_{x_j} = \sum_{i=1}^{n} |s|_{x_i} \cdot |\sigma(x_i)|_{x_j}.$$

Thus, if $M_{n,m}(\sigma)$ denotes the $n \times m$ matrix whose rows are the vectors $\vec{v}_m(\sigma(x_i))$, i.e.

$$M_{n,m}(\sigma) := \begin{pmatrix} |\sigma(x_1)|_{x_1} & \cdots & |\sigma(x_1)|_{x_m} \\ \vdots & & \vdots \\ |\sigma(x_n)|_{x_1} & \cdots & |\sigma(x_n)|_{x_m} \end{pmatrix},$$

then applying σ to s corresponds to multiplying the vector $\vec{v}_n(s)$ by the matrix $M_{n,m}(\sigma)$:

Lemma 10.3.3 $\vec{v}_m(\sigma(s)) = \vec{v}_n(s) \cdot M_{n,m}(\sigma)$.

For example, if $s := x_1^2 x_2$ and $\sigma := \{x_1 \mapsto x_2 x_3, x_2 \mapsto x_1^2 x_3\}$, then $\sigma(s) = (x_2 x_3)^2 x_1^2 x_3 \approx_{AC1} x_1^2 x_2^2 x_3^3$, $\vec{v}_2(s) = (2\ 1)$,

$$M_{2,3}(\sigma) = \begin{pmatrix} 0 & 1 & 1 \\ 2 & 0 & 1 \end{pmatrix} \quad \text{and} \quad \vec{v}_3(\sigma(s)) = (2\ 2\ 3) = (2\ 1) \cdot \begin{pmatrix} 0 & 1 & 1 \\ 2 & 0 & 1 \end{pmatrix}.$$

10.3.2 *AC1-unification*

Let $S := \{s_1 \approx_{AC1}^? t_1, \ldots, s_k \approx_{AC1}^? t_k\}$ be an elementary *AC1*-unification problem, let $X_n := \{x_1, \ldots, x_n\}$ be the set of all variables occurring in S, and let σ be a substitution. We may (without loss of generality) assume that $\mathcal{D}om(\sigma) \subseteq X_n$, and that there exists $m \geq 1$ such that $\sigma(x_i) \in T(\Sigma_1, X_m)$ for all $x_i \in X_n$.

Lemma 10.3.4 *The following statements are equivalent:*

1. *σ is an AC1-unifier of S.*
2. *$\vec{v}_n(s_i) \cdot M_{n,m}(\sigma) = \vec{v}_n(t_i) \cdot M_{n,m}(\sigma)$ for all $i = 1, \ldots, k$.*

Proof By Lemma 10.3.1, $\sigma(s_i) \approx_{AC1} \sigma(t_i)$ iff $\vec{v}_m(\sigma(s_i)) = \vec{v}_m(\sigma(t_i))$. Thus, Lemma 10.3.3 yields the above equivalence.   □

Let $M_{k,n}(S)$ be the integer matrix whose rows are the vectors $\vec{v}_n(s_i) - \vec{v}_n(t_i)$, i.e. the matrix whose entry at position (i, j) is $|s_i|_{x_j} - |t_i|_{x_j}$. The above lemma can now be reformulated as follows:

Lemma 10.3.5 σ *is an AC1-unifier of S iff the columns of $M_{n,m}(\sigma)$ are (non-negative integer) solutions of the system of* **homogeneous linear diophantine equations** $DE(S)$:

$$
M_{k,n}(S) \cdot \begin{pmatrix} y_1 \\ \vdots \\ y_n \end{pmatrix} = \begin{pmatrix} 0 \\ \vdots \\ 0 \end{pmatrix}.
$$

We call $DE(S)$ a system of *diophantine* equations since the entries of the matrix $M_{k,n}(S)$ are integers, and we are only interested in (non-negative) integer solutions. The meaning of *homogeneous* and *linear* is as in linear algebra.

Example 10.3.6 The *AC1*-unification problem $S := \{x_1 x_2 \approx_{AC1}^? x_3^2\}$ corresponds to the homogeneous linear diophantine equation

$$
(1 \ \ 1 \ \ -2) \cdot \begin{pmatrix} y_1 \\ y_2 \\ y_3 \end{pmatrix} = \begin{pmatrix} 0 \\ 0 \\ 0 \end{pmatrix}. \tag{$*$}
$$

The substitution $\sigma := \{x_1 \mapsto x_1 x_2^2, x_2 \mapsto x_1, x_3 \mapsto x_1 x_2\}$ is an *AC1*-unifier of S, and it yields the matrix

$$
M_{3,2}(\sigma) = \begin{pmatrix} 1 & 2 \\ 1 & 0 \\ 1 & 1 \end{pmatrix},
$$

whose columns solve $(*)$. Conversely, the solution $y_1 = 1$, $y_2 = 3$, and $y_3 = 2$ of $(*)$ can be turned into the following *AC1*-unifier of S:

$$
\tau := \{x_1 \mapsto x_1, x_2 \mapsto x_1^3, x_3 \mapsto x_1^2\}.
$$

Obviously, the substitution that replaces all variables x_i occurring in an elementary *AC1*-unification problem S by 1 is an *AC1*-unifier of S. This trivial unifier corresponds to the trivial solution of $DE(S)$, which replaces all y_i by 0. Thus, the decision problem for elementary *AC1*-unification is decidable in constant time: just say "yes" without looking at the problem.

Fact 10.3.7 *Every elementary AC1-unification problem has a solution.*

In order to obtain a most general *AC1*-unifier of S, we must determine a *finite generating set* for the set of all solutions of $DE(S)$. In the following, we denote column vectors by $v\downarrow$ to distinguish them from row vectors, which we write as $\vec{v}$. By a slight abuse of notation, we write $v\downarrow \in \mathbb{N}^n$ to express that all entries of the column vector $v\downarrow$ are non-negative integers, and we write $0\downarrow$ for column vectors having only 0 as entry, without explicitly distinguishing different dimensions in the notation.

Definition 10.3.8 Let $M_{k,n}$ be a $k \times n$ integer matrix, and let

$$M_{k,n} \cdot y\downarrow = 0\downarrow \qquad (*)$$

be the system of homogeneous linear diophantine equations induced by $M_{k,n}$. A finite set $V := \{v_1\downarrow, \ldots, v_r\downarrow\} \subseteq \mathbb{N}^n$ is a **generating set** for the set of all (non-negative integer) solutions of $(*)$ iff every element of V solves $(*)$, and for each $v\downarrow \in \mathbb{N}^n$ that solves $(*)$ there exist $a_1, \ldots, a_r \in \mathbb{N}$ such that

$$v\downarrow = v_1\downarrow \cdot a_1 + \cdots + v_r\downarrow \cdot a_r.$$

Theorem 10.3.9 *For every system of homogeneous linear diophantine equations there exists a finite generating set, and this set is computable.*

We defer the proof of this theorem to Subsection 10.3.4.

Given a finite generating set $W := \{v_1\downarrow, \ldots, v_r\downarrow\}$ for $DE(S)$, we can construct a most general $AC1$-unifier of S as follows. Let $M_{n,r}(W) := (v_1\downarrow \cdots v_r\downarrow)$ be the matrix that has the vectors $v_i\downarrow$ as its columns, and let σ_W be the substitution satisfying $M_{n,r}(\sigma_W) = M_{n,r}(W)$. (Note that, modulo $\approx_{AC1}$, there exists exactly one such substitution σ_W for every matrix $M_{n,r}(W)$.)

Theorem 10.3.10 *The substitution σ_W induced by the finite generating set W of all non-negative integer solutions of $DE(S)$ is a most general $AC1$-unifier of S.*

Proof Since the columns $v_i\downarrow$ of $M_{n,r}(\sigma) = M_{n,r}(W)$ are solutions of $DE(S)$, σ_W is an $AC1$-unifier of S by Lemma 10.3.5.

To show that σ_W is most general, we consider an arbitrary $AC1$-unifier τ of S. Let $M_{n,s}(\tau) := (u_1\downarrow \cdots u_s\downarrow)$ be the matrix corresponding to τ. By Lemma 10.3.5, the columns $u_j\downarrow$ of this matrix are solutions of $DE(S)$. Since W is a generating set for these solutions, there exist $a_{1,j}, \ldots, a_{r,j} \in \mathbb{N}$ such that $u_j\downarrow = v_1\downarrow \cdot a_{1,j} + \cdots + v_r\downarrow \cdot a_{r,j}$. Let $A_{r,s}$ be the matrix whose entries at position (i,j) are the numbers $a_{i,j}$, and let δ be the substitution corresponding to this matrix, i.e. the substitution that satisfies $M_{r,s}(\delta) = A_{r,s}$. By definition of $A_{r,s}$ we have $M_{n,s}(\tau) = M_{n,r}(\sigma_W) \cdot M_{r,s}(\delta)$, and it is easy to see that this implies $\tau(x_i) \approx_{AC1} \delta(\sigma_W(x_i))$ for all $x_i \in X_n$. This shows that τ is an $AC1$-instance of σ_W on $X_n = Var(S)$. $\qquad\square$

Example 10.3.11 Let us again consider the *AC1*-unification problem $S :=$ $\{x_1 x_2 \approx^?_{AC1} x_3^2\}$ of Example 10.3.6. In this case, $DE(S)$ consists of the single equation $(1 \ 1 \ -2) \cdot y{\downarrow} = 0{\downarrow}$. It is easy to verify that the following is a generating set for all non-negative integer solutions of this equation:

$$W := \left\{ \begin{pmatrix} 1 \\ 1 \\ 1 \end{pmatrix}, \begin{pmatrix} 2 \\ 0 \\ 1 \end{pmatrix}, \begin{pmatrix} 0 \\ 2 \\ 1 \end{pmatrix} \right\}.$$

This set yields the mgu $\sigma_W = \{x_1 \mapsto x_1 x_2^2, x_2 \mapsto x_1 x_3^2, x_3 \mapsto x_1 x_2 x_3\}$ of S. The unifier $\tau := \{x_1 \mapsto x_1, x_2 \mapsto x_1^3, x_3 \mapsto x_1^2\}$ of S yields a matrix with just one column:

$$M_{3,1}(\tau) = \begin{pmatrix} 1 \\ 3 \\ 2 \end{pmatrix} = \begin{pmatrix} 1 \\ 1 \\ 1 \end{pmatrix} \cdot 1 + \begin{pmatrix} 2 \\ 0 \\ 1 \end{pmatrix} \cdot 0 + \begin{pmatrix} 0 \\ 2 \\ 1 \end{pmatrix} \cdot 1.$$

The substitution $\delta := \{x_1 \mapsto x_1, x_2 \mapsto 1, x_3 \mapsto x_1\}$, which is induced by the above representation of $M_{3,1}(\tau)$ as a linear combination of the solutions $v_i{\downarrow}$, obviously satisfies $\delta(\sigma_W(x_i)) \approx_{AC1} \tau(x_i)$ for $i = 1, 2, 3$.

Corollary 10.3.12 *AC1 is unitary for elementary unification.*

AC1-unification with constants is no longer unitary (see Exercise 10.16), but still finitary. Also, the decision problem for *AC1*-unification with constants is no longer trivial, but NP-complete (see Exercise 10.17 for the NP-hardness result).

10.3.3 *AC*-unification

An (elementary) *AC*-unification problem S is an *AC1*-unification problem in which the unit 1 does not occur. By Lemma 10.3.2, any *AC*-unifier of S is also an *AC1*-unifier of S. The converse is not true since *AC1*-unifiers may replace certain variables by 1, whereas this is not possible for *AC*-unifiers. In the matrix representation of an *AC*-unifier of S this restriction means that every row of $M_{n,m}(\sigma)$ must contain a non-zero entry. In particular, the trivial *AC1*-unifier $\{x_1 \mapsto 1, \ldots, x_n \mapsto 1\}$ of S is not an *AC*-unifier. The decision problem for elementary *AC*-unification is nontrivial, but not very hard.

Lemma 10.3.13 *The elementary AC-unification problem S is solvable iff the system of homogeneous linear diophantine equations $DE(S)$ has a solution in the positive integers.*

Proof If $v\downarrow \in (\mathbb{N} - \{0\})^n$ is a solution of $DE(S)$, then the corresponding substitution σ (i.e. the substitution satisfying $M_{n,1}(\sigma) = v\downarrow$) is an $AC1$-unifier of S by Lemma 10.3.5. Since all entries of $v\downarrow$ are non-zero, it is also an AC-unifier by Lemma 10.3.2.

Conversely, let σ be an AC-unifier of S, and assume (without loss of generality) that $\mathcal{D}om(\sigma) \subseteq X_n = \mathcal{V}ar(S)$, and that there exists $m \geq 1$ such $\sigma(x_i) \in T(\Sigma, X_m)$ for all $x_i \in X_n$. If we define $\delta := \{x_1 \mapsto x_1, \ldots, x_m \mapsto x_1\}$, then $\delta\sigma$ is also an AC-unifier of S. The corresponding matrix $M_{n,1}(\delta\sigma)$ consists of a single column, which solves $DE(S)$ and has only entries > 0.   □

As an example, we consider the unification problem $S := \{x_1 x_2 \approx^?_{AC} x_3^2\}$ of Example 10.3.6 as an AC-unification problem. This problem yields the system of homogeneous linear diophantine equations

$$(1 \ \ 1 \ \ -2) \cdot \begin{pmatrix} y_1 \\ y_2 \\ y_3 \end{pmatrix} = \begin{pmatrix} 0 \\ 0 \\ 0 \end{pmatrix}. \tag{$*$}$$

The solution $y_1 = 1, y_2 = 1, y_3 = 1$ of $(*)$ yields the AC-unifier $\{x_1 \mapsto x_1, x_2 \mapsto x_1, x_3 \mapsto x_1\}$ of S, whereas the solution $y_1 = 2, y_2 = 0, y_3 = 1$ yields $\{x_1 \mapsto x_1^2, x_2 \mapsto 1, x_3 \mapsto x_1\}$, which is an $AC1$-unifier of S, but not an AC-unifier.

Theorem 10.3.14 *Solvability of elementary AC-unification problems is decidable in polynomial time.*

Proof by reduction to linear programming, which is known to be polynomial:

By the previous lemma, it is sufficient to show that the following problem is decidable in polynomial time: given a $k \times n$ integer matrix A, does the system of equations

$$A \cdot y\downarrow = 0\downarrow \tag{i}$$

have a solution in $(\mathbb{N} - \{0\})^n$? This is equivalent to asking whether the system of equations and inequalities

$$A \cdot y\downarrow = 0\downarrow, \ y_1 > 0, \ldots, y_n > 0 \tag{ii}$$

has a solution in $\mathbb{Z}^n$, which in turn is equivalent to asking whether

$$A \cdot y\downarrow = 0\downarrow, \ y_1 \geq 1, \ldots, y_n \geq 1 \tag{iii}$$

has a solution in $\mathbb{Q}^n$ (i.e. a rational solution). This last problem can easily be turned into a linear programming problem (see Exercise 10.19), which is solvable in polynomial time [137].   □

For AC-unification with constants, things are not so rosy: the decision problem is NP-complete (see Exercise 10.18 for the NP-hardness result).

Now, we consider the problem of computing a complete set of AC-unifiers of a given AC-unification problem S. Let σ be the most general $AC1$-unifier of S. An AC-unifier θ of S is also an $AC1$-unifier of S, and thus an $AC1$-instance of σ on $Var(S)$. Nevertheless, σ need not be a most general AC-unifier of S:

1. The most general $AC1$-unifier σ need not be a Σ-substitution since it may introduce the unit $1 \in \Sigma_1 - \Sigma$. Consequently, it need not be an AC-unifier of S.
2. Even if σ is a Σ-substitution, it need not be most general with respect to AC-instantiation.

The first problem can only occur if S, considered as an AC-unification problem, is not solvable.

Lemma 10.3.15 *S has an AC-unifier iff the most general $AC1$-unifier of S is ($\approx_{AC1}$-equivalent to) a Σ-substitution.*

Proof If the most general $AC1$-unifier σ of S is $\approx_{AC1}$-equivalent to a Σ-substitution σ' (i.e. a substitution that does not introduce 1), then σ' is an AC-unifier of S by Lemma 10.3.2. Conversely, assume that σ is not $\approx_{AC1}$-equivalent to a Σ-substitution. This means that $\sigma(x) \approx_{AC1} 1$ for some $x \in Var(S)$. Consequently, $\delta(\sigma(x)) \approx_{AC1} 1$ for all substitutions δ, which shows that no $AC1$-instance of σ can be a Σ-substitution. $\square$

The reason for the second problem is that an $AC1$-instance of σ need not be an AC-instance of σ.

Example 10.3.16 In Example 10.3.11 we have seen that $\sigma_W = \{x_1 \mapsto x_1 x_2^2, x_2 \mapsto x_1 x_3^2, x_3 \mapsto x_1 x_2 x_3\}$ is a most general $AC1$-unifier of $S := \{x_1 x_2 \approx_{AC}^? x_3^2\}$. Obviously, σ_W is a Σ-substitution, and thus σ_W is an AC-unifier of S. The substitution $\tau := \{x_1 \mapsto x_1, x_2 \mapsto x_1^3, x_3 \mapsto x_1^2\}$ is also an AC-unifier of S, and we have seen that it is an $AC1$-instance of σ_W on $Var(S)$. However, the substitution $\delta := \{x_1 \mapsto x_1, x_2 \mapsto 1, x_3 \mapsto x_1\}$, which yields this $AC1$-instance relationship, is not a Σ-substitution. It is easy to see that τ cannot be obtained as an AC-instance of σ_W.

The Σ_1-substitution δ can, however, be split into the *erasing* substitution $\kappa := \{x_2 \mapsto 1\}$ and the Σ-substitution $\delta' := \{x_1 \mapsto x_1, x_3 \mapsto x_1\}$. Since $\delta = \delta'\kappa$, the AC-unifier τ is an AC-instance of $\kappa\sigma_W$.

From a given most general $AC1$-unifier σ of S, we construct a complete set of AC-unifiers of S by applying all *admissible erasing substitutions* to σ.

Definition 10.3.17 Let X and Y be finite sets of variables.

1. The Σ_1-substitution κ is called an **erasing substitution** on Y iff there exists a set $Z \subseteq Y$ such that $\mathcal{D}om(\kappa) = Z$ and $\kappa(z) = 1$ for all $z \in Z$.
2. The erasing substitution κ is **admissible** on X for the Σ-substitution σ iff $\kappa(\sigma(x)) \not\approx_{AC1} 1$ for all $x \in X$.

Theorem 10.3.18 *Let S be a solvable elementary AC-unification problem, σ a most general AC1-unifier of S, $X := \mathcal{V}ar(S)$, and $Y := \bigcup_{x \in X} \mathcal{V}ar(\sigma(x))$. The set*

$$\mathcal{C} := \{\kappa\sigma \mid \kappa \text{ is an erasing substitution on } Y \text{ and admissible on } X \text{ for } \sigma\}$$

is a complete set of AC-unifiers of S.

Proof As instances of the AC1-unifier σ of S, all substitutions $\kappa\sigma \in \mathcal{C}$ are AC1-unifiers of S. By definition of admissibility, they are ($\approx_{AC1}$-equivalent to) Σ-substitutions, i.e. they can be considered as AC-unifiers of S.

To show that $\mathcal{C}$ is complete, we consider an AC-unifier θ of S. Because θ is also an AC1-unifier of S, and σ is the most general AC1-unifier of S, there exists a substitution δ such that $\theta(x) \approx_{AC1} \delta(\sigma(x))$ for all $x \in X$. We may assume without loss of generality that $\mathcal{D}om(\delta) \subseteq Y$. We define the erasing substitution κ on Y as follows:

$$\kappa := \{y \mapsto 1 \mid y \in Y \wedge \delta(y) \approx_{AC1} 1\}.$$

For all $y \in Y$ such that $\delta(y) \not\approx_{AC1} 1$, there exists a Σ-term s_y satisfying $\delta(y) \approx_{AC1} s_y$. Thus, if we define

$$\delta' := \{y \mapsto s_y \mid y \in Y \wedge \delta(y) \not\approx_{AC1} 1\},$$

then δ' is a Σ-substitution, and it is easy to see that $\delta(y) \approx_{AC1} \delta'(\kappa(y))$ holds for all $y \in Y$. Obviously, this implies $\theta(x) \approx_{AC1} \delta'(\kappa(\sigma(x)))$, and thus it only remains to be shown that κ is admissible for σ on X. Assume to the contrary that $\kappa(\sigma(x)) \approx_{AC1} 1$ for some $x \in X$. However, this implies $\theta(x) \approx_{AC1} \delta'(\kappa(\sigma(x))) \approx_{AC1} 1$, which contradicts our assumption that θ is a Σ-substitution. $\square$

Corollary 10.3.19 *AC is finitary for elementary unification.*

Proof Since the set $Y = \bigcup_{x \in \mathcal{V}ar(S)} \mathcal{V}ar(\sigma(x))$ is finite, there are only finitely many different erasing substitutions on Y. $\square$

As an example, again consider the most general AC1-unifier

$$\sigma_W = \{x_1 \mapsto x_1 x_2^2,\ x_2 \mapsto x_1 x_3^2,\ x_3 \mapsto x_1 x_2 x_3\}$$

of Example 10.3.11. There are $2^3 = 8$ erasing substitutions (corresponding to the subsets of $Y := \{x_1, x_2, x_3\}$), of which 5 are admissible (corresponding to the sets $\emptyset$, $\{x_1\}$, $\{x_2\}$, $\{x_3\}$, and $\{x_2, x_3\}$). This yields the following complete set of AC-unifiers of $S = \{x_1 x_2 \approx^?_{AC} x_3^2\}$:

$$\left\{ \begin{array}{lll} \{x_1 \mapsto x_1 x_2^2, & x_2 \mapsto x_1 x_3^2, & x_3 \mapsto x_1 x_2 x_3\}, \\ \{x_1 \mapsto x_2^2, & x_2 \mapsto x_3^2, & x_3 \mapsto x_2 x_3\}, \\ \{x_1 \mapsto x_1, & x_2 \mapsto x_1 x_3^2, & x_3 \mapsto x_1 x_3\}, \\ \{x_1 \mapsto x_1 x_2^2, & x_2 \mapsto x_1, & x_3 \mapsto x_1 x_2\}, \\ \{x_1 \mapsto x_1, & x_2 \mapsto x_1, & x_3 \mapsto x_1\} \end{array} \right\}.$$

10.3.4 Homogeneous linear diophantine equations

Let $M_{k,n}$ be a $k \times n$ integer matrix, and let

$$M_{k,n} \cdot y\!\downarrow = 0\!\downarrow \qquad\qquad (*)$$

be the system of homogeneous linear diophantine equations induced by $M_{k,n}$. First, we show by a non-constructive argument that there exists a *finite* generating set for the non-negative integer solutions of $(*)$. Then, we turn to the problem of how to compute such a set.

Let $\geq$ denote the component-wise order on $\mathbb{N}^n$ induced by $\geq$ on $\mathbb{N}$, and let $>$ denote its strict part (i.e. $u\!\downarrow > v\!\downarrow$ iff $u\!\downarrow \geq v\!\downarrow$ and $u\!\downarrow \neq v\!\downarrow$).

Lemma 10.3.20 *The component-wise order $\geq$ on $\mathbb{N}^n$ is a well-partial order.*

Proof This is an immediate consequence of Lemma 5.4.5, since the usual order $\geq$ of natural numbers is obviously a wpo. $\qquad\square$

Definition 10.3.21 A solution $v\!\downarrow \in \mathbb{N}^n$ of $(*)$ is a **minimal nontrivial solution** iff $v\!\downarrow \neq 0\!\downarrow$, and $v\!\downarrow > u\!\downarrow$ implies $u\!\downarrow = 0\!\downarrow$ for all solutions $u\!\downarrow \in \mathbb{N}^n$ of $(*)$.

Theorem 10.3.22 *The set of all minimal nontrivial solutions of $(*)$ is finite, and it is a generating set for the non-negative integer solutions of $(*)$.*

Proof (1) Obviously, the set of all minimal nontrivial solutions of $(*)$ is an anti-chain w.r.t. $\geq$, i.e. a set of pairwise incomparable elements. Thus, it must be finite since otherwise it would yield an infinite bad sequence.

(2) We show by well-founded induction on $\geq$ that every (non-negative integer) solution of $(*)$ can be obtained as a non-negative linear combination of the minimal nontrivial solutions of $(*)$. Obviously, the trivial solution $0\!\downarrow$ can be obtained as such a linear combination (where all coefficients are 0).

Thus, assume that $u{\downarrow}$ is a nontrivial solutions of $(*)$. If $u{\downarrow}$ is minimal nontrivial, then we are done since $u{\downarrow} = u{\downarrow} \cdot 1$. Otherwise, there exists a nontrivial solution $v_1{\downarrow}$ such that $u{\downarrow} > v_1{\downarrow}$. Either $v_1{\downarrow}$ is minimal nontrivial, or there exists a nontrivial solution $v_2{\downarrow}$ such that $v_1{\downarrow} > v_2{\downarrow}$, etc. Since $\geq$ is a wpo, there cannot be an infinite descending $>$-chain, which shows that there exists a minimal nontrivial solution $v{\downarrow}$ such that $u{\downarrow} > v{\downarrow}$.

Consequently, $u{\downarrow}' := u{\downarrow} - v{\downarrow}$ is a non-negative integer solution of $(*)$, which obviously satisfies $u{\downarrow} > u{\downarrow}'$. By induction, we know that $u{\downarrow}'$ can be obtained as a non-negative linear combination of the minimal nontrivial solutions of $(*)$, and thus also $u{\downarrow} = u{\downarrow}' + v{\downarrow}$. $\qquad\square$

This proof does not show how the (finite) set of minimal nontrivial solutions of $(*)$ can be computed. One possibility for solving this problem is to determine a bound for the size of the components of minimal nontrivial solutions of $(*)$. Assume that we can compute a number $B \in \mathbb{N}$ such that $v{\downarrow} \in \{0, 1, \ldots, B\}^n$ holds for all nontrivial minimal solutions $v{\downarrow}$ of $(*)$. Then we can compute the set of all nontrivial minimal solutions of $(*)$ as follows: simply enumerate all vectors in $\{0, 1, \ldots, B\}^n$, test whether they are solutions of $(*)$, collect all these solutions and then remove the non-minimal ones.

In the following, we describe one method for obtaining a (fairly good) bound.

Definition 10.3.23 For an integer (column) vector $x{\downarrow} \in \mathbb{Z}^k$ we denote its components by $x_1, \ldots, x_k$, and define

$$\|x{\downarrow}\| := \sum_{i=1}^{k} |x_i|,$$

where $|x_i|$ denotes the absolute value of the integer x_i. For a $k \times n$ integer matrix $M_{k,n} := \left(x{\downarrow}^{(1)} \cdots x{\downarrow}^{(n)} \right)$ we define

$$\|M\| := \max\{\|x{\downarrow}^{(j)}\| \mid 1 \leq j \leq n\}.$$

Theorem 10.3.24 Let $M_{k,n}$ be a $k \times n$ integer matrix, and let $x{\downarrow} \in \mathbb{N}^n$ be a minimal nontrivial solution of $M_{k,n} \cdot y{\downarrow} = 0{\downarrow}$ $(*)$. Then

$$\|x{\downarrow}\| \leq (1 + \|M_{k,n}\|)^k.$$

Before proving the theorem, let us first note two obvious facts:

1. Since $x{\downarrow} \in \mathbb{N}^n$, the inequality $\|x{\downarrow}\| \leq B_0 := (1 + \|M_{k,n}\|)^k$ implies that every component x_i of $x{\downarrow}$ satisfies $x_i \leq B_0$.

2. If $\|x{\downarrow}\| = p$ for a vector $x{\downarrow} \in \mathbb{N}^n$, then $x{\downarrow}$ can be obtained from $0{\downarrow}$ by adding p unit vectors. We denote the unit vector that has 1 in position i and 0 in all other positions by $e{\downarrow}^{(i)}$.

The *intuitive idea* underlying the proof of Theorem 10.3.24 is as follows. Assume that $x{\downarrow} \in \mathbb{N}^n$ is a minimal nontrivial solution of $(*)$ such that $p := \|x{\downarrow}\| > B_0$. We go from $0{\downarrow}$ to $x{\downarrow}$ by adding appropriate unit vectors, and take care that we don't stray "too far" from the straight route to $x{\downarrow}$, which is the line (in $\mathbb{R}^n$) from $0{\downarrow}$ to $x{\downarrow}$ (see Fig. 10.2). Since every point on this line is a solution of $(*)$, this makes sure that the intermediate vectors $y{\downarrow}^{(j)} \in \mathbb{N}^n$ reached by adding unit vectors have the property that $M_{k,n} \cdot y{\downarrow}^{(j)}$ is not "far" away from $0{\downarrow}$. This in turn makes sure that there cannot be "many" different vectors $M_{k,n} \cdot y{\downarrow}^{(j)}$. Since p is large (larger than B_0), we can then conclude that there exist $\ell < \ell'$ such that $M_{k,n} \cdot y{\downarrow}^{(\ell)} = M_{k,n} \cdot y{\downarrow}^{(\ell')}$. Consequently, $y{\downarrow}^{(\ell')} - y{\downarrow}^{(\ell)}$ is a nontrivial non-negative integer solution of $(*)$ that is smaller than $x{\downarrow}$, which contradicts the minimality of $x{\downarrow}$.

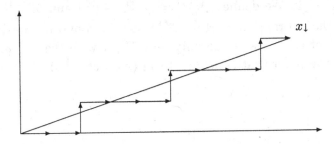

Fig. 10.2. An illustration for the proof of the theorem.

To make this intuition more precise, we must introduce some notation. Let $[0, 1]$ denote the interval of real numbers between 0 and 1 (including 0 and 1). For a vector $y{\downarrow} \in \mathbb{R}^n$, we denote the unit cube with lower left corner $y{\downarrow}$ by $C_{y{\downarrow}}$, i.e.

$$C_{y{\downarrow}} := \left\{ z{\downarrow} \in \mathbb{R}^n \mid z{\downarrow} = y{\downarrow} + \sum_{i=1}^{n} e{\downarrow}^{(i)} \cdot r_i \text{ for some } r_i \in [0, 1] \right\},$$

and the line between $0{\downarrow}$ and $y{\downarrow}$ by $[0{\downarrow}, y{\downarrow}]$, i.e.

$$[0{\downarrow}, y{\downarrow}] := \{y{\downarrow} \cdot r \mid r \in [0, 1]\}.$$

Lemma 10.3.25 *Let $x{\downarrow} \in \mathbb{N}^n$ and $p := \|x{\downarrow}\|$. There exist sequences of vectors $y{\downarrow}^{(0)}, \ldots, y{\downarrow}^{(p)} \in \mathbb{N}^n$ and $z{\downarrow}^{(0)}, \ldots, z{\downarrow}^{(p)} \in \mathbb{R}^n$ such that*

1. $y{\downarrow}^{(0)} = 0{\downarrow} < y{\downarrow}^{(1)} < \cdots < y{\downarrow}^{(p)} = x{\downarrow}$,

2. $y{\downarrow}^{(i+1)} = y{\downarrow}^{(i)} + e{\downarrow}^{(j_i)}$ for some $j_i, 1 \leq j_i \leq n$,

3. $z\!\downarrow^{(i)} \in C_{y\downarrow^{(i)}} \cap [0\!\downarrow, x\!\downarrow]$.

Proof We define the required sequences by induction. In the base case, we set $y\!\downarrow^{(0)} := 0\!\downarrow$ and $z\!\downarrow^{(0)} := 0\!\downarrow$. Now, assume that $0 \leq \ell < p$, and that we already have vectors $y\!\downarrow^{(0)}, \ldots, y\!\downarrow^{(\ell)}$ and $z\!\downarrow^{(0)}, \ldots, z\!\downarrow^{(\ell)}$ satisfying

$$y\!\downarrow^{(0)} = 0\!\downarrow < y\!\downarrow^{(1)} < \cdots < y\!\downarrow^{(\ell)} < x\!\downarrow,$$

and parts (2) (for $0 \leq i < \ell$) and (3) (for $0 \leq i \leq \ell$) of the lemma. The elements of $C_{y\downarrow^{(\ell)}} \cap [0\!\downarrow, x\!\downarrow]$ are the vectors $x\!\downarrow \cdot r = \sum_{i=1}^{n} e\!\downarrow^{(i)} \cdot x_i \cdot r$ such that $r \in [0,1]$ and, for $i = 1, \ldots, n$,

$$y_i^{(\ell)} \leq x_i \cdot r \leq y_i^{(\ell)} + 1. \tag{$**$}$$

Let r_ℓ be the largest element of $[0,1]$ that satisfies $(**)$. Such a real number r_ℓ exists since $C_{y\downarrow^{(\ell)}} \cap [0\!\downarrow, x\!\downarrow]$ is nonempty (it contains $z\!\downarrow^{(\ell)}$). In addition, since $y\!\downarrow^{(\ell)} < x\!\downarrow$, it is easy to see that there exists $j_\ell, 1 \leq j_\ell \leq n$, such that $x_{j_\ell} \cdot r_\ell = y_{j_\ell}^{(\ell)} + 1$. We define $y\!\downarrow^{(\ell+1)} := y\!\downarrow^{(\ell)} + e\!\downarrow^{(j_\ell)}$ and $z\!\downarrow^{(\ell+1)} := x\!\downarrow \cdot r_\ell$. Intuitively, the appropriate vector $z\!\downarrow^{(\ell+1)}$ can be found by considering the intersections of the faces of the unit cube $C_{y\downarrow^{(\ell)}}$ with the line $[0\!\downarrow, x\!\downarrow]$, and then taking the point that is nearest to $x\!\downarrow$ (see Fig. 10.3).

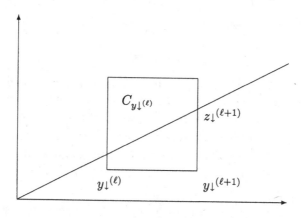

Fig. 10.3. How to find $z\!\downarrow^{(\ell+1)}$.

By construction, $z\!\downarrow^{(\ell+1)} \in C_{y\downarrow^{(\ell+1)}} \cap [0\!\downarrow, x\!\downarrow]$. In addition, $y\!\downarrow^{(\ell+1)} \leq x\!\downarrow$ since $y_{j_\ell}^{(\ell+1)} = y_{j_\ell}^{(\ell)} + 1 = x_{j_\ell} \cdot r_\ell \leq x_{j_\ell}$. Since $\|x\!\downarrow\| = p$, and $y\!\downarrow^{(\ell+1)}$ is obtained as the sum of $\ell + 1$ unit vectors, we know that $y\!\downarrow^{(\ell+1)} = x\!\downarrow$ iff $\ell + 1 = p$. $\square$

Lemma 10.3.26 *If $x\!\downarrow \in \mathbb{N}^n$ is a nontrivial solution of $(*)$ such that $p := \|x\!\downarrow\| > B_0$, then $x\!\downarrow$ is not a minimal nontrivial solution of $(*)$.*

Proof Let $y_\downarrow^{(0)}, \ldots, y_\downarrow^{(p)} \in \mathbb{N}^n$ and $z_\downarrow^{(0)}, \ldots, z_\downarrow^{(p)} \in \mathbb{R}^n$ be the two sequences of vectors satisfying 1–3 of Lemma 10.3.25. We define $d_\downarrow^{(\ell)} := z_\downarrow^{(\ell)} - y_\downarrow^{(\ell)}$ for $\ell = 0, \ldots, p$. Since $z_\downarrow^{(\ell)} \in [0_\downarrow, x_\downarrow]$, it is a (real) solution of $(*)$, and since $z_\downarrow^{(\ell)} \in C_{y_\downarrow^{(\ell)}}$, we know that $0 \le d_i^{(\ell)} \le 1$. Consequently, we obtain the following identities for the absolute value of the ith component of $M_{k,n} \cdot d_\downarrow^{(\ell)}$:

$$|(M_{k,n} \cdot d_\downarrow^{(\ell)})_i| = |(M_{k,n} \cdot z_\downarrow^{(\ell)})_i - (M_{k,n} \cdot y_\downarrow^{(\ell)})_i| = |(M_{k,n} \cdot y_\downarrow^{(\ell)})_i|.$$

Let $a_{i,j}$ denote the entry of $M_{k,n}$ at position (i,j). Since $0 \le d_i^{(\ell)} \le 1$, we can deduce that $(M_{k,n} \cdot y_\downarrow^{(\ell)})_i$ is an integer satisfying

$$- \sum_{\substack{1 \le j \le n \\ a_{i,j} < 0}} |a_{i,j}| \;\le\; (M_{k,n} \cdot y_\downarrow^{(\ell)})_i \;\le\; \sum_{\substack{1 \le j \le n \\ a_{i,j} \ge 0}} |a_{i,j}|.$$

Thus, for all i there are at most $1 + \sum_{1 \le j \le n} |a_{i,j}| \le 1 + \|M_{k,n}\|$ possible values for $(M_{k,n} \cdot y_\downarrow^{(\ell)})_i$. Since $p > B_0 = (1 + \|M_{k,n}\|)^k$, there exist $0 < \ell < \ell' \le p$ such that $M_{k,n} \cdot y_\downarrow^{(\ell)} = M_{k,n} \cdot y_\downarrow^{(\ell')}$. This implies that $y_\downarrow^{(\ell')} - y_\downarrow^{(\ell)} \in \mathbb{N}^n$ is a nontrivial solution of $(*)$ that is smaller than $x_\downarrow \in \mathbb{N}^n$. $\qquad\square$

This concludes the proof of Theorem 10.3.24.

Exercises

10.14 Let $C := \{f(x,y) \approx f(y,x)\}$, $R := \{f(f(x,y),z) \to f(x, f(y,z))\}$, and $S := \{f(x, f(y,z)) \to f(f(x,y),z)\}$. Show that the relations $\approx_C \circ \to_R$ and $\approx_C \circ \to_S$ do not terminate.

10.15 Compute the mgu of $x_1 x_2 \approx^?_{AC1} x_3 x_4$.

10.16 Show that the *AC1*-unification problem (with constants a, b)

$$x_1 x_2 \approx^?_{AC1} ab$$

has a minimal complete set of *AC1*-unifiers of cardinality 4.

10.17 Show that the decision problem for *AC1*-unification with constants is NP-hard. (*Hint:* use a reduction of positive 1-in-3-SAT where the clause $p \vee q \vee r$ is translated into the equation $x_p x_q x_r \approx^?_{AC1} a$.)

10.18 Show that the decision problem for *AC*-unification with constants is NP-hard. (*Hint:* use a reduction of positive 1-in-3-SAT where the clause $p \vee q \vee r$ is translated into the equation $x_p x_q x_r \approx^?_{AC} abb$.)

10.19 An instance of the linear programming problem is given by an $r \times s$ integer matrix B, a row vector $\vec{c} \in \mathbb{Z}^s$, a column vector $d_\downarrow \in \mathbb{Z}^r$, and an integer $b \in \mathbb{Z}$. The question is whether there exists a solution $y_\downarrow \in \mathbb{Q}^s$ of the inequalities

$$B \cdot y_\downarrow \le d_\downarrow, \quad \vec{c} \cdot y_\downarrow \ge b.$$

Show that the problem (iii) in the proof of Theorem 10.3.14 can be turned into an instance of the linear programming problem. (*Hint:* define $\vec{c} := \vec{0}$, $b := 0$,

$$B := \begin{pmatrix} A \\ -A \\ -E_n \end{pmatrix} \quad \text{and} \quad d_\downarrow := \begin{pmatrix} 0 \\ \vdots \\ 0 \\ -1 \\ \vdots \\ -1 \end{pmatrix},$$

where E_n denotes the $n \times n$ unit matrix (with 1 in the diagonal and 0 in all other positions), and the first $2k$ entries of $d_\downarrow$ are 0, and the remaining n entries are -1.)

10.20 Compute a complete set of AC-unifiers of $x_1 x_2 \approx^?_{AC} x_3 x_4$.

10.21 Let σ_1 and σ_2 be AC-unifiers of the AC-unification problem S. Show that the substitution

$$\{x \mapsto \sigma_1(x) * \sigma_2(x) \mid x \in \mathcal{D}om(\sigma_1) \cup \mathcal{D}om(\sigma_2)\}$$

is also an AC-unifier of S.

10.22 Let S be a solvable AC-unification problem, W the set of all minimal nontrivial solutions of $DE(S)$, and σ_W the most general $AC1$-unifier of S induced by W (see Theorem 10.3.10). Show that the complete set of AC-unifiers $\mathcal{C}$ obtained from σ_W with the help of Theorem 10.3.18 is a *minimal* complete set of AC-unifiers of S.

10.23 Is the statement in the previous exercise also true if we take an arbitrary most general $AC1$-unifier of S for constructing the complete set $\mathcal{C}$?

10.4 Boolean rings

Boolean algebra (the theory of $\wedge$, $\vee$ and $\neg$) is fundamental for mathematics and computer science because it formalizes propositional logic, digital circuits and sets. Boolean ring theory formalizes the same concepts in the language of ring theory. There are two constants 0 and 1, and two operations

+ and $*$ subject to the following set of identities:

$$B := \left\{ \begin{array}{rcl} x + y & \approx & y + x, \\ (x + y) + z & \approx & x + (y + z), \\ x + x & \approx & 0, \\ 0 + x & \approx & x, \\ x * (y + z) & \approx & (x * y) + (x * z), \end{array} \quad \begin{array}{rcl} x * y & \approx & y * x, \\ (x * y) * z & \approx & x * (y * z), \\ x * x & \approx & x, \\ 0 * x & \approx & 0, \\ 1 * x & \approx & x \end{array} \right\}.$$

As is customary in ring theory, $*$ binds more tightly than $+$, and we frequently drop $*$ altogether, e.g. we write xy instead of $x * y$. Because both $+$ and $*$ are associative, many further parentheses become redundant.

Two consequences of B worth keeping in mind are

$$x * (x + 1) \approx_B 0,$$
$$x \approx_B y \iff x + y \approx_B 0.$$

Because many of our arguments will be semantic, let $\mathcal{B}_2$ be the two-element Boolean ring with carrier $\mathbf{2} := \{0, 1\}$ where $*$ and $+$ are "and" and "exclusive or" (i.e. multiplication and addition modulo 2). It is easy to see that $\mathcal{B}_2$ is indeed a model of B. In fact, it is the initial model of B, i.e. every ground term is equivalent to 0 or 1 modulo B (see Exercise 10.24). Note that the constants 0 and 1 coincide with the values $0, 1 \in \mathbf{2}$. Hence we take the liberty of treating elements of $\mathbf{2}$ as ground terms.

It is easy to translate between Boolean algebra and Boolean ring theory:

$$\begin{array}{rcl} x \wedge y & \mapsto & x * y, \\ x \vee y & \mapsto & x + y + x * y, \\ \neg x & \mapsto & 1 + x. \end{array} \qquad \begin{array}{rcl} x * y & \mapsto & x \wedge y, \\ x + y & \mapsto & (x \wedge \neg y) \vee (\neg x \wedge y), \end{array}$$

We prefer to work with $+$ and $*$ because the identities in B are close to those of ordinary arithmetic and more pleasant to use than their counterparts for Boolean algebra. In particular, terms have a very convenient normal form, the polynomial form. In the sequel all terms are elements of $T(\Sigma, V)$ where $\Sigma = \{0, 1, +, *\}$. Including free constants merely complicates technicalities. Therefore we ignore them in this section.

10.4.1 Polynomials

We call a product of distinct variables a **monomial** and a sum of distinct monomials a **polynomial**. We compare monomials and polynomials modulo associativity and commutativity of $+$ and $*$. For example, we do not distinguish between $xy + z$ and $z + yx$. More abstractly, we can view a monomial as a set of variables and a polynomial as a set of monomials. Every term can be transformed into a unique $\approx_B$-equivalent polynomial, its polynomial form. This is the Boolean ring counterpart of the conjunctive/disjunctive normal form of Boolean algebra terms. To accommodate 0 and 1 we identify 0 with the empty polynomial and 1 with (the polynomial containing only) the empty monomial. The **polynomial form** of a term is obtained in the same way as with polynomials over $\mathbb{R}$, except that one also applies $x * x \approx_B x$ and $x + x \approx_B 0$. These two rules are responsible for the absence of coefficients and exponents in our polynomials. The polynomial form can be computed recursively as follows:

$x, 0, 1$: Every variable and the constants 0 and 1 are polynomials already.

$t_1 + t_2$: Let p_1 and p_2 be the polynomial forms of t_1 and t_2. The polynomial form of $t_1 + t_2$ is obtained from $p_1 + p_2$ by cancelling all equivalent monomials, i.e. removing both occurrences of the same monomial in p_1 and p_2 ($x + x \approx_B 0$).

$t_1 * t_2$: Let $p = m_1 + \cdots + m_k$ and $q = n_1 + \cdots + n_l$ be the polynomial forms of t_1 and t_2. The polynomial form of $t_1 * t_2$ is obtained by cancelling all equivalent monomials from the sum

$$(m_1 * n_1 + \cdots + m_1 * n_l) + \cdots + (m_k * n_1 + \cdots + m_k * n_l)$$

obtained by multiplying out the product $p * q$. The product $m * n$ of two monomials $m = x_1 \cdots x_r$ and $n = y_1 \cdots y_s$ is the monomial obtained by removing repeated occurrences of the same variable from $x_1 \cdots x_r y_1 \cdots y_s$ ($x * x \approx_B x$).

Note that certain simplifications are implicit in the representation of 1 and 0 as the empty monomial and polynomial. For example, the product of the two monomials 1 and x is the monomial x because 1 is empty.

The polynomial form of t is denoted by $t{\downarrow}_P$. Because each step of the algorithm is justified by identities in B, we conclude that the following holds:

Fact 10.4.1 $t \approx_B t{\downarrow}_P$.

The following is an example of the step by step computation of the polynomial form:

$$
\begin{aligned}
(y+1) * (x+y) + xy \quad &\approx_B \quad (y*x+y*y+1*x+1*y) + xy \\
&\approx_B \quad (yx+y+x+y) + xy \\
&\approx_B \quad (yx+x) + xy \approx_B x.
\end{aligned}
$$

It turns out that two terms are $\approx_B$-equivalent iff they have the same polynomial form. The proof of the $\Leftarrow$-direction is straightforward:

$$s{\downarrow}_P = t{\downarrow}_P \;\Rightarrow\; s \approx_B s{\downarrow}_P = t{\downarrow}_P \approx_B t.$$

We prove the other direction by means of a semantic lemma.

Lemma 10.4.2 $\mathcal{B}_2 \models s \approx t \;\Rightarrow\; s{\downarrow}_P = t{\downarrow}_P.$

Proof We show the contrapositive. Assume that $s{\downarrow}_P \neq t{\downarrow}_P$. Hence there is a monomial in one of the two normal forms which is not in the other. Let m be such a monomial which is of minimal length. For concreteness assume m is in $s{\downarrow}_P$. Therefore $s{\downarrow}_P$ is of the form $M + m + G$ and $t{\downarrow}_P$ of the form $M + H$, where M contains the monomials that are shorter than m, and G and H contain the remaining monomials, i.e. those monomials different from and not shorter than m.

Now define a mapping $\varphi : V \to \mathbf{2}$ which assigns 1 to all variables in m and 0 to all other variables. Let $\hat{\varphi} : \mathcal{T}(\Sigma, V) \to \mathcal{B}_2$ be the homomorphic extension of φ. This means $\hat{\varphi}(m) = 1$. Because m is of minimal length, all monomials in G and H must contain some variable not contained in m. Therefore $\hat{\varphi}(m') = 0$ for all monomials m' in G and H, and hence $\hat{\varphi}(G) = \hat{\varphi}(H) = 0$. Thus we can show that $\hat{\varphi}(s) \neq \hat{\varphi}(t)$ which yields $\mathcal{B}_2 \models s \not\approx t$:

$$\begin{aligned}
\hat{\varphi}(s) &= \hat{\varphi}(s{\downarrow}_P) = \hat{\varphi}(M) + \hat{\varphi}(m) + \hat{\varphi}(G) = \hat{\varphi}(M) + 1 \\
&\neq \hat{\varphi}(M) = \hat{\varphi}(M) + \hat{\varphi}(H) = \hat{\varphi}(t{\downarrow}_P) = \hat{\varphi}(t). \qquad \square
\end{aligned}$$

Now we can easily obtain a fundamental theorem about Boolean rings:

Theorem 10.4.3 *The following statements are equivalent:*

1. $s \approx_B t$,
2. $s{\downarrow}_P = t{\downarrow}_P$,
3. $\mathcal{B}_2 \models s \approx t$.

Proof Lemma 10.4.2 proves $3 \Rightarrow 2$, the implication $2 \Rightarrow 1$ was already dealt with above, and $1 \Rightarrow 3$ follows because $s \approx_B t$ means $s \approx t$ holds in all Boolean rings, in particular in $\mathcal{B}_2$. $\qquad \square$

In particular, this shows that $\approx_B$ is decidable, either by comparing polynomial forms (which are computable), or by testing semantic equality in $\mathcal{B}_2$ (which is decidable because $\mathcal{B}_2$ is finite).

10.4.2 Unification

Unification in Boolean rings (**Boolean unification**) means solving equations of the form $s \approx_B^? t$. (Exercise 10.26 justifies the restriction to a single equation.) As a consequence of Theorem 10.4.3 we obtain that Boolean unification is closely related to equation solving in $\mathcal{B}_2$:

Lemma 10.4.4

1. *Every solution of $s \approx^? t$ in $\mathcal{B}_2$ can be viewed as a B-unifier.*
2. *If $s \approx^?_B t$ has a unifier then $s \approx^? t$ has a solution in $\mathcal{B}_2$.*

Proof (1) Let $\varphi : V \to \mathbf{2}$ be a solution of $s \approx t$ in $\mathcal{B}_2$, i.e. $\widehat{\varphi}(s) = \widehat{\varphi}(t)$. Because we identify the constants 0 and 1 with their respective values 0 and 1 in $\mathcal{B}_2$, we can also view φ as a mapping to ground terms, in which case we denote its homomorphic extensions by $\tilde{\varphi} : \mathcal{T}(\Sigma, V) \to \mathcal{T}(\Sigma, V)$. Because any homomorphism $\psi : \mathcal{T}(\Sigma, V) \to \mathcal{B}_2$ must be the identity on $\mathbf{2}$, i.e. it has to map the terms 0 and 1 to their respective values 0 and 1 in $\mathcal{B}_2$, we obtain $\widehat{\varphi} = \psi\tilde{\varphi}$ (both sides agree on V). Thus we have $\psi(\tilde{\varphi}(s)) = \widehat{\varphi}(s) = \widehat{\varphi}(t) = \psi(\tilde{\varphi}(t))$ for every ψ and hence $\mathcal{B}_2 \models \tilde{\varphi}(s) \approx \tilde{\varphi}(t)$. Theorem 10.4.3 yields $\tilde{\varphi}(s) \approx_B \tilde{\varphi}(t)$, i.e. the solution φ, when viewed as a substitution, is a unifier.

(2) Let σ be a unifier of $s \approx_B t$, i.e. $\sigma(s) \approx_B \sigma(t)$. Theorem 10.4.3 yields $\mathcal{B}_2 \models \sigma(s) \approx \sigma(t)$ and hence in particular $\widehat{\varphi}(\sigma(s)) = \widehat{\varphi}(\sigma(t))$ where $\varphi : V \to \mathbf{2}$ is arbitrary. Hence $\widehat{\varphi}\sigma : V \to \mathbf{2}$ is a solution in $\mathcal{B}_2$. □

It turns out that Boolean unification is unitary, a rare property. Because $x \approx_B y \Leftrightarrow x + y \approx_B 0$, we can transform every unification problem into the form $t \approx^?_B 0$, which is the standard form from now on. For example, $x * y \approx_B 0$ has an mgu $\sigma := \{x \mapsto x * (1+y)\}$. Because $\sigma(x * y) = (x * (1+y)) * y \approx_B 0$, σ is a unifier. It is less obvious that σ is most general.

We will now study two unification algorithms, *Löwenheim's formula* and *successive variable elimination*, which are based on completely different principles.

10.4.3 Löwenheim's formula

Löwenheim [163] discovered the following amazing formula for turning any unifier into an mgu. Given a unifier τ of $t \approx^?_B 0$, i.e. $\tau(t) \approx_B 0$, the substitution σ defined by

$$\sigma(x) := (t + 1) * x + t * \tau(x)$$

for all $x \in \mathcal{V}ar(t)$ and $\sigma(x) := x$ for all $x \notin \mathcal{V}ar(t)$, is an mgu. The following lemma is the key to proving that σ is a unifier:

Lemma 10.4.5 *If $\sigma(x) = (s+1) * \sigma_1(x) + s * \sigma_2(x)$ for all $x \in \mathcal{V}ar(t)$, then $\sigma(t) \approx_B (s+1) * \sigma_1(t) + s * \sigma_2(t)$.*

Proof by induction on t. The base cases (variable, 0, 1) are trivial.
$t = t_1 + t_2$: Using the induction hypothesis we can easily verify that

$$
\begin{aligned}
\sigma(t) &= \sigma(t_1) + \sigma(t_2) \\
&\approx_B ((s+1) * \sigma_1(t_1) + s * \sigma_2(t_1)) + ((s+1) * \sigma_1(t_2) + s * \sigma_2(t_2)) \\
&\approx_B (s+1) * (\sigma_1(t_1) + \sigma_1(t_2)) + s * (\sigma_2(t_1) + \sigma_2(t_2)) \\
&= (s+1) * \sigma(t) + s * \sigma(t).
\end{aligned}
$$

$t = t_1 * t_2$: Using the induction hypothesis we can easily verify that

$$
\begin{aligned}
\sigma(t) &= \sigma(t_1) * \sigma(t_2) \\
&\approx_B ((s+1) * \sigma_1(t_1) + s * \sigma_2(t_1)) * ((s+1) * \sigma_1(t_2) + s * \sigma_2(t_2)) \\
&\approx_B (s+1) * \sigma_1(t_1) * \sigma_1(t_2) + s * \sigma_2(t_1) * \sigma_2(t_2) \\
&= (s+1) * \sigma(t) + s * \sigma(t). \qquad \square
\end{aligned}
$$

Because Löwenheim's σ has exactly the form required by the above lemma (define $\sigma_1(x) := x$ and $\sigma_2(x) := \tau(x)$ for all x) we obtain $\sigma(t) \approx_B (t+1) * t + t * \tau(t) \approx_B 0 + t * 0 \approx_B 0$, i.e. σ is a unifier of $t \approx_B^? 0$. It is even easier to show that σ is most general by showing that it has a yet stronger property:

Definition 10.4.6 A unifier σ of $t \approx_B 0$ is a **reproductive unifier** if $\tau(\sigma(x)) \approx_B \tau(x)$ for every unifier τ of $t \approx_B 0$ and every x.

Observe that a reproductive unifier is an mgu in a strong sense: every other unifier is a B-instance of it, not just on $Var(t)$ but on all variables.
    Let τ be a unifier of $t \approx_B^? 0$. If $x \in Var(t)$ then

$$
\begin{aligned}
\tau(\sigma(x)) &= \tau((t+1) * x + t * \tau(x)) \\
&\approx_B (\tau(t) + 1) * \tau(x) + \tau(t) * \tau(\tau(x)) \\
&\approx_B (0+1) * \tau(x) + 0 * \tau(\tau(x)) \approx_B \tau(x),
\end{aligned}
$$

and if $x \notin Var(t)$ then $\sigma(x) = x$ and hence $\tau(\sigma(x)) \approx_B \tau(x)$ is trivial. Thus σ is a reproductive unifier and hence an mgu.

Example 10.4.7 The equation $xy \approx_B^? 0$ has three ground solutions:

$$
\begin{aligned}
x = 0, y = 0: \quad \sigma(x) &= (xy+1) * x + xy * 0 \approx_B x + xy, \\
\sigma(y) &= (xy+1) * y + xy * 0 \approx_B xy + y. \\
x = 0, y = 1: \quad \sigma(x) &= (xy+1) * x + xy * 0 \approx_B x + xy, \\
\sigma(y) &= (xy+1) * y + xy * 1 \approx_B y. \\
x = 1, y = 0: \quad & \text{symmetric to } x = 0, y = 1.
\end{aligned}
$$

We obtain three different mgus, depending on which ground solution we use. Some mgus are simpler than others: the first mgu replaces both x and y, whereas the other two are the identity on x or y.

In order to turn Löwenheim's formula into an algorithm, we still need to find a unifier τ to start from. Fortunately, we can resort to truth tables at this point: simply try all possible assignments $\varphi : V \to \mathbf{2}$ and check if $\widehat{\varphi}(t) = 0$. There are only finitely many relevant φ because the value of φ outside $Var(t)$ is immaterial. Lemma 10.4.4 shows that a solution φ is a unifier and guarantees that this search finds a unifier if one exists.

10.4.4 Why Löwenheim's formula works

The proof of Löwenheim's formula is surprisingly painless, but at the same time quite mysterious. Fortunately, there is a simple intuitive explanation, if we adopt a semantic point of view: we reduce Boolean unification to equation solving in $\mathcal{B}_2$. This is facilitated by some new notation. For the rest of the subsection let t be a fixed term and let $Var(t) = \{x_1, \dots, x_n\}$.

We can view a term t as a Boolean function of type $\mathbf{2}^n \to \mathbf{2}$ by defining $t(\overline{b_n}) := \widehat{\varphi}(t)$, where $\overline{b_n} \in \mathbf{2}^n$ and $\widehat{\varphi} : \mathcal{T}(\Sigma, V) \to \mathcal{B}_2$ is the homomorphic extension of the mapping $x_i \mapsto b_i$. We emphasize the functional nature of t by writing $t(\overline{x_n})$.

Because the effect of a substitution σ on t depends only on $u_i := \sigma(x_i)$ for $i = 1, \dots, n$, we can write σ as the n-tuple $(u_1, \dots, u_n)$. Emphasizing the functional nature of the u_i, this becomes $(u_1(\overline{y_k}), \dots, u_n(\overline{y_k}))$ (where $\{\overline{y_k}\}$ is the set of all variables in the u_i), which we abbreviate to $\overline{u_n}(\overline{y_k})$.

So much for the notation. The real reason why Löwenheim's σ works is that in $\mathcal{B}_2$ the term $(x + 1) * y + x * z$ behaves like a conditional: if $x = 0$, it evaluates to y, if $x = 1$, it evaluates to z. Hence we can rephrase Löwenheim's σ in $\mathcal{B}_2$ as follows:

$$\sigma(x_i) = \texttt{if } t = 0 \texttt{ then } x_i \texttt{ else } \tau(x_i).$$

We define $a_i := \tau(x_i)$ and assume for simplicity that $a_i \in \mathbf{2}$. Using the above vector notation, σ becomes

$$\overline{u_n}(\overline{x_n}) := \texttt{if } t(\overline{x_n}) = 0 \texttt{ then } \overline{x_n} \texttt{ else } \overline{a_n},$$

where we have extended the conditional to vectors, a purely syntactic abbreviation. Now it is apparent that $\overline{u_n}(\overline{b_n})$ is a ground unifier for every $\overline{b_n} \in \mathbf{2}^n$: it evaluates either to $\overline{b_n}$, if that is a unifier already, or to the default unifier $\overline{a_n}$. Therefore $\overline{u_n}(\overline{x_n})$ is a *reproductive solution*:

Definition 10.4.8 An n-tuple of terms $\overline{u_n}(\overline{x_n})$ is a **reproductive solution** of $t(\overline{x_n}) \approx_B^? 0$ if for all $\overline{b_n} \in \mathbf{2}^n$

1. $t(\overline{u_n}(\overline{b_n})) = 0$ (σ is a solution),
2. $t(\overline{b_n}) = 0 \Rightarrow \overline{u_n}(\overline{b_n}) = \overline{b_n}$ (σ is reproductive).

Theorem 10.4.9 *Every reproductive solution is a reproductive unifier.*

Proof We claim that if $\overline{u_n}(\overline{x_n})$ is a reproductive solution of $t(\overline{x_n}) \approx^?_B 0$, then the substitution σ, which maps x_i to u_i and is the identity everywhere else, is a reproductive unifier of $t \approx^?_B 0$. Because $\overline{u_n}$ is a solution, we have $\mathcal{B}_2 \models t(\overline{u_n}) \approx 0$ and hence, by Theorem 10.4.3, $\sigma(t) = t(\overline{u_n}) \approx_B 0$, i.e. σ is a unifier. To show that σ is reproductive, let δ be a unifier of $t \approx^?_B 0$. Define $\overline{s_n}(\overline{y_k}) := (\delta(x_1), \ldots, \delta(x_n))$. From $\delta(t) \approx_B 0$ it follows by Theorem 10.4.3 that $\mathcal{B}_2 \models \delta(t) \approx 0$ and hence that $t(\overline{s_n}(\overline{b_k})) = 0$ for all $\overline{b_k} \in 2^k$. Because $\overline{u_n}$ is reproductive, this implies $\overline{u_n}(\overline{s_n}(\overline{b_k})) = \overline{s_n}(\overline{b_k})$ for all $\overline{b_k} \in 2^k$. By definition of $\models$ this means $\mathcal{B}_2 \models u_i(\overline{s_n}) \approx s_i$ and hence, by Theorem 10.4.3, $u_i(\overline{s_n}) \approx_B s_i$ for $i = 1, \ldots, n$. Thus we have $\delta(\sigma(x_i)) = \delta(u_i) = u_i(\overline{s_n}) \approx_B s_i = \delta(x_i)$, and $\delta(\sigma(x)) = \delta(x)$ for all other variables x. $\square$

The correctness proof given in Subsection 10.4.3 is purely syntactic, which is why it needs an additional lemma. Reinterpreting Lemma 10.4.5 in the light of this subsection, we find it expresses the following transformation rule:

$$t(\text{if } p \text{ then } \overline{x_n} \text{ else } \overline{y_n}) \approx_B \text{if } p \text{ then } t(\overline{x_n}) \text{ else } t(\overline{y_n}).$$

10.4.5 Successive variable elimination

The idea of this unification algorithm is to reduce a unification problem $t \approx^?_B 0$ to one $t' \approx^?_B 0$ by eliminating (at least) one variable from t, so that an mgu of $t' \approx^?_B 0$ can be turned into an mgu of $t \approx^?_B 0$.

Every term t can be written as $x * r + s$ so that $x \notin Var(r, s) \subset Var(t)$. For example, you can split the polynomial form of t into two sets of monomials, those that do contain x (r_x) and the rest (s). Now r is the result of removing every occurrence of x from r_x. This simple observation is the basis of successive variable elimination.

Theorem 10.4.10 *Let $t \approx_B x * r + s$ such that $x \notin Var(r, s)$ and define $t' := (r + 1) * s$.*

1. *Every unifier of $t \approx^?_B 0$ is a unifier of $t' \approx^?_B 0$.*
2. *If σ is a reproductive unifier of $t' \approx_B 0$ and $x \notin Dom(\sigma)$, then*

$$\sigma' := \sigma \cup \{x \mapsto x * (\sigma(r) + 1) + \sigma(s)\}$$

is a reproductive unifier of $t \approx_B 0$.

Proof (1) Let τ be a unifier of $t \approx_B^? 0$ and hence $\tau(x) * \tau(r) + \tau(s) \approx_B 0$. Multiplication by $\tau(r) + 1$ yields $(\tau(r) + 1) * \tau(s) \approx_B 0$, i.e. τ is also a unifier of $(r + 1) * s \approx_B^? 0$.

(2) Let σ be a reproductive unifier of $(r+1)*s \approx_B^? 0$. It is easy to calculate that σ' is a unifier of $t \approx_B^? 0$:

$$\sigma'(t) \quad \approx_B \quad \sigma'(x) * \sigma'(r) + \sigma'(s) \quad = \quad (x * (\sigma(r) + 1) + \sigma(s)) * \sigma(r) + \sigma(s)$$
$$\approx_B \quad \sigma(s) * \sigma(r) + \sigma(s) \quad \approx_B \quad \sigma((r+1) * s) \quad \approx_B \quad 0.$$

Now we show that σ' is also reproductive. Let τ be a unifier of $t \approx_B^? 0$. As we saw above, this implies that τ is a unifier of $t' \approx_B^? 0$ and hence, because σ is a reproductive unifier, $\tau(\sigma(y)) \approx_B \tau(y)$ for all y. Therefore $\tau(\sigma'(y)) = \tau(\sigma(y)) \approx_B \tau(y)$ if $y \neq x$. Otherwise

$$\tau(\sigma'(x)) = \quad \tau(x * (\sigma(r) + 1) + \sigma(s)) = \tau(x) * (\tau(\sigma(r)) + 1) + \tau(\sigma(s))$$
$$\approx_B \quad \tau(x) * (\tau(r) + 1) + \tau(s) \approx_B \tau(x) * \tau(r) + \tau(x) + \tau(s)$$
$$\approx_B \quad \tau(t) + \tau(x) \approx_B \tau(x). \qquad \square$$

This theorem justifies an obvious recursive unification algorithm which reduces $t \approx_B^? 0$ to $t' \approx_B^? 0$. Termination is guaranteed because $Var(t') \subset Var(t)$ (provided we have chosen x, r and s sensibly, i.e. $x \in Var(t)$ and $Var(r, s) \subset Var(t)$). The base case $Var(t) = \emptyset$ is trivial: if $t \approx_B 0$ then the identity substitution is a reproductive unifier, and if $t \approx_B 1$ then there is no unifier. Finally note that the condition $x \notin Dom(\sigma)$ is always satisfied because the unification algorithm returns a unifier σ such that $Dom(\sigma) \subseteq Var(t')$.

Example 10.4.11 Solving $x * y \approx_B^? 0$ by eliminating x leads to $r = y$ and $s = 0$ and the new equation $((y+1)*0) \approx_B^? 0$. In order to eliminate the next variable, we compute the polynomial form of $(y + 1) * 0$, which is simply 0. Therefore the identity substitution is an mgu of $((y + 1) * 0) \approx_B^? 0$. Hence an mgu of $x * y \approx_B^? 0$ is $\{x \mapsto x * (r+1) + s \approx_B x * (y+1)\}$, which is also one of the mgus obtained by Löwenheim's formula (see Example 10.4.7). This example demonstrates that more than one variable may disappear in each step: eliminating x also eliminated y.

A slightly more interesting example is $x + y + xy \approx_B^? 0$. Eliminating x using $r := y+1$ and $s := y$ yields the new equation $y \approx_B^? 0$ since $((r+1)*s)\downarrow_P = y$. Eliminating y from this equation yields $0 \approx_B^? 0$ since the polynomial form of $(1 + 1) * 0$ is 0. The identity substitution is an mgu of $0 \approx_B^? 0$, and thus $\{y \mapsto y * (1 + 1) + 0 \approx_B 0\}$ is an mgu of $y \approx_B^? 0$. Consequently, $\{x \mapsto x * (0 + 1 + 1) + 0 \approx_B 0, \ y \mapsto 0\}$ is an mgu of the original equation, which shows that the algorithm has correctly concluded that $x + y + xy$, which expresses "or", can only be 0 if both x and y are 0.

10.4.6 Complexity

It is well-known that the problem of deciding whether a Boolean term t is satisfiable, i.e. whether there exists an assignment $\varphi : V \to \mathbf{2}$ such that $\widehat{\varphi}(t) = 1$, is NP-complete [95]. Therefore the problem of deciding if $t \approx_B^? 0$ has a unifier is also NP-complete because the satisfiability question can be reduced to it in constant time according to Lemma 10.4.4: t is satisfiable iff $t + 1 \approx_B 0$ has a solution in $\mathcal{B}_2$ iff $t + 1 \approx_B 0$ has a unifier.

Of course we are really interested in the problem of finding a (most general) unifier, rather than just determining if one exists. The former problem is clearly no easier than the latter, and hence it is unlikely that a polynomial-time Boolean unification algorithm exists.

Löwenheim's method has time complexity $O(s(n) + n)$, where n is the size of t, $s(n)$ is the time to find a unifier τ, and $+n$ is the overhead for substituting τ into the formula for σ. Because we can restrict the search for τ to ground substitutions of 0 and 1, it reduces to the problem of finding a satisfying assignment for a Boolean term, again a problem for which no polynomial- but only exponential-time algorithms are known.

The time complexity of successive variable elimination is likewise exponential, although this is more complicated to show, because the term manipulations are more involved. Hence we do not go into the details.

10.4.7 Boolean unification in ML

We present a simple implementation of successive variable elimination. Variables are implemented as integers, terms as polynomials:

```
type monomial = int list;
type polynomial = monomial list;
```

Note that this means the monomial [] is 1, the polynomial [] is 0, and the polynomial [[]] is 1. Monomials and polynomials have a unique representation because variables are ordered.

```
(* ordVar: int * int -> order *)
fun ordVar(i,j:int) = if i=j then EQ else if i>j then GR else NGE;
```

To guarantee uniqueness, monomials are represented as ascending lists of variables and polynomials as ascending lists of monomials. Monomials are compared lexicographically. We have chosen the lexicographic extension $>_{Lex}$ which we have called *Lex* in ML (see Exercise 2.27). This means that

$x_1 + x_2 + x_1 x_2 + 1$ is represented by `[[],[1],[1,2],[2]]` as opposed to `[[],[1],[2],[1,2]]`, had we chosen $>^*_{lex}$. This simplifies matters below marginally.

Much more compact representations of Boolean terms are possible, but they require more sophisticated data structures [35].

A straightforward implementation of addition and multiplication of monomials and polynomials is shown in Fig. 10.4. It relies on the fact that monomials and polynomials are ordered.

```
(* addPP: polynomial * polynomial -> polynomial *)
fun addPP(p,[]) = p
  | addPP([],q) = q
  | addPP(m::p,n::q) = (case Lex ordVar (m,n) of
                          GR => n::addPP(m::p,q)
                        | EQ => addPP(p,q)
                        | NGE => m::addPP(p,n::q));

(* mulMM: monomial * monomial -> monomial *)
fun mulMM([],n) = n
  | mulMM(m,[]) = m
  | mulMM(a::m,b::n) = (case ordVar(a,b) of
                          EQ => a::mulMM(m,n)
                        | GR => b::mulMM(a::m,n)
                        | NGE => a::mulMM(m,b::n));

(* mulMP: monomial * polynomial -> polynomial *)
fun mulMP(m,[]) = []
  | mulMP(m,n::p) = addPP([mulMM(m,n)], mulMP(m,p));

(* mulPP: polynomial * polynomial -> polynomial *)
fun mulPP([],p) = []
  | mulPP(m::p,q) = addPP(mulMP(m,q), mulPP(p,q));
```

Fig. 10.4. Polynomial arithmetic.

Substitutions have their usual association list representation:

```
type subst = (int * polynomial) list;
```

Application of substitutions to monomials and polynomials is implemented using polynomial arithmetic:

```
(* substM: subst * monomial -> polynomial *)
fun substM(s,[]) = [[]]
  | substM(s,i::m) = if indom i s then mulPP(app s i, substM(s,m))
                     else mulMP([i], substM(s,m));

(* substP: subst * polynomial -> polynomial *)
fun substP(s,[]) = []
  | substP(s,m::p) = addPP(substM(s,m),substP(s,p));
```

The functions *indom* and *app* were already defined in Section 4.7.

An implementation of successive variable elimination is shown in Fig. 10.5. It is a direct translation of Theorem 10.4.10. Because terms are represented by polynomials, the test $t \approx_B 0$ can be implemented by pattern matching with [], and the test $t \approx_B 1$ by pattern matching with [[]].

```
exception BUnify;

fun bu [] = []
  | bu [[]] = raise BUnify
  | bu t =
      let val (x,(r,s)) = decomp t
          val r1  = addPP([[]],r)
          val u   = bu(mulPP(r1,s))
          val r1u = substP(u,r1)
          val su  = substP(u,s)
      in (x,addPP(mulMP([x],r1u),su)) :: u end;
```

Fig. 10.5. Successive variable elimination.

If the argument to *bu* is neither 0 nor 1, *decomp* decomposes t into $x * r + s$: *decomp* picks out the first (and hence smallest) variable x, and *decomp2* computes r and s:

```
(* decomp2: int * polynomial * polynomial * polynomial
            -> polynomial * polynomial *)
fun decomp2(_, [], r, s) = (r,s)
  | decomp2(x, (y::m)::p, r, s) =
      if x=y then decomp2(x, p, r@[m], s) else (r, s@(y::m)::p);

(* decomp: polynomial -> int * (polynomial * polynomial) *)
fun decomp ([]::(x::m)::p) = (x, decomp2(x,p,[m],[[]]))
  | decomp ((x::m)::p) = (x, decomp2(x,p,[m],[]));
```

Note that *decomp2* relies on the fact that polynomials are ascending w.r.t. $>_{Lex}$ because it stops decomposing once it has found a monomial which does not start with x (and hence does not contain x), assuming that the remaining monomials do not contain x either.

Exercises

10.24 Show that $t \approx_B 0$ or $t \approx_B 1$ holds for every ground term t.

10.25 Solve the following equation using both Löwenheim's formula and successive variable elimination.

$$x + y + z + xy + xz + yz \approx_B^? 0.$$

10.26 Show that the unification problem $\{t_1 \approx_B^? 0, \ldots, t_n \approx_B^? 0\}$ has the same set of unifiers as the equation $(t_1 + 1) * \cdots * (t_n + 1) \approx_B^? 1$.

10.27 The powerset of a set S can be regarded as a Boolean ring. Clearly 0 should be the empty set. Find appropriate interpretations for 1, + and * which satisfy the identities B.

10.28 Show that $t \approx_B x * (t_0 + t_1) + t_0$ where $t_b := \{x \mapsto b\}(t)$ for $b = 0, 1$.

10.29 Show that for every term t and variable x there are terms u and v such that $t \approx_B x * u + (x + 1) * v$ and $x \notin Var(u, v)$.

10.30 Prove the following analogue of Theorem 10.4.10:

Theorem *Let* $t \approx_B x * u + (x + 1) * v$ *be such that* $x \notin Var(u, v)$ *and define* $t' := u * v$.

(a) *Every unifier of* $t \approx_B^? 0$ *is a unifier of* $t' \approx_B^? 0$.

(b) *If* σ *is a reproductive unifier of* $t' \approx_B 0$ *and* $x \notin Dom(\sigma)$, *then* $\sigma' := \sigma \cup \{x \mapsto x * (\sigma(u) + \sigma(v) + 1) + \sigma(v)\}$ *is a reproductive unifier of* $t \approx_B 0$.

10.31 Show that $\approx_B^I$, the inductive theory induced by B, is decidable.

10.5 Bibliographic notes

In this chapter, we have only introduced the basic notions of unification theory, and have investigated the unification properties of three equational theories in more detail. There are many other interesting topics in this area that we have not addressed at all. Exhaustive overviews on unification theory, providing references to most of the relevant literature, can be found in [12, 125, 233].

The notion of a minimal complete set of E-unifiers was first introduced (under the name "maximally general set of unifiers") by Plotkin in [205], where he already conjectured that such a set need not always exist. The first example of an equational theory for which this worst case occurs (i.e. of a theory of unification type zero) was given by Fages and Huet [89]. The notion "unification type" and the corresponding unification hierarchy were developed by Siekmann [231]. Plotkin's definition of E-instantiation already differed from the original definition of the instantiation quasi-order used for syntactic unification [216] in that it was restricted to the variables occurring in the unification problem. An example that shows that the unification type of an equational theory may become worse if one uses an instantiation quasi-order that compares substitutions on all variables can be found in [10].

The simple C-unification algorithm of Exercise 10.13 was used in the theorem prover by Guard [102]. Completeness of this algorithm was shown by Siekmann [232], who also pointed out that this method generates many redundant solutions. Other C-unification algorithms have been described in [87, 110, 139], but none of them produces a minimal complete set (without an additional minimization phase). NP-completeness of the decision problem for C-unification with constants is mentioned in [95], where it is attributed to Sethi (private communication, 1977). The simple proof that we have given in this chapter is due to Narendran (private communication, 1993), who also pointed out that similar reductions can be employed for AC and $AC1$.

The first proof of NP-hardness of AC-unification with constants can be found in [25]. Polynomiality of the decision problem for elementary AC-unification was first pointed out in [80]. In [135], it is shown that solvability of general AC-unification problems is in NP. The first algorithms for AC-unification with constants have been independently developed by Stickel [236] and Livesey and Siekmann [160]. Both algorithms reduce AC-unification to the problem of solving linear diophantine equations, but they differ in the treatment of free constants. Stickel first solves an elementary AC-unification problem, which is obtained by treating free constants as variables, and then modifies the solutions of the elementary problem to obtain solutions of the problem with constants. Livesey and Siekmann handle free constants with the help of inhomogeneous linear diophantine equations. In [237], Stickel presented an algorithm for general AC-unification, but could not show that it terminates. This gap was closed by Fages in [88]. More recent algorithms for AC-unification are, for example, described in [139, 92, 46, 111, 159, 31, 29, 30]. The bound on the size of minimal nontrivial solutions of a system of homogeneous linear diophantine equations presented in this chapter is due to Pottier [208]. Other results on this topic can, for example, be found in [118, 154, 53, 31, 80, 57, 91].

Two interesting lines of research in unification theory have been triggered by the investigation of AC-unification. On the one hand, it turned out that there are large classes of theories for which unification can be reduced to solving systems of linear equations in appropriate semirings [9, 191]. For example, unification modulo the theory of Abelian groups can be reduced to solving linear diophantine equations in $\mathbb{Z}$ [157]. On the other hand, the problem of how to construct an algorithm for general AC-unification from a given algorithm for AC-unification with constants has been generalized to the so-called *combination problem* for unification algorithms (which is the unification counterpart to the problem of combining decision procedures for the word problem): given equational theories E_1 and E_2 over disjoint signatures, how can algorithms for E_i-unification be combined into an algorithm for unification modulo $E_1 \cup E_2$? Rather general solutions to this problem have been presented in [223, 11].

Boolean unification goes back to Boole himself [28], who solved the one-variable case by variable elimination. A modern treatment of Boolean equations can be found in the book by Rudeanu [219]. Boolean unification was rediscovered for computer science by Büttner and Simonis [47] (who use variable elimination) and Martin and Nipkow [167, 168] (who reinvent Löwenheim's method). Martin and Nipkow also deal with the issue of additional constants in Boolean terms. Nipkow has generalized Boolean unification to primal algebras [187].

We have made use of semantic arguments to show that two Boolean terms are equal iff their polynomial forms are equal. There are two approaches to computing polynomial forms and obtaining this result that rely on rewriting alone: rewriting modulo associativity and commutativity [116, 203], and ordered rewriting [169, 202]. Both approaches generate a terminating rewrite relation despite the fact that $+$ and $*$ are commutative (see Chapter 11 for more information).

11

Extensions

Term rewriting is an extensive subject area, and this book covers only the basic concepts. Therefore we would like to give our readers a glimpse of further important topics. We concentrate mainly on extensions of term rewriting that are motivated by the inability of the basic framework to deal with certain common problems, such as inherently nonterminating identities and weaknesses of first-order equational logic. Note that this chapter is only meant to whet the reader's appetite and provide pointers to the literature, where precise treatments can be found.

11.1 Rewriting modulo equational theories

Probably the most infuriating limitation of the basic rewriting framework is the inability to deal gracefully with commutative operators: commutativity cannot be oriented into a terminating rewrite rule. An obvious idea is not to use commutativity as a rewrite rule, but to take it into account when applying some other rewrite rule. For example, if $+$ is commutative, the rewrite rule $0 + x \to x$ can reduce $t + 0$ to t. Commutativity is built into the rewrite process. More abstractly, we can split a set of identities into a set E that contains problematic identities like commutativity, and the remainder R. This gives rise to a new rewrite relation $\to_{R/E}$, which is defined on equivalence classes of terms:

$$[s]_{\approx_E} \to_{R/E} [t]_{\approx_E} \;:\Leftrightarrow\; \exists s', t'.\; s \approx_E s' \to_R t' \approx_E t.$$

It is easy to see that

$$s \approx_{R \cup E} t \;\Leftrightarrow\; [s]_{\approx_E} \stackrel{*}{\leftrightarrow}_{R/E} [t]_{\approx_E}.$$

If $\to_{R/E}$ is convergent then $s \approx_{R \cup E} t \Leftrightarrow ([s]_{\approx_E}{\downarrow}_{R/E}) = ([t]_{\approx_E}{\downarrow}_{R/E})$ holds.
Of course the main problem with this rather general approach is that in

order to reduce $[s]_{\approx_E}$ w.r.t. $\rightarrow_{R/E}$ we need to explore all of $[s]_{\approx_E}$, i.e. we need to enumerate all terms that are E-equivalent to s to find one that is reducible via $\rightarrow_R$. This requires all E-equivalence classes to be finite. Although this works for some popular sets of identities like AC, it is quite impractical from an efficiency point of view. Hence we need to refine $\rightarrow_{R/E}$.

Huet's approach [119] is quite radical: use $\rightarrow_R$ instead of $\rightarrow_{R/E}$. He shows that under certain termination and critical pair conditions (involving critical pairs not just between rules in R but also between rules in R and identities in E), $s \approx_{R \cup E} t \Leftrightarrow s{\downarrow}_R \approx_E t{\downarrow}_R$. The main restriction of his approach is that R needs to be left-linear.

A compromise between $\rightarrow_R$ and $\rightarrow_{R/E}$ is studied by Peterson and Stickel [203] and generalized by Jouannaud and Kirchner [127]:

$$ s \rightarrow_{R,E} t :\Leftrightarrow \exists (l \rightarrow r) \in R, p \in \mathcal{P}os(s), \sigma.\ s|_p \approx_E \sigma l \wedge t = s[\sigma r]_p. $$

This means that each rewrite step involves matching modulo $\approx_E$.

Note that $\rightarrow_{R,E}$ is weaker than $\rightarrow_{R/E}$: if $E = \{(x+y)+z \approx x+(y+z)\}$ and $R = \{0 + x \rightarrow x\}$, then $[(a + 0) + b]_{\approx_E} \rightarrow_{R/E} [a + b]_{\approx_E}$ because $(a+0)+b \approx_E a+(0+b) \rightarrow_R a+b$, but $(a+0)+b$ is in normal form w.r.t. $\rightarrow_{R,E}$.

Jouannaud and Kirchner develop a critical pair lemma and a completion procedure for $\rightarrow_{R,E}$ where the critical pair computation involves E-unification. Although R need not be left-linear, E-equivalence classes must be finite. Bachmair reformulates this completion procedure using inference rules and proof orders [14, 6].

An important application of $\rightarrow_{R,E}$ is the following convergent (modulo $\approx_E$) rewrite system for Boolean rings [116] (see Section 10.4):

$$ E := \left\{ \begin{array}{llll} x + y & \approx & y + x, & \quad x * y \approx y * x, \\ (x + y) + z & \approx & x + (y + z), & \quad (x * y) * z \approx x * (y * z) \end{array} \right\}, $$

$$ R := \left\{ \begin{array}{llll} x + x & \rightarrow & 0, & \quad x * x \rightarrow x, \\ 0 + x & \rightarrow & x, & \quad 0 * x \rightarrow 0, \quad \dots \\ x * (y + z) & \rightarrow & (x * y) + (x * z), & \quad 1 * x \rightarrow x, \end{array} \right\}. $$

R contains so-called "extended" rules like $(x + x) + y \rightarrow 0 + y$, which are shown as "$\dots$" above. They can be generated automatically from the basic rules of R.

Not only do we have $s \approx_B t \Leftrightarrow (s{\downarrow}_{R,E}) \approx_E (t{\downarrow}_{R,E})$, i.e. a rewriting-based decision procedure for $\approx_B$. Confluence of $\rightarrow_{R,E}$ modulo $\approx_E$ can even be checked automatically using an AC-unification algorithm (see Section 10.3) for computing critical pairs.

In general, the main drawback of $\to_{R,E}$ is that rewriting requires E-matching and critical pair computations require E-unification, which is harmful for efficiency and decidability.

11.2 Ordered rewriting

Ordered rewriting addresses a similar problem to rewriting modulo an equational theory: how to deal with nonterminating rules like commutativity. It does so without the need for E-unification or even E-matching.

The basic idea is to shift the termination proof from "compile time" to "run time". In both cases, we need a reduction order $\succ$. In ordinary term rewriting, termination of $\to_R$ is proved once and for all by showing that R is contained in $\succ$. In ordered rewriting, termination is enforced by admitting a rewrite step only if it decreases the term w.r.t. $\succ$. For example, if $R = \{x * y \to y * x\}$ and $\succ$ is such that $b * a \succ a * b$ (e.g. the lexicographic path order induced by $b > a$), then $b * a$ rewrites to $a * b$, but here the process stops because $a * b \not\succ b * a$ ($\succ$ is well-founded). As termination is enforced in each step, identities can be used in both directions, provided the order decreases. This leads to the rewrite relation $\to_{E\succ}$:

$$s \to_{E\succ} t \quad :\Leftrightarrow \quad \exists (l \approx r) \in E \cup E^{-1}, \ p \in \mathcal{P}os(s), \ \sigma.$$
$$s|_p = \sigma l \ \wedge \ t = s[\sigma r]_p \ \wedge \ \sigma l \succ \sigma r,$$

where E is an arbitrary set of identities. An identity $l \approx r$ such that $l \succ r$ is usually written $l \to r$.

Since $\to_{E\succ}$ is meant to decide $\approx_E$, we would like the following to hold:

$$s \leftrightarrow_E t \ \Leftrightarrow \ s \leftrightarrow_{E\succ} t. \tag{$*$}$$

However, this is a bit too ambitious: if $E = \{x * y \approx y * x\}$, then we have in particular $x * y \leftrightarrow_E y * x$, but there is no reduction order $\succ$ such that either $x * y \succ y * x$ or $y * x \succ x * y$. Therefore we settle for the weaker requirement that $(*)$ should hold for all ground terms s and t. This restriction to ground terms is unproblematic as far as deciding $\approx_E$ is concerned, because we can always replace all variables by new free constants (see the remark after Definition 4.1.2). Therefore $\succ$ is required to be total on ground terms (for an example of such a reduction order see Exercise 5.20), which immediately guarantees $(*)$ for all ground terms s and t.

On ground terms, ordinary rewriting is a special case of ordered rewriting provided R terminates: if $\succ = \xrightarrow{+}_R$ then $s \to_R t \Leftrightarrow s \to_{R\succ} t$ for all ground terms s and t.

Because $\to_{E\succ}$ is terminating ($\succ$ is a reduction order), it follows from $(*)$

that $s \approx_E t \Leftrightarrow s\!\downarrow_{E\succ} = t\!\downarrow_{E\succ}$ holds for all ground terms s and t provided $\to_{E\succ}$ is (locally) ground confluent, i.e. confluent for all ground terms. Unfortunately, ground confluence of terminating term rewriting systems is undecidable in general [136]. Because ordered rewriting covers ordinary rewriting, the undecidability carries over.

Fortunately, there is an extended Critical Pair Lemma [14, 18, 252] which requires checking that all ground instances of all "extended" critical pairs (where both sides of an identity are used) are joinable. Although the latter property is necessarily also undecidable, there are sufficient conditions for establishing it, which work for many practical examples [169, 202]. Under suitable assumptions about $\succ$ (which, for example, the lexicographic path order meets), the following two systems are ground convergent:

$$
\begin{aligned}
(x * y) * z &\to x * (y * z), \\
x * y &\approx y * x, \\
x * (y * z) &\approx y * (x * z).
\end{aligned}
$$

This one merely shows that $\approx_{AC}$ can be decided by sorting, and that ordered rewriting can simulate bubble-sort.

$$
\begin{array}{rclcrcl}
(x + y) + z &\to& x + (y + z), & \quad & (x * y) * z &\to& x * (y * z), \\
x + y &\approx& y + x, & & x * y &\approx& y * x, \\
x + (y + z) &\approx& y + (x + z), & & x * (y * z) &\approx& y * (x * z), \\
x * (y + z) &\to& x * y + x * z, & & (x + y) * z &\to& x * z + y * z, \\
0 + x &\to& x, & & x + 0 &\to& x, \\
1 * x &\to& x, & & x * 1 &\to& x, \\
0 * x &\to& 0, & & x * 0 &\to& 0, \\
x + x &\to& 0, & & x * x &\to& x, \\
x + (x + y) &\to& y, & & x * (x * y) &\to& x * y.
\end{array}
$$

This one uses the sorting trick for ordered rewriting in Boolean rings (see Section 10.4), thus providing an alternative decision procedure for $\approx_B$, which does not need AC-matching.

Extending completion to ordered rewriting leads to "unfailing completion". Because ordered rewriting can handle non-orientable identities, unfailing completion does not fail. Under certain reasonable assumptions one can even show that unfailing completion will find a convergent system if it exists. For details see [14, 18, 252].

11.3 Conditional identities and conditional rewriting

Equational logic is only a small fragment of first-order logic and of limited expressiveness. For example, a classical result by Redko [215, 96] shows that there is no finite set of identities which axiomatizes equivalence of regular expressions using only the basic operators "concatenation", "union" and "Kleene star". However, there is a finite set of **conditional identities**, i.e. formulae

$$s_1 \approx t_1 \wedge \ldots \wedge s_n \approx t_n \;\Rightarrow\; s \approx t,$$

which does the job using only the basic operators [148].

A simpler example of this kind is based on the integers generated by the constant 0, the successor function s and the predecessor function p, subject to the identities $E_{\mathbb{Z}} := \{p(s(x)) \approx x,\ s(p(x)) \approx x\}$. It is not hard to show that there is no finite set of identities $E \supseteq E_{\mathbb{Z}}$ defining a function pos such that $pos(t) \approx_E$ *true* iff t represents a positive integer, and $pos(t) \approx_E$ *false* otherwise. Again, E may only mention the basic operators 0, s, p and pos; *true* and *false* can be encoded as $s(0)$ and 0. (Exercise: find a finite set E containing additional operators.) However, using conditional identities, the axiomatization is easy:

$$pos(s(0)) \approx true, \qquad pos(x) \approx true \;\Rightarrow\; pos(s(x)) \approx true,$$
$$pos(0) \approx false, \qquad pos(x) \approx false \;\Rightarrow\; pos(p(x)) \approx false.$$

The above examples show that in many cases conditional identities are more expressive than unconditional ones. Fortunately, much of the algebraic theory of equational classes as presented in Section 3.5 can be generalized to the conditional case [246]. In particular, given a set of conditional identities E, one can again define a relation $\approx_E$, the set of identities valid in all models of E, and there is a complete proof system for $\approx_E$ [227].

However, rewriting with conditional identities, also known as **conditional rewriting**, differs from its unconditional relative in many important aspects. For a start, there are (at least) two potentially interesting definitions of $\to_E$, where E is a set of conditional identities:

$$s \to_E t \;\Leftrightarrow\; \exists (l_1 \approx r_1 \wedge \ldots \wedge l_n \approx r_n \Rightarrow l \approx r) \in E, p \in \mathcal{P}os(s), \sigma.$$
$$s|_p = \sigma l \;\wedge\; t = s[\sigma r]_p \;\wedge\; \sigma l_1 \sim \sigma r_1 \wedge \ldots \wedge \sigma l_n \sim \sigma r_n.$$

In the more equational definition, $\sim$ is $\overset{*}{\leftrightarrow}_E$, in the more rewriting oriented one, $\sim$ is $\downarrow_E$. To distinguish the two interpretations we write $\to_{\leftrightarrow E}$ and $\to_{\downarrow E}$.

Note that the above "definition" of $\to_E$ is recursive and hence not a definition at all. Strictly speaking $\to_E$ is the least relation that satisfies the above equivalence, which can also be expressed as an inductive definition.

Although $\overset{*}{\leftrightarrow}_{\leftrightarrow E}$ and $\approx_E$ coincide, we only have $\overset{*}{\leftrightarrow}_{\downarrow E} \subseteq \approx_E$: given $F :=$ $\{c \approx a,\ c \approx b,\ a \approx b \Rightarrow d \approx e\}$, which consists of two unconditional identities and a conditional one, where $a, \ldots, e$ are distinct constants, $d \approx_F e$ is valid but $d \overset{*}{\leftrightarrow}_{\downarrow F} e$ does not hold. In case $\to_{\downarrow E}$ is confluent (which $\to_{\downarrow F}$ is not!), $\overset{*}{\leftrightarrow}_{\leftrightarrow E}$ and $\overset{*}{\leftrightarrow}_{\downarrow E}$ coincide. Despite the discrepancy between $\approx_E$ and $\overset{*}{\leftrightarrow}_{\downarrow E}$, the latter is the standard interpretation of conditional rewriting because it has an obvious operational reading. That is, unless the premises of a rule contain "extra variables", i.e. variables which do not occur on the lhs of the conclusion, e.g. as in $x \approx y * y \Rightarrow sqrt(x) \approx y$. In this case rewriting turns into "narrowing" (see Section 11.6). But even if conditions do not contain extra variables, there is a nasty surprise: $\to_{\downarrow E}$ need not be decidable and the normal form of a term need not be computable. Nevertheless, conditional rewriting is essential in many applications of rewriting.

The basic theory of conditional rewriting, including termination and confluence, goes back to [134, 26, 78]. Completion is studied by Ganzinger [94], modularity by Middeldorp [177, 178]. A more detailed guide to the extensive literature is beyond the scope of this book.

11.4 Higher-order rewrite systems

Term rewriting systems deal well with first-order objects like numbers and lists, but fail to accommodate higher-order functions. For example, the standard definition of the well-known *map* function, which applies a function to all elements of a list,

$$
\begin{aligned}
map(f, empty) &\;\to\; empty, \\
map(f, cons(x, xs)) &\;\to\; cons(f(x), map(f, xs)),
\end{aligned}
$$

is a legal functional program but not a legal TRS: in the second rule, f appears both as a variable and as a function symbol.

A second example is the manipulation of terms with bound variables. Although term rewriting can deal with propositional logic, for example via Boolean rings, predicate logic is another matter. A simple tautology like $(\forall x.(P(x) \wedge Q(x))) \Leftrightarrow ((\forall x.P(x)) \wedge (\forall x.Q(x)))$ is outside the scope of term rewriting because of the bound variables.

The solution to these problems is the λ-calculus [21, 113], a rewriting-based formalism where variable binding and substitution are primitive. It is the core of all functional programming languages [182] and many theorem provers [97, 200]. Because we cannot possibly explain the λ-calculus too, the following remarks are intended for those already familiar with it.

Higher-order rewrite systems (HRS) are simply sets of rewrite rules between (typed) λ-terms. For example, the above definition of *map* is an HRS. Because λ-terms generalize first-order terms, every TRS is also an HRS.

The transformation of the above rule for $\forall$ is a bit more subtle. Instead of $\forall x.P(x)$ we need to write $all(\lambda x.P(x))$, where *all* is a higher-order function representing the universal quantifier. This encoding of quantifiers as λ-terms is due to Church [50]. The rewrite rule now becomes

$$all(\lambda x.P(x) \wedge Q(x)) \;\rightarrow\; all(\lambda x.P(x)) \wedge all(\lambda x.Q(x)).$$

So far we have said nothing about how the rules of an HRS interact with the primitive conversion rules (α, β and η) of the λ-calculus. There are two different approaches:

1. Rewriting is performed modulo the conversion rules of λ-calculus, i.e. the latter are part of the matching process. This idea goes back to Klop [140, 144], although he did not use the λ-calculus itself but had his own meta-language to deal with binding and substitution and called the resulting calculus "Combinatory Reduction Systems". Nipkow suggested the simply-typed λ-calculus as a meta-language and extended a number of critical-pair-based confluence criteria to the higher-order setting [189, 190]. Termination orders are also beginning to emerge [207, 129].

   Van Oostrom and van Raamsdonk [197, 195, 212, 196] generalize the framework further by abstracting from the substitution calculus of the meta-language. They derive very strong confluence results in this setting.

2. The rewrite rules are combined with the reduction rules of the λ-calculus, i.e. β reduction steps are performed explicitly and not as part of other rewrite steps. The main question is when confluence and termination are preserved in this combination. This line of research was started by Tannen [33] and has continued to flourish [34, 20, 22, 128].

11.5 Reduction strategies

Throughout this book we have pretended that rewrite systems only come in two flavours: terminating and nonterminating. This is too simplistic. Due to the possible choice between different redexes in a term, some reduction sequences from a given term may terminate while others do not: the TRS $\{f(x) \rightarrow b, \; a \rightarrow a\}$ induces both the terminating reduction $f(a) \rightarrow b$ and the nonterminating one $f(a) \rightarrow f(a) \rightarrow \cdots$. Especially when term rewriting is viewed as an abstract form of program execution, it is vital to control this nondeterminism by a *reduction strategy*. Because functional programs can be viewed as orthogonal term rewriting systems (see Section 6.3), the study of reduction strategies is mostly confined to orthogonal systems.

Reduction strategies are often defined in terms of the position of a redex: **outermost** means that it is not properly contained in another redex, and **leftmost** refers to the order of subterms in linear notation. Important strategies are:

leftmost-outermost reduces the leftmost of the outermost redexes in each step. This corresponds to the evaluation mechanism "call-by-name" in programming languages.

parallel-outermost reduces all outermost redexes simultaneously in each step. This is unproblematic because different outermost redexes must always be in separate subterms.

It can be shown that parallel-outermost is a **normalizing** strategy for orthogonal systems, i.e. repeated parallel-outermost reduction leads to a normal form if one exists. This strategy can be a bit expensive because it may reduce more redexes than necessary for reaching a normal form. Leftmost-outermost, an obvious cheaper alternative, fails to be normalizing: $\{f(x,c) \to d,\ a \to a, b \to c\}$ induces the infinite leftmost-outermost reduction $f(a,b) \to f(a,b) \to \cdots$. If we require the TRS to be both orthogonal and **left-normal**, i.e. in all left-hand sides the function and constant symbols occur to the left of all variables (in linear notation), then leftmost-outermost is also normalizing. As a consequence, leftmost-outermost reduction for combinatory logic is normalizing (see Example 4.1.3, where you have to write "." as a prefix rather than an infix symbol to verify left-normality).

Huet and Lévy's landmark study [122] of reduction strategies covers all of the above results. In particular they identify a subclass of orthogonal systems called **strongly sequential** which admit an efficient normalizing strategy. Strongly sequential systems include left-normal systems but exclude systems such as combinatory logic extended by the following rules:

$$B := \{f(a,b,x) \to c,\ f(b,x,a) \to c,\ f(x,a,b) \to c\}.$$

This TRS is orthogonal but not strongly sequential. It requires some kind of pseudo-parallel reduction strategy. When normalizing $f(t_1, t_2, t_3)$ we cannot fix on just two of the arguments because we cannot decide which arguments terminate (thanks to Turing-completeness of combinatory logic).

The study of reduction strategies goes back to the λ-calculus and combinatory logic [61, 62, 21]. O'Donnell [192] was the first to consider reduction strategies for orthogonal term rewriting systems. Klop [141] gives a nice overview of the whole area and also covers the results by Huet and Lévy (see also [142]). Middeldorp [179] adapts the theory to the situation where proper normal forms may not exist, as is the case in lazy functional programming. Durand and Middeldorp [83] generalize and simplify Huet and Lévy's work using tree automata techniques, an idea due to Comon [56]. Kennaway [138] proves the remarkable theorem that every orthogonal TRS has a computable "sequential" reduction strategy, which appears to contradict our intuition about system B above. Antoy and Middeldorp [5] generalize and simplify this result while also surveying the related literature. Van Raamsdonk [212, 213] shows that for a certain subclass of (almost) orthogonal higher-order rewrite systems, "outermost-fair" reduction is normalizing.

11.6 Narrowing

Narrowing is a process that can be used as a general E-unification procedure, which in turn leads to an execution model for combined functional and logic programming languages. Formally, narrowing can be seen as a generalization of term rewriting where the matching process is replaced by unification: both the rewrite rule and the term to be rewritten are instantiated.

Let E be a set of identities, and assume that R is a convergent term rewriting system that is equivalent to E. If σ is an E-unifier of the equation $s \approx_E^? t$, then $\sigma(s)$ and $\sigma(t)$ have a common R-normal form, that is, there are chains of reductions starting from $\sigma(s)$ and $\sigma(t)$ that lead to the same R-irreducible term. The main idea underlying narrowing is to construct the unifier and the corresponding chains of reductions simultaneously.

As an example, consider the set of identities $E := \{0 + x \approx x\}$ and let R be the corresponding convergent TRS. In order to solve the E-unification problem $y + z \approx_E^? 0$, we look for an *instance* of $y + z$ to which the rule $0 + x \to x$ applies. Such an instance can be found by (syntactically) unifying $y + z$ with the left-hand side $0 + x$, which yields the mgu $\sigma_1 := \{y \mapsto 0, z \mapsto x\}$. If we apply σ_1 to $y + z$, we obtain first the term $0 + x$, and then, by rewriting with R, the term x. This yields the new equation $x \approx_E^? 0$, which has the (syntactic) mgu $\tau := \{x \mapsto 0\}$. By this process, we have simultaneously constructed the E-unifier $\sigma := \tau\sigma_1 = \{x \mapsto 0, y \mapsto 0, z \mapsto 0\}$ of $y + z \approx_E^? 0$, and the rewrite chain $\sigma(y + z) = 0 + 0 \to_R 0 = \sigma(0)$.

Formally, the **narrowing relation** $\leadsto_R$ induced by a TRS R is defined as follows. Let s be a term. If $p \in \mathcal{P}os(s)$ is a non-variable position, $l \to r$ is a renamed rule of R such that s and $l \to r$ have no variables in common, and σ is a (syntactic) mgu of l and $s|_p$, then $s \leadsto_R \sigma(s)[\sigma(r)]_p$.

We write $s \leadsto_R^\sigma \sigma(s)[\sigma(r)]_p$ to indicate which substitution was used in the narrowing step. The narrowing relation is extended to equations as follows: $(s \approx_E^? t) \leadsto_R^\sigma (s' \approx_E^? t')$ iff $s \leadsto_R^\sigma s'$ and $t' = \sigma(t)$ or $t \leadsto_R^\sigma t'$ and $s' = \sigma(s)$.

If R is a convergent TRS that is equivalent to the set of identities E, then the narrowing relation induced by R gives rise to the following E-unification procedure: In order to enumerate a complete set of E-unifiers of $s \approx_E^? t$, generate *all* narrowing sequences

$$(s \approx_E^? t) \leadsto_R^{\sigma_1} (s_1 \approx_E^? t_1) \leadsto_R^{\sigma_2} \cdots \leadsto_R^{\sigma_{n-1}} (s_{n-1} \approx_E^? t_{n-1}) \leadsto_R^{\sigma_n} (s_n \approx_E^? t_n).$$

If $s_n =_E^? t_n$ has the (syntactic) mgu τ, then this narrowing sequence yields the E-unifier $\tau\sigma_n \cdots \sigma_1$ of $s \approx_E^? t$. Note that this is a search procedure because there may be any number of narrowing sequences starting from a given equation due to the choice of which rule to apply where. Narrowing is in general neither confluent nor terminating, even if R is.

The idea of narrowing was first mentioned by Slagle [234] and Lankford [155] as an optimization of the general paramodulation rule in cases where a canonical TRS is available. The first description of narrowing as a general E-unification procedure is due to Fay [90].

In the simple unoptimized form described above, the E-unification procedure obtained by narrowing usually does not terminate (even for finitary theories), and the complete set of E-unifiers generated this way is usually not minimal. Most of the research on narrowing as a general equational unification procedure has been concerned with finding methods to prune the search space. In principle, these optimizations of narrowing depend on the fact that, for a convergent TRS, one can fix an arbitrary strategy for computing normal forms. Thus, it is sufficient to generate all narrowing derivations that are obtained from rewriting derivations conforming to the fixed strategy. For a survey see [103] and for recent results [180].

Narrowing can also be generalized to conditional rewriting [123, 180] and rewriting modulo equational theories [126]. A combination of both generalizations is described in [27]. Narrowing with higher-order rewrite rules has also been studied [209, 211, 210, 162, 7, 105].

Finally, narrowing can combine first-order functional and logic programming. Functional programs can be viewed as orthogonal term rewriting systems. A clause $p \Leftarrow p_1, \ldots, p_n$ of a logic program can be viewed as a conditional identity $p_1 \approx true \wedge \ldots \wedge p_n \approx true \Rightarrow p \approx true$ (where the conditions may contain "extra" variables!). Therefore conditional identities subsume functional and logic programs. A query in the sense of logic programming becomes an equation $q \approx_E^? true$. Evaluating a term t in the sense of functional programming corresponds to solving the equation $t \approx_E^? x$.

Narrowing with conditional identities constitutes a unified evaluation mechanism for such queries. However, narrowing for convergent systems is slightly different from narrowing in the context of functional programming, where termination cannot be assumed. For the latter see, for example, [4]. For surveys of combined functional and logic programming see [103, 104].

Appendix 1
Ordered Sets

A1.1 Basic definitions

Let $\rhd$ be a binary relation on a set A. Recall that $\rhd$ is

transitive	iff $\forall x, y, z \in A.\ x \rhd y \wedge y \rhd z \Rightarrow x \rhd z$,
reflexive	iff $\forall x \in A.\ x \rhd x$,
irreflexive	iff $\forall x \in A.\ \neg(x \rhd x)$,
symmetric	iff $\forall x, y \in A.\ x \rhd y \Rightarrow y \rhd x$,
antisymmetric	iff $\forall x, y \in A.\ x \rhd y \wedge y \rhd x \Rightarrow x = y$.

An **equivalence relation** is a reflexive, transitive and symmetric relation. An equivalence relation $\sim\ \subseteq A \times A$ induces an **equivalence class** $[a]_\sim :=\ \{a' \in A \mid a \sim a'\}$ for each $a \in A$ and a **quotient set** $A/_\sim := \{[a]_\sim \mid a \in A\}$.

Note that equivalence classes form a partition of A: two equivalence classes $[a]_\sim$ and $[b]_\sim$ are either identical (if $a \sim b$) or disjoint (if not $a \sim b$).

A **partial order** is a reflexive, transitive and antisymmetric relation which is usually written $\geq$. The pair $(A, \geq)$ consisting of a set A and a partial order $\geq$ on A is called a **partially ordered set** or **poset**. A **strict order** is a transitive and irreflexive relation usually written $>$. Note that $x \leq y$ means $y \geq x$ and $x \not\geq y$ means $\neg(x \geq y)$ (and similarly for $>$).

Partial orders and strict orders are interdefinable:

- Every partial order $\geq$ induces a strict order

$$x > y \ :\Leftrightarrow\ x \geq y \wedge x \neq y,$$

the **strict part** of $\geq$.

- Every strict order $>$ induces a partial order

$$x \geq y \ :\Leftrightarrow\ x > y \vee x = y,$$

the reflexive closure of $>$.

A transitive and reflexive relation is a **quasi-order**. If $\gtrsim$ is a quasi-order,

$$x > y \;:\Leftrightarrow\; x \gtrsim y \wedge \neg(y \gtrsim x)$$

is the associated strict order and

$$x \sim y \;:\Leftrightarrow\; x \gtrsim y \wedge y \gtrsim x$$

the associated equivalence. The quasi-order $\gtrsim$ induces a partial order on $A/\!\!\sim$:

$$[x]_\sim \geq [y]_\sim \;:\Leftrightarrow\; x \gtrsim y.$$

A relation $\vartriangleright$ is called **linear** or **total** if $x \vartriangleright y \vee x = y \vee y \vartriangleright x$ for all x and y. For example, a partial order $\geq$ is linear if $x \leq y \vee x \geq y$ for all x and y; in this case $\geq$ is simply called a linear order.

Definition A1.1.1 Let $(A, \geq)$ be a poset and let $M \subseteq A$.

- $m \in M$ is a **maximal** element of M if $\forall n \in M.\; n \geq m \Rightarrow n = m$.
- $m \in M$ is the **greatest** element of M if $\forall n \in M.\; m \geq n$.
- $u \in A$ is an **upper bound** of M if $\forall m \in M.\; u \geq m$.

The notions of **minimal** and **least** element and **lower bound** are defined dually, i.e. by reversing the order.

Appendix 2
A Bluffer's Guide to ML

This appendix assumes that the reader is familiar with the ideas and principles of functional programming and merely introduces (some of) their concrete syntax in ML. For a full exposition of ML see Paulson's textbook [201].
To aid readability, we distinguish **keywords** from *identifiers*.

A2.1 Types

ML is a strongly typed language. In the sequel, types are denoted by τ.

Basic types are *bool*, *int* and *string*. In addition to the basic types, there
are type constructors for forming new types. Given a type constructor t
of n arguments and types $\tau_1, \ldots, \tau_n$, ML uses postfix syntax $(\tau_1, \ldots, \tau_n)t$ to
denote the compound type. If $n = 1$ we can write $\tau\,t$ instead of $(\tau)t$. There
are three predefined type constructors:

τ_1 -> τ_2 is the type of functions from τ_1 to τ_2.

τ_1 * $\cdots$ * τ_n is the Cartesian product $\tau_1 \times \cdots \times \tau_n$.

τ *list* is the type of lists whose elements have type τ.

Note that -> and * are infixes. To disambiguate the syntax, -> binds less
tightly than *, which binds less tightly than postfix notation. Function
arrows associate to the right. Therefore

> *int* * *int list* -> *bool* -> *string*

is short for

> (*int* * ((*int*) *list*)) -> (*bool* -> *string*)

Types may also contain type variables which we write α, β, etc.

A2.2 Expressions

In the sequel, the letter e denotes an expression. If expression e has type τ we write $e:\tau$.

A2.2.1 Basic values

The type *bool* has two constants *true* and *false*. String constants are enclosed in double quotes, as in "ML".

The basic list constructors are [], the empty list, and the infix ::, which puts an element in front of a list. For example, 1::(2::[]) is the list [1,2]. A list of n elements is written $[e_1,\ldots,e_n]$, where all elements need to have the same type, say τ, in which case the whole list has type τ *list*.

Tuples are written as usual: if $e_i:\tau_i$ for $i = 1,\ldots,n$ then $(e_1,\ldots,e_n)$ is an expression of type $\tau_1 * \cdots * \tau_n$.

A2.2.2 Compound expressions

Larger expressions are formed by function application. If $f: \tau_1 \rightarrow \tau_2$ and $e:\tau_1$ then $f\ e$ (also written $(f\ e)$ or $f(e)$) denotes the application of f to e and is of type τ_2. ML is an eager language: e is evaluated first and the result is passed to f.

If f is a function of type $\tau_1 \rightarrow \cdots \rightarrow \tau_n \rightarrow \tau$ we write the application of f to arguments $e_1,\ldots,e_n$ as $f\ e_1\ \ldots\ e_n$. This is short for $(\ldots(f\ e_1)\ldots e_n)$, which means that first f is applied to e_1, then the result to e_2, and so on: application associates to the left. We need not supply all of f's arguments at once: $(f\ e_1)$ is a perfectly legal expression of type $\tau_2 \rightarrow \cdots \rightarrow \tau_n \rightarrow \tau$.

Complex expressions can be structured using the let-in-end syntax for local bindings, as in

```
let val x = 42
    val y = x*x
in y+y end
```

The evaluation of this expression proceeds as follows:

1. The value 42 is locally bound to x.
2. The value 1764 is locally bound to y.
3. The value of the whole expression is $y+y$, i.e. 3528.

This evaluation does not affect the bindings of x or y outside the expression.

A2.3 Function declarations

Functions are declared with the keyword **fun** and the following syntax:

fun $f\ x_1 \dots x_n$ = e

This defines a curried function of n arguments. Its type is

τ_1 -> $\cdots$ -> τ_n -> τ

where τ_i is the type of x_i and τ the type of e.

ML's type system lets us deduce the type of a function automatically from its definition, so the user is not required to annotate it with types. For example, the ML system infers from the definition

fun *add1* x y = $x+y+1$;

that *add1*: *int* -> *int* -> *int*. You can now evaluate *add1* 5 7, which yields 13, or apply *add1* to only one argument: *add1* 5 is a well-formed expression of type *int* -> *int*. In fact, you can treat *add1* 5 like any other function. For example,

let val *add6* = *add1* 5 **in** (*add6* 10) + (*add6* 20) **end**;

evaluates to 42.

Parentheses may be required to disambiguate an expression. For example, *add1 add1* 2 3 4 means (((*add1 add1*) 2) 3) 4, which is a nonsense, and should have been *add1* (*add1* 2 3) 4.

The function *add1* may only be applied to integers. ML functions can also be polymorphic, in which case they can be applied to arguments of different types. A simple example is

fun *id* x = x;

where *id* is assigned the type α -> α because it can take arguments of an arbitrary type α and return a result of the same type. Another simple example is

fun *swap* (x,y) = (y,x);

of type $\alpha * \beta$ -> $\beta * \alpha$. At this point we have already used pattern matching, an extended form of function definition. In general, the arguments of the function being defined need not be individual variables but could be arbitrary patterns, for example

fun *perm* $((x,y),z)$ = (z,y,x);

which has type $(\alpha * \beta) * \gamma$ -> $\gamma * \beta * \alpha$.

Patterns are expressions which contain only variables and constructors. Standard constructors are tuples and the list constructors [] and ::. Pattern matching allows functions to be defined by a list of clauses instead of just a single one. A simple example is

```
(* zip: α list * β list -> (α * β) list *)
fun zip ([], [])      = []
  | zip (x::xs, y::ys) = (x,y) :: zip(xs,ys);
```

Clearly $zip([x_1,\ldots,x_n], [y_1,\ldots,y_n])$ is $[(x_1,y_1),\ldots,(x_n,y_n)]$. The first clause takes care of the case where both lists are empty, and the second clause of the case where both lists are nonempty. Pattern matching automatically decomposes the lists into their first elements x and y and the remainders xs and ys. Note that *zip* is not defined if the two lists are of different lengths. In that case the execution stops with an exception at the point where *zip* is called with one empty and one nonempty list.

In the definition of *zip*, the order of the two clauses does not matter. In general, it does.

```
fun length (x::xs) = 1 + length(xs)
  | length xs      = 0
```

The function *length* has type α *list* -> *int* and computes the length of a list. The second clause is used only if the argument does not match the first clause. Reversing the order of the clauses results in a function which is 0 everywhere. Fortunately, in that case the ML system would at least issue a warning that the second clause is redundant. Variables which are not used on the rhs can be replaced by "_":

```
fun length (_::xs) = 1 + length(xs)
  | length _       = 0
```

The above definition of *length* is not very elegant because one can write the second lhs more clearly as *length* [], which also removes the dependence on the order.

The generalized form of function definition is

```
fun f patterns₁ = e₁
  | f patterns₂ = e₂
    ⋮
  | f patternsₙ = eₙ
```

The declaration of mutually recursive functions uses the keyword **and** to separate the functions:

```
fun even 0 = true
  | even n = odd(n-1)
and odd 0 = false
  | odd n = even(n-1);
```

Not every function must have a name. The keyword **fn** introduces an anonymous function: **fn** x **=>** e is the function which takes an argument x and returns the result e. For example, *add6* above could also be written as **fn** x **=>** x**+6**. Pattern matching is allowed as well:

    fn *pattern*$_1$ **=>** e_1 **|** ... **|** *pattern*$_n$ **=>** e_n

Pattern matching is also allowed in **case** expressions:

    case e **of** *pattern*$_1$ **=>** e_1 **|** ... **|** *pattern*$_n$ **=>** e_n

The above can be regarded as a shorthand for

    (**fn** *pattern*$_1$ **=>** e_1 **|** ... **|** *pattern*$_n$ **=>** e_n)(e)

A2.4 Standard functions

A2.4.1 Booleans

The two infix operations **andalso** and **orelse** realize conditional "and" and "or": b_1 **andalso** b_2 is equivalent to   **if** b_1 **then** b_2 **else false**;
b_1 **orelse** b_2 is equivalent to   **if** b_1 **then true else** b_2.

A2.4.2 Lists

The following is a collection of standard functions from the literature, some of which are part of ML already.

```
(* null: α list -> bool *)
fun null []       = true
  | null (_::_) = false;

(* map: (α -> β) -> α list -> β list *)
fun map f []        = []
  | map f (x::xs) = f(x) :: map f xs;

(* exists: (α -> bool) -> α list -> bool *)
fun exists p []       = false
  | exists p (x::xs) = p(x) orelse exists p xs;

(* forall: (α -> bool) -> α list -> bool *)
fun forall p []       = true
  | forall p (x::xs) = p(x) andalso forall p xs;

(* concat: α list list -> α list *)
fun concat []       = []
  | concat (x::xs) = x @ (concat xs);
```

The infix **@** appends two lists: $[x_1, \ldots, x_m]$ **@** $[y_1, \ldots, y_n]$ evaluates to $[x_1, \ldots, x_m, y_1, \ldots, y_n]$.

A2.5 Datatypes

ML offers a datatype definition facility which is strongly related to the concept of a term algebra: roughly speaking, the elements of a datatype correspond to the terms over a given signature. For example, binary trees with integer labels can be introduced as follows:

`datatype` *btree* `=` *Mt* `|` *Node* `of` *btree* `*` *int* `*` *btree*

This says that a value of type *btree* is either the constant *Mt* or of the form *Node*(t_1, i, t_2), where $i : int$ and $t_1, t_2 : btree$. The functions *Mt*: *btree* and *Node*: *btree* `*` *int* `*` *btree* `->` *btree* are called **constructors** because they construct the values of the datatype.

In general, a datatype definition of the form

`datatype` t `=` C_1 `of` τ_1 `|` $\ldots$ `|` C_n `of` τ_n

introduces a new type t and constructor functions $C_i : \tau_i \to t$. If C_i is a constant, `of` τ_i is omitted.

A2.6 Exceptions

Exceptions arise naturally because inbuilt functions, e.g. division, but also user-defined ones, e.g. *zip* above, are undefined (as opposed to nonterminating) for certain arguments. In that case the function *raises* an exception, which interrupts the current evaluation. However, exceptions can also be *handled*, i.e. the interruption can be caught before it propagates to the top level. Hence there are three ML constructs dealing with exceptions:

`exception` E`;`
> declares a user-defined exception named E.

`raise` E
> is an expression which has no value but raises exception E.

e_1 `handle` E `=>` e_2
> is an expression which is evaluated as follows. If e_1 evaluates to a normal value, then this is the value of the whole expression. If the evaluation of e_1 raises exception E, handle that exception by evaluating e_2 instead. If the evaluation of e_1 raises some other exception, the whole expression raises that exception.

Bibliography

LNCS = Lecture Notes in Computer Science.

[1] Wilhelm Ackermann. *Solvable Cases of the Decision Problem*. North-Holland, 1954.

[2] William W. Adams and Philippe Loustaunau. *An Introduction to Gröbner Bases*, volume 3 of *Graduate Studies in Mathematics*. AMS, 1994.

[3] Alfred V. Aho, John E. Hopcroft, and Jeffrey D. Ullman. *The Design and Analysis of Computer Algorithms*. Addison-Wesley, 1974.

[4] Sergio Antoy, Rachid Echahed, and Michael Hanus. A needed narrowing strategy. In *Proc. 21st ACM Symp. Principles of Programming Languages*, pages 268–279, 1994.

[5] Sergio Antoy and Aart Middeldorp. A sequential reduction strategy. *Theoretical Computer Science*, 165:75–95, 1996.

[6] Jürgen Avenhaus. *Reduktionssysteme*. Springer-Verlag, 1995.

[7] Jürgen Avenhaus and Carlos Loría-Sáenz. Higher-order conditional rewriting and narrowing. In J.-P. Jouannaud, editor, *Constraints in Computational Logics*, volume 845 of *LNCS*, pages 269–284. Springer-Verlag, 1994.

[8] Franz Baader. Unification in idempotent semigroups is of type zero. *J. Automated Reasoning*, 2:283–286, 1986.

[9] Franz Baader. Unification in commutative theories. *J. Symbolic Computation*, 8:479–497, 1989.

[10] Franz Baader. Unification, weak unification, upper bound, lower bound, and generalization problems. In R.V. Book, editor, *Rewriting Techniques and Applications*, volume 488 of *LNCS*, pages 86–97. Springer-Verlag, 1991.

[11] Franz Baader and Klaus Schulz. Unification in the union of disjoint equational theories: Combining decision procedures. In D. Kapur, editor, *Automated Deduction — CADE-11*, volume 607 of *LNCS*, pages 50–65. Springer-Verlag, 1992.

[12] Franz Baader and Jörg H. Siekmann. Unification theory. In D.M. Gabbay, C.J. Hogger, and J.A. Robinson, editors, *Handbook of Logic in Artificial Intelligence and Logic Programming*. Oxford University Press, 1994.

[13] Franz Baader and Cesare Tinelli. A new approach for combining decision procedures for the word problem, and its connection to the Nelson-Oppen combination method. In W. McCune, editor, *Automated Deduction*

— *CADE-14*, volume 1249 of *LNCS*, pages 19–33. Springer-Verlag, 1997.

[14] Leo Bachmair. *Canonical Equational Proofs*. Progress in Theoretical Computer Science. Birkhäuser, 1991.

[15] Leo Bachmair and Bruno Buchberger. A simplified proof of the characterization theorem for Gröbner-bases. *ACM SIGSAM Bulletin*, 14(4):29–34, 1980.

[16] Leo Bachmair and Nachum Dershowitz. Critical pair criteria for completion. *J. Symbolic Computation*, 6:1–18, 1988.

[17] Leo Bachmair, Nachum Dershowitz, and Jieh Hsiang. Orderings for equational proofs. In *1st IEEE Symp. on Logic in Computer Science*, pages 346–357. IEEE Computer Society Press, 1986.

[18] Leo Bachmair, Nachum Dershowitz, and David A. Plaisted. Completion without failure. In H. Aït-Kaci and M. Nivat, editors, *Resolution of Equations in Algebraic Structures*, volume 2: Rewriting Techniques, pages 1–30. Academic Press, 1989.

[19] Leo Bachmair and Harald Ganzinger. Buchberger's algorithm: A constraint-based completion procedure. In J.-P. Jouannaud, editor, *Constraints in Computational Logics*, volume 845 of *LNCS*, pages 285–301. Springer-Verlag, 1994.

[20] Franco Barbanera, Maribel Fernández, and Herman Geuvers. Modularity of strong normalization and confluence in the algebraic λ-cube. In *9th IEEE Symp. Logic in Computer Science*, pages 406–415. IEEE Computer Society Press, 1994.

[21] Hendrik Pieter Barendregt. *The Lambda Calculus, its Syntax and Semantics*. North-Holland, 2nd edition, 1984.

[22] Gilles Barthe and Herman Geuvers. Modular properties of algebraic type systems. In G. Dowek, J. Heering, K. Meinke, and B. Möller, editors, *Higher Order Algebra, Logic and Term Rewriting*, volume 1074 of *LNCS*, pages 37–56. Springer-Verlag, 1996.

[23] David Basin and Harald Ganzinger. Complexity analysis based on ordered resolution. In *11th IEEE Symp. Logic in Computer Science*, pages 456–465. IEEE Computer Society Press, 1996.

[24] Lewis Denver Baxter. *The Complexity of Unification*. PhD thesis, University of Waterloo, Ontario, Canada, 1976.

[25] Dan Benanav, Deepak Kapur, and Paliath Narendran. Complexity of matching problems. *J. Symbolic Computation*, 3:203–216, 1987.

[26] Jan A. Bergstra and Jan Willem Klop. Conditional rewrite rules: Confluence and termination. *J. Computer and System Sciences*, 32:323–362, 1986.

[27] Alexander Bockmayr. Conditional narrowing modulo a set of equations. *Applicable Algebra in Engineering, Communication and Computing*, 4:147–168, 1993.

[28] George Boole. *The Mathematical Analysis of Logic*. Macmillan, 1847. Reprinted 1948, B. Blackwell.

[29] Alexandre Boudet. Competing for the AC-unification race. *J. Automated Reasoning*, 11:185–212, 1993.

[30] Alexandre Boudet and Evelyne Contejean. "Syntactic" AC-unification. In J.-P. Jouannaud, editor, *Proc. Constraints in Computational Logics*, volume 845 of *LNCS*, pages 136–151. Springer-Verlag, 1994.

[31] Alexandre Boudet, Evelyne Contejean, and Hervé Devie. A new AC-unification algorithm with a new algorithm for solving diophantine equa-

tions. In *5th IEEE Symp. Logic in Computer Science*, pages 141–150. IEEE Computer Society Press, 1990.

[32] Alexandre Boudet, Jean-Pierre Jouannaud, and Manfred Schmidt-Schauß. Unification in Boolean rings and Abelian groups. *J. Symbolic Computation*, 8:449–477, 1989.

[33] Val Breazu-Tannen. Combining algebra and higher-order types. In *3rd IEEE Symp. Logic in Computer Science*, pages 82–90. IEEE Computer Society Press, 1988.

[34] Val Breazu-Tannen and Jean Gallier. Polymorphic rewriting conserves algebraic confluence. *Information and Computation*, 114:1–29, 1994.

[35] Randal E. Bryant. Graph based algorithms for boolean function manipulation. *IEEE Trans. Comp.*, 35(8):677–691, 1986.

[36] Bruno Buchberger. *Ein Algorithmus zum Auffinden der Basiselemente des Restklassenringes nach einem nulldimensionalen Polynomideal*. PhD thesis, Mathematisches Institut der Universität Innsbruck, 1965.

[37] Bruno Buchberger. Ein algorithmisches Kriterium für die Lösbarkeit eines algebraischen Gleichungssystems. *Aequationes Mathematicae*, 4, 1970.

[38] Bruno Buchberger. Some properties of Gröbner-bases for polynomial ideals. *ACM SIGSAM Bulletin*, 10(4):19–24, 1976.

[39] Bruno Buchberger. A theoretical basis for the reduction of polynomials to canonical forms. *ACM SIGSAM Bulletin*, 10(3):19–29, 1976.

[40] Bruno Buchberger. Gröbner bases: An algorithmic method in polynomial ideal theory. In N. K. Bose, editor, *Multidimensional Systems Theory*, pages 184–232. Reidel, 1985.

[41] Bruno Buchberger. Basic features and development of the critical pair completion procedure. In J. P. Jouannaud, editor, *Rewriting Techniques and Applications*, volume 202 of *LNCS*, pages 1–45. Springer-Verlag, 1986.

[42] Bruno Buchberger. History and basic features of the critical-pair/completion procedure. *J. Symbolic Computation*, 3:3–38, 1987.

[43] Bruno Buchberger. Applications of Gröbner bases in non-linear computational geometry. In R. Janssen, editor, *Trends in Computer Algebra*, volume 296 of *LNCS*, pages 52–80. Springer-Verlag, 1988.

[44] Bruno Buchberger and Rüdiger Loos. Algebraic simplification. *Computing*, Supplement 4:11–43, 1982.

[45] Reinhard Bündgen. Simulating Buchberger's algorithm by Knuth-Bendix completion. In R.V. Book, editor, *Rewriting Techniques and Applications*, volume 488 of *LNCS*, pages 386–397. Springer-Verlag, 1991.

[46] Wolfram Büttner. Unification in the data structure multiset. *J. Automated Reasoning*, 2:75–88, 1986.

[47] Wolfram Büttner and Helmut Simonis. Embedding boolean expressions into logic programming. *J. Symbolic Computation*, 4:191–205, 1987.

[48] Philippe Le Chenadec. *Canonical Forms in Finitely Presented Algebras*. Research Notes in Theoretical Computer Science. Pitman, 1986.

[49] Ahlem Ben Cherifa and Pierre Lescanne. Termination of rewriting systems by polynomial interpretations and its implementation. *Science of Computer Programming*, 9(2):137–160, 1987.

[50] Alonzo Church. A formulation of the simple theory of types. *J. Symbolic Logic*, 5:56–68, 1940.

[51] Alonzo Church and J. Barkley Rosser. Some properties of conversion. *Trans. AMS*, 39:472–482, 1936.

[52] Adam Cichon and Pierre Lescanne. Polynomial interpretations and the complexity of algorithms. In D. Kapur, editor, *Automated Deduction — CADE-11*, volume 607 of *LNCS*, pages 139–147. Springer-Verlag, 1992.

[53] Michael Clausen and Albrecht Fortenbacher. Efficient solution of linear diophantine equations. *J. Symbolic Computation*, 8:201–216, 1989.

[54] William F. Clocksin and Christopher S. Mellish. *Programming in Prolog*. Springer-Verlag, 2nd edition, 1984.

[55] Paul M. Cohn. *Universal Algebra*. Reidel, 2nd edition, 1981.

[56] Hubert Comon. Sequentiality, second-order monadic logic and tree automata. In *10th IEEE Symp. Logic in Computer Science*, pages 508–517. IEEE Computer Society Press, 1995.

[57] Evelyne Contejean and Hervé Devie. An efficient incremental algorithm for solving systems of linear diophantine equations. *Information and Computation*, 113:143–172, 1994.

[58] Jacques Corbin and Michel Bidoit. A rehabilitation of Robinson's unification algorithm. In R. Pavon, editor, *Information Processing 83*, pages 909–914. North-Holland, 1983.

[59] Thomas H. Cormen, Charles E. Leiserson, and Ronald L. Rivest. *Introduction to Algorithms*. MIT Press, 1990.

[60] Bruno Courcelle. Fundamental properties of infinite trees. *Theoretical Computer Science*, 25:95–169, 1983.

[61] Haskell B. Curry and Robert Feys. *Combinatory Logic, Vol. I*. North-Holland, 1958.

[62] Haskell B. Curry, J. Roger Hindley, and Jonathan P. Seldin. *Combinatory Logic, Vol. II*. North-Holland, 1972.

[63] David Cyrluk, Patrick Lincoln, and Natarajan Shankar. On Shostak's decision procedure for combinations of theories. In M. McRobbie and J. Slaney, editors, *Automated Deduction — CADE-13*, volume 1104 of *LNCS*, pages 463–477. Springer-Verlag, 1996.

[64] Max Dauchet. Simulation of Turing machines by a left-linear rewrite rule. In N. Dershowitz, editor, *Rewriting Techniques and Applications*, volume 355 of *LNCS*, pages 109–120. Springer-Verlag, 1989.

[65] Max Dauchet. Simulation of Turing machines by a regular rewrite rule. *Theoretical Computer Science*, 103:409–420, 1992.

[66] Max Dauchet, Thierry Heuillard, Pierre Lescanne, and Sophie Tison. Decidability of the confluence of finite ground term rewrite systems and of other related term rewrite systems. *Information and Computation*, 88:187–201, 1990.

[67] Max Dauchet and Sophie Tison. Decidability of confluence for ground term rewriting systems. In *Fundamentals of Computation Theory*, volume 199 of *LNCS*, pages 80–89. Springer-Verlag, 1985.

[68] Max Dauchet and Sophie Tison. The theory of ground rewrite systems is decidable. In *5th IEEE Symp. Logic in Computer Science*, pages 242–248. IEEE Computer Society Press, 1990.

[69] Martin Davis. Hilbert's tenth problem is unsolvable. *The Amer. Math. Monthly*, 80:233–269, 1973.

[70] Nachum Dershowitz. A note on simplification orderings. *Information Processing Letters*, 9(5):212–215, 1979.

[71] Nachum Dershowitz. Termination of linear rewriting systems. In S. Even and O. Kariv, editors, *Automata, Languages and Programming*, volume 115

of *LNCS*, pages 448–458. Springer-Verlag, 1981.

[72] Nachum Dershowitz. Orderings for term-rewriting systems. *Theoretical Computer Science*, 17:279–301, 1982.

[73] Nachum Dershowitz. Termination of rewriting. *J. Symbolic Computation*, 3:69–115, 1987.

[74] Nachum Dershowitz and Jean-Pierre Jouannaud. Rewrite systems. In J. van Leeuwen, editor, *Formal Models and Semantics, Handbook of Theoretical Computer Science, Vol. B*, pages 243–320. Elsevier—MIT Press, 1990.

[75] Nachum Dershowitz, Jean-Pierre Jouannaud, and Jan Willem Klop. Open problems in rewriting. In R.V. Book, editor, *Rewriting Techniques and Applications*, volume 488 of *LNCS*, pages 445–456. Springer-Verlag, 1991.

[76] Nachum Dershowitz and Zohar Manna. Proving termination with multiset orderings. *Communications of the ACM*, 22(8):465–476, 1979.

[77] Nachum Dershowitz, Leo Marcus, and Andrzej Tarlecki. Existence, uniqueness, and construction of rewrite systems. *SIAM J. Computing*, 17:629–639, 1988.

[78] Nachum Dershowitz, Mitsuhiro Okada, and G. Sivakumar. Canonical conditional rewrite systems. In E. Lusk and R. Overbeek, editors, *9th Int. Conf. on Automated Deduction*, volume 310 of *LNCS*, pages 538–549. Springer-Verlag, 1988.

[79] Jeremy Dick, John Kalmus, and Ursula Martin. Automating the Knuth Bendix ordering. *Acta Informatica*, 28:95–119, 1990.

[80] Eric Domenjoud. *Outils pour la déduction automatique dans les théories associatives-commutatives*. Thèse de Doctorat, Université de Nancy I, France, 1991.

[81] Peter J. Downey, Ravi Sethi, and Robert Endre Tarjan. Variations on the common subexpression problem. *J. ACM*, 27(4):758–771, 1980.

[82] Klaus Drosten. *Termersetzungssyteme*, volume 210 of *Informatik-Fachberichte*. Springer-Verlag, 1989.

[83] Irène Durand and Aart Middeldorp. Decidable call by need computations in term rewriting (extended abstract). In W. McCune, editor, *Automated Deduction — CADE-14*, volume 1249 of *LNCS*, pages 4–18. Springer-Verlag, 1997.

[84] Cynthia Dwork, Paris Kanellakis, and John Mitchell. On the sequential nature of unification. *J. Logic Programming*, 1:35–50, 1984.

[85] Cynthia Dwork, Paris Kanellakis, and Larry Stockmeyer. Parallel algorithms for term matching. *SIAM J. Computing*, 17:711–731, 1988.

[86] Elmar Eder. Properties of substitutions and unifications. *J. Symbolic Computation*, 1:31–46, 1985.

[87] François Fages. *Formes Canoniques dans les Algèbres Booléennes, et Application à la Démonstration Automatique en Logique de Premier Ordre*. Thèse de 3ème cycle, Université Paris VI, 1983.

[88] François Fages. Associative-commutative unification. In R. Shostak, editor, *7th Int. Conf. Automated Deduction*, volume 170 of *LNCS*. Springer-Verlag, 1984.

[89] François Fages and Gérard Huet. Complete sets of unifiers and matchers in equational theories. *Theoretical Computer Science*, 43:189–200, 1986.

[90] Michael Fay. First-order unification in an equational theory. In *Proc. 4th Workshop on Automated Deduction*, pages 161–167, Austin, Texas, 1979.

[91] Miguel Filgueira and Ana P. Tomás. A fast method for finding the ba-

sis of nonnegative solutions to a linear diophantine equation. *J. Symbolic Computation*, 19:507–526, 1995.

[92] Albrecht Fortenbacher. An algebraic approach to unification under associativity and commutativity. In J.-P. Jouannaud, editor, *Rewriting Techniques and Applications*, volume 202 of *LNCS*, pages 381–397. Springer-Verlag, 1985.

[93] Jean Gallier, Paliath Narendran, David Plaisted, Stan Raatz, and Wayne Snyder. An algorithm for finding canonical sets of ground rewrite rules in polynomial time. *J. ACM*, 40:1–16, 1993.

[94] Harald Ganzinger. A completion procedure for conditional equations. *J. Symbolic Computation*, 11:51–81, 1991.

[95] Michael R. Garey and David S. Johnson. *Computers and Intractability. A Guide to the Theory of NP-Completeness*. Freeman and Company, 1979.

[96] Ferenc Gécseg and Istvan Peák. *Algebraic Theory of Automata*. Akadémiai Kiadó, Budapest, 1972.

[97] M.J.C. Gordon and T.F. Melham. *Introduction to HOL: a theorem-proving environment for higher order logic*. Cambridge University Press, 1993.

[98] Bernhard Gramlich. Generalized sufficient conditions for modular termination of rewriting. *Applicable Algebra in Engineering, Communication and Computing*, 5:131–158, 1994.

[99] Bernhard Gramlich. Confluence without termination via parallel critical pairs. In H. Kirchner, editor, *Trees in Algebra and Programming — CAAP '96*, volume 1059 of *LNCS*, pages 211–225. Springer-Verlag, 1996.

[100] George Grätzer. *Universal Algebra*. Springer-Verlag, 2nd edition, 1979.

[101] Wolfgang Gröbner. Über die Eliminationstheorie. *Monatshefte für Mathematik*, 54:71–78, 1950.

[102] J.R. Guard, F.C. Oglesby, J.H. Bennett, and L.G. Settle. Semi-automated mathematics. *J. ACM*, 16:49–62, 1969.

[103] Michael Hanus. The integration of functions into logic programming: From theory to practice. *J. Logic Programming*, 19&20:583–628, 1994.

[104] Michael Hanus and Herbert Kuchen. Integration of functional and logic programming. *ACM Computing Surveys*, 28:306–308, 1996.

[105] Michael Hanus and Christian Prehofer. Higher-order narrowing with definitional trees. In H. Ganzinger, editor, *Rewriting Techniques and Applications*, volume 1103 of *LNCS*, pages 138–152. Springer-Verlag, 1996.

[106] Jean van Heijenoort. *From Frege to Gödel. A Source Book in Mathematical Logic, 1879–1931*. Harvard University Press, 1967.

[107] Jacques Herbrand. *Recherches sur la théorie de la démonstration*. PhD thesis, University of Paris, 1930.

[108] Jacques Herbrand. *Logical Writings*. Reidel, 1971.

[109] Gabor T. Herman. Strong computability and variants of the uniform halting problem. *Z. Math. Logik Grundl. Math.*, 17:115–131, 1971.

[110] Alexander Herold. *Combination of Unification Algorithms in Equational Theories*. PhD thesis, Universität Kaiserslautern, 1987.

[111] Alexander Herold and Jörg H. Siekmann. Unification in Abelian semigroups. *J. Automated Reasoning*, 3:247–283, 1987.

[112] J. Roger Hindley. *The Church-Rosser Property and a Result in Combinatory Logic*. PhD thesis, University of Newcastle-upon-Tyne, 1964.

[113] J. Roger Hindley and Jonathan P. Seldin. *Introduction to Combinators and λ-Calculus*. Cambridge University Press, 1986.

[114] Heisuke Hironaka. Resolution of singularities of an algebraic variety over a field of characteristic zero: I, II. *Annals of Math.*, 79:109–326, 1964.

[115] Dieter Hofbauer and Clemens Lautemann. Termination proofs and the length of derivations. In N. Dershowitz, editor, *Rewriting Techniques and Applications*, volume 355 of *LNCS*, pages 167–177. Springer-Verlag, 1989.

[116] Jieh Hsiang. Refutational theorem proving using term rewriting systems. *Artificial Intelligence*, 25:255–300, 1985.

[117] Gérard Huet. Résolution d'équations dans les langages d'ordre $1, 2, ..., \omega$. Thèse d'Etat, Université Paris VII, 1976.

[118] Gérard Huet. An algorithm to generate the basis of solutions to homogeneous linear diophantine equations. *Information Processing Letters*, 7:144–147, 1978.

[119] Gérard Huet. Confluent reductions: Abstract properties and applications to term rewriting systems. *J. ACM*, 27:797–821, 1980.

[120] Gérard Huet. A complete proof of correctness of the Knuth-Bendix completion procedure. *J. Computer and System Sciences*, 23:11–21, 1981.

[121] Gérard Huet and Dallas Lankford. On the uniform halting problem for term rewriting systems. Technical Report 283, IRIA, 1978.

[122] Gérard Huet and Jean-Jacques Lévy. Computations in orthogonal rewriting systems. In Jean-Louis Lassez and Gordon Plotkin, editors, *Computational Logic: Essays in Honor of Alan Robinson*, pages 395–443. MIT Press, 1991.

[123] Heinrich Hußmann. Unification in conditional equational theories. In B. Caviness, editor, *EUROCAL'85, Proc. Vol. 2*, volume 204 of *LNCS*, pages 543–553. Springer-Verlag, 1985.

[124] Nathan Jacobson. *Basic Algebra, Vol. 1*. Freeman, 2nd edition, 1985.

[125] Jean-Pierre Jouannaud and Claude Kirchner. Solving equations in abstract algebras: A rule-based survey of unification. In Jean-Louis Lassez and Gordon Plotkin, editors, *Computational Logic: Essays in Honor of Alan Robinson*, pages 257–321. MIT Press, 1991.

[126] Jean-Pierre Jouannaud, Claude Kirchner, and Hélène Kirchner. Incremental construction of unification algorithms in equational theories. In J. Diaz, editor, *Automata, Languages and Programming*, volume 154 of *LNCS*, pages 361–373. Springer-Verlag, 1983.

[127] Jean-Pierre Jouannaud and Hélène Kirchner. Completion of a set of rules modulo a set of equations. *SIAM J. Computing*, 15:1155–1196, 1986.

[128] Jean-Pierre Jouannaud and Mitsuhiro Okada. Abstract data type systems. *Theoretical Computer Science*, 173:349–391, 1997.

[129] Jean-Pierre Jouannaud and Albert Rubio. A recursive path ordering for higher-order terms in η-long β-normal form. In H. Ganzinger, editor, *Rewriting Techniques and Applications*, volume 1103 of *LNCS*, pages 108–122. Springer-Verlag, 1996.

[130] Samuel Kamin and Jean-Jacques Lévy. Two generalizations of the recursive path ordering. University of Illinois at Urbana-Champaign. Unpublished manuscript, 1980.

[131] Abdelilah Kandri-Rody and Deepak Kapur. Computing a Gröbner basis of a polynomial ideal over a Euclidean domain. *J. Symbolic Computation*, 6:37–57, 1988.

[132] Abdelilah Kandri-Rody, Deepak Kapur, and Franz Winkler. Knuth-Bendix procedure and Buchberger algorithm—a synthesis. In *Proc. ACM-SIGSAM Int. Symp. Symbolic and Algebraic Computation, ISSAC '89*, pages 55–67.

ACM Press, 1989.

[133] Paris Kanellakis and Peter Z. Revesz. On the relationship of congruence closure and unification. *J. Symbolic Computation*, 7:427–444, 1989.

[134] Stéphane Kaplan. Conditional rewrite rules. *Theoretical Computer Science*, 33:175–193, 1984.

[135] Deepak Kapur and Paliath Narendran. Complexity of unification problems with associative-commutative operators. *J. Automated Reasoning*, 9:261–288, 1992.

[136] Deepak Kapur, Paliath Narendran, and Friedrich Otto. On ground-confluence of term rewriting systems. *Information and Computation*, 86:14–31, 1990.

[137] Narendran K. Karmarkar. A new polynomial-time algorithm for linear programming. *Combinatorica*, 4:373–395, 1984.

[138] J. Richard Kennaway. Sequential evaluation strategies for parallel-or and related reduction systems. *Ann. of Pure and Applied Logic*, 43:31–56, 1989.

[139] Claude Kirchner. *Méthodes et Outils de Conception Systématique d'Algorithmes d'Unification dans les Théories Équationelles*. Thèse d'état, Université de Nancy I, France, 1985.

[140] Jan Willem Klop. *Combinatory Reduction Systems*. Mathematical Centre Tracts 127. Mathematisch Centrum, Amsterdam, 1980.

[141] Jan Willem Klop. Term rewriting systems. In S. Abramsky, D.M. Gabbay, and T.S.E. Maibaum, editors, *Handbook of Logic in Computer Science*, volume 2, pages 2–116. Oxford University Press, 1992.

[142] Jan Willem Klop and Aart Middeldorp. Sequentiality in orthogonal term rewriting systems. *J. Symbolic Computation*, 12:161–195, 1991.

[143] Jan Willem Klop, Aart Middeldorp, Yoshihito Toyama, and Roel de Vrijer. Modularity of confluence: A simplified proof. *Information Processing Letters*, 49:101–109, 1994.

[144] Jan Willem Klop, Vincent van Oostrom, and Femke van Raamsdonk. Combinatory reduction systems: Introduction and survey. *Theoretical Computer Science*, 121:279–308, 1993.

[145] Donald E. Knuth and P.B. Bendix. Simple word problems in universal algebra. In J. Leech, editor, *Computational Problems in Abstract Algebra*, pages 263–297. Pergamon Press, 1970.

[146] Dexter Kozen. *Complexity of Finitely Presented Algebras*. PhD thesis, Cornell University, May 1977.

[147] Dexter Kozen. Complexity of finitely presented algebras. In *Proc. 9th ACM Symp. Theory of Computing*, pages 164–177, 1977.

[148] Dexter Kozen. A completeness theorem for Kleene algebras and the algebra of regular events. In *6th IEEE Symp. Logic in Computer Science*, pages 214–225. IEEE Computer Society Press, 1991.

[149] Mukkai S. Krishnamoorthy and Paliath Narendran. On recursive path ordering (note). *Theoretical Computer Science*, 40:323–328, 1985.

[150] J. B. Kruskal. Well-quasi-ordering, the tree theorem, and Vazsonyi's conjecture. *Trans. AMS*, 95:210–225, 1960.

[151] Wolfgang Küchlin. A confluence criterion based on the generalized Newman lemma. In B. Caviness, editor, *EUROCAL'85, Proc. Vol. 2*, volume 204 of *LNCS*, pages 543–553. Springer-Verlag, 1985.

[152] Masahito Kurihara and Azuma Ohuchi. Modularity of simple termination of term rewriting systems with shared constructors. *Theoretical Computer*

Science, 103:273–282, 1992.

[153] Masahito Kurihara and Azuma Ohuchi. Modularity in noncopying term rewriting. Theoretical Computer Science, 152:139–196, 1995.

[154] Jean-Luc Lambert. Une borne pour les générateurs des solutions entières positives d'une équation diophantienne linéaire. Comptes Rendus de l'Académie des Sciences de Paris, 305:39–40, 1987.

[155] Dallas Lankford. Canonical algebraic simplification in computational logic. Technical Report ATP-25, Department of Mathematics, University of Texas, Austin, 1975.

[156] Dallas Lankford. On proving term rewriting systems are Noetherian. Technical Report MTP-3, Mathematics Department, Louisiana Tech University, Ruston, 1979.

[157] Dallas Lankford, G. Butler, and B. Brady. Abelian group unification algorithms for elementary terms. Contemporary Mathematics, 29:193–199, 1984.

[158] Jean-Louis Lassez, Michael Maher, and Kim Mariott. Unification revisited. In Jeff Minker, editor, Foundations of Deductive Databases and Logic Programming, pages 587–625. Morgan Kaufman, 1987.

[159] Patrick Lincoln and Jim Christian. Adventures in associative-commutative unification. J. Symbolic Computation, 8:217–240, 1989.

[160] Mike Livesey and Jörg H. Siekmann. Unification of AC-terms (bags) and ACI-terms (sets). Internal report, University of Essex, 1975. Also published as Technical Report 3-76, Universität Karlsruhe, 1976.

[161] Rüdiger Loos. Term reduction systems and algebraic algorithms. In J. Siekmann, editor, Proc. 5th German Workshop on Artificial Intelligence, GWAI'81, volume 47 of Informatik Fachberichte, pages 214–234. Springer-Verlag, 1981.

[162] Carlos Alberto Loría-Sáenz. A Theoretical Framework for Reasoning about Program Construction Based on Extensions of Rewrite Systems. PhD thesis, Universität Kaiserslautern, 1993.

[163] Leopold Löwenheim. Über das Auflösungsproblem im logischen Klassenkalkül. Sitzungsberichte Berliner Math. Gesell., 7:89–94, 1908.

[164] Zohar Manna and Steven Ness. On the termination of Markov algorithms. In Proc. Third Hawaii Int. Conf. System Science, pages 789–792, 1970.

[165] Alberto Martelli and Ugo Montanari. An efficient unification algorithm. ACM Trans. Programming Languages and Systems, 4(2):258–282, 1982.

[166] Alberto Martelli and Gianfranco Rossi. Efficient unification with infinite terms in logic programming. In Proc. Int. Conf. Fifth Generation Computer Systems, pages 202–209. ICOT, 1984.

[167] Ursula Martin and Tobias Nipkow. Boolean unification. J. Automated Reasoning, 4:381–396, 1988.

[168] Ursula Martin and Tobias Nipkow. Boolean unification — the story so far. J. Symbolic Computation, 7:275–293, 1989. Reprinted in C. Kirchner, Unification, pages 437–455. Academic Press, 1990.

[169] Ursula Martin and Tobias Nipkow. Ordered rewriting and confluence. In M.E. Stickel, editor, 10th Int. Conf. Automated Deduction, volume 449 of LNCS, pages 366–380. Springer-Verlag, 1990.

[170] Yuri Matijasevich. Simple examples of undecidable associative calculi. Soviet Mathematics (Doklady), 8(2):555–557, 1967.

[171] Yuri Matiyasevich and Géraud Sénizergues. Decision problems for semi-

Thue systems with a few rules. In *11th IEEE Symp. Logic in Computer Science*, pages 523–531. IEEE Computer Society Press, 1996.

[172]   Kurt Mehlhorn. *Data Structures and Algorithms 1: Sorting and Searching.* EATCS Monographs on Theoretical Computer Science. Springer-Verlag, 1984.

[173]   Karl Meinke and John Tucker. Universal algebra. In S. Abramsky, D.M. Gabbay, and T.S.E. Maibaum, editors, *Handbook of Logic in Computer Science*, volume 1, pages 189–411. Oxford University Press, 1992.

[174]   Yves Métivier. About the rewriting systems produced by the Knuth-Bendix completion algorithm. *Information Processing Letters*, 16:31–34, 1983.

[175]   Aart Middeldorp. A sufficient condition for the termination of the direct sum of term rewriting systems. In *4th IEEE Symp. Logic in Computer Science*, pages 396–401. IEEE Computer Society Press, 1989.

[176]   Aart Middeldorp. *Modular Properties of Term Rewriting Systems.* PhD thesis, Vrije Universiteit, Amsterdam, 1990.

[177]   Aart Middeldorp. Modular properties of conditional term rewriting systems. *Information and Computation*, 104:110–158, 1993.

[178]   Aart Middeldorp. Completeness of combinations of conditional constructor systems. *J. Symbolic Computation*, 17:3–21, 1994.

[179]   Aart Middeldorp. Call by need computations to root-stable form. In *Proc. 24th ACM Symp. Principles of Programming Languages*, pages 94–105, 1997.

[180]   Aart Middeldorp and Erik Hamoen. Completeness results for basic narrowing. *Applicable Algebra in Engineering, Communication and Computing*, 5:213–253, 1994.

[181]   Aart Middeldorp and Hans Zantema. Simple termination revisited. In A. Bundy, editor, *Automated Deduction — CADE-12*, volume 814 of *LNCS*, pages 451–465. Springer-Verlag, 1994.

[182]   John C. Mitchell. *Foundations for Programming Languages.* MIT Press, 1996.

[183]   C. St. J. A. Nash-Williams. On well-quasi-ordering finite trees. *Proc. Cambridge Philosophical Society*, 59:833–835, 1963.

[184]   Greg Nelson and Derek C. Oppen. Fast decision procedures based on congruence closure. *J. ACM*, 27:356–364, 1980.

[185]   M. H. A. Newman. On theories with a combinatorial definition of 'equivalence'. *Annals of Mathematics*, 43(2):223–243, 1942.

[186]   Tobias Nipkow. Combining matching algorithms: The regular case. In N. Dershowitz, editor, *Rewriting Techniques and Applications*, volume 355 of *LNCS*, pages 343–358. Springer-Verlag, 1989.

[187]   Tobias Nipkow. Unification in primal algebras, their powers and their varieties. *J. ACM*, 37:742–776, 1990.

[188]   Tobias Nipkow. Combining matching algorithms: The regular case. *J. Symbolic Computation*, 12(6):633–653, 1991.

[189]   Tobias Nipkow. Higher-order critical pairs. In *6th IEEE Symp. Logic in Computer Science*, pages 342–349. IEEE Computer Society Press, 1991.

[190]   Tobias Nipkow. Orthogonal higher-order rewrite systems are confluent. In M. Bezem and J.F. Groote, editors, *Proc. Int. Conf. Typed Lambda Calculi and Applications*, volume 664 of *LNCS*, pages 306–317. Springer-Verlag, 1993.

[191]   Werner Nutt. Unification in monoidal theories. In M.E. Stickel, editor,

Bibliography

10th Int. Conf. Automated Deduction, volume 449 of *LNCS*, pages 618–632. Springer-Verlag, 1990.

[192] Michael J. O'Donnell. *Computing in Systems Described by Equations*, volume 58 of *LNCS*. Springer-Verlag, 1977.

[193] Enno Ohlebusch. A simple proof of sufficient conditions for the termination of the disjoint union of term rewriting systems. *Bull. European Association for Theoretical Computer Science*, 49:178–183, 1993.

[194] Enno Ohlebusch. On the modularity of termination of term rewriting systems. *Theoretical Computer Science*, 136:333–360, 1994.

[195] Vincent van Oostrom. *Confluence for Abstract and Higher-Order Rewriting*. PhD thesis, Vrije Universiteit, Amsterdam, 1994.

[196] Vincent van Oostrom. Developing developments. *Theoretical Computer Science*, 175:159–181, 1997.

[197] Vincent van Oostrom and Femke van Raamsdonk. Weak orthogonality implies confluence: The higher-order case. In A. Nerode, editor, *Logical Foundations of Computer Science*, volume 813 of *LNCS*, pages 379–392. Springer-Verlag, 1994.

[198] Mike S. Paterson and Mark N. Wegman. Linear unification. *J. Computer and System Sciences*, 16:158–167, 1978.

[199] Lawrence C. Paulson. Verifying the unification algorithm in LCF. *Science of Computer Programming*, 5:143–169, 1985.

[200] Lawrence C. Paulson. *Isabelle: A Generic Theorem Prover*, volume 828 of *LNCS*. Springer-Verlag, 1994.

[201] Lawrence C. Paulson. *ML for the Working Programmer*. Cambridge University Press, 2nd edition, 1996.

[202] Gerald E. Peterson. Complete sets of reductions with constraints. In M.E. Stickel, editor, *10th Int. Conf. Automated Deduction*, volume 449 of *LNCS*, pages 366–380. Springer-Verlag, 1990.

[203] Gerald E. Peterson and Mark E. Stickel. Complete sets of reductions for some equational theories. *J. ACM*, 28:223–264, 1981.

[204] David A. Plaisted. Equational reasoning and term rewriting systems. In D.M. Gabbay, C.J. Hogger, and J.A. Robinson, editors, *Handbook of Logic in Artificial Intelligence and Logic Programming*, volume 1, pages 274–367. Oxford University Press, 1993.

[205] Gordon Plotkin. Building-in equational theories. *Machine Intelligence*, 7:73–90, 1972.

[206] Detlef Plump. Implementing term rewriting by graph reduction: Termination of combined systems. In S. Kaplan and M. Okada, editors, *Conditional and Typed Rewriting Systems — CTRS'90*, volume 516 of *LNCS*, pages 307–317. Springer-Verlag, 1991.

[207] Jaco van de Pol and Helmut Schwichtenberg. Strict functionals for termination proofs. In M. Dezani-Ciancaglini and G. Plotkin, editors, *Typed Lambda Calculi and Applications*, volume 902 of *LNCS*, pages 350–364. Springer-Verlag, 1995.

[208] Loïc Pottier. Minimal solutions of linear diophantine equations: Bounds and algorithms. In R.V. Book, editor, *Rewriting Techniques and Applications*, volume 488 of *LNCS*, pages 162–173. Springer-Verlag, 1991.

[209] Christian Prehofer. Higher-order narrowing. In *9th IEEE Symp. Logic in Computer Science*, pages 507–516. IEEE Computer Society Press, 1994.

[210] Christian Prehofer. A call-by-need strategy for higher-order functional-logic

programming. In J. Lloyd, editor, *Logic Programming*, pages 147–161. MIT Press, 1995.

[211] Christian Prehofer. Solving higher-order equations: From logic to programming. Technical Report I9508, Technische Universität, München, 1995. PhD Thesis.

[212] Femke van Raamsdonk. *Confluence and Normalization for Higher-Order Rewriting*. PhD thesis, Vrije Universiteit, Amsterdam, 1996.

[213] Femke van Raamsdonk. Outermost-fair rewriting. In J.R. Hindley, editor, *Typed Lambda Calculi and Applications*, volume 1210 of *LNCS*, pages 284–299. Springer-Verlag, 1997.

[214] Jean-Claude Raoult and Jean Vuillemin. Operational and semantic equivalence between recursive programs. *J. ACM*, 27:772–796, 1980.

[215] V.N. Redko. On defining relations for the algebra of regular events. *Ukrainskii Matematicheskii Zhurnal*, 16:120–126, 1964. In Russian.

[216] J.A. Robinson. A machine-oriented logic based on the resolution principle. *J. ACM*, 12:23–41, 1965.

[217] Barry K. Rosen. Tree-manipulating systems and Church-Rosser theorems. *J. ACM*, 20:160–187, 1973.

[218] Joseph G. Rosenstein. *Linear Orderings*. Academic Press, 1982.

[219] Sergiu Rudeanu. *Boolean Functions and Equations*. North-Holland, 1974.

[220] Michael Rusinowitch. On termination for the direct sum of term rewriting systems. *Information Processing Letters*, 26:65–70, 1987.

[221] Andrea Sattler-Klein. About changing the ordering during Knuth-Bendix completion. In *STACS 94, Symposium on Theoretical Aspects of Computer Science*, pages 175–186, 1994.

[222] Manfred Schmidt-Schauß. Unification under associativity and idempotence is of type nullary. *J. Automated Reasoning*, 2:277–282, 1986.

[223] Manfred Schmidt-Schauß. Combination of unification algorithms. *J. Symbolic Computation*, 8:51–100, 1989.

[224] Manfred Schmidt-Schauß. *Computational Aspects of an Order-Sorted Logic with Term Declarations*, volume 395 of *LNCS*. Springer-Verlag, 1989.

[225] Manfred Schmidt-Schauß, Massimo Marchiori, and Sven Eric Panitz. Modular termination of r-consistent and left-linear term rewriting systems. *Theoretical Computer Science*, 149:361–374, 1995.

[226] Robert Sedgewick. *Algorithms*. Addison-Wesley, 1983.

[227] A. Selman. Completeness of calculi for axiomatically defined classes of algebras. *Algebra Universalis*, 2:20–32, 1972.

[228] Géraud Sénizergues. On the termination-problem for one-rule semi-Thue systems. In H. Ganzinger, editor, *Rewriting Techniques and Applications*, LNCS, pages 302–316. Springer-Verlag, 1996.

[229] Robert E. Shostak. An algorithm for reasoning about equality. *Communications of the ACM*, 21:583–585, 1978.

[230] Robert E. Shostak. Deciding combinations of theories. *J. ACM*, 31:1–12, 1984.

[231] Jörg H. Siekmann. *Unification and Matching Problems*. PhD thesis, Essex University, 1978. Memo CSA-4-78.

[232] Jörg H. Siekmann. Unification of commutative terms. In *Proc. Int. Symposium on Symbolic and Algebraic Manipulation, EUROSAM-79*, volume 72 of *LNCS*, pages 531–545. Springer-Verlag, 1979.

[233] Jörg H. Siekmann. Unification theory: A survey. *J. Symbolic Computation*, 7:207–274, 1989.

[234] James R. Slagle. Automated theorem proving for theories with simplifiers, commutativity and associativity. *J. ACM*, 21:622–642, 1974.

[235] Wayne Snyder. A fast algorithm for generating reduced ground rewriting systems from a set of ground equations. *J. Symbolic Computation*, 15:415–450, 1993.

[236] Mark E. Stickel. A complete unification algorithm for associative-commutative functions. In *Proc. 4th Int. Joint Conf. Artificial Intelligence, IJCAI-75*, pages 71–82, Tblisi, USSR, 1975.

[237] Mark E. Stickel. A unification algorithm for associative-commutative functions. *J. ACM*, 28:423–434, 1981.

[238] Sabine Stifter. A generalization of reduction rings. *J. Symbolic Computation*, 4:351–364, 1987.

[239] Alfred Tarski. *A Decision Method for Elementary Algebra and Geometry*. University of California Press, 1951.

[240] Erik Tidén. *First-Order Unification in Combinations of Equational Theories*. PhD thesis, Royal Institute of Technology, Stockholm, 1986.

[241] Yoshihito Toyama. On the Church-Rosser property of term rewriting systems. Technical Report NTT ECL TR 17672, NTT, 1981. In Japanese.

[242] Yoshihito Toyama. Counterexamples to termination for the direct sum of term rewriting systems. *Information Processing Letters*, 25:141–143, 1987.

[243] Yoshihito Toyama. On the Church-Rosser property for the direct sum of term rewriting systems. *J. ACM*, 34:128–143, 1987.

[244] Yoshihito Toyama. Commutativity of term rewriting systems. In K. Fuchi and L. Kott, editors, *Programming of Future Generation Computers*, volume II, pages 393–407. Elsevier Science, 1988.

[245] Yoshihito Toyama, Jan Willem Klop, and Henk Pieter Barendregt. Termination for direct sums of left-linear complete term rewriting systems. *J. ACM*, 42:1275–1304, 1995.

[246] Wolfgang Wechler. *Universal Algebra for Computer Scientists*. EATCS Monographs on Theoretical Computer Science. Springer-Verlag, 1992.

[247] Volker Weispfenning and Thomas Becker. *Gröbner Bases: A Computational Approach to Commutative Algebra*. Graduate Texts in Mathematics. Springer-Verlag, 1993.

[248] Franz Winkler. Reducing the complexity of the Knuth-Bendix completion algorithm: A 'unification' of different approaches. In B. Caviness, editor, *EUROCAL'85*, volume 204 of *LNCS*, pages 378–389. Springer-Verlag, 1985.

[249] Franz Winkler and Bruno Buchberger. A criterion for eliminating unnecessary reductions in the Knuth-Bendix algorithm. In *Proc. Coll. on Algebra, Combinatorics and Logic in Computer Science*, pages 849–869, 1983.

[250] Hans Zantema and Alfons Geser. A complete characterization of termination of $0^p1^q \rightarrow 1^r0^s$. In *Rewriting Techniques and Applications*, volume 914 of *LNCS*, pages 41–55. Springer-Verlag, 1995.

[251] Hantao Zhang and Deepak Kapur. Consider only general superpositions in completion procedures. In N. Dershowitz, editor, *Rewriting Techniques and Applications*, volume 355 of *LNCS*, pages 513–527. Springer-Verlag, 1989.

[252] Jieh Hsiang and Michael Rusinowitch. On word problems in equational theories. In T. Ottmann, editor, *Automata, Languages and Programming*, volume 267 of *LNCS*, pages 54–71. Springer-Verlag, 1987.

Index

Page numbers given in boldface refer to definitions.

Printed in the United States
By Bookmasters